Receptions of the Ancient Near East in Popular Culture and Beyond

Receptions of the Ancient Near East in Popular Culture and Beyond

edited by

Lorenzo Verderame and Agnès Garcia-Ventura

LOCKWOOD PRESS

2020

RECEPTIONS OF THE ANCIENT NEAR EAST IN POPULAR CULTURE AND BEYOND

ISBN: 978-1-948488-24-2

Front cover: Walter Andrae, draft of the stage setting act I, first scene of *Sardanapal*, 1907. Staatsbibliothek zu Berlin —Preußischer Kulturbesitz, estate Andrae 235[1].

Back cover: "Torre di Babele 2" by Piero Passone, acrylic on brick.

Cover design by Susanne Wilhelm.

Library of Congress Cataloging-in-Publication Data

Names: Verderame, L. (Lorenzo), editor. | Garcia-Ventura, Agnès, editor.
Title: Receptions of the Ancient Near East in popular culture and beyond / edited by Lorenzo Verderame and Agnès Garcia Ventura.
Description: First. | Atlanta, GA : Lockwood Press, [2020] | Includes bibliographical references and index.
Identifiers: LCCN 2019057239 (print) | LCCN 2019057240 (ebook) | ISBN 9781948488242 (paperback) | ISBN 9781948488259 (ebook)
Subjects: LCSH: Civilization, Western--Middle Eastern influences. | Civilization, Ancient, in popular culture. | Civilization, Ancient--Middle East. | Middle East--Civilization--To 622.
Classification: LCC CB251 .R37 2020 (print) | LCC CB251 (ebook) | DDC 909/.09821--dc23

Printed in the United States of America on acid-free paper.

Contents

Foreword

Receptions of the Ancient Near East in Popular Culture and Beyond

Paul Collins

This book is an enthusiastic celebration of the ways in which popular culture has consumed aspects of the ancient Near East to construct new realities. The editors are distinguished experts in the literature and cultures of ancient Mesopotamia and its historiography and they have brought together an equally impressive line-up of colleagues—archaeologists, philologists, historians, and art historians—to reflect on how objects, ideas, and interpretations of the ancient Near East, many of which are the focus of their individual scholarship, have been remembered, constructed, reimagined, mythologized, or indeed forgotten within our shared cultural memories. The exploration of cultural memories has revealed how they inform the values and structures and daily life of societies over time (Connerton 1989; Halbwachs 1992). This is therefore not a collection of essays about the deep past but rather about the stories we tell ourselves about ourselves.

There are a number of ancient societies that have a greater presence in the public consciousness than those of the ancient Near East, and they have attracted much interest in academic explorations of popular culture and issues of representation (de Groot 2016). Greece and Rome, for example, have come to embody in the West (problematic as this term is) notions of perfection and order, especially in aesthetics and politics (Kallendorf 2007; Hardwick and Stray 2008). Equally, ancient Egypt occupies a seemingly very familiar place in our lives; through the "mysteries" of hieroglyphs, pyramids, and mummies, it presents a heady mix of otherness and imagined accessibility (Riggs 2017). In the essays offered here, however, we discover just how significant the ancient Near East has been in influencing popular culture.

If, as David Lowenthal (2015) suggests, the past is a foreign country, for the nonspecialist the ancient Near East can appear as very foreign indeed: a mysterious "Orient," encompassing as it does an enormous geographical area containing an apparently impenetrable mosaic of diverse peoples, languages, and cultures. In popular understanding this can sometimes take the shape of a threatening and distant alien world but it also "charms *because* it is little known" (Lowenthal 2015, 13). Ideas about Mesopotamia (Babylonian and Assyrian "civilizations") were already embedded in cultural memory, filtered through descriptions in biblical and classical writings, long before the mid-nineteenth century when Western explorers began to uncover its ancient physical remains. Mesopotamia was understood as the cradle of civilization—or human culture's infancy (Bahrani, Çelik, and Eldem 2011, 56). The first real excavations started at a time when colonial adventurers were planting flags of occupation and ownership in foreign lands, and the "discoveries" in the Near East allowed the region's past to be simultaneously claimed and incorporated into the West's myths of origins. Mesopotamia became Orientalized for Western consumption (Bahrani, Çelik, and Eldem 2011, 62). Yet access to this ancient past was immensely challenging and only slowly revealed through the heroic decipherment of the lost cuneiform script and the languages it recorded. Popular reception was shaped by the historical reconstructions of these pioneers, which inevitably reflected the concepts and forms of argument of their own times (Couldry and Hepp 2017).

Although many of the scholarly approaches to construct Mesopotamia's past over the last century and a half are no longer considered as legitimate fields of inquiry, conclusions derived from them still echo within our cultural memories. This becomes apparent, for example, in popular understandings of the Sumerians. From the 1870s a bitter controversy developed about whether or not the Sumerian language, as had recently been identified in cuneiform texts, belonged to a distinct ethnic group. Racial science underpinned these debates and eventually would come to contrast the Sumerians (identified as "Aryans") with "Semites" (Akkadians) (Cooper 1993). Throughout the first half of the twentieth century, the academic reconstruction of Mesopotamia remained essentially a story of racial conflict with the Sumerians viewed as the founders of civilization, ultimately crushed by Semitic conquerors—notions that have never entirely gone away, existing at their most extreme in the diatribe of white supremacists. As Sumerian literary texts were discovered and translated, myth, legend, and history were often conflated so that by the 1950s the Sumerians were viewed as lying at the root of the modern world, having invented not only writing, urbanism, and the wheel, but having even experimented with democracy (Kramer 1963). The themes or, perhaps better, the myths of the origin of civilization have proved highly resilient in popular imagination despite recent arguments that the Sumerians as a people are in some sense the invention of modern Assyriologists (Cooper 2010, 331). So, for example, ancient Sumer is one of the options available for teachers to explore the achievements of the world's earliest civilizations in the UK national history curriculum for primary school children (Department for Education 2013).

Alongside understandings (or misunderstandings) of the ancient Near East generated from the publications of specialists, museums have probably played the most significant role in shaping the Western public's reception of the region's past (Evans 2012,

77–78). During the nineteenth century, European national museums began amassing collections as a result of control over their colonies or through political and economic influence in neighboring regions (e.g., Duthie 2011). As imperial institutions, the museums came with authority and popular reach, and the decisions on the selection of the objects that entered their collections, their display practices, and the dissemination of information about those choices beyond their doors have had a significant impact. Through their ethnographic representations, the museum displays contributed to the domestication of not only the contemporary colonized non-Western world but also its past. Thus, as described above, the ancient Near East came to serve as a starting point for describing the rise of Western civilization (a familiar trope even today). The cultures of Mesopotamia dominated these narratives, partly because sites like Ur, Nineveh, and Babylon could be mined for objects to fill museums (often with spectacular results), but also because many of these same sites and their inhabitants were already deeply embedded in cultural memory (Seymour 2014; Millerman 2015; Petit and Morandi 2017). Museum displays thus presented an "Orient" that seemed both familiar and exotic. Neighboring regions, such as Turkey or Arabia, however, were often viewed as peripheral to this central story, being perceived as underdeveloped or uncivilized. Modern attempts to unpack or even "decolonize" such displays can be disquieting to a public familiar with, and thereby reassured by, these versions of ancient and recent pasts (Chambers et al. 2014).

European and American museums with large ancient Near Eastern collections continue to attract enormous numbers of visitors, and many such collections are destinations on tourist itineraries. Their galleries of objects, however, can no longer be viewed as passive displays that simply transmit knowledge. Rather, it has become apparent that they actually construct meaning and define cultures through their arrangement and presentation; the displays actually create knowledge, shaping our understanding of science, culture, and history (Alpers 1991; Kaplan 1995; Moser 2006, 2010). Through museum displays ancient objects take on new lives as modern artworks (Azara and Marin 2018), and the stories they tell reveal as much about contemporary interests and concerns as they do about the objects themselves, reshaping further our understanding of their ancient roles and meanings.

Perhaps the most surprising way in which understanding of the ancient Near Eastern past has come to influence popular culture is through its reconstruction by the ancients themselves. They consciously chose either to remember or to forget parts of it. This is evidenced most famously by the Sumerian King List, a document constructed as a succession of cities and their rulers, starting at the beginning of time "before the Flood" (that theme of origins again), that had achieved the political unity of southern Mesopotamia. Yet the deletion of a number of regional states from the list by its compilers and the creation of the myth of a single dynasty in control of territory at any one time demonstrates that this is a contrived view of reality but one, nevertheless, that continues to support popular notions of deep antiquity, including the presence of aliens (e.g., Kraychir 2017). Other Mesopotamian inscriptions, especially those associated with glorious rulers of the past, were used from the second millennium BCE onwards as models in the production of contemporary works and stories; the origins and successes of kings that these describe have been understood by both scholars and the public as historical fact (Foster 2016, especially chapter 12).

The modern Near East has been much in the news over recent decades because of invasions, occupations, wars, and terrorism, which have had a devastating impact on the lives of its inhabitants. The Western press, however, has reacted with particular horror at the destruction, often targeted, of the region's rich cultural heritage, especially its archaeological sites, religious buildings, museums, and archives (Emberling and Hanson 2008). This response is strengthened by the notion of a shared global heritage—a sense of ownership in a postcolonial context—and ultimately derived from the popular understandings that the ancient Near East lies at the root of today's Western urban, literate societies (Meskell 2015). Public interest has turned to the ancient history of the Near East to try and understand the importance of this ongoing loss of heritage, and it should perhaps not come as a surprise that dominant constructs within popular culture have contributed to explanations of its significance—such as in 2016 when the then Iraqi transport minister described the ziggurat at Ur as an airport to launch spaceships from five thousand years ago (Forster 2016).

Ultimately, there is no definitive ancient Near East, because the surviving physical remains are always interpreted through the concerns of the present day and filtered through cultural memories. Academia and popular culture have created their own versions of the past with many points of contact. Among these constructions are simulacra that, in the concept developed by the French philosopher Jean Baudrillard (1994), are copies of things that never existed but feel as though they should have. Popular culture has inherited these along with stereotypes about the Near East to construct memories out of the remnants of the past. Investigating these cultural memories is surely as important as probing the ancient records as they challenge our ideas and our ways of looking at the past. As such, the enlightening essays in this volume they will prove of enormous interest not only to specialists of the ancient world, but to all those concerned with society's attitude to its own history and culture.

Bibliography

Alpers, S. 1991. "The Museum as a Way of Seeing." In I. Karp and S. Lavine (eds.), *Exhibiting Cultures: The Poetics and Politics of Museum Display*, 25–32. Washington, DC: Smithsonian Institution Press.

Azara, P., and M. Marin. 2018. "Ancient 'Art' in the White Cube? Or How Contemporary Art Creates Ancient 'Art.'" In G. Emberling and L. Petit (eds.), *Museums and the Ancient Middle East: Curatorial Practice and Audiences*, 27–38. Abingdon, UK: Routledge.

Bahrani, A., Z. Çelik, and E. Eldem. 2011. *Scramble for the Past: A Story of Archaeology in the Ottoman Empire, 1753–1914*. Istanbul: SALT.

Baudrillard, J. 1994. *Simulacra and Simulation*. Translated by Sheila Faria Glaser. Ann Arbor: University of Michigan Press.

Chambers, I., A. De Angelis, C. Ianniciello, M. Orabona, and M. Quadraro, eds. 2014. *The Postcolonial Museum: The Arts of Memory and the Pressures of History*. Abingdon, UK: Routledge.

Connerton, P. 1989. *How Societies Remember*. Cambridge: Cambridge University Press.

Cooper, J. 1993. "Sumerian and Aryan: Racial Theory, Academic Politics and Parisian Assyriology." *Revue de l'Histoire des Religions* 210(2):169–205.

———. 2010. "'I Have Forgotten My Burden of Former Days!' Forgetting the Sumerians in Ancient Iraq." *Journal of the American Oriental Society* 130(3):327–35.

Couldry, N., and A. Hepp. 2017. *The Mediated Construction of Reality*. Cambridge: Polity Press.

de Groot, J. 2016. *Consuming History: Historians and Heritage in Contemporary Popular Culture*. London: Routledge.

Department for Education. 2013. *History Programmes of Study: Key Stages 1 and 2*. Accessed 5 August 2018. https://assets.publishing.service.gov.uk/government/uploads/system/uploads/attachment_data/file/239035/PRIMARY_national_curriculum_-_History.pdf.

Duthie, E. 2011. "The British Museum: An Imperial Museum in a Post-Imperial World." *Public History Review* 18:12–25.

Emberling, G., and K. Hanson, eds. 2008. *Catastrophe! The Looting and Destruction of Iraq's Past*. Oriental Institute Museum Publications 28. Chicago: University of Chicago Press.

Evans, J. 2012. *The Lives of Sumerian Sculpture: An Archaeology of the Early Dynastic Temple*. Cambridge: Cambridge University Press.

Forster, K. 2016. "Iraqi Transport Minister Claims First Airport Was Built 7,000 Years Ago in Iraq by Ancient Sumerians." *Independent*, 1 October. Accessed 15 August 2018. https://www.independent.co.uk/news/world/middle-east/iraq-spaceships-transport-minister-kazem-finjan-iraqi-sumerians-space-travel-7000-years-ago-a7340966.html.

Foster, B. R. 2016. *The Age of Agade: Inventing Empire in Ancient Mesopotamia*. Abingdon, UK: Routledge.

Halbwachs, M. 1992. *On Collective Memory*. Translated by L. A. Coser. Chicago: University of Chicago Press.

Hardwick, L., and C. Stray. 2008. *A Companion to Classical Receptions*. Malden, MA: Blackwell.

Kallendorf, C. 2007. *A Companion to the Classical Tradition*. Oxford: Blackwell.

Kaplan, F. 1995. *Museums and the Making of "Ourselves."* Leicester: Leicester University Press.

Kramer, S. N. 1963. *The Sumerians: Their History, Culture, and Character*. Chicago: University of Chicago Press.

Kraychir, H. 2017. "Ancient Sumerian Writings Reveal Eight Immortal Kings Ruled for 241,200 Years." *Gosimasonry*, 1 March. Accessed 21 August 2018. https://gnosismasonry.wordpress.com/2017/03/01/ancient-sumerian-writings-reveal-eight-immortal-kings-ruled-for-241200-years/.

Lowenthal, D. 2015. *The Past Is a Foreign Country—Revisited*. Cambridge: Cambridge University Press.

Meskell, L., ed. 2015. *Global Heritage: A Reader*. Chichester, UK: Blackwell.

Millerman, A. J. 2015. "The Spinning of Ur, How Sir Leonard Woolley, James R. Ogden and the British Museum Interpreted and Represented the Past to Generate Funding for the Excavation of Ur in the 1920's and 1930's." PhD diss., University of Manchester.

Moser, S. 2006. *Wondrous Curiosities: Ancient Egypt at the British Museum*. Chicago: Chicago University Press.

———. 2010. "The Devil Is in the Detail: Museum Displays and the Creation of Knowledge" *Museum Anthropology* 33:22–32.

Petit, L. P., and D. Morandi, eds. 2017. *Nineveh, the Great City: Symbol of Beauty and Power.* Leiden: Sidestone.

Riggs, C. 2017. *Egypt: Lost Civilizations.* London: Reaktion.

Seymour, M. 2014. *Babylon: Legend, History and the Ancient City.* London: Tauris.

Receptions of the Ancient Near East in Popular Culture and Beyond

Preliminary Considerations

Agnès Garcia-Ventura and
Lorenzo Verderame

The present volume brings together eighteen essays dealing with the reception of ancient Near Eastern motifs in the popular culture of the last two centuries. The essays correspond to a series of lectures and workshops organized from January to May 2016 by the editors of the volume at "Sapienza," Università degli Studi di Roma, under the title *Storia degli studi sul Vicino Oriente Antico*.[1]

The idea to hold these meetings arose in response to a twofold concern. The first was the lack of a debate within the ancient Near Eastern disciplines on the modern and contemporary reception, and the reconstruction, of the ancient Near Eastern past. This subject is only rarely addressed by scholars whose main field of expertise is the study of the primary sources at our disposal—that is, philologists, archaeologists, and art historians. The second was the fact that the reception and reconstruction of the past has become an independent discipline labeled "reception studies." This prolific new research field explores the reception of antiquity in recent years by modern and contemporary historians, art historians, musicologists, and even students of cinema. The "antiquity" usually meant in these studies, however, is antiquity from a European and Western culture perspective—that is, classical antiquity, with a few forays into the biblical world.[2] From this point of view, the status of the ancient Near East (and in par-

---

1. The initiative has been funded by a grant program organized by "Sapienza," Università degli Studi di Roma ("Giornate di storia degli studi sul Vicino Oriente Antico"; C26C157SL3). We want to thank Lockwood Press and the anonymous reviewer who read our first manuscript for their professionalism and meticulous work. Moreover, we are particularly grateful to Billie Jean Collins, the director of Lockwood Press, for a further thorough revision of the manuscript and for her valuable suggestions to improve it, including the ordering of the contributions.

2. For these studies, for example, in the history of art or for the debate within the history of science, see Evans 2012 and Rochberg 2016, respectively.

ticular Mesopotamia) is ambiguous, undetermined, and often speculative. Defined as the "cradle of civilization" (*Western* civilization, of course), it is considered a necessary but undeveloped forerunner of Greek culture; and it is the "miracle" of Greek culture that is the real mark of "our" civilization that distinguishes it from the "others." Furthermore, as a remote and exotic culture, and as the *East* seen in opposition to the *West*, the ancient Near East is often relegated to the margins of the scholarly debate on antiquity or even treated as an ethnographic subject.

Thus, with the exception of Babylon[3] the Near Eastern past is often ignored in reception studies. Nevertheless, a few monographs have been devoted to it, often focusing on its visual art or approaching it from an art historical perspective,[4] or from a spatial and chronological viewpoint, focusing on the experience of Victorian Britain.[5] In general, other monographs and collections of essays authored or edited by scholars of ancient Near Eastern disciplines have focused on historiography, and deal with the reception only rarely or tangentially.[6] By tackling reception studies from the perspective of scholars of the ancient Near East, we aim to offer a different approach on these topics, particularly the cultural output of scholarly research and its diffusion in popular culture.

To address our two concerns, we decided to organize the series of meetings mentioned above, which included some thirty lectures and presentations and were held at "Sapienza" in 2016.[7] The texts of these lectures on the reception of the ancient Near East in popular culture and on the reconstruction (and also the reception) of this past through archaeology have now been collected and are published here alongside papers from other guest contributors.[8]

3. See, for instance, Seymour 2014, Liverani 2016, or Polaschegg and Weichenhan 2017; for the reception in Western literature see Scheil 2016, and in Arabic literature see Janssen 1995. A recent example of the relevance and omnipresence of Babylon considered in both primary sources and in its reception is the temporary exhibition *Babylon: Myth and Reality* held at the British Museum (London) 2008–2009 (see Finkel and Seymour 2008 for the catalogue).

4. Bohrer (2003) analyzed Orientalism and the image of Mesopotamia in nineteenth-century England, France, and Germany, mainly in visual culture. Brusius wrote a monograph and several articles on the development of photography and archaeology in the ancient Near East. Both scholars are art historians focusing on visual arts and culture (as example of this perspective, see for instance the collective volume edited by Brusius, Dean and Ramaligam 2013). Malley's monograph (2012) on Layard and Nineveh applies a different approach, dealing with the imperialistic appropriation of Mesopotamia's past during Victorian times and the figure of Layard.

5. See the extensive three-volume study by McGeough 2015, as well as Brusius, Dean, and Ramalligam 2013, Malley 2012, and, in part, Bohrer 2003.

6. See, among others, Lehmann 1994; Larsen 1996; Hanisch and Schönig 2001; Hanisch 2003; Da Riva and Vidal 2005; Holloway 2006; Evans 2012.

7. For a detailed program with titles and participants, see: http://lorenzoverderame.site.uniroma1.it/attivita-1/2016storiastudi (accessed 14 November 2019).

8. The lectures on the historiography of ancient Near Eastern studies have been collected and ed-

1. Starting Points: The Terms and Perspectives under Debate

As is customary, we use the term "ancient Near East" as a label to include ancient Mesopotamia (the "Land between the Rivers" Tigris and Euphrates) as well as some parts of modern-day Iran and Syria. From the chronological point of view, the term covers some three thousand years, from the end of the fourth millennium BCE until the conquest by Alexander the Great in 331 BCE.[9]

At this point, we need to outline briefly two concepts that are essential to a clear understanding of the points of departure and the approaches applied in the chapters compiled here. These two concepts are Orientalism and popular culture.

The way in which Western culture has created its own Orient—or, better, its *Orients*, according to the context, the place, and the time—has had a huge impact on the reception and creation of ancient Near Eastern motifs in Western culture.[10] Said's "Orientalism," for all the criticism it has received, remains a landmark and a necessary premise for any conscientious study of the discipline, its aims, and the election and construction of the subjects by scholars in response to contemporary concerns, in both the past and the present.[11] Interestingly enough, the debate on Orientalism has had little or no impact on ancient Near Eastern studies. If we exclude some works and authors as well as occasional contributions and monographic collections focusing specifically on the topic,[12] Orientalism is not only absent from the scholarly discussion within those disciplines, but it has not even generated an epistemological debate regarding the approach and construction of the research itself. Historical, philological, and archaeological research on ancient Near Eastern cultures have had both an indirect and a direct impact on the construction of the political discourse of the last two centuries, from colonialism to the creation of modern nations, from racial theories to the debate over antiquities. All this has been ignored in academia, where the naïve claim is widespread

---

ited by the two present writers in the volume *Following in the Footsteps of Our Predecessors: Studies on the History of Assyriology* (forthcoming, to be published by Eisenbrauns/Pennsylvania State University Press).

9. In academic works, Egypt is not generally considered among the disciplines included in ancient Near Eastern studies. For this reason, both Egyptology and Egyptomania (a fertile area for research) are beyond the scope of this volume.

10. The way the modern Near Eastern cultures have received and built their own past, either independently or adopting and elaborating on Western "Oriental" models, is a different, parallel issue, which has not been researched properly until now. For postcolonial archaeology in the ancient Near East, see for instance Porter 2010; for the general debate on Western models within the Islamic intellectual world, see Laroui 1987 and Shariati 1982.

11. Said 1978. For a general overview of Said's Orientalism and its critics, see MacKenzie 1995 and Varisco 2007.

12. Orientalism is one of the focuses (or indeed the main focus) of the works cited in the previous notes and is part of the epistemological approach of scholars such as Mario Liverani or Zainab Bahrani. For single contributions in collected essays see, for example, Kohl, Larsen, and Rowlands in Miller, Rowlands, and Tilley 1989, and Meyer-Zwiffelhoffer and Wiesehöfer in Rollinger, Luther, and Wiesehöfer 2007.

that we "only" study the past; a past that, from this point of view, would have nothing to do with the present.[13] On the contrary, a critical reflection on the origin and role of Near Eastern studies with regard to political involvement in the affairs of the area would lead to a mature awareness about our disciplines and the way we "do culture." The further step would be, of course, a dialogic reflection on how modern Near Eastern people perceive their own past, especially considering that Near Eastern disciplines are creations of "Western" scholars, while Arab scholars are heavily underrepresented in the scholarly debate, apart from archaeology.[14]

As for "popular culture," we use it here in its broadest meaning, embracing a wide range of manifestations over the course of approximately two centuries. From the arts to mass media, the subject under investigation is the reception of ancient Near Eastern cultures and motifs outside academic circles. Here we do not apply the customary distinction between "popular culture" and "high culture" for two main reasons. First, when applying this distinction, the focus is on the audience receiving the cultural product, not in the cultural product itself as we intend to do in this volume. Second, because this distinction has been constructed from a certain point of view—boosted from academic circles and from elites—privileging some cultural expressions while despising others. There is, then, a clear social class discourse of self-legitimation. Consequently, this distinction has embedded a value judgment we want to avoid.[15]

The focus is thus the cultural products resulting from the use of either direct or indirect information from archaeological digs, translations of ancient texts, and images from the ancient Near East that have been sources of inspiration for modern-day creators. It is the popular culture, understood in this broad meaning alluded to by the "beyond" in the title of this compilation of essays, that generates these cultural products. From this point of view, the present volume applies an original approach by rejecting any chronological, geographical, or genre limits on how these motifs have found their way, or have been received, in the productions of individual artists or in the mass media.

Moving on now to the perspectives of the study, in this volume we present essays that deal with themes relevant to both reception studies and archaeology, two areas that are not usually considered side by side in collective volumes (for the reasons briefly outlined above regarding specialization and academic traditions). The only exception

---

13. The naïve approach of Jean Bottéro (1982) in his "Eloge d'une science inutile" is quite surprising, not only because the author dismissed the role of Near Eastern archaeology and philology in racial theories and forgot how these had influenced the life of scholars and the development of the discipline, but also because his work continues to be quoted and considered the starting point for a positive reflection on the future of the discipline.

14. Since the independence of modern Near Eastern countries, local archaeologists have had an increasing involvement in excavations, resulting in the development of their own schools and traditions.

15. For an overview of the use and definition of "popular culture" in opposition to "high culture," as well as the difficulties and variants when establishing these boundaries, see Grig 2017, 3–14 (with previous references).

to this rule might be the relationship between archaeology and architecture in ancient Near Eastern studies, where reflections on (re)construction as well as collaboration between architects and archaeologists have been present since the end of the nineteenth century CE. Both Robert Koldewey (1855–1925) and Walter Andrae (1875–1956), who worked on the pioneering archaeological campaigns at the settlement of Babylon, were trained architects. The research carried out recently by scholars like Brigitte Pedde, Davide Nadali, and Maria Gabriella Micale also offers food for thought in this direction,[16] as does Mario Liverani's monograph *Immaginare Babele* (2013; for the English translation of the volume see Liverani 2016), a masterly overview of the relation between archaeology and architecture and between construction and reconstruction.

Starting from these perspectives, and in an attempt to broaden the topics and issues analyzed, in this volume we aim to prompt a discussion of the ontological construction of the archaeological thought concerning the ancient Near East. We contend that the various disciplines devoted to the study of the ancient Near East potentially create an idea (or create their own ideas) of the region and the period. This idea might be based on preconceptions and on primary sources at one and the same time. The product of this first mixture would become, in its turn, the starting point for further reception studies of the ancient Near East.

However, as we see in some of the chapters of this volume (especially those devoted to opera) this is not always the case. In fact, often the starting point does not even necessarily contain the flavor of the primary sources. The reception of the ancient Near East is of course possible without material culture—that is, without referring to archaeological sources, or also consciously (or unconsciously) ignoring the sources if they exist. This may be fostered by the unavailability of anthologies of translated texts or popular books on the topic, as well as to the recentness of the discoveries and the ambiguous status within the development of the "Western Civilization" and thus the minor appeal in comparison with ancient Egypt and classical cultures. In this scenario, then, neither accuracy nor the availability of materials are perceived as necessary: they are just potential inspirational sources that archaeology might provide. This is clear for instance in the way Cubism took so-called "primitive" art (to name a well-known and well-studied topic) and also in some case studies included in the present volume (particularly the ones related to futurist worlds).[17]

In short, through the range of perspectives and case studies compiled in this volume, we intend to show that the reception of the ancient Near East, like all the receptions of antiquity in popular culture and arts, can be constructed either in continuity or in discontinuity with respect to the primary sources. In fact, few of the case studies

16. See for instance the volume edited by Micale and Nadali 2015, with previous references.

17. For the interpretation and reception of early Mesopotamian statuary, see for example Evans 2012, especially chapters 1 and 2; for a classic and general analysis of the relationship between ethnography, literature, and art, see Clifford 1988.

correspond totally to one of the two extremes. Very often, the boundaries are blurred. Continuity and discontinuity are thus flexible and variable, mixed in different proportions, conferring complexity on the way a distant past such as the ancient Near East is received, reshaped, and reimagined in media as diverse as opera, Black Metal, films, photographs, architecture, comics, sculpture, or paintings.

2. *Contents of the Volume*

As we have seen above, reception studies are often limited both geographically and chronologically, and in fact the most discussed scenarios for case studies are Victorian Britain and Germany in the first half of the twentieth century. As a result, it is often the scholars linked in some way to these academic traditions who are the ones most involved in these studies. With the present volume, we intend to offer a collection of essays that complement but also go beyond these conventional frameworks. To do so, we invited scholars from different backgrounds and areas of expertise to present their approaches to the reception of ancient Near Eastern studies through a case study. As a result of their insights, the volume benefits from a variety of geographical and chronological frameworks, analyzing the reception of the ancient Near East in popular culture in Norway, the Czech Republic, and Spain (countries often considered as "peripheral" in reception studies) and also covering a wide time span that both predates and postdates the standard period in reception studies of the late-nineteenth and early-twentieth centuries. The case studies in this volume also explore the precedents, for instance the Baroque, as well as the final decades of the twentieth century and the beginning of the twenty-first with a clear concern with the most recent examples of the reception and reconstruction of this past.

The book consists of eighteen articles. It opens with a foreword by Paul Collins and closes with an afterword by Frances Pinnock. The other sixteen essays are presented in the five thematic sections we list below. This thematic arrangement may help the reader to better navigate through a volume that encompasses a high degree of heterogeneity. However, as most contributions present points of contact and divergence, we also encourage the reader to find these dialogues between chapters beyond the thematic sections here proposed and even to see the other possible arrangements.

The first section, devoted to visual arts and narratives, includes the chapters by Pedro Azara and Marc Marín, Jean Evans, and Silvana di Paolo. Those by Azara and Marín and by Evans concentrate, respectively, on two leading names in contemporary art, Joan Miró (1893–1983) and Michael Rakowitz (1973–). Di Paolo deals with photography with a special focus on the snapshots of Persepolis by the Neapolitan Luigi Pesce (1818–1891).

The second section, devoted to performing arts, includes the contributions by Kerstin Droß-Krüpe, Valeska Hartmann, and Daniele Rosa, ranging from opera (Droß-Krüpe and Hartmann) to Black Metal (Rosa). They cover a broad scope of musical performances, both from the geographical and from the chronological point of view, from the Baroque to the twentieth century, from Italy to Norway.

The third section is devoted to the reception of ancient Near Eastern motifs either on the big screen or in television series and includes the contributions by Kevin McGeough, Eva Miller, and Lorenzo Verderame. From the history of Gilgamesh quoted in *Star Trek* to Near Eastern elements in biblical productions and Mesopotamian demons in horror movies, these articles discuss how ancient Near Eastern cultures have been received and elaborated in order to adapt to, or create, new poetics.

The fourth section revolves around written narratives, from novels and crime fiction to comics, and includes the chapters by Jana Mynářová and Pavel Kořínek, Luigi Turri, Francesco Pomponio, and Ryan Winters. The articles deal with topics such as the reception of the *Epic of Gilgamesh* (Turri) or of ancient Near Eastern elements and motifs in crime stories (Pomponio) and in Czech comics (Mynářová and Kořínek), while Winters discusses the alien origin of Mesopotamian civilization prompted by Zecharia Sitchin.

The fifth and last section reflects on the role of the modern archaeologists as receivers as well as transmitters of ancient Near Eastern material culture, dealing with aspects of reception, reconstruction, and revival of these remains from the past. This section includes the contributions by Davide Nadali, Juan-Luis Montero Fenollós, and Silvia Festuccia. The primary sources used by these authors, particularly by Nadali and Montero Fenollós, include drawings, photographs, site reconstructions, and even academic reports on the organization of archaeological campaigns. Their contributions, then, provide not only a historiographical approach to archaeology, but also a reflection on the current praxis and deontology of the profession. Festuccia, meanwhile, studies this material culture to approach a topic often overlooked in studies on the past: the role of sport and what can be (or not) labelled as such from our current point of view.

The present volume has its origin in the editors' curiosity about historical and contemporary concerns and specifically about the modern-day reception of ancient Near Eastern cultures. Their interest has found support from a group of committed colleagues from the very beginning, and many more whom they met or contacted during the course of the work. The result is a collection of a wide and diversified range of topics related to reception studies, in which all authors enthusiastically shared their own knowledge, interest, and personal experience. The editors wish to thank all the authors for their dedication and for helping to make this volume a tangible reality. All in all, we believe this volume is a vivid reflection of these scholars' interests in the field and we hope that it will encourage others to make further advances in this stimulating area of research.

Bibliography

Bohrer, F. N. 2003. *Orientalism and Visual Culture: Imagining Mesopotamia in Nineteenth-Century Europe*. Cambridge: Cambridge University Press.

Bottéro, J. 1982. "Eloge d'une science inutile: l'orientalisme." *Akkadica* 30:12–26.

Brusius, M., K. Dean, and C. Ramalingam. 2013. *William Henry Fox Talbot: Beyond Photography*. New Haven: Yale University Press.

Clifford, J. 1988. *The Predicament of Culture*. Cambridge, MA: Harvard University Press.

Da Riva, R., and J. Vidal. 2005. *Descubriendo el Antiguo Oriente: Pioneros y arqueólogos de Mesopotamia y Egipto a finales del s. XIX y principios del s. XX*. Barcelona: Bellaterra Arqueología.

Evans, J. M. 2012. *The Lives of Sumerian Sculpture: An Archaeology of the Early Dynastic Temple*. Cambridge: Cambridge University Press.

Finkel, I., and M. Seymour. 2008. *Babylon: Myth and Reality; British Museum Exhibition, London, 2008.11.13–2009.03.15*. London: British Museum Press.

Grig, L. 2017. *Popular Culture in the Ancient World*. Cambridge: Cambridge University Press.

Hanisch, L. 2003. *Die Nachfolger der Exegeten: Deutschsprachige Erforschung des Vorderen Orients in der ersten Hälfte des 20. Jahrhunderts*. Wiesbaden: Harrassowitz.

Hanisch, L. and H. Schönig, eds. 2001. *Ausgegrenzte Kompetenz: Porträts vertriebener Orientalisten und Orientalistinnen 1933–1945; eine Hommage anlässlich des XXVIII. Deutschen Orientalistentags in Bamberg, 26.–30. März 2001*. Halle: Orientwissenschaftliches Zentrum.

Holloway, S. W. 2006. *Orientalism, Assyriology and the Bible*. Hebrew Bible Monographs 10. Sheffield, UK: Sheffield Phoenix.

Janssen, C. 1995. *Bābil, the City of Witchcraft and Wine: The Name and Fame of Babylon in Medieval Arabic Geographical Texts*. Mesopotamian History and Environment Series 2. Ghent: University of Ghent.

Kohl, P. L. 1989. "The Material Culture of the Modern Era in the Ancient Orient: Suggestions for Future Work." In D. Miller, M. Rowlands, and C. Tilley (eds.), *Domination and Resistance*, 239–45. One World Archaeology 3. London: Routledge.

Laroui, A. 1987. *Islam et modernité*. Paris: La Découverte.

Larsen, M. T. 1989. "Orientalism and Near Eastern Archaeology." In D. Miller, M. Rowlands, and C. Tilley (eds.), *Domination and Resistance*, 229–39. One World Archaeology 3. London: Routledge.

———. 1996. *The Conquest of Assyria: Excavations in an Antique Land, 1840–1860*. London: Routledge.

Lehmann, R. G. 1994. *Friedrich Delitzsch und der Babel-Bibel-Streit*. Orbis Biblicus et Orientalis 133. Freiburg: Universitäts-Verlag; Göttingen: Vandenhoeck & Ruprecht.

Liverani, M. 2016. *Imagining Babylon: The Modern Story of an Ancient City*. Studies in Ancient Near Eastern Records 11. Berlin: de Gruyter. Translation of *Immaginare Babele: Due secoli di studi sulla città orientale antica*. Rome: Laterza, 2013.

MacKenzie, J. 1995. *Orientalism: History, Theory and the Arts*. Manchester: Manchester University Press.

Malley, S. 2012. *From Archaeology to Spectacle in Victorian Britain: The Case of Assyria, 1845–1854*. Farnham, UK: Ashgate.

McGeough, K. 2015. *The Ancient Near East in the Nineteenth Century: Appreciations and Appropriations*. 3 vols. Sheffield, UK: Sheffield Phoenix.

Meyer-Zwiffelhoffer, E. 2007. "Orientalismus? Die Rolle des Alten Orients in der deutschen Altertumswissenschaft und Altertumsgeschichte des 19. Jahrhunderts (ca. 1785–1910)." In A. Luther, R. Rollinger, and J. Wiesehöfer (eds.), *Getrennte Wege? Kommunikation, Raum und Wahrnehmung in der Alten Welt*, 501–94. Oikumene 2. Frankfurt: Verlag Antike 2007.

Micale, M. G., and D. Nadali, eds. 2015. *How Do We Want the Past to Be? On Methods and Instruments of Visualizing Ancient Reality*. Regenerating Practices in Archaeology and Heritage 1. Piscataway, NJ: Gorgias.

Miller, D., M. Rowlands, and C. Tilley, eds. 1989. *Domination and Resistance*. One World Archaeology 3. London: Routledge.

Polaschegg, A., and M. Weichenhan, 2017. *Berlin-Babylon: eine deutsche Faszination 1890–1930*. Berlin: Klaus Wagenbach.

Porter, B. W. 2010. "Near Eastern Archaeology: Imperial Pasts, Postcolonial Presents, and the Possibilities of a Decolonized Future." In J. Lydon and U. Z. Rizvi (eds.), *Handbook of Postcolonial Archaeology*, 51–60. Abingdon, UK: Routledge.

Rochberg, F. 2016. *Before Nature: Cuneiform Knowledge and the History of Science*. Chicago: University of Chicago Press.

Rollinger, R. 2011–2013. "Sport und Spiel." In *Reallexikon der Assyriologie und vorderasiatischen Archäologie* 13:6–16.

Rollinger, R., A. Luther, and J. Wiesehöfer, eds. 2007. *Getrennte Wege? Kommunikation, Raum und Wahrnehmung in der Alten Welt*. Oikumene 2. Frankfurt: Verlag Antike.

Rowlands, M. 1989. "A Question of Complexity." In D. Miller, M. Rowlands, and C. Tilley (eds.), *Domination and Resistance*, 28–39. One World Archaeology 3. London: Routledge.

Said, E. W. 1978. *Orientalism*. New York: Pantheon.

Scheil, A. 2016. *Babylon Under Western Eyes: A Study of Allusion and Myth*. Toronto: University of Toronto Press.

Seymour, M. 2014. *Babylon: Legend, History, and the Ancient City*. New York: Tauris.

Shariati, A. 1982. *Histoire et destinée*. Paris: Sindbad.

Varisco, D. M. 2007. *Reading Orientalism*. Seattle: University of Washington Press.

Wiesehöfer, J. 2007. "Alte Geschichte und alter Orient, oder: Ein Pladoyer fur Universalgeschichte." In A. Luther, R. Rollinger, and J. Wiesehöfer (eds.), *Getrennte Wege? Kommunikation, Raum und Wahrnehmung in der Alten Welt*, 595–616. Oikumene 2. Frankfurt: Verlag Antike.

Mesopotamia in Miró. Miró in Mesopotamia

Pedro Azara and Marc Marín

This article deals with the reception of Mesopotamian art and culture through the eyes of the Spanish artist Joan Miró.[1] The artist's interest in Mesopotamia had not been explored until recently (Marín 2017; Azara and Marín 2018). Previous studies on his use of traditional, collective, "primitive," or archaeological art as sources of inspiration have not been successful in identifying Mesopotamian material among his references. So far, the influence of early Mesopotamian visual culture has been identified in the artist's statuary, in his drawings, and even in theater scenography designed by him. Mesopotamian iconography has been spotted in his studios in Palma de Mallorca, Spain, as well as in the artist's personal library and personal booklets. This essay thus presents the evidence in support of the idea that Miró's interest on and knowledge of Mesopotamia was deeper than expected.

These facts are presented with the aim of understanding the way Miró observed and used Mesopotamian art, focusing on identifying the reasons for his interest; when and how the artist encountered these objects—either live or through publications; whether he was interested in the object, or in the image of it; and whether he showed predilection for any specific Mesopotamian material culture over another. An analysis of his work spaces, as well as the significance of the objects sheltered in them, will be presented together with questions of anonymity or collectivity in his art. Our approach will be contextualized among previous studies on the relation between Miró and traditional, popular, and, mostly, "primitive" arts. This text aspires, ultimately, to contribute to the studies of the western reception of Mesopotamian art during the twentieth century.

1. This research has been possible thanks to the help and the generosity of Pilar Ortega and Gloria Moragues (Miró Succession, Palma de Mallorca), Maria Esther Molina Costa (Pilar and Joan Miró Foundation, Palma de Mallorca), Rosa Maria Malet, Elena Escobar and Teresa Montaner (Joan Miró Foundation, Barcelona), and Margarita Cortadella and Fèlix Bota (Picasso Museum, Barcelona).

This research is related to a previous study by the authors on how modern artists understood and eventually used Mesopotamian material in their own work.[2] Painters and sculptors like Henry Moore, Alberto Giacometti, and Willem de Kooning were declared to have been deeply inspired by Sumerian statues, such as statues of Gudea and other worshipper statues, seen in the British Museum (London), the Louvre Museum (Paris), and the Metropolitan Museum of Art (New York), triggering a series of paintings, drawings, and engravings in the 1930s and 1950s (see Evans 2012; Bahrani 2014). Likewise, texts by writers and critics such as Georges Bataille, Michel Leiris, Christian Zervos, Jurgis Baltrušaitis, and even Agatha Christie (Max Mallowan's spouse), together with later poems by Charles Olson, were among the first authors to describe "Sumerian" artifacts as works of art.

These first publications and museum displays of Sumerian material attracted the attention, first of all, of surrealistic artists. That surrealistic artists were some of the first to appreciate Sumerian artifacts as works of art was due to the fact that these compositions were perceived as new ways of expressing emotions far away from classical ones and at the same time different from the already known African, pre-Columbian, and other so-called "primitive" artifacts. Some of these artists, such as Henry Moore, had already declared their fascination with all kinds of nonclassical compositions, and even wrote on Mesopotamian sculpture as early as 1935 (Moore 1935, 995). Clasping hands and large, wide-opened eyes were features of Sumerian worshipper statues, capable of expressing emotions in a way understandable to modern Westerners. Some artists reacted to Sumerian artifacts similarly to the way some cubist and expressionist Western artists and architects had reacted, at the beginning of the twentieth century, to "primitive" artifacts, when African, Iberian, pre-Columbian, and Southeast Asian "idols" and cultic or magical items were shown for the first time in Western countries, in international and colonial exhibitions resulting from the Western colonial occupation of parts of Africa and Asia. Sumerian images and items were likewise perceived as "primitive" and were therefore saturated with the "magic aura" that "primitive" art was supposed to hold, though in a somehow different or innovative way. For these artists, Sumerian artifacts were new items, never before seen, and, at the same time, items that could be compared to other non-Western anti-naturalistic items. In a sense, they were new but already known.

1. Son Boter

Early in his career, the artist Joan Miró expressed his intention to build himself a singular space from which he could focus on sculpture. He understood that the works he would conceive in this space would be significantly related, on the one hand, to the con-

2. This research was pursued in the context of the exhibition *From Ancient to Modern: Archaeology and Aesthetics* at the Institute for the Study of the Ancient World at NYU, 12 February–7 June 2015. See Chi and Azara 2015.

Figure 1. Front view of the building known as Son Boter, in Palma de Mallorca (Spain). Courtesy of Marc Marín and Pedro Azara.

tainer—that is, to the architecture of the building—and, on the other, to the objects and images contained within its walls. He wanted to feel that when he accessed this space he would be "entering the earth," and thus his sculpture would be "more natural and spontaneous." The sculptures in this space should resemble "living creatures inhabiting the workshop" that would provoke in the visitor "a strong impression of being in a new world," in "another world" (Rowell 2002, 251–77).

This desire, which he expressed in his personal notebooks in the 1940s, would materialize in the following decade when he acquired a traditional house from the eighteenth century, thanks to the Guggenheim International Award he received in 1958 (*Miró Sert* 2007), a typical Majorcan *possessió* called Son Boter (fig. 1). Miró found in Son Boter a refuge, a place where he could create in close connection to tradition from within a vernacular architecture. Son Boter is frequently presented in scholarly publications, as well as in quotes by the artist, as a "prehistoric cave." This fact is not surprising, given that the interest of the artist for prehistoric techniques and cultures is widely acknowledged. It is attested in his notebooks, particularly from the 1940s, where he wrote down a series of instructions for the development of different techniques (etchings, engravings, sculpture, painting), inspired by the techniques of "the dawn of time" (Rowell 2002, 249–77; Picon 2002, 131, 143, 172). Also well-known is the deep impression felt by the artist and his ceramist colleague Llorenç Artigas when they visited the Paleolithic caves of Altamira, in Spain, in 1957.[3]

3. This visit took place in the context of the development of two ceramic murals for the UNESCO Headquarters (Calzada 2001, 183–93; Stavrinaki 2011, 574–79).

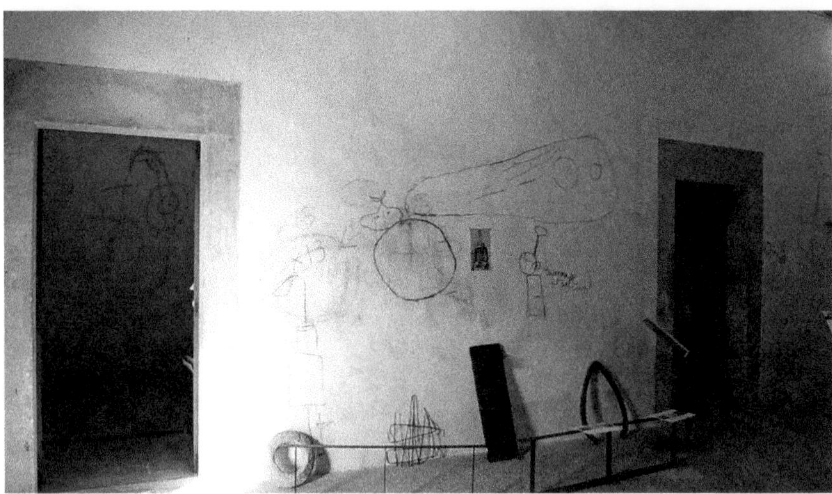

Figure 2. View of the lower floor at the studio of Joan Miró at Son Boter, in Palma de Mallorca (Spain). Courtesy of Marc Marín and Pedro Azara.

Today Son Boter is part of the complex of buildings that compose the *Fundació Pilar i Joan Miró a Mallorca,* which includes another building designed in the 1950s by the Spanish architect Josep Lluís Sert, used as a studio known as *Son Abrines,* and the museum, opened in 1992, designed by the Spanish architect Rafael Moneo. Son Boter became the shelter and birthplace of most of Miró's sculptures from the 1960s onwards; however, the first floor was also intensely employed for the painting of large canvases. One accesses Son Boter through a large central hall with four separate rooms at each side and a staircase at the end, which connects both floors. All the rooms are paved with terracotta tiles, and the walls are all white, plastered, irregular surfaces. Most of these walls are covered with black charcoal graffiti (fig. 2). Unfortunately, the lines are fading away today due to the humid conditions of the walls, and the protection of the graffiti is not ensured due to lack of funding.[4]

Miró used the white walls of Son Boter as large blank sheets of paper where he could draw scale projects. Miró declared that he was unable to produce art in a space with no qualities, just as he was unable to paint on a spotless canvas. He felt the need to fill the space with items and images that caught his attention, and he needed to be surrounded by them. He was keen to use spots in sheets of paper and random markings on the canvases as starting points for his paintings, and in a similar way he used to collect random objects that would trigger new creations. These could be either human-made objects (toys, traditional art figurines, industrial items with shapes that could be seen

4. Recent and past photographs of the walls of the studio can be found in numerous publications (Miró 1987; Punyet and del Moral 2015).

as human or animal shapes) or objects he found in nature (shells, stones with certain shapes, small branches). Most of these items were small, cheap objects with a personal value to him, and, most importantly, whose author was not known. These anonymous objects allowed him to be in contact with his surroundings "in a very lively manner" (Rowell 2002, 251–77).

For Joan Miró, the studio represented a place to capture images. These images were disposed throughout the space in a noncasual manner, just as the different elements that compose a collage are not placed randomly on a canvas. Miró used to pin printed photograph cuttings and postcards on the walls of Son Boter. He arranged these cuttings along the four walls that configure the rooms, approximately at eye level. They conform, together with nearby graffiti, objects and words and expressions "inscribed" on the walls, a continuous work, a sort of spatial collage or mural tryptic. Over time the different individual meanings of these objects and the architecture bonded together. Each individual element in Son Boter is thus not to be understood independently. These images, objects, and texts persisted for the last thirty years of his life in his studio, and when he donated the house to the Spanish government, he clearly specified that everything should be kept as it was. Thanks to this wish, most of these photographs hanging on the walls are still on view.[5]

Words and expressions in Catalan and French are written on the walls, next to some of the sketches and photographs. Some of these words resemble titles of works of art common in Miró's production and can thus be easily related to other paintings, drawings, engravings, and sculptures holding the same titles: *Femme, Femme et oiseau, Femme et coquillage, Personnage, Personnage dans la nuit, Personnage et oiseau, Tête d'homme et Femme, Objets dans le calme, Monument à un couple d'amoureux.* Other expressions are less common and might probably refer to the surrounding objects and drawings: *Beau comme une cathédrale gothique, clau, sense cabellera ni forats*—Catalan words for "key," and "without hair or holes." Other expressions are almost unreadable due to erasures and to superposition of words. It is notable how the titles of the works by Miró show a clear intention to erase any trace of singularity. These titles were used repeatedly during the life of the artist to refer to different works. Already in 1934, he declared to the gallerist Pierre Matisse that he preferred to employ "very ordinary and unpretentious titles: figure, '*personnage*,' figures, '*personnages*.'"[6]

---

5. They were just recently replaced by copies. Most of the originals are kept in the archives of the Miró Foundation in Palma, and one of them is preserved in the Joan Miró Foundation in Barcelona.

6. Letter to Pierre Matisse, 12 October 1934 (Rowell 2002, 185). On the titles of poems of Miró, Rowell writes: "En la mayoría de los casos, los títulos poéticos se le ocurrían mientras pintaba. Eran expresiones verbales que entraban en resonancia con las imágenes que se formaban sobre el lienzo. El contenido de esas imágenes verbales, o de esos títulos, mezcla temas reales (mujeres, pájaros) con acontecimientos o circunstancias no reales, creando así una realidad mítica que quebranta nuestras costumbres mentales. Esta poesía verbal paralela, nunca denotativa ni descriptiva, enriquece -y, de hecho, mitologiza- la iconografía de las pinturas" (Rowell 2002, 237).

These rooms were documented up from the 1950s by the Spanish photographers Francesc Català-Roca, Pedro Coll, Josep Planas i Montanyà, and Joan Gomis, and their photographs are among the most valuable documents to trace the evolution of Miró's workspaces. A picture of the studio showing Miró in front of one of the walls allows us to interpret the now blurred word *Objets* from the expression or title: *Objets dans le calme*. Recent visits to the archives of these photographers have unfortunately not shed more light on the questions addressed in the current essay.

In Son Boter, the pictures hanging from the walls show various items that might be classified as either archaeological, ancient, ethnic, or popular. Among them, two Catalan Romanesque frescoes showing a winged bull[7] (Miró was always interested in winged or flying figures, such as butterflies, dragonflies, birds, or angels); a fragment of a sculpture (probably from Cyprus); an ancient Balkan bell-shaped idol; a bronze scepter from Palestine (currently at the Israel Museum in Jerusalem); an Iranian (Amlash) female idol or "mother goddess" from the first millennium BCE; a terracotta horse apparently of Chinese origin; an African statue; and, last but not least, a series of well-known early Mesopotamian artifacts, including statues, terracotta figurines, masks, and reliefs.[8]

The inclusion of these cuts on the walls permitted the cohabitation of two realities in a single place. On the one hand, the photographs, understood as fixed (pinned) windows from which to access another world—either past or imaginary—were cut and disposed throughout the space without representing a scene by their own. Instead, they were the initial traces that the artist would later encounter, and from which would emanate new forms that would "domesticate" the space. On the other hand, the charcoal graffiti belonged to another reality—an ephemeral and ever changing one—in which the figures of the cuts would develop through small gestures,[9] suffer violent transformations, expand throughout the space, and enter the artist's own visual language. Ancient forms were interpreted and deformed—or translated—through the eyes of the artist.

---

7. This symbol of Luke the Evangelist was in fact studied by Jurgis Baltrušaitis (1934) as an example of Neo-Assyrian iconography in Romanesque art.

8. A film showing some of the photograph cuttings and graffiti on the walls of Son Boter is available at https://vimeo.com/229230900. Among the Mesopotamian artifacts: a terracotta male figurine from Eridu, first half of the fourth millennium (IMB 54931); a terracotta female figurine, unknown provenance, second half of the fourth millennium (IMB 42610); the "mask of Warka," late fourth millennium to early third millennium (IMB 45434); "lion-hunt stele," Uruk, end of the fourth millennium to the early third millennium (IMB 23477); Copper support with worshipper statue, Khafadje, first half of the third millennium (IMB 8969); worshipper statuette, Ashnunnak, first half of the third millennium (IMB 19754); warrior figurine, Tello-Lagash, Neo-Sumerian (IMB 16303); female figurine, first Babylonian dynasty (IMB 21399). The captions and inventory numbers have been taken from the catalogue of the exhibition *Trésors du Musée de Bagdad: des origines à l'Islam* (*Trésors* 1966).

9. Miró: "Picasso told me one day: pure creation is a graffiti, a small gesture on a wall. This is why it is so important for me" (Raillard 1978, 153).

2. *Mesopotamia in Miró*

The cut photographs hanging on the walls of Son Boter have been on view since Joan Miró hanged them on the walls between 1966 and 1968.[10] Dozens of pictures by the aforementioned photographers, some published as early as the 1960s, show him in this studio next to the cut photographs, which are clearly visible and easily recognizable. Moreover, since the passing of Joan Miró in the 1980s, the studio has been open to the public. However, until recently, we were unaware of any publication that either accurately identified these images in the photographs of Son Boter or that described any relation between Miró and Mesopotamia.

This realization encouraged us to contact the Miró Foundation in Barcelona, the Pilar and Joan Miró Foundation, and the Miró Succession in Palma de Mallorca.[11] None of them had previously noticed the early Mesopotamian origin of some of the archaeological objects in photographs in Son Boter. Our research led to a publication by the German historian of ancient art, Brigitte Pedde, including a paper presented at a colloquium in London in 2010 on a theme related to her studies: the influence of Mesopotamian art in modern art, especially in architecture (Pedde 2012, 89–100). Pedde focused on the influence of Sumerian art in the works of various twentieth-century artists, and, among other examples, she mentioned the case of Miró and Son Boter. Previously, the "mask of Warka," or "Lady of Uruk" (IMB 45434)—one of the artifacts shown in the photograph cuts in Son Boter—had been correctly identified by María José Balsach (2007).[12]

Apart from these two publications, the interest of Miró in Mesopotamian culture had not been explored further. Most scholarly articles on the various influences on Miró's work mentioned either pre-Columbian art (Katchina dolls and Maya sculpture), art from Easter Island, "Eastern" art (meaning Far Eastern art from China or Japan), Greek art, Catalan Romanesque frescoes, and traditional Mediterranean or Balearic terracotta painted figurines (called "siurells"). Besides, on numerous occasions, Miró manifested his fascination for certain ancient and traditional arts, although he rarely cited his references individually. A review of the artist's own words, through the study of his epistolary corpus, interviews, and personal notebooks, reveals numerous quotes and expressions that illustrate his conception of antiquity in relation to tradition.[13] A good example of this connection are the "siurells." Of them, Miró said:

---

10. Photographs by Josep Planas i Montanyà taken in 1968 show the cuts hanging on the walls. The magazine out of which these images were cut was published in 1966.

11. From the beginning, the research presented in this essay has been developed in parallel by Miró's heirs, by the curators, librarians, and personnel from the three institutions in Barcelona and Palma, as well as by ourselves, between Barcelona, Palma, Saint-Paul-de-Vence, and Paris.

12. We thank Pilar Ortega (Successió Miró, Palma de Mallorca) for providing this information.

13. About the influence traditional and ancient arts on Miró, the Catalan writer Baltasar Porcel interviewed the artist: "J.M.: Necessito estar en contacte amb la terra ... Em rodejo d'objectes d'ar-

> C'est beau, n'est-ce pas, les siurells? Je les ai découverts dès ma première enfance à Majorque, et j'en emportais toujours quelques-uns lorsque je retournais à Barcelone. Les siurells ne devraient pas disparaître. L'artisanat est l'art les plus pur, l'art du peuple, que j'ai constamment admiré. Est-il vrai que les siurells relèvent d'une très ancienne tradition de l'île, dont les origines remontent aux Phéniciens?[14]

The evocation of "primitive," prehistoric, or archaic imaginary when describing Miró or his creation is ubiquitous throughout the specialized publications.[15] Penrose, for instance, was fascinated by Miró's ability to "invent" abstract forms that "seem significant and somehow akin to the prehistoric signs," figures that find "their preceding archetypes" in "the oldest known works of art" (Penrose 1970, 66–67). Penrose suggested that Miró's interest for "primitive" rituals and art would date back to his first trips to Paris, in the early 1920s, influenced by poets like Robert Desnos, Michel Leiris, and Antonin Artaud.[16] The fierceness of the "savage" and the innocence of the "primeval" in Miró's work would exalt, according to the author, our own "primitive" emotions.

---

tesania popular ... B.P.: S'ha dit que havíeu begut a moltes fonts ... Han influït sobre vós l'art romanic, l'Orient i la Xina, els miniaturistes perses dels segles disset i divuit..." (Porcel 1989, 18). Miró wrote on his notebooks: "I have to have always in mind Iberian prehistoric paintings"; "a magnificence [Miró is writing about a female sculpture he made in the early forties] that evokes sculptures from the Eastern Islands"; "On *A Woman*, I have to think on prehistoric idols reproduced on the first volume of the Spanish History" (Picon 2002, 131, 143, 151). From the same notebook, the renowned Miró specialist Margit Rowell selected the following thoughts by the artist: "In Mexican prehistory, there were vases with a dark red surface (brilliantly smooth), and at the top a drawing in black, as in Greek vases" (Rowell 1995, 197). In an interview with Francis Lee, Miró said: "My favorite painting schools belonged to a time as remote as possible: paintings from prehistoric grottoes–primitives" (Rowell 1995, 225). For Miró's relation to traditional and ancient cultures, see Catoir 1995; Calzada 2001; Dupin 1993; Fitzsimmons 1958; Juncosa 2002; Labrusse 2001; Panicelli and Rico 1994; Penrose 1970; Queneau 1949; Rowell 2002; Schneider 1963; Serra 1984; Stavrinaki 2011.

14. Serra 1984, 22. Miró referenced to the Siurells frequently in relation to his works: "Como punto de partida usar raíces de caña, arreglarlas un poco con cuchillo y hacer un moulage o simplemente darle una capa de yeso e ir trabajándolo; se puede hacer una reproducción en yeso, como los silbatos de Mallorca, y colorearlo" (Rowell 2002, 251–77). Also Penrose (1970, 141) highlights Miró's admiration for these "Catalan" traditional terracotta figures, and their resemblance to "the archaic sculptures of all primitive cultures." The author particularly highlights the simplicity of their shapes, "in which one can still perceive the fingers that molded them." The author presumes that the textures, the colors and the vitality of these figures would have made these statuettes more meaningful for the artist.

15. Among numerous examples: the same building of Son Boter is described as "the most primitive house" of the hill (Penrose 1970, 127); the artist is said to evoke "a shine like that of an antediluvian firefly" (Rowell 2002, 148); the figures in his collage-drawings are said to suggest "dancing shadows executing a mysterious ritual, or painted or incised signs on the walls of a cavern of a prehistoric man" (Penrose 1970, 76–77); his art is said to "successfully adapt a modern technique to primitive themes," with a notable "sense of the ancient mysteries, of the irrational, of the magical powers within things" (Fitzsimmons 1958).

16. Penrose 1970, 195. Artaud, poet, but also actor and theatre director, described Syria in his

This habit of confining Miró's references within a vague category of "primitive" arts certainly contributed to the erroneous identification of the Mesopotamian objects hanging from the walls of Son Boter. Recent publications mentioning these clipped photographs indicate, for instance:

> Ritagli di riviste fissati con puntine da disegno alle porte e alle controfinestre … Le cartoline postali e le ritagli di carta, di eterogenea iconografia—sculture precolombine, galloromane e iberiche. (Panilleci and Rico 1994, 23)[17]

In other publications on Son Boter, the Mesopotamian references have gone unnoticed:

> El grafiti titulado "Femme" presenta evidentes similitudes formales y sígnicas con el conjunto de figuras arqueológicas que Miró clavó a su lado. Incluso el mismo sentido estilizado de esas figuras puede seguirse en el proyecto escultórico apenas abocetado al carboncillo. (Interiores 1993, 190)

> Miró was keenly interested in the early civilizations of the Mediterranean area and enthralled by their common preoccupation with the fertility of the soil, beasts, and humankind, which came as a revelation to him. He visited archaeological museums in order to study objects that would inspire his three-dimensional work, but he also created an imaginary museum at home by plastering the walls of his studios with photographic newspaper clippings, illustrations from books and magazines, and sketches of his own … The planetary choreography of the chairs in the studio is matched by the little slips of paper and objects that stud the walls …: magazine photographs of archaeological finds, predominantly from the Mediterranean area—from Cyprus, Greece, North Africa, Sicily, Asia Minor. This sea of papers testifies to Miró's keen eye and his predilection for three-dimensional form, which applied as much to the primitive idols of the Cyclades as to the simple but masterly ceramics and bronzes of earlier civilizations. (Catoir 1995, 16, 20)

> Without any doubt, Miró will keep the taste, the nostalgia of a collective, magic, mythic art. Soon, before leaving, we shall look at the reproductions that hold on the wall of the ground floor of the studio: primitive Catalan art [this means, Romanesque frescoes], Oceanic, African, Maya art—no individual art. Nevertheless, these are shapes that serve him as a springboard, like these cut photographs from a paper from yesterday or from a magazine forty years old, these heteroclite objects, these Eastern eggs, these "siurells." (Picon 2002, 109)

---

famous book *Héliogabale* as a "land where the earth lives, and where there are living stones," where "stones live like the plants and the animals, and it can also be said that the sun is a living being" (196).

17. N.B.: there are no Gallo-Roman or Iberian sculptures in Son Boter.

Even recently, an exhibition in Italy showing both works of art and documentation by Miró asked for the loan of one of these clipped photographs to emulate the studio of the artist. The clip, however, was not included in the catalogue individually, but only in a caption indicating "Image of Human Figures."[18]

The relations between the photographs, the graffiti around them, and subsequent works he would conceive in this space have been studied by previous authors. However, the redefinition of the identity of the artifacts shown in the photographs will require future revisions to some of the previous approaches to the works he produced in this space. Pedde (2012, 91–92) has suggested possible formal relations between the position of the arms and the gesture of the hands of a Sumerian statue and nearby graffiti; hands and eyes were common features in Miró's anthropomorphic representations. She also highlights the resemblance between one big terracotta worshipper statue and the sculpture *Woman* (1968, FJM 7281). Next to this terracotta figurine the artist drew a series of anthropomorphic figures on charcoal on the wall.[19] These graffiti have been put in relation with the marble sculpture called *Femme échevelée*, exhibited in the garden of the Fondation Marguerite et Aimée Maeght in Saint-Paul-de-Vence, France. A writing on the wall located near the graffiti, reading "without hair or holes," seems to suggest the process by which this sculpture was engendered from the Sumerian terracotta figurine. Another formal similarity can be identified between the bow that a warrior is handling in the "lion-hunt stele" from Uruk (IMB 23477) and the moon in the nearby graffiti (fig. 3). The moon is a motif related to female figures that constantly appears in Miró's work from his early paintings. In this case, the bow is being transformed into a crescent moon.[20]

Beyond the walls of Son Boter the formal similarities between some Sumerian artifacts and works by Miró are surprising. Some of these relations have been studied in a recent exhibition at the Joan Miró Foundation in Barcelona (Azara 2017), such as the resemblance between the heads of some Syro-Mesopotamian terracotta statuettes from the second millennium and some sculptures by Miró.[21] The curved peak of the bird-like anthropomorphic figure fits beautifully within the artist's imaginary of the

18. *Miró: L'impulso creativo* (Palazzo del Te in Mantua, Italy, 26 November 2014—6 April 2015). The catalogue also reproduces one of the cut photographs from Son Boter, showing three Sumerian figurines: one bronze worshipper and two terracotta lizard-head female figurines from the fifth millennium BCE. The caption says: "Ritaglio con immagini di figure." Despite that these statuettes are well known, there is no mention of their origin.

19. For more suggestions on possible relations between the cuts and different works by Miró see Pedde 2012, 91–92.

20. The comparison between the moon and the horns of a bull was frequent among Spanish surrealists.

21. For instance, Proyecto para un monumento (1954, FJM 7245); Proyecto para un monumento (1954, FJM 7246), Proyecto para un monumento (1954, FJM 7247); Middle Bronze Age figurines from Syria, held at the Département des Antiquités Orientales at the Musée du Louvre (Azara 2017, 55, 56)

femmes-oiseau. One is led to speculate about the artist's interest in or fascination with these statues, terracotta statuettes, and hard stone reliefs. It can be thought that these ancient figures might have attracted Miró because they aligned with his taste or his conception of what art should be or represent, or how it should represent the world. Large hypnotic eyes and schematic shapes, as well as mythological or ancient figures had always attracted him.[22] We imagine that maybe these early Mesopotamian items evoked in Miró an iconography of his interest, which triggered in him the need to hang the photographs on the walls.

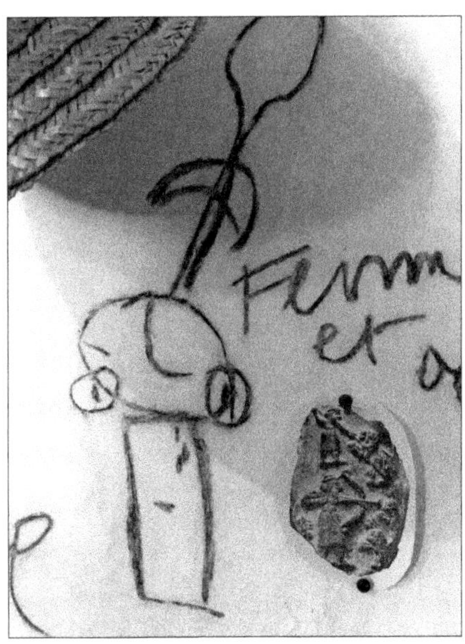

Figure 3. Graffiti and stone relief. Courtesy of Marc Marín and Pedro Azara.

Almost all the photographs hanging from the walls of Son Boter belonged to two different issues from the same month of the magazine *Arts & Loisirs* from 1966 (fig. 4).[23] Fortunately for us, the complete collection of this magazine, which was published between 1966 and 1967, is held at the library of the National Museum of Catalan Art (MNAC) in Barcelona. *Arts & Loisirs* was a popular French cultural magazine managed by the journalist André Parinaud, who was at that time also the director of the modern art magazine *Arts.* New artistic, sociological, and philosophical themes were the main concern of this magazine, together with articles on modern art and cultural movements, artists, and exhibitions. The French Assyriologist Jean Bottéro also published an illustrated text—precisely one of the two articles that caught Miró's attention.[24]

22. Miró: "L'œil, ça m'a toujours fasciné. Est-ce que je redoute l'œil? Non, nullement. Je n'ai aucune méfiance à son égard. Non, aucune crainte. L'œil c'est, pour moi, de la mythologie. Qu'est-ce que j'entends par mythologie? Par mythologie j'entends quelque chose qui est doté d'un caractère sacré comme une civilisation antique." (Rowell 1995, 300)

23. *Arts & Loisirs* 19 (2–9 and 9–16 February 1966). We thank the personnel at the archives at the Picasso Museum in Barcelona for tracking down the magazine from which these images were cut. We have not yet been able to identify the origin of two other small illustrations that Miró stuck to the walls. These, however, are also images of Mesopotamian iconography. One represents a Syro-Mesopotamian terracotta female figurine, the other an Iranian steatopygious terracotta female figure belonging to a private collection in Paris. One of the images was given on temporary loan to Italy at the time of this research, and we have not yet been able to look at its reverse.

24. Some well-known writers, such as Georges Perec, wrote regularly in *Arts & Loisirs.* A conversa-

AU LOUVRE LES TRÉSORS DE BAGDAD

SUMER

TOUT A COMMENCÉ LA !

Figure 4. *Arts & Loisirs*, 19 (2–9 February 1966), 46–47. Courtesy of Marc Marín and Pedro Azara.

Both articles illustrated with early Mesopotamian artifacts were published on the occasion of a travelling exhibition, called *Trésors du Musée de Baghdad: des Origines à l'Islam,* opened at the Louvre Museum in Paris in 1966.[25] It was an international travelling exhibition of masterpieces belonging to the Baghdad Archaeological Museum (as it was known then; now the National Museum of Iraq in Baghdad), ranging from Sumerian until Islamic times and curated by André Parrot, at the time chief curator of the *Département des Antiquités Orientales* at the Louvre Museum in Paris. It was shown in Hamburg (1964), Lisbon, and Turin (1965), and finally Bordeaux and Paris (1966).[26] This international travelling exhibition was possible due to the closure of the old Bagh-

tion between the philosopher Michel Foucault, already renowned by the time of the publication, and Claude Bonnefoy, the reputed literature critic, was published in June 1966.

25. The exhibition was hosted in the Mollien Gallery at the Louvre Museum from 28 January to 28 March 1966. The exhibition was organized thanks to the proposal of the Iraqi government by the Réunion des Musées Nationaux under the patronage of the Ministère des Affaires Culturelles, managed at that time by the Ministre d'État in charge of Cultural Affairs, the known writer and art historian M. André Malraux. A small catalogue with black and white photographs and a text by André Parrot was published.

26. The exhibition received mixed reviews. *Arts & Loisirs,* for instance, rated it with only two stars, and considered that despite the glimmering masterpieces, the exhibition was not able to give a broad view on Mesopotamian cultures.

dad Archaeological Museum while the new National Museum of Iraq was still under construction.

So far, the first documented evidence from the contact between Miró and Mesopotamia dates to 7 August 1934, when the artist Henri Matisse sent him a postcard he had bought in the Louvre Museum, showing the photograph of a copper head of a bull from Tello (ancient Girsu), excavated at the beginning of the twentieth century (fig. 5).[27] During the 1930s, Miró wrote on his personal booklets a list of readings of his interest, in which he included a special volume by the magazine *Cahiers d'Art* dedicated to Mesopotamian art (1935).[28] The study of the personal library of the artist, kept in a room with restrictive access at the library of the Joan Miró Foundation in Barcelona, reveals numerous volumes dedicated partially or completely to Mesopotamian culture. André Malraux sent Miró a dedicated volume of his work *Les voix du silence* (Galérie Pléiade, 1951), of the three volumes of *Le Musée Imaginaire de la sculpture mondiale* (Galérie Pléiade, 1952–54) and of the first edition of *La métamorphose des dieux* (Nouvelle Revue Française, 1957). In these publications appeared black and white photographs of some of the artifacts Miró would later, in the late 1960s, hang from the walls of Son Boter. Miró also kept a first edition of Samuel Noah Kramer's *L'histoire commence à Sumer* (1957), and a Spanish edition of André Parrot's *Assur* (1961).

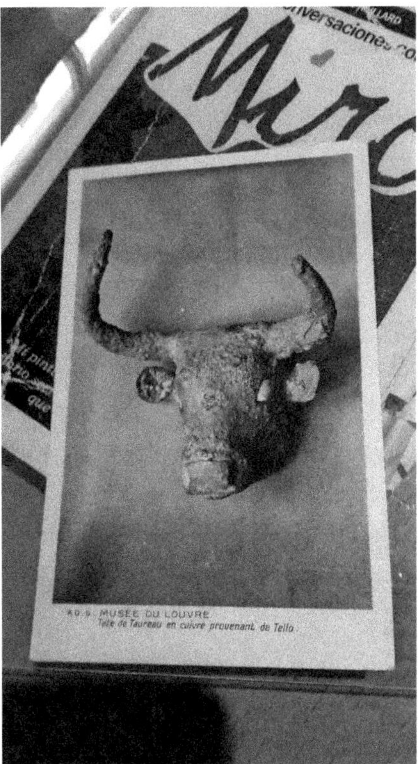

Figure 5. Postcard sent by Henri Matisse to Miró, showing a copper head of a bull from Tello (Iraq). Courtesy of Marc Marín and Pedro Azara.

In December 1963, the art critic Pierre Schneider published an interview that represents the only attested case of a direct "dialogue" between the artist and Mesopotamia.[29] This interview took place in the Louvre Museum in Paris. Miró asked Schneider

27. The postcard is held at the Successió Miró in Palma de Mallorca. When Matisse sent the postcard, Miró's use of bull iconography was already common, both in paintings and in sculpture.

28. Miró wrote: "L'art de la Mésopotamie (Cahiers d'Art)" in a personal booklet from the 1930s through 1940s (Ref. 1323–1411; Fundació Joan Miró, Barcelona). He referred to *L'Art de la Mésopotamie de la fin du quatrième millénaire au XVe siècle avant notre ère* (Zervos 1935).

29. Schneider 1963. The interview was published again in 1972, in *Les dialogues du Louvre*

to walk through the rooms of the museum without any particular direction, suggesting that the objects would somehow call him and not vice versa. In other words, he wanted to wander through the different galleries in search of subjects that would attract him and objects with whom to interact. Throughout the interview, Miró identified and compared Sumerian, Akkadian, Babylonian, Assyrian, Persian, and Egyptian objects. Among them, he particularly highlighted the "small objects from Tello [ancient Girsu]," the statues of Gudea, king of Lagash, past whom, he considered, one could not "walk quickly,"[30] a collection of bronzes from Luristan (Iran), and the statue of "Manishinsu" (Susa, Iran).[31] Among the objects of Tello-Girsu, Miró was amazed by one in particular, which he identified as "a sort of butterfly-woman."[32] He was probably referring to the Presargonid terracotta figure known as "statue fontaine" (AO4596). A frontal black and white photograph of this object had been included in the *Cahiers d'Art* dedicated to Mesopotamian art. Schneider describes how Miró, when standing in front of the figure, first lifted his hand and then let it fall down, "as a gesture of desperation and admiration." The fact that Miró interpreted—or transformed—the figure into a winged woman was common in his way of relating with the objects he found. The figure only acquired the wings through the eyes of Miró, who conferred upon her the ability to fly and thus translated her into his own visual language.

In contrast, in front of the Stele of Naram-Sin (ca. 2254–2218 BCE), the first Mesopotamian monarch who dared to represent himself wearing a divine tiara and thus as a divinity, Miró expressed his dissatisfaction: "It smells like ministries, like a consulate." The artist declared: "you don't receive that little 'shock,' like in the previous ones. It's too official." Schneider interprets this to mean that Miró rejected the stele for being an example of "established orders"; for being what he understands as an art imposed by "tyranny." In a similar manner, he showed no interest for Babylonian, Assyrian, or Egyptian objects. They appeared too political (Schneider 1963, 31–42).

Schneider understands Miró to be fascinated by objects of "bizarre shape, asymmetrical, tattooed with inscriptions," by those he considered to have "concentrations of a vital energy seized at the critical moment of their birth," those capable of giving a "shock," of hurting and cruelly deforming previous forms. It is remarkable that Miró, while wandering through the museum, asked Schneider to go to "his neighborhood." Schneider specifies: "Son quartier, c'est Sumer." It was in the first Mesopotamian rooms at the Département des Antiquités Orientales where the atmosphere was "calmed, si-

(Schneider 1972). We have accessed the edition of 1991. We thank Pilar Ortega and Gloria Moragas (Successió Miró, Palma) for providing this valuable information.

30. Miró: "A la vue du Prince [sic] de Lagash (Goudéa): On ne peut pas passer en vitesse" (Schneider 1963, 85).

31. It is possible that Schneider was referring to Manishtusu, king of Akkad, ca. 2270–2255 BCE (Sb47).

32. Miró: "Cette espèce de femme papillon, avec ses petits yeux, quelle merveille … Ça, et la statue colossale de Goudéa" (Schneider 1963, 113).

lent, warmly anonymous." His neighborhood: a welcoming place, where one is familiar with his neighbors, where one does not feel like a stranger.

Miró felt close to some Early Mesopotamian objects, either by its forms or by the meaning the artist attributed to them. It is certainly hard to know the level of knowledge that Miró had about the social or political history of early Mesopotamia, but he showed a high degree of familiarity with the aforementioned objects. He was probably familiar with the main Mesopotamian locations and figures, some of which he would recall from biblical passages, which he knew well.[33] In 1967, the surrealist poet Yvan Goll published *Bouquet de rêves pour Neila,* including a series lithographs by Miró. One of the poems, titled *De toutes les reines de Tyr,* read:

> De toutes les reines de Tyr et de Babylone
> De toutes les chanteuses de la Crète
> Des palmes de Palmyre
> Tu as hérité la sagesse
> Et le secret du sang.
> Écroulée est la coupole de Sodome
> Mais ses oiseaux égarés
> Commencent à dormir sur moi … (Miró 1976, 146–47)

Another Mesopotamian image that the artist hung on the walls of his studio shows a worshipper statue from Mari belonging to the National Museum of Damascus, Syria.[34] This image was used as the cover of the small guide of an exhibition dedicated to André Malraux that took place in the Fondation Marguerite et Aimée Maeght in Saint-Paul-de-Vence, France, in 1973.[35] The exhibition, inspired by Malraux's Imaginary Museum, was an ambitious display of art encompassing cultures from various periods and locations, that included significant archaeological material.

One of the images contained in the *Arts & Loisirs* magazines, showing a Syro-Mesopotamian masculine figure from the beginning of the second millennium BCE, was first hung on the walls of Son Boter, to be later removed with the aims of using it for a different purpose.[36] This image is now contained within a paper envelope labeled by Miró himself with the words "Miró" and "Ballet," held at the Joan Miró Foundation in Barcelona (FJM 1161). This envelope contains a series of images—postcards and photograph cuts—showing an amalgam of popular and traditional art. These were in-

33. Miró: "Mientras hago escultura tener siempre la Biblia abierta, esto me dará un sentimiento de grandiosidad y de gestación del mundo" (Personal booklets, 1941–42; Rowell 2002, 251–77).

34. Archives of the Pilar and Joan Miró Foundation in Palma de Mallorca.

35. André Malraux et le Musée Imaginaire, Fondation Marguerite et Aimé Maeght en Saint-Paul-de-Vence (13 July—30 September 1973)

36. A photograph by Josep Planas i Montanyà (1968) shows this cut hanging from a wall from the ground floor of Son Boter, close to a similar figurine interpreted as a female. Next to them, Miró had written "monument à un couple d'amoureux."

tended to be projected in the representation of the ballet *L'Oeil Oiseau*, in the gardens of the Fondation Marguerite et Aimée Maeght (Saint-Paul-de-Vence). This representation never took place, given the political instability during the summer of 1968 in France (the so called *Mai 68*). A later version of the ballet, *L'Ucello Luce*, would be presented thirteen years later in Venice and Bologna.

Miró had participated in the design of theatre scenography already in the 1920s. He worked on the script and the design of a ballet between 1927 and 1935. The scheme was a succession of unrelated scenes dealing with human connections with the outer and inner worlds (some exalting, some terrifying). A labyrinth—a metaphor of the inner self—was a most important space. Miró, however, abandoned the project since he felt incapable of writing a structured plot. The idea was taken up again at the beginning of the 1960s. Miró had designed, by then, a real labyrinth, a stone garden filled with statues at the new Maeght Foundation in Saint-Paul-de-Vence, built, again, by the Spanish architect Josep Lluís Sert. Miró gave this old plot to the French poet Jacques Dupin who, following Miró's sketches and notes written in his notebooks from the 1930s, tried to write a scheme that could be used as a plot for the ballet entitled *L'Oeil Oiseau*. He wrote that "*On Fire* [the title of one of the scenes], that would end with a projection of rapid images on a screen in order to evoke the painter, his studio, his work and his universe, would take place in the museum [Maeght Foundation] courtyard."[37] The script indicated:

> Interlude: Irruption of images. A large number of still images are projected onto a white screen at a rapid but irregular rate. Found images that Miró collected in sketchbooks or on the walls of his studio [sic]. (Bravo, Escudero, and Malet 1995, 211, 389)

The postcards contained in the paper envelope may help explain why Miró chose the Syro-Mesopotamian figurine. Most postcards collected by the artist illustrate traditional or folk topics. The objects shown in them are anonymous. Miró was fond of objects and buildings whose author was not remembered because for him names of artists were not important at all. These objects and spaces were not the creation of a single mind, they were not personal creations; instead, they were created following traditional patterns, materials, techniques, and shapes that did not belong to anyone.

Miró's defense of anonymity in art is well-known.[38] In spite of the limited written or spoken thoughts of his on record, Miró made very clear that anonymous art was

37. Dupin 1993, 346. This description, however, does not fully coincide with what Dupin wrote in another more-detailed text on this ballet (Bravo, Escudero, and Malet 1995, 207). Unfortunately, Dupin is dead, and there are some impediments to consulting his texts and letters.

38. In an interview undertaken by the French poet Georges Duthuit, Miró answered to Duthuit's questions: "G.D.: Vous m'avez également dit que l'œuvre d'art doit être anonyme parce qu'elle doit s'intégrer dans le cadre dans lequel on la place. J.M.: En effet … Une peinture murale est dictée par l'architecture, par les plans, par les formes, par les volumes, par l'entourage, jusqu'à ce qu'il y ait une

the greatest and that what was called "primitive" art, which certainly included some manifestations of "Early Mesopotamian art," as well as popular art,[39] were the acme of art for him. So, in order to find true art, which for Miró comprised "primitive," popular art, early archaeological artifacts, as well as objects of folklore, it was necessary to go back in time, to follow the path to the origins of art: "il faut remonter jusqu' aux sources de l'expression pour retrouver le collectif" (Rowell 1995, 241). Or, if one would like to stay in tune with modern times, ballet was the solution; ballet was a collective artistic creation: "le ballet est le type même de l'art collectif" (Rowell 1995, 244). Ballet, "primitive" and popular art, or anonymous art were all intimately connected for Miró.

Early Mesopotamian sculptures, figurines, and reliefs were motifs for his inspiration because they revealed some of the first human creations. By using them, he was looking at the roots of the creative human impulse. Early Mesopotamian items were valuable for Miró not because they were old but because there were timeless, showing that great art was not ahead of time but was out of time, relevant in any period of time. Miró was inspired by these images because he was trying to create shapes and creatures as relevant and vital as the ancient ones. This permanence of shapes and techniques may have fascinated Miró. These figurines were thousands of years old and yet they looked like modern traditional ones, like those that Miró collected in his studios. The notion of author, as a personal creator, was abolished for him.

3. *Miró in Mesopotamia*

We started this study by asking ourselves about the significance of the magazine cuts hanging from the walls of Son Boter. Although the obtaining of these images might have been a matter of chance, the location of the cuts within the room was hardly fortuitous, as has been discussed. Their presence triggers comparisons of Son Boter with a canvas, an "imaginary museum," a prehistoric cavern, and a collage. Their placement marks the starting of the transfiguration of the space into a work of art. The essence or meaning of the photographed artifacts expands throughout the different halls of the building through the graffiti and is later transmitted to the different sculptures and *personnages* conceived within its walls. The cuts represented for Miró a window or a passage to the origins. From there, Mesopotamian shapes were translated into *mironian*

fusion complète entre paysage, architecture et peinture. C'est donc une œuvre tout à fait anonyme, impersonnelle. Il en est toujours ainsi dans les grandes époques. Les fresques anciennes n'ont pas été signées par leurs auteurs. Les pyramides non plus" (Rowell 1995, 165); "Ninguna escuela, [declaró] ningún artista me interesa; ninguno. Sólo lo anónimo, lo que sale del esfuerzo inconsciente de la masa" (Rowell 2002, 174).

39. "L'art populaire universel est une des sources de [mon] inspiration. Les racines humaines puissent aux mêmes sources de cette planète" (Rowell 1995, 257). "Plus une chose est locale, plus elle est universelle. D'où l'importance de l'art populaire: il y a une grande unité entre les sifflets de Majorque et les choses grecques" (Rowell 1995, 274).

forms, saturating the artist's creations with the archaic essence of the "dawn of times," making the past present.

His workshops were spaces where he collected images and objects that would allow him to liaise with their forms and meanings, triggering the germination of new ideas strongly connected to tradition. They were spaces where one could connect with the transcendent. Miró perceived no differences between past and present.[40] He was aware that calling these artifacts "works of art" was controversial, since a modern concept of art did not exist in early Mesopotamia.[41] And still, the "impact" or the "shock" of these figures was greater than later works of art. They were admirable because he perceived them as spontaneous and anonymous. He was not only attracted to their images—indirectly through photographs and publications—but he was keen to visit the ancient Near Eastern galleries at the Louvre, especially those dedicated to Sumer, which he called "his neighborhood." We know, therefore, that he was not only moved by the image of the object but by the object itself. This allows us to infer that his interest did not only reside in the shapes of the objects, but also in their essence or meaning.

In Schneider's interview, Miró shows a predilection for those forms and figures that, he understands, do not fit into a canon or an official order established by institutions ("by tyranny"). These preferred shapes are described by Schneider as abstract, bizarre, asymmetrical, or tattooed with inscriptions. Miró tends to interpret these figures in his own language, and in this process, even if he shows familiarity with most of the objects identified, he does not show a preoccupation for their accurate identification. The "*statue fontaine*," for instance, is perceived as a *femme-papillon*. This transformation of reality into his own language was common in the way he related to the world.

We might also infer from this realization that the artist rejected later forms of ancient Near Eastern figurative art because he presumed figurative realism to be an expression of official ideology. If so, Miró's perception of the history of art would recall Henri Frankfort's revision on the history of abstract art, presuming a nonfigurative origin of human artistic creation, against the classical idea that abstraction was always the manifestation of a degeneration from a previous figurative period (Frankfort 1939, 1943; see Evans 2012, 46–75). Frankfort's publications, together with works by other authors, such as Georges Bataille, Michel Leiris, and Christian Zervos, contributed to establishing a theoretical scheme thanks to which early Mesopotamian art was considered a thoughtful and valid alternative to Western works of art, facilitating their embrace by modern artists who believed these objects would allow for a new

40. The artist insists on this idea during his interview with Schneider, with statements such as: "Time does not exist for me" (Schneider 1971, 35).

41. Miró, in front of small objects from the site of Tello (ancient Girsu): "Ah. Tremendous. Do they think of this as great art, or what? These little things, they fill an enormous room. How can you respond to paintings after you've seen these things? (Silence) Art? They probably never heard of the word" (Schneider 1971, 35).

conception of art and thought, contrary to the classical paradigm (see Evans 2012; Bahrani 2017, 136).

Miró's case is far from unique. Artists and poets such as Pablo Picasso,[42] Henry Moore, Alberto Giacometti, Barbara Hepworth, Willem de Kooning, Willy Baumeister, or Charles Olson, in the 1920s and 1930s, also received Mesopotamian sculpture and writing as admirable arts, with which they could communicate and which were capable of inspiring their new creations. Some of these authors allowed early Mesopotamian sculpture to enter the realm of art through the "legitimate" frame of "primitive art." It is hard to determine to what extent this frame is still accepted nowadays outside of academia, in the popular culture, although the influence of this initial reception of early Mesopotamian material culture as "primitive" seems evident in the fact that the relation between Miró and Mesopotamia has gone unnoticed until now. Artifacts and images in his studios were rendered anonymous either by the artist or by specialists who sustained and legitimized the inaccurate identification of these artifacts.

It is fair to point out how throughout this process modern artists contributed to steer the Western perception of ancient Near Eastern art. Miró's perception, shared among some aforementioned artists and critics, that these objects were "spontaneous" and "anonymous"—characteristics commonly attributed to "primitive" arts—contrasts, however, with the views of scholars such as Evans (2012), who clearly recognizes a canon that tends to regulate the style of Early Dynastic temple statuary.[43] Miró's case seems to support Evans's thesis that the present reception of this statuary is still primarily formal, and that the influence of the first archeological reconstructions and exhibitions of this material is still present in current functional interpretations. It seems clear that the emergence and sustenance of the paradigm of early Mesopotamian art as a form of "primitivism" was forged through the interaction of not only a few artists and art historians, but also gallerists, art collectors, curators, critics, editors, and even some archaeologists, throughout the twentieth century. An interesting question for further analysis would be whether this paradigm of a "Mesopotamian primitivism" is still recognizable in contemporary artists whose work is inspired by ancient Near Eastern cultures.

Bibliography

Arts & Loisirs. 1966. Issue 19 (2–9 and 9–16 February).

Azara, P., ed. 2017. *Sumer and the Modern Paradigm.* Barcelona: Fundació Joan Miró.

Azara, P., and M. Marín. 2018. "An Archaeological Exhibition without Archaeology? Joan Miró's

---

42. Picasso interpreted Neo-Assyrian winged bulls in some of his drawings and engravings of the Vollard Suite in the 1930s.

43. She identifies, however, a certain degree of diversity among statues, which she attributes to geographical and temporary variations, as well as to a certain degree of individualization of the statuary according to gender and to the inscriptions they bear.

Look at Sumerian Masterpieces." In G. Emberling and L. P. Petit (eds.), *Museums and the Ancient Middle East: Curatorial Practice and Audiences*, 138–50, London: Routledge.

Bahrani, Z. 2014. *The Infinite Image: Art, Time and the Aesthetic Dimension in Antiquity*. London: Reaktion.

———. 2017. *Mesopotamia: Ancient Art and Architecture*. London: Thames & Hudson.

Bravo, I., C. Escudero, and R. Mª Malet. 1995. *Miró a escena*. Barcelona: Fundación Joan Miró.

Catoir, B. 1995. *Miró on Mallorca*. Munich and New York: Prestel.

Calzada, C. 2001. "Aproximaciones a la relación de Miró con el arte prehistórico." *Anuario del Departamento de Historia y Teoría del Arte (Universidad Autónoma de Madrid)* 13:183–93.

Chi, J. and P. Azara, eds. 2015. *From Ancient to Modern: Archaeology and Aesthetics*. Princeton: Princeton University Press.

Dupin, J. 1993. *Joan Miró*. Barcelona: La Polígrafa.

Evans, J. M. 2012. *The Lives of Sumerian Sculpture: An Archaeology of the Early Dynastic Temple*. Cambridge: Cambridge University Press.

Fitzsimmons, J. 1958. *Miró: 'Peintures Sauvages' 1934 to 1953*. New York: Pierre Matisse Gallery.

Frankfort, H. 1939. *Sculpture of the Third Millennium B.C. from Tell Asmar and Khafajah*, Oriental Institute Publications 44. Chicago: University of Chicago Press.

———. 1943. *More Sculpture from the Diyala Region*. Oriental Institute Publications 60. Chicago: University of Chicago Press.

Juncosa P. 2002. "*De lo anónimo en lo construido. Primitivismo y Modernidad en el espacio de Miró y Sert.*" Ph.D. diss., Escuela Técnica Superior de Arquitectura de Barcelona Aproximaciones a la relación de Miró con el arte prehistórico – UPC, Spain.

Interiores de Miró: En el Pabellón Mudéjar de Sevilla. 1993. Seville: Centro Andaluz de Arte Contemporáneo.

Joan Miró: Son Abrines i Son Boter; Olis, dibuixos y graffitis. 1987. Palma de Mallorca: Fundació Pilar i Joan Miró.

Labrusse, R. 2001. *Miró: Un feu dans les ruines*. Paris: Hazan.

Marín, M. 2017. "Miró: el 'impacto' sumerio." In P. Azara, M. Marín, B. Pedde, Z. Bahrani (eds.), *Sumeria y el paradigma moderno*, 119–25. Barcelona: Fundación Joan Miró.

Miró Sert: La construcció d'una amistat. 2007. Palma de Mallorca: Fundació Pilar i Joan Miró a Mallorca.

Miró, J. 1976. *Joan Miró: Litographe III (1964–1969)*. Paris: Maeght Éditeur.

Moore, H. 1935. "Mesopotamian Art." *The Listener* 5(June):944–96.

Panicelli, I., and P. Rico Lacasa, eds. 1994. *Gi ultimi sogni di Miró*. Milan: Edizioni Charta.

Pedde, B. 2012. "Ancient Near Eastern Motifs in the European Art of the 20th Century AD." In R. Matthews and J. Curtis (eds.), *Proceedings of the 7th International Congress on the Archaeology of the Ancient Near East, 12th to 16th April 2010, Vol. 2*, 89–100. London: British Museum and University College.

Penrose, R. 1970. *Miró*. Barcelona: Destino.

Picon, G., ed. 2002. *Joan Miró: Los cuadernos catalanes, dibujos y escritos inéditos presentados por Gaëtan Picon*. Valencia: Institut Valencià d'Art Modern; Murcia: Colegio Oficial de Aparejadores y Arquitectos Técnicos de la Región de Murcia.

Porcel, B. 1989. "Joan Miró o l'Equilibri fantastic." In *Els tallers de Miró*. Barcelona: Institut Català d'Estudis Mediterranis.

Punyet, J., and J.-M. del Moral. 2015. *El ojo de Miró*. Madrid: La Fábrica.

Queneau, R. 1949. *Joan Miró ou le poète préhistorique*. Paris: Albert Skira.

Raillard, G. 1978. *Conversaciones con Miró*. Barcelona: Granica.

Rowell, M., ed. 1995. "Joan Miró: Notes de Travail, 1940–41, 1941–42." In *Joan Miró: Écrits et entretiens*, 183–216. Paris: Lelong.

———. 2002. *Joan Miró: Escritos y conversaciones.* Valencia: Institut Valencià d'Art Modern; Murcia: Colegio Oficial de Aparejadores y Arquitectos Técnicos de la Región de Murcia.

Schneider, P. 1963. "Au Louvre avec Miró." *Preuves* 154:35–44. Reprinted in *Les dialogues du Louvre* Paris: A. Biro, 1972, 1991.

Serra, P. 1984. *Miró et Mallorca.* Paris: Éditions Cercle d'Art.

Stavrinaki, M. 2011. "Modernité préhistorique: techniques 'd'auto-imitation' et temporalités à rebours chez Max Ernst et Joan Miró." *Perspective* 1:574–79.

Trésors du Musée de Bagdad: des origines à l'Islam. 1964. Paris: Musée du Louvre, Ministère des Affaires Culturelles – Réunion des Musées Nationaux.

Zervos, C. 1935. *L'Art de la Mésopotamie De la fin du quatrième millénaire au XVe siècle avant notre ère: Elam, Sumer, Akkad.* Paris: *Éditions* Cahiers d'Art.

Case Studies in the Popular Reception of the Tell Asmar Sculpture Hoard

Jean M. Evans

The great impression made by the Early Dynastic sculpture hoard from Tell Asmar cannot be underestimated. Henri Frankfort, director of the Iraq Expedition of the Oriental Institute of the University of Chicago, published the Asmar sculpture hoard in the first of his two volumes devoted to sculpture excavated in the Diyala region east of Baghdad (Frankfort 1939, 1943). Frankfort's treatment of Early Dynastic sculpture signaled an abandonment of the dominant anthropological research model with its emphasis on the "Sumerian Problem" (Jones 1969; Evans 2012, 46–75). Frankfort instead adopted art-historical methodologies, focusing on style and its evolution. The geometric-style sculpture in the Asmar sculpture hoard was designated a chronological marker, contemporary wherever it appeared, and it was largely on the basis of sculpture style that a tripartite subdivision of the Early Dynastic period was articulated (Evans 2007).

Aesthetic inquiry with its emphasis on stylistic analysis has been steadfast in research on Early Dynastic sculpture since the early twentieth century. It is a way of seeing, a gaze from which it is difficult to turn. As I argue here, the aesthetic reception of Sumerian sculpture and its positioning at the beginning of art history has permeated popular culture, too. Three case studies in the popular reception of the Asmar sculpture hoard beyond the scope of scholarly research are presented below. That this popular reception is primarily visual is not accidental. Rather, it reflects the aesthetic inquiry that has dominated the Asmar sculpture hoard.

The first case study considers an online sighting of a Sumerian (Early Dynastic) statue on Mars. The description of this Martian-Sumerian statue demonstrates how prevalent the early twentieth-century reception of Sumerian sculpture still is today. Its steadfastness is bolstered by the affinities early twentieth-century Western artists felt with Sumerian sculpture. These affinities were universal responses applicable to any artistic tradition understood as "primitive."

Next, I examine the reception of the Asmar sculpture hoard in Meg Saligman's mural *Common Threads*, which includes the largest figure in the Asmar sculpture hoard. The mural reflects the treatment of the Asmar sculpture hoard in art history textbooks, which frequently place the statues at the origins of broader themes and developments. Similar to the way early twentieth-century Western artists embraced Sumerian sculpture, the framing of Sumerian sculpture within an origins narrative perpetuates universal responses. It is this sense of connectivity in framing Sumerian sculpture within an origins narrative that is explored visually by Saligman.

Finally, the artist Michael Rakowitz considers the role of the present in two projects that incorporate elements of the Oriental Institute's Mesopotamian collection in general and the Asmar sculpture hoard in particular. Rakowitz's projects signal a turn away from the aesthetic object as somehow fixed at the moment of inception. The archaeologist and the contested space of archaeology within a post-colonial history is a central theme, as is loss and the paradox of reconstruction. Rakowitz's visual biographies of Early Dynastic sculpture and other Mesopotamian artifacts pose questions that, if addressed also in ancient Near Eastern scholarship, would suggest different methodologies for a renewed approach to these artifacts.

1. *The Cone-Shaped Beard of a Sumerian Statue on Mars*

The U.S. National Aeronautics and Space Administration (NASA) launched the Curiosity rover on Mars in 2012. Equipped with seventeen cameras, the rover has captured thousands of images of the surface of Mars as part of its mission to determine whether the planet is habitable to microbial life. The rover's images, which have been made available online, have captured the public's imagination. Among the surface formations on Mars, enthusiasts have identified everything from utilitarian objects to the face of Donald Trump. More specifically, online ufologists and alien conspiracy theorists have found evidence of extraterrestrial life—Morse-code messages and humanoid aliens—among the surface formations on Mars. Sumerian sculpture is also part of this evidence. In December 2015, a formation in one rover image was interpreted as the head from a Sumerian statue (fig. 1; McKeown 2015; Ivan 2017).

The possibility of a Sumerian statue on Mars is of particular importance for Anunnaki believers (see Winters, this volume). In early Sumerian texts, Anunnaki is a general term for deities (Black and Green 1992, 32). To modern believers, the Anunnaki in Sumerian myth are extraterrestrial beings who used Mars as a way station en route to colonizing Earth in antiquity. These and other similar beliefs are categorized as ancient astronaut hypotheses. What these hypotheses have in common is the premise that extraterrestrial beings made contact with ancient civilizations on Earth and brought with them technology so advanced that they were accorded divine status (Lieb 1998).

The tenets of Anunnaki believers are largely based on the writings of Zecharia Sitchin (1920–2010), a graduate of the London School of Economics who was self-taught in the ancient languages he claimed supported his theories. Drawing on analyses of primarily Sumerian texts, Sitchin (2015) argued that the Anunnaki were extraterrestrial beings who had traveled to Earth from the planet Nibiru. Ultimately, they created

Figure 1. NASA image from the Mars Curiosity rover with enhancement by author, to reproduce the methods used by Ufologists to identify forms among the surface formations. Courtesy NASA/JPL-Caltech. Courtesy NASA/JPL-Caltech.

humankind in the form of the Sumerians who worshiped them. The Anunnaki eventually left Earth but it is believed they may return one day—possibly in 2022.

Although scholars have dismissed Sitchin, belief in the Anunnaki has developed into a subculture. His popularity is undeniable. *The 12th Planet*—Sitchin's first book in the Earth Chronicles series—has gone through forty-five printings. His books have sold millions of copies worldwide and have been translated into over twenty-five languages. This popularity is not a purely theoretical exercise. The Office of Museum Education and Public Programs at the Oriental Institute, for example, receives inquiries about Anunnaki beliefs. On occasion, enthusiasts have offered to teach our Museum visitors about the Anunnaki.

In the rover image, "ufologists believe we can clearly make out the face of the statue, two eyes, a nose, a mouth and the typical cone-shaped beard we see in nearly all Ancient Sumerian Statues on our planet" (Ancient Code 2015). The sculpture in the

Figure 2. Tell Asmar, Abu Temple, Early Dynastic sculpture hoard. The statues in the hoard are now divided among the Iraq Museum, The Oriental Institute of the University of Chicago, and The Metropolitan Museum of Art. Courtesy of the Oriental Institute of the University of Chicago.

rover image was identified by Martine Grainey, who studies NASA images and posts her findings to Facebook.[1] Grainey enhanced the rover image to make more visible a land formation resembling a male head from an Early Dynastic temple statue. More specifically, the combination of darkened long hair and beard resembles the largest male figure in the Asmar sculpture hoard (fig. 2). Some scholars have identified this statue as a representation of a deity (Jacobsen 1989). It would therefore follow that, for Anunnaki believers, the sculpture fragment on Mars preserves the appearance of these extraterrestrial beings.

My aim here is to focus on one aspect of this Sumerian statue on Mars: the criteria used for identification. Eyes, nose, and mouth are cited. Human facial features, of course, are not particular to Sumerian statues. The only specificity in the identification is the cone-shape of the beard. What is so telling about a cone?

At stake here is not the identification of a Sumerian statue on Mars. Instead, it is the articulation of that identification. For there we detect the influence of the early twentieth-century reception of the Asmar sculpture hoard. Literally beyond the furthest reaches of our planet—and, figuratively, far beyond the reaches of scholarly dis-

1. I would like to thank Ivan Petricevic of ancient-code.com who corresponded with me about this image in December 2017.

course—the early twentieth-century emphasis on geometric abstraction governs the reception of Early Dynastic sculpture.

The vocabulary used to describe Early Dynastic ("Sumerian") sculpture is still largely that of Frankfort (1939, 1943). Frankfort (1935, 121) asserted that the Asmar sculpture hoard represented the "foundation of all sculptural achievement" because it was an early example of stone sculpture. The widely held assumptions that art had evolved from its primordial origins in abstract, geometric forms particularly resonated with Frankfort. In the sculpture style of the Asmar sculpture hoard, Frankfort saw a human body that was "ruthlessly reduced to abstract plastic form" (1935, 73; 1939, 20). The result was a series of "bold simplifications which approximate, in a varying degree, the ultimate limit, namely purely geometrical bodies" (1939, 19). For all Mesopotamian sculpture, this geometry was "the cylinder or the cone" manifest in the rounded sculpture base; the encircling gesture of the hands; the patterned edge accentuating the curve of the skirt; and the inverted, cone-like face (1939, 2, 34–36, 40).

The use of this vocabulary ensconced the Asmar sculpture hoard within a discourse that prioritized aesthetics. The geometric forms of the sculpture in the hoard were particularly resonant because of the early twentieth-century aesthetic sensibility that had already embraced abstraction in art. This language of abstraction was used to describe both so-called non-Western "primitive" art as well as early twentieth-century Western art. Frankfort therefore did not invent a vocabulary for the reception of the Asmar sculpture hoard. In the early twentieth century, descriptions of fundamental shapes, masses, and forms—cylinders, spheres, and cones—comprised the commonly utilized, collective vocabulary of abstraction in art (Evans 2012, 60–61).

The Sumerians were "primitive" in the sense that they represented the earliest civilization in world history. Sumerian sculpture was itself "primitive." When the Asmar sculpture hoard was excavated in the 1930s, the understanding of so-called "primitive" art as a collection of universal visual attributes promoted comparisons among the artistic traditions of ancient cultures, non-Western cultures, and the modern West. Today, scholars prefer to interrogate the processes underlying conceptions of universal form in "primitive" art. Rejecting the notion that any actual tradition is primitive, it is understood that the primitive, like the Orient, is located in its Western reception (Connelly 1998, 89).

Recent scholarship has shown an interest in recognizing the influence of Sumerian sculpture—and Mesopotamian art in general—on early twentieth-century Western artists (Evans 2012; Bahrani 2014; Chi and Azara 2015). Alberto Giacometti, Henry Moore, and other early twentieth-century artists were taken with "primitive" Sumerian sculpture, primarily the statues of Gudea of Lagash. It is important to recognize, however, that a specifically Sumerian response cannot be extracted from the enthusiasm of these artists. That is to say, what many early twentieth-century Western artists admired about Sumerian sculpture was identical to what they admired about "primitive" art in general. Essentially, this was an aesthetic devoid of cultural relativism.

In the early twentieth-century, the "primitive" was a collection of visual attributes construed by the West as universally characteristic of primal artistic expression. Because these attributes stemmed from the "primitive," they were unencumbered and unmitigated by cultural context. When Moore declared an affinity with Sumerian sculpture, for example, he therefore felt the same affinity across a spectrum of cultures, writing that, "for me, Sumerian sculpture ranks with Early Greek, Etruscan, Ancient Mexican, Fourth and Twelfth Dynasty Egyptian, and Romanesque and early Gothic sculpture, as the great sculpture of the world" (Wilkinson 2002, 101–2). Moore and other artists celebrated the universal qualities of the "primitive" through Sumerian—among other—sculpture, but they did not attribute to Sumerian sculpture qualities unique to Sumer.

The affinities that Moore and other artists felt with Sumerian sculpture are similar to Picasso's use of the "primitive" in *Les Demoiselles d'Avignon* (1907). The painting has no direct visual borrowings from "primitive" cultures despite attempts by generations of art historians to find them (Connelly 1998, 89). When Moore admired the richness, wonder, and creative urge of Sumerian sculpture, he admired those same qualities in all other "primitive" cultures, too. As with *Les Demoiselles d'Avignon*, this reception embodied a narrow range of concepts that could be validated in opposition to the Western artistic tradition (Connelly 1998, 91). Picasso articulated this reception through visual representation, while Moore, other artists, and early scholars also articulated this reception through an established vocabulary (Evans 2012, 61–75).

Scholarly discourse has shifted to the study of primitivism as a multivalent Western reception of the "primitive" (Connelly 1998). Primitivism has been thoroughly interrogated in, for example, the study of African arts. For decades already, scholars have refuted the use of Picasso to validate African arts. But a corresponding recognition must also occur in the growing interest in documenting Sumerian sculpture at the intersection of early twentieth-century Western artists. That is, it is not necessary to use early twentieth-century art to validate Sumerian sculpture. Early twentieth-century Western artists admired, sketched, and wrote about Sumerian sculpture. But that is very different from a study of ancient Sumer. Rather, early twentieth-century Western artists admired a range of characteristics that we would consider, in retrospect, devoid of place or time. Since scholarly attempts to move beyond questions of style and aesthetics are fairly recent, it is no surprise that such conceptions have not yet reached the general public. Not even a Sumerian statue on Mars can escape the early twentieth-century formal analysis that cemented Early Dynastic sculpture in aesthetic discourse. As a result, these statues have been divorced from a fuller exploration of their use and meaning in the Early Dynastic temple. In reality, our ways of seeing these statues have changed very little since the 1930s (Evans 2012, 73–75).

2. Early Dynastic Statues, Art History Textbooks, and Sunglasses

The Asmar sculpture hoard is included in many art history textbooks, which perpetuate the vocabulary first applied by Frankfort. Some half a century after Frankfort, the

Asmar sculpture hoard is still "made up of simple forms, primarily cones and cylinders" (Gardner 1996, 45). Sumerian sculptural form, in general, is "based on the cone and cylinder" (Janson 1986, 74).

Helen Gardner authored *Art through the Ages* through three editions and thirty-nine printings up until her death in 1946. Over half a million copies were sold before the volume, arguably the first global art history survey, was simply renamed *Gardner's Art through the Ages* from the fourth edition onwards (Jaffee 2016). It is still in print. The retitled editions elaborate upon the universal significance of the enlarged eyes of Sumerian statues. The convention of enlarged eyes "is not only Sumerian but appears throughout ancient art" (Gardner 1970, 39). Similarly, another art history survey also notes that the statues in the Asmar sculpture hoard reveal "that many of the conventions of religious art in the Near East (later to be passed on to Europe and also to the Far East) were already present" (Honour and Fleming 1982, 31).

This sense of connectivity is explored visually in the mural *Common Threads* (1998; fig. 3) by Meg Saligman (American, b. 1965). The mural stands some eight stories high on the side of the Stevens Administrative Building at the intersection of Broad and Spring Garden streets in downtown Philadelphia, Pennsylvania. It is the most famous mural of the Philadelphia Mural Arts Advocates, an organization that aims to create murals that connect artists to communities.

Saligman is known for juxtaposing traditional conceptions of art with contemporary subjects. For example, her first mural at 18th and Wallace streets in Philadelphia had a composition based on Raphael's *School of Athens* (1509–1511) but substituted famous athletes as the subjects. *Common Threads* depicts "Victorian ladies, ancient heroes, historical gentlemen, and past imagery in all forms," according to Saligman (Moss 2010, 384). With the exception of the large central figure, the mural pairs these subjects with students from Benjamin Franklin High School and the School for Creative and Performing Arts who echo their poses (Golden et al. 2002, 116).

The largest statue in the Asmar sculpture hoard is depicted near the top left corner of *Common Threads*. Next to the statue is a male student standing solidly with clasped hands. He is wearing sunglasses. In preparation for the mural, Saligman met with high school students. She showed them images of sculpture and "asked them to mimic their gestures" (Golden et al. 2002, 122). Perhaps the student who imitated the pose of the Asmar statue had been taught art history from *Gardner's Art through the Ages*. The editors offered various possible interpretations for the enlarged eyes of the statues in the Asmar sculpture hoard, including the suggestion that "the modern affectation of dark glasses" was "curiously Sumerian when oversized!" (Gardner 1970, 40).[2]

Explanations for the enlarged eyes of Early Dynastic ("Sumerian") statues tend to literalism across a range of disciplines. The American psychologist Julian Jaynes

---

2. Another popular survey noted the "huge staring goggle eyes" of the statues in the Asmar sculpture hoard (Honour and Fleming 1982, 31).

Figure 3. Meg Saligman, *Common Threads* (1998). Photo by Rmarfuggi (Own work) [CC BY-SA 4.0 (https://creativecommons.org/licenses/by-sa/4.0)], via Wikimedia Commons.

(1977, 169) was struck by the "huge globular eyes" of the Asmar sculpture hoard statues "hypnotically staring out of the unrecorded past of five thousand years ago with defiant authority." In *The Social History of the Unconscious*, Frankl (1989, 170) perceived in the "huge eyes" of early Sumerian sculpture "a sense of awe and apprehension which obviously indicates the anxiety those people felt in the presence of the gods." According to Gardner (1970, 40), the "curiously Sumerian" eyes could be "a badge of attractive mystery." Another art history textbook noted, "the sight of the divine has mesmerized these substitute worshipers and they are depicted as if in a hypnotic trance" (Tanser and Kleiner 1996, 45).

The enlarged eyes of Early Dynastic statues are mysterious, eerie, hypnotic—even extraterrestrial. But might this be largely an aftereffect of having removed the statues from their ancient context? Seeing is a cultural construct, one so familiar that it is paradoxically invisible (Mitchell 2002, 166). Might this otherness of enlarged eyes be symptomatic of how we see Early Dynastic statues as somehow autonomous, already at their inception, from the culture that produced them?

Common Threads is meant to unite "allegory and portraiture in a broad commentary about the things that connect us across generations and across cultures" (Golden et al. 2002, 116). The mural resonates with art history textbooks because it performs the visual equivalent. Both emphasize similarities rather than differences. This is a continuity without contextualization, and this is the terrain where the reception of Early Dynastic sculpture is primarily located. Even the preoccupation with style and chronology in much of twentieth-century scholarship had to extract these statues from archaeological context in order to impose an orderly narrative of progress from abstraction to realism (Evans 2007). Through these and other considerations, this sculpture has achieved an otherness. Similar to the way early twentieth-century Western artists embraced Sumerian sculpture, the responses elicited by their otherness are universal. This is why even sunglasses can be, somehow, Sumerian.

3. *Michael Rakowitz, Invisible Enemy, and Special Ops Cody*

In the influential "The Way of the Shovel: On the Archaeological Imaginary in Art," Roelstraete (2009) signaled the tendency of contemporary art to look back at both its own past and the past in general. This was a literal digging—archival, historiographical, archaeological—but it was also the metaphorical deep scrutiny of psychoanalysis. There is a quality of excavation in Roelstraete's archaeological imaginary, a turn toward the past in order to understand something that is happening now.

The 2013 exhibition of the same title at the Museum of Contemporary Art (MCA) in Chicago included the work of Michael Rakowitz (American, b. 1973).[3] Rakowitz draws upon his experience of growing up with an Iraqi-Jewish mother and an American father to produce work that explores disputed social, political, and cultural histories. The looting of the Iraq Museum and the continued destruction of Middle Eastern cultural heritage are a major focus of his work. His ongoing project, *The Invisible Enemy Should Not Exist* (2007–present), was featured in the MCA exhibition. The name is from one translation of one of the names of the processional way that led through the Ishtar Gate into Babylon.

3. For the exhibition publication, see Roelstraete 2013.

Figure 4. Oriental Institute Museum, The Edgar and Deborah Jannotta Mesopotamian Gallery, 2014 installation of Michael Rakowitz, *The Invisible Enemy Should not Exist* (2007–present). Courtesy of the Oriental Institute of the University of Chicago.

Invisible Enemy attempts to recover the thousands of artifacts looted from the Iraq Museum in 2003 by recreating them using the packaging of Middle Eastern food products and newspapers. The use of ephemeral, disposable materials is a reminder that the past is literally being thrown away. These materials also embrace the inevitable failure of reconstruction. Rakowitz's sculptures are, ultimately, reconstructions, their materials reminding us that all reconstructions are only a small portion of what had once been.

There is a relationship between *Invisible Enemy* and the Oriental Institute, its "Lost Treasures of Iraq" database initially supplying some of the reference images for Rakowitz to recreate that which had been lost. In 2014, the Oriental Institute Museum exhibited a portion of *Invisible Enemy* directly opposite the permanent display of Early Dynastic statues (fig. 4). The Mesopotamian collection at the Oriental Institute was obtained legally through the division of finds practiced in the early twentieth century. Yet Rakowitz's work has become emblematic of the continued threats to Iraqi cultural heritage. The history of an archaeology that removed these artifacts from their place of origin for display in Western museums is a part of the history of cultural heritage, too. Kholeif (2017, 12) asks whether the objects of *Invisible Enemy* will be one day "resting silently like relics, dead bodies in the Pitt Rivers Museum, Oxford, or indeed, the British Museum?" For Kholeif, the Western display of antiquities is associated with imprisonment, sanitization, and, ultimately, death.

The Oriental Institute assumed a neutral stance in 2014, describing *Invisible Enemy* as "part of an ongoing commitment to recuperate the thousands of objects that are still missing."[4] It was also a continual reminder "of the ongoing challenges faced in Baghdad."[5] But this insistence on neutrality was reductive. The juxtaposition of *Invisible Enemy* and the Museum's display of Diyala sculpture did more than raise cultural awareness. What happened, instead, was the dislodging of the aesthetic object.

The ephemeral, disposable materials used by Rakowitz tell us something about these statues as we see them now—even if we were to encounter them now, in Iraq, coming out of the ground. These ancient statues are incomplete, with only rare exceptions already fragments when they were excavated. They were already ephemeral some 4,500 years ago. After they had served their dedicatory purpose in the temples, they were broken, thrown away, and otherwise taken out of commission. They were hoarded below floors, encased in the plaster and mud brick of installations, or strewn about and left behind.

Brown (2013, 257) understands an archaeological impulse that "has been precipitated by the longing for an archaeology not of the past, say, and not even of the recent past but of the recently present." What is particularly resonant about *Invisible Enemy* is the transparency of the reconstruction. *Invisible Enemy* builds another chapter into the biography of Sumerian sculpture. The present in the timeline of these artifacts repeats itself, but it is also radically different from everything that came before. Rakowitz's first solo exhibition, *Michael Rakowitz: Backstroke of the West,* opened at the Museum of Contemporary Art in September 2017. In the exhibition, the labels for *Invisible Enemy* included narratives of individuals reacting to the looting of the Iraq Museum and the ongoing loss of cultural heritage in Iraq. The paradox is that when these artifacts were looted, something was lost beyond a physical object because they were no longer only ancient. Sumerian statues and other artifacts looted from the Iraq Museum lost something of the past by being forced into becoming recently present. Rakowitz's work is therefore archaeological because it is the excavation and reconstruction of our own perception of Sumerian sculpture.

Filmed on location at the Oriental Institute in the summer of 2017, *The Ballad of Special Ops Cody* is a stop-motion film that was commissioned by MCA for Rakowitz's solo exhibition (fig. 5; Kholeif 2017). The film begins with an event that occurred in 2005, when an Iraqi insurgent group posted a photograph online of captured US soldier John Adam held hostage at gunpoint. The insurgents threatened to behead Adam if prisoners being held in US jails in Iraq were not freed. The photo, however, was a hoax. Adam was actually an action figure named Special Ops Cody.

---

4. Summary of the exhibition: https://oi.uchicago.edu/museum-exhibits/special-exhibits/michael-rakowitz-invisible-enemy-should-not-exist (accessed November 2017).

5. See Green and Evans 2015, 188. As a coauthor of the cited publication, it is possible for me to attribute this portion of the essay to Jack Green, Chief Curator of the Oriental Institute Museum from 2011 to 2015.

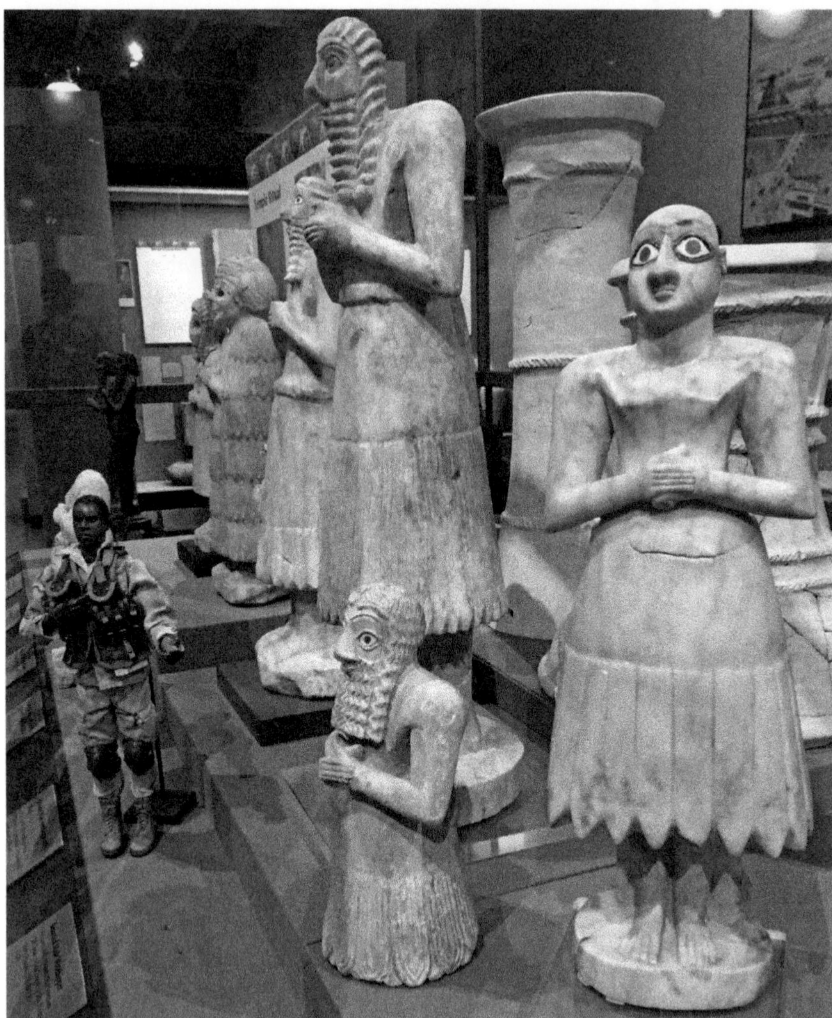

Figure 5. Oriental Institute Museum, The Edgar and Deborah Jannotta Mesopotamian Gallery during the 2017 filming of Michael Rakowitz, *The Ballad of Special Ops Cody*. Photo by author.

In *Ballad,* Special Ops Cody walks off a stage set similar to what was used in the hoax and visits the Oriental Institute Museum. Retired Sergeant Gin McGill-Prather narrates as Special Ops Cody looks at the displays in the Mesopotamian gallery. "I never knew stuff like that really existed," voices the narrator, "not for real ... but when you see these things up close and for real, something ... there aren't words for."

The narration is accompanied by close shots of individual artifacts. The assumption is that the narrator is voicing a sense of awe at what is being encountered in the museum. But this assumption becomes distorted. When Special Ops Cody approaches the Early Dynastic statues on display, the narrator begins to recount traumatic stories about the mistreatment of Iraqi detainees. Awe turns to horror.

The narrator tells the statues they deserve to be free and asks, "Are you guys ready to come out?" Museum staff opens the display case. Special Ops Cody climbs into the case. The statues never respond to his attempts to set them free. Special Ops Cody clasps his hands like the other statues, and Museum staff closes the case.

Special Ops Cody action figures were available for sale exclusively on US bases in Kuwait and Iraq. They were often sent home to soldiers' children as a kind of surrogate. Like Special Ops Cody, the Early Dynastic statues are also surrogates who represented their donors in the temple. Across some 4,500 years, these images have a common purpose.

Why was the film shot on location at the Oriental Institute Museum? *Ballad* has parallels with the installation of *Invisible Enemy* at the Oriental Institute Museum. Both *Invisible Enemy* and the Early Dynastic statues spanned a shared heritage, but neither was a presentable option. One represented the statues destroyed in the looting of the Iraq Museum, and the other was the ensconcing of the antiquity in a museum display case. The dilemma was made transparent by the narrator of *Ballad*: "We keep you locked up, fragile, temperature-controlled, humidity-controlled, without the chance of human hands touching you."

Both of Rakowitz's projects show an interest in biography. The missing eye inlays of the Diyala statues are part of what attracts Special Ops Cody. The narrator tells the statues, "I see your faces without eyes, and I think of that day." What begins in the museum with a sense of awe ends with pristine objects behind glass. But parts are already missing. These statues have not ended up in the museum with the same things they once had. This has also happened to the narrator of *Ballad*, who has had something taken away. We know that something is missing from Special Ops Cody, too, because the case closes, and he becomes a part of the missing.

Archaeology will always occupy a contested space. The way forward is recognition. As a part of the reception of the ancient Near East, Rakowitz provokes something new at the intersection of scholarly research and contemporary representation. In his refusal to neglect the present, temple sculpture is no longer fixed at its inception, and it is no longer solely aesthetic. Yet something is also perpetuated, something that draws us back into the past but also into something new. It is rare that scholarship can achieve such a dislodging on its own. Ultimately, an exterior provocation is required. For this reason, it may be the artists who will be able to help us tell new stories about the lives of ancient objects.

Bibliography

Ancient Code. 2015. "Ancient Anunnaki statue found on Mars? NASA Rover snaps curious image." *Ancient Code* 29 December. Accessed November 2017. https://www.ancient-code.com/has-nasa-accidentally-found-an-ancient-sumerian-statue-on-the-surface-of-mars/.

Bahrani, Z. 2014. *The Infinite Image: Art, Time, and the Aesthetic Dimension in Antiquity*. London: Reaktion Books.

Black, J., and A. Green. 1992. *Gods, Demons and Symbols of Ancient Mesopotamia: An Illustrated Dictionary*. London: The British Museum Press.

Brown, B. 2013. "Anarchéologie: Object Worlds & Other Things, Circa Now." In D. Roelstraete (ed.), *The Way of the Shovel*, 250–64. Chicago: University of Chicago Press.

Chi, J. Y., and P. Azara. 2015. "Glam-UR-ous: The Art of Archaeology and Aesthetics." In J. Chi and P. Azara (eds.), *From Ancient to Modern: Archaeology and Aesthetics*, 22–53. Princeton: Princeton University Press.

Connelly, F. S. 1998. "Primitivism." In M. Kelly (ed.), *Encyclopedia of Aesthetics*, Volume 4, 88–92. Oxford: Oxford University Press.

Evans, J. M. 2007. "The Square Temple at Tell Asmar and the Construction of Early Dynastic Mesopotamia, ca. 2900–2350 B.C.E." *American Journal of Archaeology* 111:599–632.

———. 2012. *The Lives of Sumerian Sculpture: An Archaeology of the Early Dynastic Temple*. Cambridge: Cambridge University Press.

Frankfort, H. 1935. "Sumerian Sculpture." *Burlington Magazine* 66:110–21.

———. 1936. *Progress of the Work of the Oriental Institute in Iraq, 1934/35: Fifth Preliminary Report of the Iraq Expedition*. Oriental Institute Communications 20. Chicago: University of Chicago Press.

———. 1939. *Sculpture of the Third Millennium B.C. from Tell Asmar and Khafājah*. Oriental Institute Publications 44. Chicago: University of Chicago Press.

———. 1943. *More Sculpture from the Diyala Region*. Oriental Institute Publications 60. Chicago: University of Chicago Press.

Gardner, H. 1970. *Gardner's Art through the Ages*. Fifth edition, revised by H. de la Croix and R. G. Tansey. New York: Harcourt, Brace, & World.

———. 1996. *Gardner's Art through the Ages*. Tenth edition, revised by R. G. Tansey and F. S. Kleiner. Fort Worth: Harcourt Brace College Publishers.

Golden, J. R., M. Rice, M. Y. Kinney, D. Graham, and J. Ramsdale. 2002. *Philadelphia Murals and the Stories They Tell*. Philadelphia: Temple University Press.

Green, J. D. M., and J. M. Evans. 2015. "Ground to Gallery: The Discovery, Interpretation, and Display of Early Dynastic Sculpture of the Iraq Expedition of the Oriental Institute." In J. Chi and P. Azara (eds.), *From Ancient to Modern: Archaeology and Aesthetics*, 163–93. Princeton: Princeton University Press.

Honour, H., and J. Fleming. 1982. *The Visual Arts: A History*. Englewood Cliffs, NJ: Prentice-Hall.

Jacobsen, T. 1989. "God or Worshipper." In A. Leonard, Jr. and B. B. Williams (eds.), *Essays in Ancient Civilization Presented to Helene J. Kantor*, 125–30. Studies in Ancient Oriental Civilization 47. Chicago: University of Chicago Press.

Jaffee, B. 2016. "Art History's Other Global Moment: Chicago, 1948." *Panorama: Journal of the Association of Historians of American Art* 2(2). Accessed November 2017. http://journal-panorama.org/barbara-jaffee-associate-professor-art-history-division-northern-illinois-university/.

Janson, H. W. 1986. *History of Art*. Third edition, revised and expanded by A. F. Janson. New York: Harry N. Abrams.

Jaynes, J. 1977. *The Origin of Consciousness in the Breakdown of the Bicameral Mind*. Boston: Houghton Mifflin.

Jones, T., ed. 1969. *The Sumerian Problem*. New York: John Wiley & Sons.

Kholeif, O. 2017. *Michael Rakowitz: Backstroke of the West*. Chicago: Museum of Contemporary Art.

Lieb, M. 1998. *Children of Ezekiel: Aliens, UFOs, the Crisis of Race, and the Advent of End Time.* Durham, NC, and London: Duke University Press.
Mitchell, W. J. T. 2002. "Showing Seeing: A Critique of Visual Culture." *Journal of Visual Culture* 1:165–81.
Moss, K. 2010. "Cultural Representation in Philadelphia Murals: Images of Resistance and Sites of Identity Negotiation." *Western Journal of Communication* 2010(July):372–95.
Roelstraete, D. 2009. "The Way of the Shovel: On the Archaeological Imaginary in Art. " *e-flux journal,* March. Accessed November 2017. http://www.e-flux.com/journal/04/68582/the-way-of-the-shovel-on-the-archeological-imaginary-in-art/.
———. 2013. *The Way of the Shovel.* Chicago: University of Chicago Press.
Sitchin, J. ed. 2015. *The Anunnaki Chronicles: A Zecharia Sitchin Reader.* Rochester, VT: Bear & Co.
Wilkinson, A. ed. 2002. *Henry Moore, Writings and Conversations.* Berkeley and Los Angeles: University of California Press.

Images of Ruins as Metaphorical Places of Transformation

The Case of Persepolis

Silvana Di Paolo

1. *Images of Ruins: Objectivity and Artificiality*

The circulation of photographs of ruined monuments and artifacts had considerable influence on the visual culture of antiquity from the mid-nineteenth century onwards. In the specific case of Persepolis, this form of art was used to produce both memory-images of the past and future visions of reality.

The invention of photography profoundly changed the way in which people perceived their reality. By capturing items in an objective manner using light and chemicals, photography modified how people perceived and experienced the external world, via reinterpretation through the camera lens. The macroscopic result of its advent seems to have been the substitution of interpretation with objectivity in the picturing of scientific subjects, thanks to the "production" of perfect mimetic copies of the subject rather than something new (when compared with painting, for instance).[1] The dialectic between human products (conditioned by skill, sensibility, theories of art, and so on) and mechanical and neutral media seems to be solved with the loss of the "exceptionality" of the architectural remains no longer reproduced by painters with artistic license, deviations from the original, wanting imperfections, or, in some cases, misinterpretations. Instead, photography seems to magnify the documentary value of the subject by returning infinite images of ruins, decay, and destruction. But, if compared with the contemporary multiple images conveying "a shock of vanishing materiality"[2] through

1. On the dialectic between unicity and multiplicity, as well as the change of direction towards the perfect replication of the physical world introduced by the photography, see Saltz 2015, 197–207. On the painting as a means to convey the image of the Orient in the Western world, see the contribution by D. Nadali in this volume.

2. Boym (2010, 58) investigates the value of "shocking" ruins (the inversion of the "wish" images) contra the idea of the perfectibility of the progress.

different means—among which are the distortion of the tonal range of photographs,[3] the celebration of single "frozen" episodes, and the potential production of an infinite series of copies—the early photography also highlighted the importance of *how* the subject is reproduced, the role that the angle of view plays in the final appearance of an image, and the choice of an appropriate focal length to capture meaningful details of the inanimate subject. This produces a new concept of originality associated with the uniqueness of each replica.[4]

The authenticity of a thing is the quintessence of all that is transmissible in it from its origin on, ranging from its physical duration to the historical testimony relating to it. Since the historical testimony is founded on the physical duration, the former, too, is jeopardized by reproduction in which the physical duration plays no part. And what is really jeopardized when the historical testimony is affected is the authority of the object, the weight it derives from tradition (Benjamin 2008, 22).

In the opinion of W. Benjamin, who exalted the role of technological arts such as photography and cinema, the "aura" of artwork is eliminated in the age of mechanical reproduction: the "copied" object is detached from the domain of tradition and gains independence from the ritual. More copies can become originals, each for reasons inherent in their nature and characteristics (Batchen 2010, 20–26).

The variety of uses of the new medium included the reproduction of archaeological remains or ancient artifacts. From the earliest experiments in this field, the study of ruins was inextricably linked to the photography's development, although still in a chaotic or nuanced form, because, before creating new epistemologies, photography assimilated *already existing* cultural "icons" (as, for instance, the biblical sites).[5]

As static, formally complex, and artistic subjects, historic sites, architecture, and ruins have been constantly reinterpreted within this specific landscape, producing a new "art" matching the virtuosity of the painting, incision, and so on. On the one hand, photography has been technically a potent embodiment for the ongoing industrial and political transformation of Western culture during the nineteenth century (Heilbrun 1998). On the other hand, study, research, and meditation on the subject has facilitated

3. Kushinski (2016) explores, for instance, how contemporary art (including photography) can manipulate or subvert the meaning also beyond the art context: the control of the luminosity produces a "disturbed reality" for representation of modern man-made catastrophes.

4. In the twentieth century, photography, as well as other technological arts (like cinema), have triggered new thoughts and a renewed research agenda on the relationship between original and copy in antiquity, as well as on the copy as producer of new knowledge available for multiple perspectives. See Settis, Anguissola, and Gasparotto 2015. On the apparent opposition between original and copy in the ancient Near East, see Di Paolo 2018.

5. On the early photographs as tools for archaeological study, see Lyons et al. 2005. On the eccentricities and peculiarities of the relationship between archaeology and photography, see Brusius 2016, 255–56.

imagination and mental representations, extending archaeology's influence into other spheres of social and cultural life (see below).

Since the second half of the nineteenth century, the photographical documentation of the Middle East intensified and contributed to the support of an "Orientalist vision" in the Western world.[6] The historical and cultural experiences of ancient sites (Persepolis, Palmyra, Jerusalem, and so on) have acquired a plethora of meanings over time that have focused on the relationship between relics and time, the profane time of historical memory and sacred time, namely symbolical and mythological.

Without going into the well-studied topic of the development of the archaeological photography also in the Orient (Bahrani, Çelik, and Eldem 2011; Bohrer 2011; Brusius 2016), I want to emphasize that explorations intended to take pictures reflected not so much aesthetic or even preservationist interests (the latter being a very modern concern), but a political agenda and, at a more personal level, an attempt to build *ex novo* or "regenerate" existing ideas and images of the Orient. In fact, at the political level, the systematic photographical surveys were essential to convey images of ruins and abandonment, as well as spiritual decadence and moral decline (through the contrast between the ancient splendors of Greco-Roman civilization and the modern degeneration attributed to Muslims; Liverani 2018). On the more intimate level, a consciously or unconsciously artificial archaeological culture has been constructed for specific aims (Warwick and Willis 2012).

2. *Imagining Buildings, Narrating Ruins*

Photography, as with other technologies of image-making aimed at recording ruined monuments, can be subject to cultural or ideological manipulation, because they provide opportunities for reflections on their ability to "activate forms" of diverse origins and tradition into original narratives.

To be provocative, I would like to focus on two images to explain my point better. They are two different views of the same subject. The first one is a realistic view (a photo) of the ruins of the Western Portal belonging to the "Gate of All Nations" (the only entrance to the monumental terrace) built by King Xerxes at Persepolis during the first half of the fifth century BCE. This image, taken by the archaeological mission sponsored by the Oriental Institute of Chicago and directed by A. Schmidt (1953) between 1935–1939 (fig. 1) shows the debris visible at that time and belonging to the west entrance to the gate with a couple of incomplete "guardian" bulls and a very small portion of the inner colonnade (the column on the left side).

6. On this aspect and the role of the local photography, see Behdad and Gartlan 2013; Behdad 2015 with preceding bibliography.

Figure 1. Persepolis. Western Portal of the "Gate of the Nations" (Schmidt 1953, pl. 54). https://oi.uchicago.edu/gallery/gate-xerxes#3A1_72dpi.png.

In the background, it is possible to recognize what was left of the Apadana with his hundred columns, while on the right side there is the monumental stairway giving access to the terrace from the countryside.

The second picture (fig. 2) is an imagined view of the same portal, again taken from the northwest side, although more oriented toward west and seen from above.[7] Here, the virtual representation of the monumental entrance to the terrace of Persepolis serves to enlarge the body of archaeological knowledge. The compact body of the buildings, different heights, colors (not visible here) applied to distinguish architectural elements (animals, capitals, walls) all contribute to an imaginative vision offering means of additional interpretation, although is not completely "artificial" but strictly based on texts, photos, and a reconstruction model created by Friedrich Krefter.[8]

As architect and archaeologist, Krefter had been invited to Iran by Ernst Herzfeld and worked at the excavations of Persepolis between 1931 and 1935, producing plans and sketches of the site. During the 1960s, he built the first wooden architectural model

7. This image is part of the project of virtual reconstruction of Persepolis born by a German-Iranian cooperation and developed by architects W. Gambke and K. Afhami. See the website: www.persepolis3D.com.

8. On a different view on reconstruction and representation, see the remarks by D. Nadali in this volume.

Figure 2. Grand Stairway and West Portal of the "Gate of All Nations" (from Persepolis3D.com).

of Persepolis (scale 1:200) presented as a coronation gift by the President of the Federal Republic of Germany, Heinrich Lübke, to Mohammad Reza Shah Pahlavi (Krefter 1969, 123–37; 1971). Krefter had to face the thorny issue of the reconstruction of the upper part of walls, as well as the cornices, ceilings and roofing. He also had to "imagine" how the buildings were originally interrelated within the city plan: he hypothesized isolated structures including the "Gate of all Nations," that were reconstructed as separate from the outer defense walls.

The work of the architect was imaginative because he invented what is not there. But imagination is a process and not a "revelation." Conceptualized in this way, imagination appears intentional rather than fanciful. In Krefter's work, structures have been considered as radically isolated from one another and not conceived as elements contributing to a comprehensive built environment. Krefter saw a potential whole in the single parts. This modern vision of architecture (but now partially outdated) has also been attributed to an exemplary past (distant in time and space). What *could be* or *ought to be* is considered superior to *what* is. This plan remained unsurpassed until the end of the twentieth century, despite the later excavations, and considerably influential because it inspired new projects aimed to virtually reconstruct the site: the developers, conjugating "vision" and "view," received the suggestions of the archaeologists and architects involved in the excavations, opting for what they considered the best solution among various possibilities.

The juxtaposition of the two images allows a preliminary observation. What has been in the past and what is today the role of the imagination and representation in archaeology; that is, if imagination is to be considered a factor "in excess" in a rigorous scientific method, or if it is part of a more complex mental process that uses images to construct creative forms of thought by producing new forms of knowledge. Therefore, it does not seem an exaggeration to say that the virtual is not opposed to the reality, but to the possibility. The virtual is not lacking reality. Instead, it is a way of being "fruitful" in which there is space for creation.

The images correspond to deep layers of reality at increasingly intimate levels of memory and thought. In the search of more extensive forms of knowledge, therefore, the images should be related to other types of representation, images intended as *memory* that retain elements of a recent or distant past and images as *projection* that constructs visions of reality for the future. Reality is therefore an uneasy world, a world in which virtuality is the place of a complex multiplicity that implies both current and virtual elements. In this framework, imagination is a specific form of representation which plays an important role as ideas and words. To discuss and analyze these phenomena of reprocessing and interpretation of perceived data, Persepolis seemed to me particularly paradigmatic of the cognitive function of imagination: reproducing archaeological data previously perceived, on one hand (we will see this subsequently), and producing a synthesis of isolated perceptions in more complex constructions, on the other: as Susan Sonntag said, "Interpretation is the revenge of the intellect upon art" (Sonntag 1966, 7).

3. *Images-Dream: The Materialization of the Future*

The archaeological imagination does not precede archaeology as a practice. There is not a Maginot Line between the rational, on the one hand, and the imaginative, on the other. Rather, interpretation serves to enlarge the complexity of the archaeological experience.[9]

Persepolis has given birth to a kind of image-dream, becoming the site of excellence of an ideological vision, a promising image of what is going to materialize into a vision for future generations. The idealized image of its monuments has given impetus to well-defined representation strategies that have deconstructed a series of images with the intention of replacing them with others. There was thus an overlap between the project and its external representation, a very effective means of communication and persuasion. The mental images, charged with symbolism, have therefore become a powerful means for launching new projects and the political and social transformations underlying the projects themselves. Through its glorious past, Persepolis becomes a means of the country's potential for rebirth.

---

9. On different imaginative responses to archaeology, see the collection of essays, *The Nineteenth-Century Archaeological Imagination* (2012).

With the transition from the Qajar to the Pahlavi dynasty, Persepolis has been identified as "the true spirit of the nation." Taking inspiration from the actions of Mustafa Kemal Atatürk in Turkey, Reza Shah undertook an ambitious modernization project in Iran.

In this political agenda, the nationalist use of archaeology took a new direction: the Achaemenid past was embedded in a nationalist rhetoric by transferring the cultural primacy from Susa to Persepolis, which became the most significant and authentic site of "national unity" (Grigor 2009, 273–90). Susa, in fact, was an expression of the policy of the Qajar dynasty which, thanks to an agreement with France, had granted the great Western power the exclusive right to carry out excavations in the country. In 1899, with the creation of the *Délégation en Perse,* the French obtained a total concession for all archaeological excavations in Iran for an indefinite period. Despite this, Susa gradually became their exclusive center of interest and particularly important for the French expansion and influence (Chevalier 2003, 512–16; Nasiri-Moghaddam 2004, 347–49, 357–62).

Obviously, this development did not, of course, reflect a historical or cultural judgment. It was the result of a choice dictated by the desire to subvert the ideological system created by the Qajar sovereigns who in the Pahlavi eyes had accepted the colonialist policy of the Western powers (specifically, France). Thus, the will to make the country homogeneous from a cultural point of view and, above all, to oppose the previous policy resulted in the promotion of the historical and cultural value of ancient Persepolis, as well as the invention or reinvention of an official architectural language inspired by the ancient accomplishments (Grigor 2009, 273–90).

The grandeur of the ruins, the complexity of the architectural system, and the figurative program with the long theories of dignitaries and subjects moving ideally towards the political and ideological center of the empire (the Achaemenid king) was closely functional to the political project, becoming also the iconic symbol of celebrations for the 2,500th anniversary of the foundation of the monarchy by Cyrus the Great in 1971. Under Mohammed Reza Pahlavì, these celebrations mixed together the modernity of the initiatives and the antiquity of vestiges, creating a new image of the country. Images of the archaeological sites were also places of "transformation." They, reproducing reality, were brought into relationships and sometimes merged with other types of representation: archaeological ruins were functional for reconstruction and cultural re-elaboration.[10]

4. *Images-Memory: Capturing the Concreteness of the Nation*

Antiquities in the Near East have witnessed the encounter between East and West in many ways. Their manipulation has given rise to particular mental constructions: on

---

10. On the photography in this period, see Tahmasbpour 2018.

the one hand, Europe and its "interpretation" of the Eastern world, and on the other, in a specular way, the Oriental world reinterpreted in the light of the encounter with the Other, sometimes obeying external stresses, sometimes following autonomous paths.[11]

In the framework of the imperialist pushes of European powers in the nineteenth and early twentieth centuries, interest in Iran (and, consequently, in its past) was part of the process of modernizing the country and seeking new markets. England and Russia saw Iran as an interesting market for new investors and sought to extend their influence in this country, which represented a key route to reaching India and, access to Arabian Sea also through Afghanistan, especially for Russia (Poulson 2005, 77–81). As a result, Iran survived as a buffer state between the expanding Russia towards the Persian Gulf and the British strategy of defending her own interests in India. In this situation of rivalry, a growing interest in the Western world developed under Nasir al-din Shah Qajar (1848–1896).

Under Qajar's reign, which lasted for fifty years, the presence of Westerners intensified. Europeans filtered the knowledge of Iran based on their own ideals, while the Persians did not suffer but reacted to the cultural stresses even with autonomous and original responses (Behdad 2001, 141–51). The nineteenth century promoted scientific classification and documentation projects that accompanied the progressive knowledge of culture. Through a binary division of cultures (Western vs. non-Western), differences were formalized, although the phenomenon should be explored in its entirety to capture the plurality of outcomes.

Persepolis became a field of experimentation and exploration through various kinds of art (literature, painting, photography). Here, I will focus on some aspects of the relationship between travel narratives and photography, while other research topics, such as collecting interests closely related to the development and diffusion of photographic repetitions, will be subject to specific studies.

The nostalgic and exotic trends that overlook the first photos favored the ancient vestiges, for the subject seemed to be apt for grasping the sense of decadence and abandonment of the eastern countries. Images were therefore not completely objective but always an expression of power relations between East and West. A special contribution comes from a group of Italian photographers, one of the first to undertake prolific photographic activity in Iran, even if experimentally and in many cases not professional (see Bonetti and Prandi 2010).

One of the most important sources for the documentation left on Persepolis (and one of the most significant unpublished or little-known documents) was Luigi Pesce. Born in Naples in 1818, Pesce emigrated to Persia in 1848 and became chief of the Shah infantry and later one of the founders of the Tehran Polytechnic, where he taught Persian officers the basics of photography. The collection of Pesce's photos on Perse-

11. It was suggested that especially for royal images the local photographic practices were principally indebted to the Persian painting tradition: Brusius 2015, 57–83.

polis dating from 1857 to 1858 comprised a specific series, with its own autonomous numbering, within a much wider range of images that the photographer offered for sale or in gift, for example to Nasir al-din Shah Qajar (fig. 3; Pesce 1860). In these first shots of the site of Persepolis, Pesce was "languishing" on the monuments, always inserted into the surrounding environment (a process opposed to that used by others), which obviously tended to emphasize the context in which the imposing ruins were inserted. The subjects were not selected for monumental abstraction but realistically involved in their natural atmosphere. Ruins become the subject of a representation in which they are transfigured by the constructive power of the gaze by choosing a specific point of view and a specific visual interest.

The resulting photographic series became a real reportage, an absolute novelty for Persia, which was set in the wake of photographic campaigns conducted in Europe and the Middle East in the same period. One of the most important projects was realized by Luigi Sacchi who, between 1852 and 1855, published a photographic volume entitled *Monuments, Views and Costumes of Italy* on monuments from all over Italy (Hannavy 2013, 752–57). This work was the first embryonic photographic "archive" that embodied the idea of nation through the national cultural heritage. These experiences permitted one to discover the nation, build an imagined political community and managed to envision it in symbols and images. In Iran, Luigi Pesce projected the idea of nation onto an emotional and symbolic plane. Monuments were eloquent visual evidence on which to base the historical legitimization of the "modern" nation (ruled by the Qajar dynasty). This visual evidence emphasized by Pesce and other photographers pointed both to the relationship between the territory and the populations and to the richness and variety of the land itself, which over time structured the memory of a very long past. The monuments allowed the transformation of an abstract idea of the nation, and its population into concrete images, with photography contributing to this concreteness. The survey of the antiquities of Persepolis was to be, in the Pesce project, a remarkable undertaking of historical, artistic, and archaeological interest. Before him, only Eugène Flandin, accompanied by the architect Pascal Coste and attached to a French diplomatic mission to Iran, travelled as head of an archaeological expedition to western and southern Iran on behalf of the Paris Académie des Beaux-Arts. This mission

Figure 3. Luigi Pesce. "Ruine a Persepoli." 1860. Salt paper. Paris, Musée Guimet. https://rosettaapp.getty.edu/delivery/DeliveryManagerServlet?dps_pid=IE1378533.

Figure 4. E. Flandin. Persepolis. "Vue du Palais n°. 2 du plan général." https://digitalcollections.nypl.org/items/510d47e2-8fba-a3d9-e040-e00a18064a99.

produced a six-volume album with a series of bas-reliefs, columns and other details (fig. 4; Flandin 1851–1854).

After 1870, Persepolis photographs became very common, thanks to the systematic campaigns of Jane Dieulafoy and Jacques de Morgan of the *Delegation en Perse*. After this date, there was also a greater sensitivity for a less conventional reading of places, often due to the personal history of the artist.

Antoin Sevruguin was an important photographer, belonging to a family of Russian diplomats of Armenian-Georgian origin, who was born and lived in Persia (Scheiwiller 2018, 145–69). The perception of ancient Persepolitan ruins was filtered by the taste and sensibility of the artist who was not only interested in reproducing taxonomic series of images or typological inventories of monuments (rocky tombs, colonnades, doors, etc.). Sevruguin stands out from his predecessors because he created an interaction between human and architectural vestiges: the human figure, sometimes his own, moved in the visual field and in the physical space of the ruins, thus providing information about the size of the monuments and the angle chosen for the photographic shot. The proportions, together with the quality of the light and the choice of the diagonal lines, became functional not only for the illustration of antiquity (for a wider European and local audience) but also for the creation of an aesthetic language through the familiar use of the asymmetry and decentralization of the point of view. It was an integrated landscape that entailed manipulation of existing forms. The image emphasized the manmade landscape: the natural topography was altered and transformed through the efforts of humans. Adding a human element in the landscape with monuments and ruins bridged the human connection to the "story" within the photograph. Without a historical picture of reference, the archaeological remains were understood and represented within a much larger cultural imagery that implicitly included villages, peoples, customs, and traditions.

The creation of an image-memory complex of the ancient Persepolis capital, to which both the travel reports (which I have not considered here) and the countless drawings and sketches of the ancient monuments and the first photographic series contributed, was at the same time an important source of knowledge from which European painting drew while reinterpreting it.

I would like to conclude not with a photograph but a painting (fig. 5). It equally combines both images-memory and images-dream. The subject matter of the painting (1878) by Edwin Long, a British Victorian artist, is drawn from the Old Testament book of Esther. It depicts the Queen of Persia and wife of King Xerxes in her palace at Susa while she is preparing to meet her husband and intercede for her people. In the background, there are various architectural features referring to the Persepolis monuments, including the columns and their capitals with bull protomes and the relief with the king killing the lion under the winged disk.

Figure 5. Edwin Long, *Queen Esther*, 1878.

On the one hand, there is almost a "philological" reconstruction of the room, with wall inscriptions strictly based on cuneiform script, and the architectural description depending on Esther 1:6. On the other hand, the scene is imaginatively constructed, with the royal image on the door and the combination of Assyrian and Achaemenid motives on the walls to build a "neutral" image promoting the plurality and the instability of knowledge.

Bibliography

Batchen, G. 2010. "An Almost Unlimited Variety: Photography and Sculpture in the Nineteenth Century." In R. Marcoci, G. Batchen, and T. Bezzola (eds.), *The Original Copy: Photography of Sculpture, 1839 to Today; The Museum of Modern Art, New York (August-November 1, 2010)*, 20–26. New York: The Museum of Modern Art.

Bahrani, Z., Z. Çelik, and E. Eldem, eds. 2011. *Scramble for the Past: A Story of Archaeology in the Ottoman Empire, 1753–1914*. Istanbul: SALT.

Behdad, A. 2001. "The Power-Ful Art of Qajar Photography: Orientalism and (Self)-Orientalizing in Nineteenth Century Iran." *Iranian Studies* 34:141–51.

———. 2015. *Camera Orientalis. Reflection on Photography of the Middle East*. Chicago and London: University of Chicago Press.

Behdad, A., and L. Gartlan. 2013. *Orientalism: New Essays on Colonial Representation*. Los Angeles: Getty Publications.

Benjamin, W. 2008. *The Work of Art in the Age of Its Technological Reproducibility and Other Writings on Media*, edited by M. W. Jennings, B. Doherty and T. Y. Levin. Cambridge, MA: Harvard University Press.

Bohrer, N. 2011. *Photography and Archaeology*. London: Reaktion Books.

Bonetti, M. F., and A. Prandi, eds. 2010. *La Persia Qajar: Fotografi italiani in Iran 1848–1864.* Rome: Peliti Associati.

Boym, S. 2010. "Ruins of the Avant-Garde: From Tatlin's Tower to Paper Architecture." In J. Hell and A. Schönle (eds.), *Ruins or Modernity*, 58–85. Durham, NC: Duke University Press.

Brusius, M. 2015. "Royal Photographs in Qajar Iran: Writing the History of Photography between Persian Miniature Painting and Western Technology." In T. Sheehan (ed.), *Photography, History, and Difference*, 57–83. Hanover, NH: Dartmouth College Press.

———. 2016. "Photography's Fits and Starts: The Search for Antiquity and Its Image in Victorian Britain." *History of Photography* 43:250–66.

Chevalier, N. 2003. *La recherche archéologique française au Moyen-Orient 1842–1947.* Paris: Éditions Recherche sur les Civilisations.

Di Paolo, S. 2018. "Copies and Degrees of Similarities: Accuracy in the Mimesis and Its Violations in the Ancient Near East." In S. Di Paolo (ed.), *Implementing Meanings: The Power of the Copy Between Past, Present and Future; An Overview from the Ancient Near East*, 29–70. Altertumskunde des Vorderen Orients 19. Münster: Ugarit-Verlag.

Flandin, E. 1851–1854. *Voyage en Perse de mm. Eugène Flandin, peintre, et Pascal Coste, architecte, entrepris par ordre de m.le ministre des affaires* étrangères, *d'après les instructions dressées par l'Institut.* Paris: Gide & J. Baudry. See digitized copy: https://digitalcollections.nypl.org/collections/voyage-en-perse-de-mm-eugne-flandin-peintre-et-pascal-coste-architecte-entrepris#/?tab=about.

Grigor, T. 2009. "Orientalism and Mimicry of Selfness: Archeology of the Neo-Achaemenid Style." In N. Oulebsir and M. Volait (eds.), *L'Orientalisme architectural entre imaginaires et savoirs*, 273–90. Paris: CNRS/Picard.

Hannavy, J. 2013. "Italy." In *Encyclopedia of Nineteenth-Century Photography.* New York: Taylor & Francis.

Heilbrun, F. 1998. "Around the World: Explorers, Travelers, and Tourists." In M. Frizot (ed.), *A New History of Photography.* Cologne: Könemann.

Krefter, F. 1969. "Persepolis im Modell." *Archäologische Mitteilungen aus Iran* 2:123–37.

———. 1971. *Persepolis Rekonstruktionen.* Berlin: Gebr. Mann.

Kushinski, A. 2016. "Light and the Aesthetics of Abandonment: HDR Imaging and the Illumination of Ruins." *Transformations: Journal of Media and Culture* 28. Accessed 28 September 2017. http://www.transformationsjournal.org/issues/28/03.shtml.

Liverani, M. 2018. *Paradiso e dintorni: Il paesaggio rurale dell'antico Oriente.* Bari, Rome: Laterza.

Lyons, C. L., J. K. Papadopoulos, L. S. Stewart, and A. Szegedy-Maszak. 2005. *Antiquity and Photography: Early Views of Ancient Mediterranean Sites.* Los Angeles: Getty Publications.

Nasiri-Moghaddam, N. 2004. *L'archéologie française en Perse et les antiquités nationales (1884–1914).* Paris: Connaissances et Savoirs.

The Nineteenth-Century Archaeological Imagination. 2012. Special Issue of *Journal of Literature and Science* 5(1).

Pesce, L. 1860. *Album fotografico della Persia.* Digitized version: https://rosettaapp.getty.edu/delivery/DeliveryManagerServlet?dps_pid=IE1378533

Poulson, S. C. 2005. *Social Movements in Twentieth-Century Iran: Culture, Ideology, and Mobilizing Frameworks.* Lanham, MD: Lexington.

Saltz, L. 2015. "Natural/Mechanical: Keywords in the Conception of Early Photography." In T. Sheenan and A. Zervigon (eds.), *Photography and Its Origins*, 197–207. New York: Routledge.

Schmidt, C. F. 1953. *Persepolis I: Structures, Reliefs, Inscriptions.* Chicago: University of Chicago Press.

Scheiwiller, S. G. 2018. "Relocating Sevruguin: Contextualizing the Political Climate of the Iranian Photographer Antoin Sevruguin (c. 1851–1933)." In M. Ritter and S. G. Scheiwiller (eds.), *The Indigenous Lens: Early Photography in the Near and Middle East*, 145–69. Berlin: de Gruyter.

Settis, S., A. Anguissola, and D. Gasparotto. 2015. *Serial/Portable Classic: The Greek Canon and Its Mutation*. Milan: Fondazione Prada.

Sonntag, S. 1966. "Against Interpretation." In *Against Interpretation and Other Essays*, 3–14. New York: Penguin Modern Classics.

Tahmasbpour, M. 2018. "Photography during the Qajar Era, 1842–1925." In M. Ritter and S. G. Scheiwiller (eds.), *The Indigenous Lens: Early Photography in the Near and Middle East*, 57–76. Berlin: de Gruyter.

Warwick, A., and M. Willis. 2012. "Introduction: The Archaeological Imagination." *Journal of Literature and Science* 5:1–5.

Artaserse

An Ancient Oriental Ruler on Modern Opera Stages?

Kerstin Droß-Krüpe

The ancient Near East has throughout the centuries been an object of fascination, exoticism, and longing for Western civilizations. Particularly on the opera stage, the exotic was and is often staged with great audience appeal. The exotic in particular sets dreams free for the audience. When (ancient) orient and opera meet one another plenty of stereotypes convene.[1] This connection has taken on a new dimension in recent years: Since the beginning of the increased arrival of refugees from Syria in Europe in 2015, several stages have performed plays and operas with and about refugees and their Near Eastern home countries. However, it is not only in modern times, but already in antiquity that looking across cultural borders between a "western" and "eastern" world stoked the imagination. As a result, at least since the Renaissance, the ancient Greek and Latin authors' fascination for the "oriental world" spilled over to southern and central Europe, a phenomenon certainly stimulated by European travellers and their reports as well as illustrated publications on that region, such as Paul Rycaut's *The Present State of the Ottoman Empire* (1670). Likewise, during Napoleon's campaign to Ottoman Egypt and Syria, Ottoman envoys enforced this development. All this resulted in, among other things, a growing pan-European interest in Turqueries,

---

I am very grateful to Agnès Garcia-Ventura and Lorenzo Verderame for their kind invitation to contribute to this volume. I further owe thanks to Filippo Carlà-Uhink (Potsdam), Sebastian Fink (Helsinki), Valeska Hartmann (Marburg), Helmut Hering (Weimar/Lahn), Barbara Köstner (Bonn), Florian Krüpe (Marburg), Michael Yonan (Columbia), and an unknown reviewer for invaluable critical comments, as well as for providing further ideas and for spotting inconsistencies. Falk Ruttloh (Kassel) assisted greatly in supplying reviews and newspaper articles dealing with both stagings discussed below as well as remote literature. Virginia Geisel (Marburg) and Markus Diedrich (Marburg) edited the English manuscript and valuably added to the clarity of thoughts—all remaining errors are obviously my own. I am also grateful to Georg Lang (Parnassus arts productions, Vienna) and Nils Klinger (Kassel) for providing me with photographic material from the stagings discussed.

1. On exoticism in opera, see Gurlich 1993 and Said 1994.

that is, a Turkish style of decoration and exotic "oriental" luxury. In this context several stage works were created that deal with Egyptian kings, Babylonian queens, harem abductions, or the liberation of slaves. As Edward Said pointedly puts it:

> These subaltern cultures were exhibited before Westerners as microcosms of the larger imperial domain. Little, if any, allowance was made for the non-European except within this framework. (Said 1994, 112)

Many of these "oriental" operas by Händel, Vivaldi, Hasse, and other composers nowadays enjoy a renaissance on Europe's opera stages, but lesser-known eighteenth-century opera offers even more things to discover. Among these hidden gems lies the works of Leonardo Vinci, one of the most successful Italian opera composers of his time. In particular, his scorings of libretti written by Pietro Metastasio heightened his fame. As the result of these two musical geniuses' collaboration, *Artaserse*—undoubtedly Vinci's masterpiece—was staged in Rome in 1730. The focus of this drama is on the Persian king Artaxerxes I, who is shown as a man of immense personal stature. As a typical example of Pietro Metastasio's work, it is based on a ruler who has to do the right thing and put aside or reconcile his own feelings over love and duty in the face of various dilemmas.

For centuries, the piece was almost completely forgotten.[2] In 2012, a modern revival of Vinci's *Artaserse* was staged with an all-male cast (five countertenors and one tenor). While the staged version was shown at the Opéra National de Lorraine in Nancy, the only theater willing to stage it (though only two years later it was performed at the Opéra Royal de Versailles), there was a DVD and CD release as well as a concert version, with almost the same cast, which toured Europe to great acclaim. Only a little later, in 2016, the Staatstheater Kassel staged *Artaserse*—the first scenic presentation of this opera in Germany since 1746.

Following a brief introduction to the peculiarities and functioning of baroque opera and its renaissance that also reviews the historical sources regarding Artaxerxes, this essay compares the 2012 and 2016 stagings, focusing on how differently an ancient oriental ruler is brought to the stage in the twenty-first century—or rather if there is anything oriental in *Artaserse*.

1. Baroque Opera in the Twentieth and Twenty-first centuries

No work of art allows such a multidimensional experience as opera: not only the content and the music, but also the director's engagement with them, are places of aesthetic

2. Vinci's *Artaserse* was first rediscovered by the "Musikwerkstatt Wien" in 2007. Here the main part, originally meant for soprano castrato, was performed by the British countertenor Andrews Watts who brilliantly mastered almost the whole part in the original range. See L'Artaserse, Musik Werkstatt Wien, http://www.musikwerkstatt-wien.com/produktionen/2007lartaserse.html (accessed 7 November 2019).

experience. For the art lover and the musicologist, but also for the historian, opera is an attractive field of inquiry (see Assmann 2005 and 2015; Manuwald 2013; Droß-Krüpe 2017, 9–10).

Currently, it is baroque opera in particular that is booming and gaining worldwide attention. Since the Zurich opera house, under the direction of Jean-Pierre Ponnelle and Nikolaus Harnoncourt,[3] staged three operas by Claudio Monteverdi[4] in 1975–1977 in historical performance practice—that is, played on historical instruments or their replicas and old temperaments (415 Hz)[5]—the storm of enthusiasm for eighteenth century opera has virtually never waned. But it is by no means the case that baroque opera had fallen into oblivion before 1977. G. F. Händel's operas in particular had already been "rediscovered" in 1920, when the art historian and musicologist Oskar Hagen staged *Rodelinda* in Göttingen. His production proved that not only Händel's oratorios, but also his operas still had much to offer to the audience of the twentieth century.[6]

And yet, the public interest in baroque opera in the twentieth century was different from the current wave of the baroque opera renaissance of our days: At that time, especially the presentation of highly virtuous arias in breakneck tempi challenged the sopranos (e.g., Joan Sutherland)[7] and completely awed the audience. Furthermore, until well into the late twentieth century it was common practice that scores were rewritten extensively before staging—recitatives were deleted, the characteristic DaCapo arias were rigorously shortened and rearranged, and, above all, the leading roles originally written for *castratos* or male sopranos were transposed and made singable for tenors, baritones, or even basses. These drastic interventions in music and dramaturgy were perceived as necessary modernizations that should make baroque opera acceptable for modern audiences (e.g., Peters 1989). Today's performance practice for this music is rather different: length and form are mostly left in their original way, and instrumentation, dramaturgy, and cast are mostly accepted and retained. The enthusiasm of the late twentieth and early twenty-first centuries for the baroque opera is to a large extent fed by the contrast between historical music-making on the one hand and modern staging

3. Alice Harnoncourt's role as concertmaster should not be underestimated. Fürstauer and Mika 2009, 33–34.

4. *L'Orfeo* (1975–1976); *L'incoronazione di Poppea* (1977); *Il ritorno d'Ulisse in patria* (1977).

5. Today's tendency towards a 415 Hz-pitch of the instruments is however rather a convention than a rendition of a historical fact, since obligatory tuning did not exist in the baroque period. As Quantz already stated: "[wie] die Orchester zu stimmen pflegen, ist nach Beschaffenheit der Orte und Zeiten immer sehr verschieden gewesen." Quantz [1752] 1983, § 6, 241.

6. See Thompson 2006, 19–24 and 39–44. It is particularly remarkable that Hagen was working with amateur actors whom he recruited from his colleagues and students. The Akademische Orchestervereinigung provided the instrumental accompaniment. His production is considered a starting point for Händel's renaissance and formed also the beginning of the "Göttinger Händel-Festspiele."

7. One may only think of her title role in *Alcina*, most prominently performed with the Händel Opera Society in 1957 in London, 1959 in Cologne (with Fritz Wunderlich), and 1960 in Venice (a performance which earned her the honorary title "La Stupenda") or her interpretation of Cleopatra in *Giulio Cesare in Egitto* in 1963, again with the Händel Opera Society in London.

in the sense of director's theater on the other (Eckert 1995). However, this second (or third) renaissance of the baroque opera mostly affects only the musical and dramaturgical aspects; the staging practices were virtually never concerned. Here, clearly sophisticated staging concepts dominate, which show a tendency towards modernization: staging concepts are considered an independent part of the *Gesamtkunstwerk* opera, and the latter's themes are transferred into the present and/or oriented towards political and social daily themes. The staging of Leonardo Vinci's *Artaserse* by director Silviu Purcărete in Nancy in 2012 marks a turning point here. The production has revived a baroque *Gesamtkunstwerk*, so to speak, not only by taking over the cast and music of the premiere, but also by taking up the costumes (and in parts the stage set) of the eighteenth century. In contrast, director Sonja Trebes in 2016 at the Staatstheater Kassel opted for a mixed cast with only one countertenor (for the title role) and a thoroughly modern production with a uniform stage design. But before we can turn our attention to the details of both productions, it seems necessary to illuminate the historical protagonist, the librettist and composer, as well as the *opera seria* as an art form that has lastingly been shaped by both.

2. *Artaserse: A Persian Ruler Entering Europe's Opera Stages*

Artaxerxes I, who ruled as Persian Great King after the murder of his father Xerxes in 465 BCE until his own death in 424 BCE, was a well-known and popular character on the European seventeenth- and eighteenth-century stages. From 1669 to 1737, a variety of operas and plays were performed that revolved around his figure. And yet, the sources for the actual historical Persian king are sparse. We have his own testimonies in the form of inscriptions from Persepolis (Weissbach 1911, 121; Herzfeld 1938, 45–46, no. 22). We also have historical details, which are much more important for the history of the reception of his figure, in Greek historiography and biblical texts of the Old Testament—here especially in the context of building activities in Jerusalem (Ezra 7:7–26; Neh 2:1, 13:6). Several sources describe in detail the murder of Xerxes by the chief of his life guards, Artabanos/Artapanus, as well as the accession of his young son Artaxerxes.[8] In general, Artaxerxes I is described positively in the sources; he is characterized as a kind-hearted, moderate, and exceedingly capable ruler who, however, also had abilities in matters of warfare. At the same time the Greek sources (and the Roman sources based upon them) emphasize the strong influence of his mother Amestris and his wife Amytis, who were able to manipulate Artaxerxes "so that he has also been called a weakling commanded by the harem" (Schmitt 1987, 655).

8. Ctesias (FGrHist 688) *frag.* 13–14 (Lenfant); Aristotle, *Politica* 5.10.1311b37; Diodorus Siculus 11.69–71; Justin, *Epitome* 3.1.2–9.

Against this background, it does not come as a surprise that all the important librettists of the late seventeenth and eighteenth century have dealt with the figure of Artaxerxes. The prelude was a libretto of the Venetian Aurelio Aureli with the title *L'Artaxerse overo L'Ormonda costante,* which is strongly oriented towards Plutarch's biography on Artaxerxes. It premiered on 30 December 1668 in the Teatro Santi Giovanni e Paolo in Venice in a musical setting by Antonio Cesti. Apparently, the opera was a considerable success, as it was performed for four weeks, which was not a matter of course in Venice's carnival season (Selfridge-Field 2007, 93–94). The main plot, however, does not center around the murder of Xerxes and new king Artaxerxes, but rather around the sibling rivalry between the firstborn Artaxerxes and his younger brother Cyrus. Aureli creates an Artaxerxes who is by no means heroic, but rather lascivious, unrestrained, and effeminate—thus an equivalent to contemporary imaginations of the Ottoman sultan. The opera demonstrates that in the absence of reason, absolute power easily can become tyranny and arbitrary rule.

In the course of the eighteenth century, the character representation of Artaxerxes changed in the libretti.[9] His seventeenth-century depiction as a rather immoral ruler increasingly gave way to a much more positive portrayal; the conflicts described are not triggered by the deficiencies of his personality, but by fateful events. What we encounter here is a clear adaption to the zeitgeist; a transformation of the ruler's image in view of "the Turk threat" and other challenges of the Habsburg Empire. Justice, which the ruler provides and must ensure, is perceived as a central problem of the present times and consequently also implemented on the opera stages of the time (see Serena 1999; Weiand 2017). Probably the most prominent and powerful example of Artaxerxes, who is shaken by fate but ultimately acts in an exemplary manner, can be found in Pietro Metastasio's libretto of 1730.

3. *Metastasio and Vinci: Two Baroque Geniuses and Their Most Fruitful Outcome,* Artaserse *(1730)*

Pietro Antonio Domenico Bonaventura Trapassi, better known under his alias Pietro Metastasio (the Hellenized version of his surname) is without any doubt the most influential opera librettist of the eighteenth century, perhaps even of the entire *opera seria.* This term, usually referred to by contemporaries as *dramma per musica,* describes the serious Italian opera that was popular throughout Europe with exception of France (Schreiber 1988, 267–73). Basically, the *opera seria* was a drama set to music modeled on the ancient tragedy. Since the middle of the sixteenth century the prevailing attitude—based on passages from Aristotle and Plato—it has been thought that the

9. To name only the most important ones: *Temistocle,* Vienna 1701 (Libretto: Apostolo Zeno); *Gli amanti generosi,* Venice 1703 (Libretto: Pietro Giovanni Candi); *Artaserse,* Venice 1705 (Libretto: Apostolo Zeno and Pietro Pariati?); *Artaserse, Re di Persia,* Naples 1713 (Libretto: Francesco Silvani).

whole tragedy, the parts of the actors and of the choirs, were supposed to be sung.[10] The consequence is obvious: in the opera, the sung text becomes binding, not the spoken dialogue as in the Singspiel (Pöhlmann 1969, 6). As Claudio Monteverdi wrote in 1607: "l'armonia serva a l'orazione."[11] The comprehensibility of the text was of immense importance, and the interpretation of the libretto in greatest possible musical expressivity was the central task of the composer. This view also explains the outstanding position of the authors of those opera texts, the librettists. Metastasio is probably the best-known and efficacious representative of these artists (Meyer 2000, 339). As Reinhard Meyer (2000, 340–41) admiringly observes:

> es dürfte bis in die Gegenwart keinen nur annähernd ähnlich erfolgreichen Librettisten gegeben haben.... Es hat bis in die Gegenwart nie wieder einen Librettisten gegeben, dessen Texte von so vielen Komponisten und über einen derart langen Zeitraum vertont worden wären.

Each of Pietro Metastasio's opera librettos was composed very strictly and formally. Their schematic structure became decisive for later librettists and shaped the entire *opera seria*. Not only the language, namely Italian, but also the formal structure of the *opera seria* was largely standardized since and by Metastasio: the typical *opera seria* consisted of three acts, each subdivided into ten to fifteen different scenes. In between acts, depending on the budget available, ballets were given, but these were not related to the theme of the opera in question (Strohm 1997, 11). The social hierarchy of the audience with the members of the aristocracy and/or the court in their loges, the bourgeoisie in the parquet, and the common people on the remotest places beneath the roof is mirrored in the role constellation on stage; the ruler, representing the top of hierarchy, appears in the end of the third act to turn the conflict—usually caused by a controversy between duties and love and seemingly leading to catastrophe—by his magnanimity or self-sacrifice for the better. Two pairs of singers (*prima donna—primo uomo; seconda donna—secondo uomo*) subordinate him or her, including several smaller roles as confidantes or keyword givers. In terms of music, the *opera seria* has been characterized since Metastasio by recitative and aria. The recitative was usually set in *versi sciolti*, irregular, rhymeless, and with seven or eleven syllables, while the text of an aria was written in lyrical verses of different meter (Schreiber 1988, 269). As a general rule it can be said that the recitative advances the action, while the aria expresses the affects (anger, love, despair, hope, etc.) of a person. Contents of the arias are more or less irrelevant for the plot; they could be exchanged, inserted, or deleted without substantially affecting the course of the opera (Schmidt-Hensel 2009, 23). Since Metastasio all arias were depar-

10. Aristotle, [*Problemata*] 19.48; Plato, *Politicus* 3.400a; Patrici 1586: "che tutta la Tragedia, che di attori era composta, e di chori, si cantava" (cited after Steinbeck 2010, 200).

11. Scherzi musicali, therein: Dichiarazione della lettera stampata nel Quinto libro de'suoi Madregali (Venice 1607).

ture arias at the end of a scene. After singing it, the singer left the stage, which meant that every scene contained only one aria (though many scenes consisted of recitatives only). The plot is arranged in such a way that figures of higher social rank perform more arias. For Metastasio it was important that the arias covered the whole range of human emotions, that they were evenly distributed over the entire opera, and that the affect changes between arias.

In accordance with the spirit of his time,[12] Metastasio's libretti are based almost exclusively on historical topics, which originate predominantly from antiquity. From the birth of the opera with the Camerata Fiorentina in Florence in the early-seventeenth century, ancient materials have been an integral component of the young musical genre of musical theater. For the opera audiences of the seventeenth and eighteenth centuries, Orpheus, Daphne, Odysseus, or Dido were familiar figures. With Claudio Monteverdi's *L'incoronazione di Poppea* that was composed after a libretto based on Tacitus by Giovanni Francesco Busenello and premiered 1642 in Venice, the librettists and composers increasingly focused on historical figures of antiquity.

Leonardo Vinci's scoring was the first of many musical settings of what was probably Metastasio's most popular libretto. Both artists had collaborated previously, as Vinci had already set five librettos by Metastasio into music: *Didone abbandonata* (first performance: January 1726, Rome, Teatro delle Dame), *Siroe Re di Persia* (first performance: February 1726, Venice, Teatro San Giovanni Crisostomo), *Catone in Utica* (first performance: January 1728, Rome, Teatro delle Dame) and *Semiramide riconosciuta* (first performance: February 1729, Rome, Teatro delle Dame), *Alessandro nell'India* (first performance: January 1730, Rome, Teatro delle Dame). Vinci's musical settings contributed crucially to the success of Pietro Metastasio and turned the latter into a celebrity, even before he was appointed to the Habsburg court in Vienna as *poeta cesareo*. But in 1730 the Neapolitan Vinci was no longer a stranger either, but belonged to the most successful opera composers of his time. Especially his last two Metastasio settings (*Alessandro nell'India* and *Artaserse*) set new standards in the genre of *opera seria*. His operas were very popular, and there were—most atypically for the opera enterprise of this time—relatively many posthumous performances,[13] which surely may be interpreted as an indication of a great and continuing appreciation.

The most famous opera of these days was undoubtedly Vinci's *Artaserse*. It premiered on 4 February 1730 in the Teatro delle Dame in Rome. With the exception of one tenor voice, *Artaserse* was originally written for castrati (or high falsetto voices) only,[14] who also had to replace all female singers, due to the fact that women were

12. As an introduction to this topic, see Weiand 2017; Walther 2010, 1–5.

13. Vinci died in May 1730 under uncertain circumstances; a poison murder is not to be excluded. Markstrom 2007, 344: "Although the story of Vinci's poisoning cannot be proven, it cannot be disproved, as is the case of similar stories connected with the deaths of Pergolesi and Mozart."

14. Also, Vinci's earlier musical settings of Metastasian libretti staged in Rome were exclusively per-

banned from the Roman theatrical stages until 1798.[15] Other performances, sometimes in a revised form, followed in fast succession in numerous cities.[16] Three performances deserve special attention: First, the performance on the occasion of the birthday of Elisabeth Christine von Braunschweig Wolfenbüttel, wife of Karl VI, on 28 August 1730 in Vienna, the first opera that Metastasio presented in his new position as *poeta cesareo* at the Habsburg court (Markstrom 2007, 320). Second, the presentations on the occasion of two inaugurations: the new Teatro San Carlo in Venice 1738 and the opera house in Dresden 1746 (Neville 1992, 220).

4. Metastasio's Artaserse*: A Complicated Plot of Love, Betrayal, Power, and Intrigue*

Before we turn to the scenic performances in Nancy and Kassel, we ought to take a closer look at the opera's plot and at the individual participants. As usual in baroque opera, the confusing story is woven around conflicts between love and obligation, loyalty and betrayal. It is set in ancient Persia of the fifth century BCE, more precisely in one of the capital cities, Susa. In the libretto's *argomento* (a kind of preface), Metastasio states that he has taken the plot from Justin's *Epitome* of Pompeius Trogus (book 3, chapter 1). However, as Charles de Brosses recognized already shortly after the premiere (De Brosses 1858, 256), Metastasio also drew on other theatrical models, especially the tragedies *Le Cid* (1637) and *Stilicon* (1660) by the French dramatist Pierre Corneille and Prosper Jolyot Crébillon's *Xerxes* (1714; see also Neville 1992, 220). From Corneille he borrowed the motif of self-sacrifice for king and country and the protection of a guilty father as the main motifs for his character Arbace. Crébillon's *Xerxes* was the inspiration for the amorous episode between Artaserse and Semira (Markstrom 2007, 309). It is important to note that Metastasio's libretto has no connections with Aureli's *Artaserse*, originally produced in Venice in 1669.[17]

Metastasio's Plot

The Persian king Serse was murdered by Artabano, the commander of his guard. Artabano directs the suspicion towards Serse's oldest son, Dario, who thereupon is ex-

---

formed by men; however, *Siroe, Re di Persia*, which premiered in Venice, also contained two roles for female artists: Marianna Benti Bulgarelli, nicknamed "La Romanina," as Emira (soprano), and Lucia Facchinelli as Laodice (soprano).

15. The ban was only lifted in the course of the French occupation in Rome.

16. For a list of performance, see http://corago.unibo.it/opera/0000052003 (accessed 7 November 2019); also Markstrom 2007, 320–25.

17. Furthermore, there are no connections to other Artaserse operas, as for example the libretto by Zeno/Pariati (1703) or the version produced at the Teatro Alibert during the Carnival season of 1721, based on Francesco Silvani's *Il tradimento traditor di se stesso* from 1711, both dealing with Artaxerxes II; Markstrom 2007, 310.

ecuted by order of his younger brother Artaserse. Artabano confesses his crime to his son Arbace, whom he hopes to install as the new Persian king. He wants Arbace to support him in the assault and murder of Serse's successor Artaserse. Since Artabano and Artaserse have been childhood friends, the former refuses to support his father—even though Serse had banned Artabano from court because of his love for Serse's daughter and Artaserse's sister, Mandane. The plot contains a second unfulfilled love: Artabano tries to force his daughter Semira to marry general Megabise, but she loves Artaserse, the new king.

When it becomes known that Dario is innocent, Arbace is accused of the murder. In order to protect his father, he does not defend himself against the false accusation and is condemned to death. Artaserse, who is not convinced of his friend's guilt, helps him to escape. In the meantime, Artabano and his henchman Megabise have incited the people of Persia against the king. Both try to poison Artaserse with an poisoned drink, but by killing Megabise, Arbace succeeds in averting their coup. Artaserse, now completely convinced of Arbace's innocence, offers him the drink to confirm on oath. Afraid of seeing his son poisoned, Artabano confesses that he had murdered Serse. Consequently, Artaserse sentences him to death, but Arbace pleads for mercy for his father. Through his intercession, the penalty becomes less severe; Artabano is banished. Arbace reunites with Mandane as his wife, while Artaserse marries Semira.

Through the course of Metastasio's opera, Artaserse undergoes a maturing character development: at first hesitant and trusting, he eventually takes on the responsibility of ruling the kingdom.

Although the historical background, the setting and the protagonists are Persian, the libretto at no point refers to Persian or oriental realia. The protagonists' motifs are not inspired by their "oriental" background, but rather by Metastasio's endeavors to present examples of good and evil. As was already the case in *Siroe, Re di Persia,* and *Semiramide riconosciuta,* this libretto rather serves to mirror the ruling class than to idealize the Orient or present an exotic subject. The libretto's main subject is not the presentation of an ancient world, or one regarded as ancient; its concern is to present a good ruler who has to overcome a conflict between love and obligation. The reason why oriental subjects in baroque opera in general and the Metastasian *Artaserse* libretto in particular enjoyed an unceasing success over decades seems to lie especially in the sociocultural, religious, and political conditions of the time. Using the apt words of musicologist Reinhard Strohm (1997, 6):

> the subjects of the dramma per musica were mostly taken from pre- or non-Christian civilizations and could therefore be used to promote enlightened tendencies without openly contradicting the Church.

To sum up: the subject is oriental, the story is set in Susa, one of the capital cities of the Persian empire, but the libretto's actual text bears not the slightest reference to foreign, exotic, oriental worlds. But what about the recent productions that make up the subject of this contribution? How do two modern dramaturges adapt this material, how oriental are their stagings, and what are their respective central aspects?

5. Artaserse *2012/2016: Two Stagings of Oriental Rulers and Miscellaneous Gender Representations*

As already suggested above, the possibilities of modern directors for producing a baroque opera as *Artaserse* are enormously versatile. One has the choice between an established or rediscovered opus, between a historical or adapted cast (a decision that is certainly determined to a large extent by the available budget for one or even several countertenors), between a baroque staging or modern director's theater. Everything is possible and a matter of conscious decisions. Exemplary for the spectrum of possibilities for staging are the two to be discussed here, the productions by Silviu Purcărete (Nancy 2012) and Sonja Trebes (Kassel 2016). Not only in terms of music, but above all in the interpretation of gender roles, these two stagings take quite different paths.

Artaserse: An Oriental Ruler in Nancy 2012

Silviu Purcărete's production of Vinci's *Artaserse* is, as Judith Malafronte rightly put it "a study in theatrical artifice."[18] When Vinci's *Artaserse* premiered in 1730, the *castrato* voice was admired for its *coloratura* and timbre. Purcărete's interpretation of *Artaserse* aims at honoring this centrality of *castrato* capabilities of those days. Five countertenors are cast here—all roles that were embodied in the premiere by male sopranos and male contraltos are thus also here cast by men, two of them embodying female figures. Five of the probably best representatives of their profession could be united on stage: Philippe Jaroussky performed the title role, Franco Fagiolo played Arbace, and Yuriy Mynenko embodied the intriguing henchman Megabise. Max Emanuel Cenčić, who was also a *spiritus rector* and responsible for the casting, presented himself as a man in female role (Mandane), as did Valer Barna Sabadus (Semira). The tenor Juan Sancho completed the cast as the intricate Artabano, a role that also in the premiere was meant for tenor voice. Concerto Köln as proven specialists for early music were responsible for the instrumental arrangement. Purcărete brings this cast, which resembles the original cast from 1730, to the Nancy stage—this modality that was quite common in the eighteenth century was acclaimed exceptionally in the European feuilletons in our times.[19]

During the overture, the audience can participate in the conversion of the singers into their Persian (or baroque) *alter egos* (figs. 1 and 2): we enter a backstage scene, where the cast is to be seen partly costumed (Sancho, Fagiolo, and Mynenko—the Persian nobles and military men), partly in T-shirt (Jaroussky—the Great King) and bathrobes (Cenčić and Barna-Sabadus—the Persian noblewomen) but already in white and

18. See Malafronte 2014.

19. E.g., "It is an event not soon to be forgotten," Loomis 2012; "uno spettacolo memorabile," Lora 2014.

rouged makeup, before proceeding into costume. At the end of the overture, Mandane and Arbace bring themselves into posture for the first scene of the first act, and the curtain always remains open.

Helmut Stürmer created baroque-seeming costumes for all roles and was also responsible for the scenery.[20] All costumes reflect both the character and gender of their wearers. The costumes for the two female roles, Semira and Mandane, are particularly sumptuous. Assisted by stagehands, wearing modern black clothing and headsets, both transform into preening divas in spectacular costumes under the eyes of the audience.[21] In the first act Mandane wears an overhanging dress whose skirt is richly decorated with gray-green feathers and which has a feather collar; in addition, there is a headdress made from white feathers.[22] Semira is wearing a white dress of similar design with white feathers, long white gloves and a head finery made from white feathers. Her white costume symbolizes her innocence, since throughout the whole story Semira is the only figure whose hands are not stained with blood. Because of their white-painted faces and the design of their high-necked dresses, which includes modeled bosoms, neither Cenčić nor Barna-Sabadus can be recognized as men. The gender illusion becomes perfect by their movements, gestures, and facial expressions, which appeared convincingly maiden-like.

Completely different, but similarly pregnant with meaning, are the male's costumes. In his first appearance, Megabise's attire stresses male and martial features: breastplate and black helmet, in addition to tight trousers beneath a long, riveted tunic, evoke immediate associations to the clothes of the Eurasian nomads, or "horse people." His costume is completed by long black feathers at the shoulders.

When Artabanos and Artaserse appear for the first time, their contrasts could not be greater: Artabanos, who brings the message of Dario's murder, is shown with a bloody sword, a horn helmet, extremely wide-cut trousers, which appear rather dress-like, and an upper part with sumptuous black skin trimming and trumpet sleeves. All this makes him appear extremely masculine and martial. Artaserse, in contrast, appears visibly unprotected and weak: Stürmer provides him in this scene with a plain, floor-length white nightgown. He is barefoot, which underlines his vulnerability. The Persian Great King does not show any royal splendor, but appears rather helpless and weak in his white shift reminiscent of women's Victorian undergarments. However, his ap-

20. Stürmer and Purcărete had already cooperated in the same season in two operas by Serguei Rachmaninoff, *Francesca da Rimini* and *Aleko* at the Teatro Colón, Buenos Aires; Lauria 2013. At the Händelfestspiele 2016 in Karlsruhe Stürmer created baroque costumes and the stage design for Händel's *Armino* with Max Emmanuel Cenčić directing and performing the title role; Roeber 2016.

21. The clothes tables remain visible during the entire performance (the bulbs at the make-up tables remain switched on) and are, just as the stagehands, included in the action.

22. On the DVD production (showing the performance from 10 November 2012 at the Opéra National de Lorraine in Nancy), the camera intensively follows her transformation, particularly during the overture. Also, several times later, the camera captures how Mandane's make-up and head finery is touched up at one of the making up tables at the edge of the stage.

Figure 1. Nancy, 2012—Artaserse, Mandane, Semira, and Artabano, © J. Laidig/ Parnassus arts productions.

Figure 2. Nancy, 2012—Arsace and Mandane, © J. Laidig/Parnassus arts productions.

pearance changes as Artaserse alone changes his costume already within the first act. In scene 8, after having ordered his own brother's execution and learning about the accusation against his friend Arbace, he appears all dressed in black: black trousers and a long black coat with oversized spiked pauldrons and long, black gloves (fig. 1). His headdress, however, is as striking as the women's: a black feather mohawk. This costume change is combined with a complete turn of character: the soft, almost effeminate, and weak Artaserse suddenly turns into a cruel king, who lets his own brother be murdered out of fear for his own life, even before the latter's guilt is clearly proven. In the second act, Artaserse is presented in the traditional baroque princely costume, and the color of his clothes changes to bright tones: Justaucorps and culottes in ivory tones, color-matching buckled shoes, and a full-bottomed wig (allonge), accompanied by a fan, a walking stick and even a mouche. In the same act, Artabano appears in a similar attire, and, however different in character and motivation, optically they are of striking resemblance. The courtly masquerade covers everything and almost functions as a uniform or disguise. The production plays with the differences in identity, not only with gender but also hierarchical identities. The full-bottomed wig serves as royal insignia: at the end of this second act (aria: "Non conosco in tal momento") the tortured Artaserse takes it off, as if he wanted to lay down his role, while he seeks support of his "twin" Artabano. His worry and distress is almost physically palpable. Again, the Great King's weakness appears, and he who appears with royal splendor, power, and ostentatious self-confidence is obviously still the unprotected young man from his first appearance in the first act. He stays in this costume also for act three, but he exchanges the full-bottomed wig for a sword, when he rushes to free his friend Arbace. While there is no trace of homoerotism between Artaserse and Arbace during in the first act (aria: "Deh respirar lasciatemi"), here some homoerotic codes may be found, less in explicit actions, but especially in Artaserse's glances (aria: "L'onda dal mar diversa"). The situation remains obscure. Is Arbace his role model or his object of desire? The decision is in the hand of the audience. It is interesting that some reviewers of this production gave special attention to the love story instead of dwelling on the aspects of gender, as one perhaps might expect in a production that presents counter tenors as female roles.[23] They come to the conclusion that Artaserse's feelings for his childhood friend Arbace go beyond friendship, and that there is a hidden homoerotic relationship. Artaserse is perceived by them as a homosexual Oriental, hiding his true sexual inclinations.[24]

In the last scene, Artaserse's clothes change again. The traditional baroque costume is replaced by a golden variant, and now explicit signs of a ruler are added: a long, white royal cloak, with a rigid, high royal collar and, again, a feather crown, which nearly appears Aztec. This final costuming visualizes Artaserse's growth into a capable, wise, and autonomous king.

Like the costumes, stage design is based on baroque models and presents them in an exaggerated form (see Hartmann 2017). The fact that the action is situated at the Persian court in Susa is optically not recognizable, there are no Persian or "oriental" realia at all, fully in keeping with the tradition of baroque opera. In the beginning of the first act, Leonardo da Vinci's Vitruvian man becomes visible, in scene seven (aria: "Sogna il guerrier le schiere") the background scenery changes and the stage prospect shows the exploding church of Monsù Desiderio (actually François de Nomé and Didi-

---

23. Exceptions are two reviews for the performance in Versailles from March 2014: Lora 2014 and Serna 2014.

24. As Tim Ashley (2012) wrote in the *Guardian*: "it is soon apparent that Artaserse's feelings for Arbace run deeper than his affection for his own fiancée, Semira." Calvin Wells expresses the same opinion in the program notes for the musical setting by Johann Adolf Hasse and the Ensemble Serse 2009 in St. Giles: "Whatever the case may be, these two men are not just friends in the traditional meaning of the word": http://www.ensembleserse.com/artaserse.html (accessed 15 March 2017).

er Barra), which also dominates the stage design of the second act. The make-up tables at the edge of the stage always remain visible. In the third act another background is added, namely José de Ribera's "Apolo y Marsias" from 1637.[25] Only towards the end of the third act, when it comes to drinking the poison, the scenery changes into a clear palace architecture with golden wall decoration, with pilasters and an enormous chandelier. But, as splendor and destruction are often closely related, the picture is framed by the exploding church from the second act.

Artaserse: An Oriental Ruler in Kassel 2016

The *Artaserse* production in Kassel is in many respects quite different. Here the theater director Ursula Benzing chose to apply slight cuts in respect to the original version and presents a mixed cast, thereby playing rather differently with the topic of gender. Only the title role was given to a countertenor (Yuriy Mynenko, who played Megabise in Nancy) who has a very strong and full voice and thereby acoustically lends Artaserse a nature of royal power.[26] For all the other roles for male sopranos and male altos, Benzing has chosen female artists.[27] This means that Arbace (Lin Lin Fan; fig. 3) and Megabise (Inna Kalinina; fig. 4) are converted to "breeches parts"—a practice that was typical since the 1970s—but stage director Sonja Trebes does not stop here, but consequently expands this approach: in her interpretation, Arbace is actually a young woman, who was raised as a man by her father Artabano (Bassem Alkhouri) because he wants to see her on the throne. Thus he pursues a prepared plan and is not an opportunist, which makes him appear more evil and heinous than in the original libretto. Consequently, Trebes changes the surtitles and also points in the thin booklet of the production explicitly to the sex of Arbace:

> Ihn [i.e. Artaserse] verbindet eine innige Freundschaft mit Arbace, die vom Vater als Junge erzogen wird, weil Artabano Arbace auf dem Thron sehen will.[28]

Trebes interprets Mandane (Maren Engelhardt), on the other hand, not as Arbace's lover but good friend, whom Serse forbade to interact with Arbace:

---

25. Originally oil on canvas, 182 × 232 cm, Museo Nazionale di San Martino, Naples. The painting shows Apollo flaying the satyr Marsyas, who dared to challenge Apollo in a context of musical skills. For his pride and hubris Marysas is punished most cruelly. Interestingly, this painting was not identified correctly by some reviewers: According to Ingobert Waltenberger (*Der neue Merkur*, 11.2012), the picture in question is Caravaggio's *Sacrificio di Isacco*.

26. Personal information form Ursula Benzing, interviewed by the author 24 February 2017.

27. The casting has consequences for the pitch—for example, the aria "Vo solcando un mar crudel" (Arbace) at the end of the first act is sung a whole tone higher than in Nancy, whereas the aria "Deh respirar lasciatemi" (Artaserse) in the first act is sung in the same tonality in both productions: see https://www.youtube.com/watch?v=XIXSRHUAxYU (accessed 7 November 2019).

28. Accompanying program of the staging © Staatstheater Kassel 2016.

Figure 3. 2016—Arbace and Artaserse, © N. Klinger/Staatstheater Kassel.

> Mandane ist ebenfalls mit Arbace befreundet, diese Freundschaft wurde von Xerxes untersagt.[29]

Trebes's interpretation of Megabise likewise being a woman completes the new range of lesbian subplots, a new and exciting interpretation which happened to be too ambiguous for some reviewers[30] or even seemed a provocative mutilation of the opera.[31]

Stage designer Dirk Becker chose a dark, plain scenery, which is dominated by an enormous X-emblem, the design of which is immediately reminiscent of the action movie "Triple X" by Rob Coban. It makes the Persian Great King Serse remain constantly present, even after his murder. Every action seems to happen under his watching eye (or in his shadow). Serse is not only the dominating shape of the Persian history in the fifth century BCE, but he is also the dominating figure of the entire stage action.[32] Especially at the beginning of the piece, his dominance makes Artaserse appear weak—

---

29. Accompanying program of the staging © Staatstheater Kassel 2016.

30. As Rudolf Hermes (2015) puts it: "Sonja Trebes spielt zwar mit den Geschlechteridentitäten, wenn die Sängerinnen von General Megabise und Prinz Arbace Spitzenunterwäsche tragen. Aber die wichtige Frage, wer Mann oder Frau ist, wird nicht eindeutig beantworten" (sic!).

31. Molke 2015: "Welches Problem Trebes nun mit diesen so genannten Hosenrolle hat, erschließt sich nicht. Jedenfalls scheint sie der Meinung zu sein, dass, wenn Arbace und Megabise jeweils von einer Frau gesungen werden, die beiden Figuren auch weiblich sein müssen."

32. This is different in Rudolf Hermes's review, which states: "Das sieht zwar schick aus, hat aber ansonsten keine Bedeutung": http://www.deropernfreund.de/kassel-12.html (accessed 7 November 2019).

Figure 4. 2016—Megabise, © N. Klinger/Staatstheater Kassel.

despite Mynenkos's stately figure and voice—in comparison to his omnipresent over-father Serse.

In regard to the costume design, Isabell Heinke created quite modern attires for all singers. Artaserse is presented in a richly decorated brocade vest covered by a uniform jacket, which is inspired by the military fashion of the nineteenth century. Arsace hides her true sex under a tight red leather jacket with gold-decorated shoulder straps, which is likewise reminiscent of a military uniform. In the end of the first act (aria: "Vo scalando un mar crudel"), Arsace takes off this disguise and appears in a white long dress: a visualized epitome of the femininity and innocence she longs for. In this costume, she is murdered in the final act of the opera. Artabano, equipped with a large disfiguring scar on the right cheek, is presented as highly decorated military man: lavish gold chains adorn his leather uniform jacket, the cut of which emphasizes his masculinity by an overemphasis of the shoulders. Megabise's costume is likewise provided with shoulder straps; her frock is made from fine, golden shimmering brocade. The proverbial wealth of the Orient is not shown here in the stage design, but in the richly decorated costumes of all persons of higher rank. Mandane's and Semira's costumes are comparatively simple, even with Mandane's dotted blue cocktail dress supplemented by an over proportioned golden necklace. Semira is, like Purcărete's Semira, dressed in a knee-length skirt in rosé with a white lace blouse, symbolizing her innocence—rightly, in fact, since everyone else in the play is somehow linked with murder.

The audience is amused by the director's idea to introduce forensic investigators with CSI manners after the murder of Serse. Besides this extremely modern element,

Trebes and Heinke also used baroque elements and in the second act presented pages as dressed in baroque clothing and a Rococo steward (aria: "Figlia, e questi il tuo sposo").

But Trebes most considerable interference with the original setting—and probably as bold as the alteration of Arsace's and Megabise's sexes—is her refusal to provide the audience with the usually mandatory *lieto fine* (happy ending). Instead, she makes Artsaserse the murderer of Arbace (still innocently dressed in white). Artaserse ends the opera in delirium, after having drained the cup of poison Artabanos presented to him. Finally, he joins his friend in death. The happy ending remains nothing but a fantasy of the dying Great King.

6. Concluding Remarks

Until the 1980s, over and over again the "authentic performance practice" of baroque opera was discussed as a formula that was intended to underscore the claim for truth, which many protagonists of this direction demanded. In the meantime, it has become generally accepted that true authenticity, in terms of a perfect realization of the past, can never be achieved. One can reconstruct circumstances of performance, playing techniques and other historical parameters, but not the actual social and individual experience of musicians and audience. We experience music, even if presented in historical performance practice, always as humans of our time and with the experiences that we make and have made. This means we perceive and experience baroque opera differently than people in earlier epochs. The Orient, which is decidedly not shown by Metastasio and Vinci, present neither in text nor music of the 1730 staging, is only present in the audiences' imagination, back then as much as today. Their figure of Artaserse is not "oriental" in its musical or lyrical structure, and neither are other oriental rulers that Metastasio brought to stage, such as Semiramis,[33] Cyrus,[34] or Siroe.[35] The choice of such historical models is certainly motivated by aesthetic and cultural factors but also strongly by the political conditions of the respective present. The same is true for the omnipresent focus on justice in all its different meanings: the oriental world serves as a background for pointing out iniquity as well as for exemplifying how an exemplary ruler might conquer them and reestablish the destroyed balance. The plot is set in Persia and not on one's own doorstep, whether in 1730 or 2012 or 2016—but Persia is not represented as being actually Persian.[36] However, in the Kassel production, the *topos* of the "rich Orient" is represented by the elaborate, precious, but nevertheless completely European articles of clothing of the represented elite and by the rich gold

33. *Semiramide riconosciuta* (first performance: 6 February 1727, Rome).

34. *Ciro riconosciuto* (first performance: 28 August 1736, Vienna).

35. *Siroe, Re di Persia* (first performance: 2 February 1726, Venice).

36. Though not made explicit, both stagings play with common western *topoi* of the Orient. One may thus agree with Said (1994, 132): "All these together create an amalgam of the arts of narrative and observation about the accumulated, dominated, and ruled territories."

jewelry of Mandane. But instead of focusing on actual oriental elements of whatever kind, both productions mainly aim to impress by playing with gender identities and homoerotic elements. Thus, on the one hand, women's roles are cast with male singers and, on the other, heterosexual relationships are reinterpreted into homosexual ones (and vice versa)—in Purcărete's production by a somewhat gay tension between Artaserse and Arsace, in Trebes's by lesbian subplots between Semira and Megabise. Even in the twenty-first century, "opera is a distant locus for gender politics" (McDonald 2001, 2), or, as Shirley Apthorp puts it: "The gender-bending in baroque operas is confusing at the best of times."[37] The ancient Near East was and still is useful as a setting, against the background of which other topics such as a princely mirror or gender bending can be negotiated. The ancient Near East is in both productions little more than an imaginative matrix, where the exotic easily becomes the erotic.

Bibliography

Apthorp, S. 2015. "Artaserse, Staatstheater Kassel, Germany — 'Simply amazing music.'" *Financial Times*. Online: https://www.ft.com/content/244f286e-a31b-11e5-8d70-42b68cfae6e4 (accessed 7 November 2019).

Ashley, Tim. 2012. Review of Vinci, *Artaserse*. *The Guardian*. https://www.theguardian.com/music/2012/nov/14/vinci-artaserse-fagioni-cencic-review (accessed 7 November 2019).

Assmann, J. 2005. *Die Zauberflöte: Oper und Mysterium*. Munich: Hanser.

———. 2015. *Die Zauberflöte: Eine Oper mit zwei Gesichtern*. Vienna: Picus.

De Brosses, Ch. 1858. *Lettre familières écrites d'Italie a quelques amis en 1739 et 1740*. Paris: Émile Perrin.

Droß-Krüpe, K. 2017. "Great Woman on Stage." In K. Droß-Krüpe (ed.), *Great Women on Stage: The Reception of Women Monarchs from Antiquity to Baroque Opera*, 9–16. Wiesbaden: Harrassowitz.

Eckert, N. 1995. *Von der Oper zum Regietheater*. Berlin: Martin Meidenbauer.

Fürstauer, J., and A. Mika. 2009. *Oper sinnlich: Die Opernwelten des Nikolaus Harnoncourt. Das Musiktheater des Nikolaus Harnoncourt, von Monteverdi bis Strawinski: Ein Leben im Spiegel der Oper*. Salzburg: Residenz.

Gurlich, R. 2013. *Exotismus in der Oper und seine szenische Realisation (1850–1910): Unter besonderer Berücksichtigung der Münchener Oper*. Anif: Müller-Speiser.

Hartmann, V. 2017. "Cleopatra in Baroque Opera: the Stage Design Between Depiction of Power and Adoption of Antiquity." in K. Droß-Krüpe (ed.), *Great Women on Stage: The Reception of Women Monarchs from Antiquity to Baroque Opera*, 49–70. Wiesbaden: Harrassowitz.

Hermes, R. 2015. Review of Leonardo Vinci, Artaserse. *Der Opfernfreund*. Online: http://www.deropernfreund.de/kassel-12.html (accessed 7 November 2019).

Herzfeld, E. 1938. *Altpersische Inschriften*. Berlin: Reimer.

Lauria, Christian. 2013. "Aleko y Francesca da Rimini de Rachmaninov. Buenos Aires." Opera World, http://www.operaworld.es/aleko-y-francesca-da-rimini-de-rachmaninov-buenos-aires/ (accessed 7 November 2019).

37. See Apthorp 2015.

Loomis, G. 2012. "Countertenors on Parade." *The New York Times*, 8 November 2012. Online: https://rendezvous.blogs.nytimes.com/2012/11/08/countertenors-on-parade (accessed 7 November 2019).

Lora, F. "'Artaserse' en travesti, fenomeno a Versailles." Il corriere musicale. Online: http://www.ilcorrieremusicale.it/2014/03/31/artaserse-en-travesti-fenomeno-a-versailles (accessed 7 November 2019).

Malafronte, J. 2014. Review of Vinci: *Artaserse*. Opera News. Online: http://www.operanews.com/Opera_News_Magazine/2014/10/Recordings/VINCI__Artaserse.html (accessed 7 November 2019).

Manuwald, G. 2013. *Nero in Opera: Librettos as Transformations of Ancient Sources*. Berlin: de Gruyter.

Markstrom, K. S. 2007. *The Operas of Leonardo Vinci, Napolitano*. Hillsdale, NY: Pendragon.

McDonald, M. 2001. *Sing Sorrow: Classics, History, and Heroines in Opera*. Westport, CT: Greenwood.

Meyer, R. 2000. "Die Rezeption der Opernlibretti Metastasios." In E. T. Hilscher and A. Sommer-Mathis (eds.), *Pietro Metastasio—uomo universale (1698–1782), Festgabe der Österreichischen Akademie der Wissenschaften zum 300. Geburtstag von Pietro Metastasio*, 311–52. Vienna: Verlag der Östereichischen Akademie der Wissenschaften.

Molke, Th. 2015. "Artaserse." *Online Musik Magazin*. Online: http://www.omm.de/veranstaltungen/musiktheater20152016/KS-artaserse.html (accessed 7 November 2019).

Neville, D. 1992. "Artaserse." In S. Sadine and C. Bashford (eds.), *The New Grove Dictionary of Opera* 1, 219–21. New York: Grove.

Patrici, F. 1586. *Della poetica*. Ferrara: Vittorio Baldini.

Peters, U. 1989. *Die Oper des 17. und frühen 18. Jahrhunderts auf der modernen Opernbühne: Eine Untersuchung zur Aufführungspraxis von Barockopern im deutschsprachigen Theaterraum zwischen 1975 und 1986*. PhD diss., University of Munich.

Pöhlmann, E. 1969. "Antikenverständnis und Antikenmißverständnis in der Operntheorie der Florentiner Camerata." *Die Musikforschung* 22:5–13.

Quantz, J. J. [1752] 1983. *Versuch einer Anweisung die Flöte traversiere zu spielen*. Berlin: Deutscher Verlag für Musik.

Roeber, Martin. 2016. "Händel-Festspiele: Cencic rehabilitiert Oper 'Arminio.'" *Musik Heute*. Online: http://www.musik-heute.de/12319/haendel-festspiele-cencic-rehabilitiert-oper-arminio/ (accessed 7 November 2019).

Said, E. 1994. "The Empire at Work: Verdi's Aida." In *Culture and Imperialism*, 111–31. New York: Vintage Books.

Schmidt-Hensel, R. D. 2009. *"La musica è del Signor Hasse detto il Sassone." Johann Adolf Hasses 'Opere serie' der Jahre 1730–1745: Quellen, Fassungen, Aufführungen*, Göttingen: Vandenbroeck & Ruprecht.

Schmitt, R. 1987. "Artaserxes I." In E. Yarshater (ed.), *Encyclopedia Iranica* 2(6), 655, London: Routledge.

Schreiber, U. 1988. *Opernführer für Fortgeschrittene: Eine Geschichte des Musiktheaters*. Bd. 1: *Von den Anfängen bis zur Französischen Revolution*. Kassel: Bärenreiter.

Selfridge-Field, E. 2007. *A New Chronology of Venetian Opera and Related Genres, 1660–1760*. Stanford: Stanford University Press.

Serena, M. 1999. *La visione della Persia achemenide nel melodramma italiano del settecento: Il caso di Artaserse*. Corso di laurea in storia, Universitá degli Studi di Bologna.

Serna, P.-R. 2014. "Artaserse à l'Opéra royal de Versailles - Feu d'artifices - Compte-rendu." Online: http://www.concertclassic.com/article/artaserse-lopera-royal-de-versailles-feu-dartifices-compte-rendu (accessed 7 November 2019).

Steinbeck, W. 2010. "'In armonia favellare': Antikenrezeption und Oper um 1600." In D. Boschung and E. Kleinschmidt (eds.), *Lesbarkeiten: Antikenrezeption zwischen Barock und Aufklärung*, 197–206. Würzburg: Königshausen & Neumann.

Strohm, R. 1997. *Dramma per Musica: Italien Opera Seria of the Eighteenth Century*. New Haven: Yale University Press.

Thompson, A. E. 2006. "Revival, Revision, Rebirth: Handel Opera in Germany 1920–1930." MA thesis, University of North Carolina, Chapel Hill. Online: https://doi.org/10.17615/4ym2-pp03 (accessed 7 November 2019).

Walther, G. 2010. "Renaissance." In F. Jaeger (ed.), *Enzyklopädie der Neuzeit 11*, 1–18. Stuttgart: Metzler.

Weiand, K. 2017. "The Polyvalence of Antiquity: Remarks on the Reception of Classical Antiquity in Early Modern Europe." In K. Droß-Krüpe (ed.), *Great Women on Stage: The Reception of Women Monarchs from Antiquity to Baroque Opera*, 17–25. Wiesbaden: Harrassowitz.

Weissbach, F. H. 1911. *Die Keilinschriften der Achämeniden*, Leipzig: Hinrichs.

When Imitation Became Reality

The Historical Pantomime *Sardanapal* (1908) at the Royal Opera of Berlin

Valeska Hartmann

> Today we shall see the creation of history. A magnificent image, embodying and imitating in all its details the archaeologists' finds and research results, shall rumble past us, mysterious, mystical, with solemnly bizarre moonlit religious rituals, yet also with martial fanfare, with colorful parades, with delightful dances. A lecture will be held for us on Assyriology, marrying wisdom-bearing scholarship with the comely grace of Terpsichore.[1]

The historical pantomime *Sardanapal*,[2] venerated with such enthusiasm by the reviewer in the arts-and-culture leaflet of *Norddeutsche Allgemeine Zeitung* after an evening's attendance at the rehearsal on 2 September 1908, to this day remains a textbook example of the vivification of archaeological findings and their dissemination as popular-science themes on the German opera stage. Never had the plot of the allegedly last ruler of Assyria[3] been told more factually or the stage design been presented more authentically, and never has a play, produced by the high order of the German Emperor, failed more spectacularly. This is somewhat surprising since the chances of success had actually been quite good. The "great historical pantomime," produced on 1 September 1908 at the Royal Opera in Berlin, was based on the ballet *Sardanapal* (1865)[4] by the maître Paulo Taglioni (1808–1884). This model also took place at the Royal Opera and is a fairly close adaptation of the lyrical tragedy *Sardanapalus* by Lord Byron (1821). It

1. *Norddeutsche Allgemeine Zeitung*, 02.09.1908, No. 206. All original quotes have been translated into English by the author for better comprehension.

2. *Sardanapal*: Great historical pantomime, in three acts, Music: Joseph Schlar, Libretto: Friedrich Delitzsch, UA: 01.09.1908, Royal Opera Berlin.

3. The legendary figure is an amalgamation of various Assyrian kings of the eighth and ninth centuries BCE, not to be identified with the historical ruler Assurbanipal (Greek Sardanapal).

4. *Sardanapal*: Great Ballet in four acts, Music: Peter Ludwig Hertel, Choreography: Paulo Taglioni, UA: 12.04.1865, Royal Opera Berlin.

tells the story of the legendary ancient Oriental king, who allegedly was a direct descendant of Nimrod and Semiramis and ruled over the Assyrian Empire until its downfall. Taglioni's *Sardanapal* was successful enough to remain a part of the program until 1890, totaling a respectable 106 productions. In 1869, the play, which was a three-hour-long monumental piece requiring immense decoration and technical efforts, became a part of the opening ceremonies at the Court Theatre at the Vienna State Opera,[5] where by 1881 it had been played one hundred times. It was this success story that Wilhelm II sought to continue, in vain, by commissioning a new version of the Taglioni ballet that was academically revised and backed by the latest archaeological findings.

In what follows, I will provide a critical analysis of the concept of a visually based intelligibility of the 1908 adaptation with respect to the academically driven revision of the popular play.[6] At the outset, this will involve studying the reception history of the mythical ruler Sardanapal from Lord Byron's tragedy to the production under Wilhelm II. I will highlight Sardanapal's poor reputation as a mythical ruler figure on the contemporary theater stages, as well as Wilhelm II's unsuccessful attempts to correct this image. The producers' ambitions to achieve authenticity in terms of both the plot and the visual aspects gave the stage a level of reality. An analysis of the effect of the emerging blurred boundary between imitation and fiction will conclude this paper.

1. *The Romantic Tyrant: Sardanapal on Stage*

The legendary figure of Sardanapal was shaped by Greek authors and enjoyed great popularity in traditional lore. In it, the storytellers merged a catalogue of rather negative character traits of a number of Assyrian rulers into a dramaturgical type that was later also applied to Roman rulers.[7] The basis for the embellished tales were the depictions by Diodorus Siculus from between 100 and 50 BCE, who in turn relied on the account by Ktesias of Knidos, personal physician at the court of the Persian king

---

5. *Sardanapal*: Great Ballet in four acts, Music: Peter Ludwig Hertel and Franz Doppler, Choreography: Paulo Taglioni, WA: 16.06.1869, Court Opera House Vienna.

6. So far only a few analyses of the 1908 historical pantomime *Sardanapal* have been published. The expert on Oriental antiquity Johannes Renger (1979, 167–69) studied the performance with respect to the development of the disciplines of ancient Oriental studies and Near Eastern archaeology in Berlin, as well as the question of the role Friedrich Delitzsch played in it. Also the Near Eastern archaeologist Kay Kohlmeyer (Kohlmeyer, Schmid, and Strommenger 1991, 13–18), who illuminated the pantomime as an expression of the emperor Wilhelm II's enthusiasm for the Orient. The expert on theater studies Dietrich Kreidt (1987, 96–97), on the other hand, provided a discussion of *Sardanapal* focusing on the exoticism of theater in the early twentieth century. As an art historian, Frederick Bohrer (2003, 297–304) addressed the question of how Mesopotamia was visually figured in general in German contemporary art. A benchmark study was provided by the theater scholar Ruth Freydank (2011). She positioned the performance within the emergence of the German Association of Oriental Studies and focused primarily on Wilhelm II's political instrumentalization of the piece.

7. Accounts, e.g., in Herodotus 2.150; Polybius 8.12.3, Dio Chrysostom 4.135; Clement of Alexandria, *Stromateis* 2.20, Diodorus Siculus 2. See Renger 2015; Rölling 2009.

Artaxerxes II (404–359 BCE) from the late fifth century BCE, as well as on writings by Marcus Junianus Justinus from the third century BCE, who made an epitome of the lost forty-four books of *Historiae Philippicae* by Trogus Pompeius (C. Müller 2001; Renger 2015; Rölling 2009). Diodorus's elaborations on Sardanapal's sensual pleasures, his insatiable desires and debaucheries, in which he is said to have surpassed all of his predecessors, have left a lasting mark on the reception history of the character. As per Diodorus's account, Sardanapal himself lived as a woman, wearing women's clothes, decorating himself with makeup and other accessories like a prostitute, and even making it a habit of speaking with a female voice. His erotic lust was supposedly directed at both men and women (Diodorus Siculus 2.23.1–4). Justinus's depiction is far shorter, but no less insistent on exposing these eccentric tendencies (Marcus Junianus Justinus 1.3). For Justinus, Sardanapal is too late in recognizing the dangers threatening him and his power position, eventually leading him to commit a spectacular suicide, the only act Justinus acknowledges as an expression of masculine willpower.

This established characterization of the allegedly last Assyrian king as the archetype of a wicked despot was a welcome model for the various forms of arts and was further embellished depending on the particular needs of the specific genres. Fulfilling these prerequisites, the figure of Sardanapal was on a par with Semiramis, Xerxes, Artaxerxes, and Cleopatra, counting among the most glamorous and most interpreted "Orientalist" figures on opera and theater stages of the seventeenth-century.[8] One of the most well-known manifestations of the Sardanapal theme is the opera *Sardanapalus* by Christian Ludwig Boxberg. The piece was originally produced in 1698 at Ansbach to honor Count Georg Friedrich of Brandenburg-Ansbach[9] and was presumably adapted from Carlo Maderni's opera *Sardanapalo*.[10] Just as the literary models, Boxberg's interpretation showed a ruler fully indulging in his desires. Embedded in a mythological context, marking and accentuating the narrative of the ruler as an example of human vice, the story is placed within an intricate web of battle and betrayal. At the close of this story arc of comedy and drama, pictured with ballets and choirs, the virtuous lovers are united, while the lecherous Sardanapal is burned at the stake along with his wife and his precious belongings.

Only George Gordon Byron's tragedy *Sardanapalus* broke with this stereotypical reception of the mythical ruler. Byron wrote to his publisher in May 1821, "I have made

---

8. Stieger 1975 and Reischert 2001, in a first approximation, count twenty-three different operas, ballets and cantatae on the figure of Sardanapal. Furthermore, there are countless interpretations on the theater stage. For detailed information of the reception of the mythical figure Sardanapal, see Bernhardt 2009.

9. *Sardanapalus*: Opera in three acts by Christian Ludwig Boxberg (Music und Libretto). UA: 1698 Ansbach.

10. *Sardanapalo*: Opera in three acts, Music: Giovanni Domenico Freschi, Libretto: Carlo Maderni, UA: 1678, Teatro S. Angelo Venezia; For a recent discussion on this opera and its approach to the sources from late antiquity, see Piffaut 2015.

Sardanapalus brave (though voluptuous, as history represents him), and also as amiable as my poor powers could render him."[11] The Byronic version of the figure is shown as being caught between his duties as a ruler demanding the virtues of a soldier and his inclination to lust and voluptuousness expressed in his love affair with the Greek slave Myrrha (Oppel 1976, 172–73). It is not until the hour of greatest danger that Sardanapalus opts in favor of the dutiful ruler and against his lustful desires. There is an overnight transformation from aesthete to brave warrior that has Sardanapalus plunge into a forlorn battle. The only act of heroism he is left with is the theatrical self destruction that he commits before his enemies and that offered a sense of horrific pleasure for the audience.

Byron's design is that of an Oriental ruler refusing to govern by force, war, and repression, embodying instead the qualities of a gentle person devoting himself mostly to the arts and to his lover. In fact, Sardanapalus declares his desires the guiding principle of his political agenda. In this choice, Byron was the first to create a separation between the unbounded ruling power of an Oriental despot and his stereotypical tyrannous behavior, which thus far had been the singular expression of both the callous and the voluptuous aspect in the character.[12] Rather than the despotic element in the character being of a piece with the tyrannous one, the decadence is (now) expressed by way of the figure's effeminate guises.[13] In the preface to the printed edition, Byron emphasized, "In publishing the following Tragedies I have only to repeat, that they were not composed with the most remote view to the stage" (Byron 1901, 9).

Notwithstanding these reminders, the piece enjoyed a highly successful history of productions over the course of the nineteenth century. First of all, the production led by actor and director Charles Kean on 13 June 1853 at the Royal Princess Theatre.[14] Kean's productions featured a stage design based on current archaeological findings on long lost civilizations and were explicitly mentioned by Kean in the announcement as an element of the historically authentic journey into the past.[15] He relied on the research

---

11. Byron 1922, 299. Although Byron, as he states himself, refers to Diodorus's accounts in his preface: "In this tragedy it has been my intention to follow the account of Diodorus Siculus; reducing it, however, to such dramatic regularity as I best could, and trying to approach the unities. I therefore suppose the rebellion to explode and succeed in one day by a sudden conspiracy, instead of the long war of the history" (Byron 1901, 9).

12. Svane 2015, 222. Byron (Byron 1901, 15)clearly expresses the voluptuousness in a stage direction on *Sardanapalus* appearance right at the beginning of the play: "Enter Sardanapalus effeminately dressed, his head crowned with flowers, and his robe negligently flowing, attended by a train of Women and young Slaves" (Act I, Scene II).

13. Svane 2015, 224–25 on the source of the principle of perverted power which is defined by the expression of femininity (she-king). See also Richardson 2004, 141–44.

14. *Sardanapalus, King of Assyria*. A Tragedy in five acts by Lord Byron. Adapted for representation by Charles Kean, Princess's Theater London, 13.06.1853.

15. "In the production of Lord Byron's Tragedy of 'Sardanapalus,' I have availed myself of the wonderful discoveries made within the last few years, by Layard, Botta, and others, on the site of the an-

on the archeological excavations in northern Mesopotamia published in the 1840s by Paul-Émile Botta, archaeologist and French consul in Mossul, and his British colleague Austen Henry Layard (Botta and Flandin 1849–1850; Layard 1849a, 1849b, 1853). The drawing reconstructions in these publications featured a close interlocking of pictorial aestheticism and scientific accuracy. With greatest imagination, Kean's stage designs assembled the sketches of relief works, outfits, and reconstructions of the palace chambers to a fantastic and sublime ensemble, leading Kean proudly to claim in his introduction to the piece:

> No pains have been spared to present to the eye the gorgeous and striking scenery, that has been so unexpectedly dug from the very bowels of the earth. The sculptures now in the British Museum have been rigidly followed; and where recent discovery has failed to give authority for minor detail, I have wherever it has been possible, borrowed designs from surrounding nations, flourishing at the same epoch. In decoration of every kind, whether scenic or otherwise, I have diligently sought for truth; and it is with some pride and satisfaction I am enabled to announce that a verdict of approval has been received from the judge most competent to speak with authority upon the surpassingly interesting subject with which I have had to deal.* (* Mr. Layard)[16]

The play was staged sixty-one times in the first run, and made the program thirty-two times also in the second run.[17] It was the *grand spectacle* of the last act offering such dramatic elements as death, fire, and destruction, together with the potential for impressive stage effects, large screens, and the display of Oriental dance that gave the performance all of the ingredients to become a countrywide success.[18]

The ballet interpretation of *Sardanapalus*, produced only twelve years later by the ballet maître Paolo Taglioni, was certainly still influenced by Charles Kean's play. His "great historical ballet" was first produced on 24 April 1865 with tremendous decora-

---

cient Nineveh ... To render visible to the eye, in connection with Lord Byron's drama, the costume, architecture, and customs of the ancient Assyrian people, verified by the bas-reliefs, which, after having been buried for nearly three thousand years, have in our own day been brought to light, was an object that might well inspire the enthusiasm of one who has learnt that scenic illustration, if it have the weight of authority, may adorn and add dignity to the noble works of genius." Libretto on *Sardanapalus, King of Assyria*. Adapted for representation by Charles Kean, London 1853, Introduction (o. P.).

16. Libretto on *Sardanapalus, King of Assyria*. Adapted for representation by Charles Kean, London 1853, Introduction (o. P.).

17. On the 1853 play *Sardanapalus* by Charles Kean, see Krengel-Strudthoff 1981; McCall 1998, 202–3; Freydank 2011, 148–50; Malley 2012, 88–101; Groth 2013.

18. Aside from various operas and cantatae, the Byronic version of the Sardanapalus theme was also met with great success in the United States. In 1876, Byron's *Sardanapalus*, adapted by Charles Calvert, played at the Booth's Theatre in Manhatten, totaling 113 shows, the longest-running performance of any of Byron's dramas ever. On the success of the *Sardanapalus* play in the United States, see Stauffer 2011.

tion and technical effort.[19] Taking a leading role not only in the choreography, but also in the composition of the libretto, Taglioni closely followed the Byronic model and created a monumental show piece which featured large groups of dancers and supernumeraries.[20] In order to compensate for the lack of speech, Taglioni added several scenes to the play, allowing his *corps de ballet* to unfold in appropriate ways. He paid particular attention to the decorations, as was noted by Karl Frenzel in his review of the ballet's premiere in *Berliner National-Zeitung*: "The glamorous set, the decorations must come to the aid of the rather weak plot, whose comprehension almost necessarily requires speech." As he explains, the playbill of the production mentions that the decorations, costumes, and stage props were copies of sculptures, bas-reliefs, and ornaments found in archaeological excavations near Nineveh whose originals were kept at museums in London, Paris, and Berlin. He goes even further, claiming that attending the ballet *Sardanapal* saves the viewer a visit to the antiquity sections at the Berlin museum. The grandeur that was lost three thousand years ago, for him, is most glamorously reestablished in front of the eyes of the viewers.[21]

In 1908, the *Berliner Volkszeitung* reminded its readers of this lavish magnificence of Taglioni's ballets and concluded, "The ballet thus represents the first piece with an authentic stage set seen on German stages."[22] This view, however, was not shared by Karl Frenzel in his 1865 review:

> Naturally, certain discrepancies between the real and the ideal past remain. It is hardly likely that the square in front of the sun temple at Nineveh actually saw the modern dances of the Third Act; the French Can-Can, the Spanish El Olé, in their styles, were unknown to the Assyrians and Babylonians. The truth about the Babylonian dances, meanwhile, must remain buried in a passage in Curtius and in Pauly's Realencyclopadie der classischen Alterthumswissenschaft. On the other hand, when the still mysterious characters of cuneiform script were deciphered to read "Death Sardanapal! Arbaces shall be king!" who did not give a smile? What is more, the attempt should be made, with such an archaic subject matter, to replace the dancers' awful puffed-up skirts which chase us with tiring monotony with unruffled gowns; the dancers in the Pompeian wall painting, the Almee's in Cairo might serve as an example.[23]

---

19. *Sardanapal*: Great Ballet in four acts, Music: Peter Ludwig Hertel, Choreography: Paulo Taglioni, UA: 12.04.1865, Royal Opera Berlin.

20. On the person of Paolo Taglioni and his work see Iden 1997 and Oberzaucher-Schüller 2011.

21. Karl Frenzel's review of the production *Sardanapal* in *Berliner National-Zeitung*, 25.04.1865 (evening issue).

22. *Berliner Volkszeitung*, 01.09.1908, No. 410 (evening issue).

23. Karl Frenzel's review of the production *Sardanapal* in *Berliner National-Zeitung*, 25.04.1865 (evening issue).

However, the lack of authenticity with regard to the dances and the costumes in no way took away from the success of the ballet, and emperor Wilhelm I (reign 1871–1888) attended the ballet frequently and with great pleasure.[24]

2. The "Real" Sardanapal and the Production by "Highest Order" 1908

The fact that the ballet *Sardanapal* was part of the program at the State Opera until 1890 strongly suggests that crown prince Wilhelm II saw the productions. His passion for archaeology caused him to have Taglioni's play restaged. He was eager to remain true to Assyriological and archaeological research of the time in order to "establish enlightenment" as he wrote in his memoirs:

> After I realized that Assyriology, which concerned so many significant people, including many religious figures of both faiths, had nonetheless not been understood and appreciated for its significance by the general public, I had my old and trusted friend, and brilliant theatrical manager, Count Hülsen-Haeseler produce Assurbanipal [sic], which was staged after a long preparation under the supervision of the German Orient Society. (Wilhelm II 1922, 169)

He transformed the play into a "great historical pantomime" featuring actors instead of dancers in the main roles.

For the scientific revision of the Taglioni model, Wilhelm II hired the Berlin-based Assyriologist Friedrich Delitzsch (1850–1922), professor at Friedrich-Wilhelms Universität and director of the Near East section at the royal museums in Berlin. Delitzsch choreographed the entries and marches of the dancers based on Assyrian bas-reliefs and also oversaw the design of the costumes and stage props.[25] This was certainly no easy task to accomplish. Placing the theatrical piece under "scientific principles" meant interfering with the authorizations of the most diverse occupations, aligning all of them with the ideas of the artistic director, Georg von Hülsen (1858–1922). Delitzsch, who

24. Especially the most realistically enacted scene with Sardanapalus's self-combustion on the enormous pyre made such an impression on him that Wilhelm I never left the theater without asking the actor, "is everything alright?" See *Berliner Volkszeitung*, 01.09.1908, No. 410 (evening issue). A similar anecdote can also be found for the *Sardanapalus* production by Charles Kean in 1853: the fire effect in the final act of the destruction of the magnificent royal hall and the entire palace was supposed to be so authentic that the insurance sent inspectors to the theater to check whether the fire may not have been "real"; Krengel-Strudthoff 1981, 20.

25. Wilhelm 1998, 6, with photographs of a costume design for an Assyrian warrior (fig. 3b–c); also found in Freydank 2011, fig. 1–2 shown with another costume design for a female role; for illustration of another group of women in costumes, see Löhlein 2010, 395, and Kohlmeyer, Schmid, and Strommenger 1991, fig. 16-9. The costumes were made by the painter Heil under the supervision of court counselor Ludwig Raupp in the royal ateliers transferring from the original monuments, as can be seen in the reference in the *Sardanapal* libretto. The person in charge of the stage props was Eugen Quaglio.

was cofounder of the German Association for Oriental Studies and who had thus far not had any experience in the world of theater, most likely accepted this task with some astonishment.[26]

Delitzsch's reworking of the piece was quite radical. Instead of conveying the dramatic elements in the protagonists' lines, he decided to silence the actors completely and tell the plot solely through the libretto, which was provided for the audience to read along. Its end section, featuring elaborate annotations and footnotes, gave it the distinct character of a scientific publication. Aside from a brief plot summary, nine pages were reserved for historical and technical background information. This included explanations on the significance of the sun god and the dances in the oriental culture, the constellations of historical figures, and the visual models for the stage designs and stage props. In some places, references to textual sources were added. The reason given was that

> Just as the dramatic plot made an effort not to present anything before the viewer's eye which was not backed by cuneiform sources or, in case they failed, by passages in the Old Testament, the outer physical form was also to be designed [...] in close consistency with original Assyrian monuments.[27]

Thus Delitzsch reassembled Byron's work in a completely new way and with distinct differences to the Taglioni interpretation. While in the Taglioni version, the female protagonists were allowed to have proper names, Delitzsch refers to them with descriptions such as "the Queen" and "the king's favourite slave." Scenes which depicted moral failures or ineptitude as a ruler on the part of Sardanapal were completely removed from the story. In Delitzsch's interpretation there is no hesitation in Sardanapal's decision to lead his soldiers into the final battle. Moreover, the Queen is allowed to stand by her King and go with him into death instead of fleeing with her son through a secret corridor. And while at the end the favorite slave is seized by madness, the King and Queen stand amongst the flames in unshakable calmness and dignity. They were placing their trust in the great gods thus escaping the fury of the Medians making their way into the palace, before it collapses in the fire with the tumbling walls opening the sight of the burning city of Nineveh.

Delitzsch thus distances himself decisively from Byron's characterization and certainly grants Sardanapalus a morally intact end. For Delitzsch, the fundamental change in the action-steering conflict leads to a key transformation in the reception of the Assyrian ruler, as he explains in the annotations at the end of the libretto:

---

26. Freydank 2011, 152. On the person of Friedrich Delitzsch and his position within the community of researchers after the "Babel-Bible" debate he initiated, see Bohrer 2003, 272–97; also Marchand 2009, 244–49, with relevant literature. On Delitzsch's time in Berlin see Renger 1979, 167–71.

27. Libretto on *Sardanapal: Great Historical Pantomime,* revised by Friedrich Delitzsch, Berlin 1908, 19.

> The King Sardanapalus coming forth in this dramatic presentation is the King Sardanapalus of history, not that of Ktesias-Diodorus. King Asurbanipal, called Sardanápallos by the classics, in Latin Sardanapālus, Sardanapallus, was one of the bravest and most fortunate war heroes ever to have occupied the Assyrian throne, an Assyrian king "unlike any" ... That is, he was the exact opposite of a despot sunken in idleness and abundance, wasting away his life dressed in women's clothes and busying himself with women's sports—the despicable distorted image through which we have come to see him since childhood following Ktesias-Diodorus.[28]

Without limitation, this production received such personal and, importantly, also financial support from the emperor as was needed to remain true to scientific principles and went far beyond the possibilities of a mere presentation of *colour locale* on stage and in the design of the set.[29]

3. *A Question of Expression: Pantomime and the Significance of Its Visual Implementation*

The choice to deprive Byron's tragedy of its speech and to stage it as a "great historical pantomime" no doubt confronted the viewer with the rather formidable task to comprehend history with other senses. The high importance given to the visual components of the theatrical performance such as stage design, decorations, and costumes has been made clear above. However, a discussion of the particularities of the pantomime is required in order to understand how this artistic genre can communicate action and plot. In the relevant theater encyclopedias of the nineteenth century written explicitly for experts and connoisseurs of the theater, the term, "pantomime" is understood as the actual miming in a narrower sense.[30] This includes silent language and the use of gestures as an independent art. According to the encyclopedias, if mimed dances are used to convey a plot, the act becomes a ballet:

> The purpose of the pantomime is to show the living figure of the human being as such in its characteristic significance; that of the ballet is to show the delightful significance and abundance of changing bodily shapes in harmoni-

---

28. Libretto on *Sardanapal: Great Historical Pantomime*, revised by Friedrich Delitzsch, Berlin 1908, 18.

29. The Berlin daily paper made it known that the outfits of the Assyrian ballet *Sardanapal* had cost the State Opera no less than 350,000 to 375,000 Marks. The sum was increased by another 30,000 Marks because of the evenings on which no show could take place due to rehearsals. See the undated newspaper article at Baden-Württemberg state archive, archive Dr. Conrad Haußmann's possessions (Q1/2 Bü11).

30. Blum, Herlosssohn, and Marggraff 1839–1846, vol. 6:41, s.v. "Pantomime," with a reference to the entry on miming, vol. 5:187–91, where the art of pantomime is equated with the art of sculpture.

> ously measured movements; both work in poetic richness and dramatic development.[31]

For Taglioni, choreographer and ballet maître as he was, the element of dance was of course essential as a narrative determinant of the 1865 *Ballet à thème Sardanapal* for the performance of the tragedy. However achieving an authentic reconstruction of antiquity unsurprisingly met with great difficulties given the specific means of the ballet, which are in direct opposition to realistic ambitions.

Also with the *corps de ballet,* the criticism of classic ballet art of the French school led to a departure from the old style in favor of character dance. This modernization process applied not only to the ballet costume but obviously to the old classic dance figures, which seemed unnatural and inappropriate in the new costumes. The 1908 version of *Sardanapal* left behind the classic ballet as a determining narrative element and instead opted for a representation of the "characteristic significance" of history through the art of pantomime. Indeed, pantomime itself was no longer meant to serve as a language of movement seeking to act out each work of an implied sentence, but embodied the artistic expression of a broader sentiment.[32] However, miming alone, with the highly praised authentic outfits as an equivalent of language, was insufficient in conveying comprehensibly and consistently the story of the Assyrian king—especially since it was the very first time the Diodorus and Ktesias interpretations had been "corrected" on stage. Along with the pantomime, verses by the writer Joseph Lauff were provided, explaining to the viewer how the events and the scenes were connected. The prologue began with a dialogue of the personifications of the *Assyrian Past* and *Science,* lamenting the fact that the splendor of Nineveh has faded from memory. However, Nineveh has been resurrected, they agree, and now the truth about Sardanapal can finally be told. The two female figures, whose role was to set the mood for the following historical episode, were joined by another speaker, the *Genius* of resurrected antiquity, who linked the individual stage scenes with historical explanations in solemn and long-winded verses.[33] Furthermore, some few scenes were also complemented with text boards.

And yet, dance was still not absent from this "great historical pantomime." It was linked to the content of the story by symbolizing the general mood of the scene.[34] The

31. Düringer 1841, 842, s.v. "Pantomime."

32. On the contemporary conception of the significance of new ballet art, see the report on the conversation with the royal ballet maître Emil Graeb: "Die Reform der Ballettkunst," in *Die Woche,* No. 36, Berlin 1908, 1547. Also, on the criticism of pantomime see the report by Leo Feld "Stumme Dramen," in *Die Schaubühne,* No. 31/32, August 1908.

33. Freydank 2011, 153–54. She also emphasizes the predominantly negative reactions to the rhymes by Joseph Lauff, who enjoyed the emperor's special appreciation because of his words endorsing the Prussian-national tendencies.

34. Dances in the second scene: *Warrior Play* and *Damascene Sword and Knee Dance* as an expression of martial courage and victory; the *Odalisque Dance* and the *Dance of Fruits and Jewels* with odalisques of Jewish, Phoenician, Chaldean, Egyptian, and Ethiopian origins as an expression of the

tension that arose from this double sequence of dance and pantomime segments effected a juxtaposition of two work conceptions that are different, yet equivalent: the outer movement, which can be perceived by the senses, and the meaning-bearing movement, which has narrative impact and communicates with the viewer through intellectual codes.[35] Just like the outfit as a whole, the element of the character dance fell in with the need for historical manner, with its design following the models of bas-reliefs from the arts possessions of the museum.[36]

The visually historicized representation went hand in hand with the moral rehabilitation of the figure of Sardanapal. The stage scenes thus created testified to this transformation, lining up to produce a truly festive and ceremonious stage action, which displayed dignity, grandeur, and strength (fig. 1). As pointed out by critics in their reviews, the attractiveness of the production stemmed not only from its enormous financial magnitude and its efforts to present historical details with great accuracy, but also, and especially, from the remarkable precision of the stage movements for which many rehearsals were required. With the accurate elaboration of each moment, these scenes became a kind of an historical image for itself. This highly stylized staging was fundamentally inconsistent to authentic naturalism. Despite being very festive and truly Assyrian, the historical pantomime became stiff and artificial[37] and thus disrupted the actual nature of the action; in other words it took away the very thing that was supposed to ensure authenticity. Stylizing action entails a removal from the human and places the action in the sphere of the holy and sublime. The excessive emphasis on historical accuracy led not only to a certain sluggishness but also to a degree of abstraction which gave a sense less of accuracy but more of a didactic character. The scenic representations became silent proof-images of history, and it is no coincidence that they were reminiscent of *tableaux vivants*. Wherever the sources left by Ktesias and Diodorus fell short of the "truth claim," Wilhelm II, aware of their narrative potential, decided to put on stage a new form of "silent" visual proof.

---

fertility and the wealth of Assyria. The *Taumelkelchtanz* in the fourth scene as an expression of the ecstasy with which Nineveh, the paramour, staggers into death while drunk from the wine. Also see *Norddeutsche Allgemeine Zeitung*, 02.09.1908, No. 206.

35. On the readability of multimedia artworks within ballet-pantomime and their twofold artistic character see Jahrmärker 2006, 21–24; on the question of the optical comprehensibility of the gesture signs pp. 52–58, and for a basic understanding of the system of theatrical semiotics see Fischer-Lichte 1983.

36. As stated by Graeb himself on his staging, in "Die Reform der Ballettkunst," in *Die Woche*, No. 36, Berlin 1908, 1547; special amusement was provoked by a parade which seemed particularly stiff to the critics because it had the actors march across the stage with unbent knees. Delitzsch's argument that this was an authentic emulation of Assyrian marches as found on ancient monument was parried with the question as to why, then, the Egyptians were not also shown to march with a sideways goose step; *Berliner Volkszeitung*, 02.09.1908, No. 412 (evening issue).

37. *Berliner Volkszeitung*, 02.09.1908, No. 411 (morning issue).

Figure 1. Scene photo of act I, second scene; Palace hall with view in the royal garden, 1908. (ullstein bild / Zander and Labisch).

4. *Playing with Reality: Stage Props and Science*

Wilhelm II was aware of both the significance and the impact of the visual performance. Aside from Friedrich Delitzsch, who was in charge of the content, he hired the archaeologist and architect Walter Andrae (1875–1958) for the conception of three stage designs.[38] Andrae was the supervisor of the excavations in Assur which were financed by the German Oriental Association. In his memoirs, he mentions the "Emperor's order" to design the architecture of the production to be "true to the period."[39] The court stage designer Hans Kautsky (1864–1937) and his assistants ensured a detailed and completely accurate transfer of the small watercolor paintings Andrae had made in Assur to the scale of the stage.[40] Andrae's draft for the first scene shows the court of the sun

38. Illustrated in Freydank 2011, fig. 4–7.

39. Andrae 1961, 180–84. His choice of words makes it clear that both he himself and Delitzsch were "made to" take part in the rehearsals and productions and were well aware of the criticism of the question of the artistic value of the production as well as of the difference between the present-day views and the ancient Assyrian form of presentation. Nevertheless, Andrae obviously saw the financial gain: "To the German Oriental Association and the museums of Berlin, the Emperor's warm interest in the Orient was of great advantage."

40. "In Berlin, anxious attention was paid to remaining true to these three drafts, and I almost fell

Figure 2. Walter Andrae, draft of the stage setting act I, first scene; court of an Assyrian temple with view of the god's sculpture, 1907. (Staatsbibliothek zu Berlin—Preußischer Kulturbesitz, estate Andrae 235[1]).

temple (fig. 2). Beside the entrance to the sanctuary, there are two colossal winged bull creatures with human heads. They open the view to the golden god sculpture to which the ceremony in the play is dedicated. The larger-than-life seated figure glows with mysticism in its niche illuminated by the light of the oil lamps. Across the lower sections of the outer façade of the temple all the way to the adjacent towers, there is an ornamental bas-relief made of enameled tiles of different colors. It shows various scenes of conquests and processions, as were known at the time from relevant research publications on Assyrian architecture.[41] Behind the temple, an impressive ziggurat rises, not only ensuring the necessary depth in the stage design, but also, thanks to its sheer size, giving the viewer the illusion of glimpsing only a small portion of the architectural scene. Kautsky transfers the watercolor design to the stage with the necessary compositional tools (fig. 3). The frame he added not only serves to reinforce the three-dimensionality,

on my back when my small colourful paintings appeared in full stage size in the State Opera" (Andrae 1961, 180–81).

41. Paul Émile Botta, Eugène Flandin, *Monument de Ninive,* 5 vols. (Paris 1849–1850); Austen Henry Layard, *Nineveh and Its Remains. With an Account of a Visit to the Chaldean Christians of Kurdistan, and the Yezidis, or Devil-Worshippers; and an Inquiry into the Manners and Arts of the Ancient Assyrians,* 2 vols. (London 1849); Austen Henry Layard, *A Second Series of the Monuments of Nineveh: Including Bas-Reliefs from the Palace of Sennacherib and Bronzes from the Ruins of Nimroud; from Drawings Made on the Spot, during a Second Expedition to Assyria* (London 1853).

Figure 3. Hans Kautsky, draft of the stage setting act I, first scene, after the draft of Walter Andrae, 1908. (J. Kapp, *200 Jahre Staatsoper im Bild*, Berlin 1942, 92, reproduction).

Figure 4. Victor Place, *Ninive et l'Assyrie*, pl. 21. Reconstruction of the Sargon palace with the gate in Khorsabad, 1867.

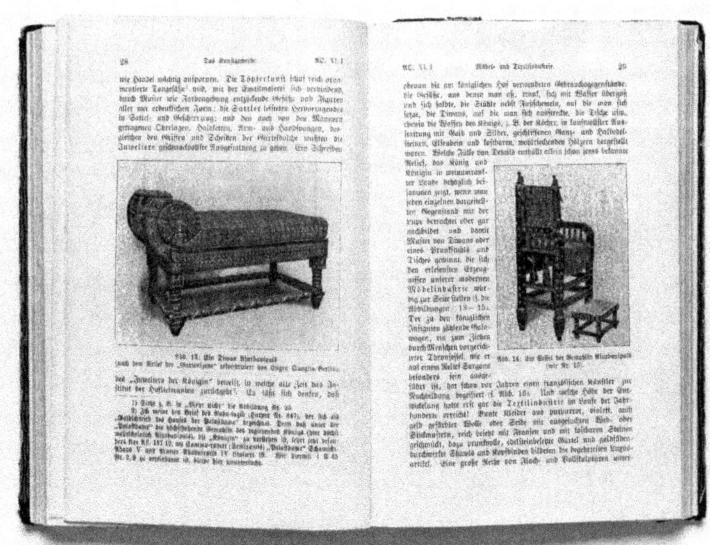

Figure 5. A divan and a chair modelled on the "Banquet Scene" relief from Assurbanipal's palace, reconstructed by Eugen Quaglio - Berlin. Delitzsch 1909, 28–29, figs. 13 and 14.

but also creates the entry alleys for the actors and dancers. Andrae's draft for his visual composition is based not only on his own reconstruction of the Assur temple site but also on the reconstructions of the southeastern façade of the Sargon palace with the gate in Khorsabad, which had already been published in 1867 by Victor Place in his volume of plates on *Ninive et l'Assyrie* (fig. 4). Kautsky's implementation is also guided by Place's reconstruction of the Sargon palace in that he added triforium windows to the two towers and leaves out two additional gateways to the temple. The design of the ornamental band that frames the arch above the gate is found in the same amount detail in the plates of the Place publication.[42]

Delitzsch seemed to be fully convinced by the historical accuracy with which the stage designs, the props, and the costumes had been created. For him, they were indeed the source of truth, as is suggested by his 1909 essay *Asurbanipal und die assyrische Kultur seiner Zeit* in the serial *Der Alte Orient*. In his report on the Assyrian dynasty of the Sargonides, Delitzsch attacks Ktesias's "far-fetched distortion of Oriental history" and condemns it as one single "historical novel." In doing so, he restores "Asurbanipal = Sardanapal" as "indeed a hero from head to toe" (Delitzsch 1909, 7–9). Aside from the "mysteries of the Assyrian victoriousness," Delitzsch also gives elaborate accounts of Sardanapal's court as an arts center—especially a crafts center. To provide visuals for the section on Assyrian furniture and textile industry, Delitzsch shows photographs of

42. Place 1867, pl. 10 and 14; details on pls. 15–17.

a divan and a table from Assurbanipal's palace, as well as a magnificent chair from his wife's possessions (fig. 5; Delitzsch 1909, figs. 13–15). As the caption states, the furniture is modeled on what is known as the Banquet Scene, a wall panel relief fragment at the North Palace of Nineveh showing Assurbanipal with his wife in the royal gardens of Nineveh after the victory over the king of the Elamites.[43] It is explained to the reader that the furniture shown here had been reconstructed by Eugen Quaglio (Berlin). The pieces, which were three-dimensionally rebuilt and portrayed against neutral background and without any additional objects, were the stage props for the 1909 pantomime *Sardanapal*. Eugen Quaglio (1857–1942) was the head of stage decorations at the Prussian State Theatres (Berlin).[44] Incidentally, no additional information is provided on his person so that it took an expert to recognize the name as one belonging to a stage designer. Without hesitation, and without explanations as to their original use, Delitzsch incorporated the stage props in his academic publication as though giving them the final confirmation of scientific authenticity. The true original relief, however, which had served as the model, is neither shown in the illustrations nor referenced in the footnotes. This may be a consequence of the series being entitled and considered, "Commonly Understandable Explanations." However, it is remarkable even for the period in question that Delitzsch would let stage props speak for themselves as reconstructions without providing visual proof of the original.

Even more astonishingly, once the show would be taken off the program, the decorations, stage props and costumes were meant to be included in the exhibitions the Royal Museums and shown next to Mesopotamian antiquities themselves.[45] This testifies not only to Quaglio's artistic mastery, but also to the dissolution of the boundary between imitation and the original, which gave the action and the objects on stage a status of reality. This form of theatrical reproduction feigned authenticity by way of meticulous truth to detail, and was naturally accompanied by a philosophy of history that subscribed fully to historicism. It was harshly criticized for the resulting exaggerated intellectualism and stage historicism. It had been the case since the turn of the century that various artistic schools like the Berlin Secession and the avant-garde had sought to dissociate themselves from the historical thinking of their period, which in their mind was conventional and outmoded. They especially turned against the cultural and educational policies of Wilhelm II, and helped art movements, such as naturalism, realism, impressionism and expressionism, to break through. Contemporary life and the problems of the social conditions were meant to feed into art and break the boundaries of the strictly hierarchical genres—an intention that was incompatible with the emperor's traditional need for harmony and ideal beauty in the arts. As different as

43. See *The British Museum*, number 124920.

44. Quaglio was from an Italian-German family of stage designers. See Boetzkes 1980.

45. Kreidt 1987, 96. Unlike Kreidt, Bohrer emphasizes that Delitzsch only had the intention, but never went through with the plan; Bohrer 2003, 302.

the modern styles may have been, they all had in common the rejection of the official cultural policy, and primarily the "Wilhelminian" supremacy of historicism and academicism in art and culture.[46] So indeed, the historical pantomime *Sardanapal* stood for a visual conception that was diametrically opposed to the contemporary debate in art and theater aesthetics.

5. The Crisis of Historicism and the Problem with Sardanapal

The emperor's idea of art, which the pantomime *Sardanapal* reflected in every way, defined the value of artistic creation close to the ideal of classical antiquity. The cultural superiority of antiquity was beyond debate for Wilhelm II. It was, after all, antiquity from which he drew the justification of the Hohenzollern Monarchy, and thus his own legitimacy, which he also defended with his reactionary cultural policy. This claim is made clear in his book *Das Königtum im alten Mesopotamien*, which appeared in 1939 in Berlin. In it, he expounds the origins of the "historical mission" bestowed upon him, going through the stages of the Persians, the ancient Babylonian monarchs and the last Assyrian kings, Alexander III and his successors, the Roman Empire, the German Holy Roman Empire in the Middle Ages, and finally the Hohenzollern.[47] This fundamental conviction was also interlocked with the art of theater. On 16 June 1898, the day of the tenth anniversary of his reign, the emperor gave the speech to the Royal Acting Staff that became famous for its closing line, "The theatre, too, is one of my weapons."[48] As Ruth Freydank noted in her article on *Sardanapal*, the German emperor took the occasion to formulate his idea of the function of theater. In keeping with the tradition of Enlightenment in a Schillerian sense, he saw in it an institution of education, linking it at the same time to his ideals of patriotic loyalty to the emperor.[49] In essence cultural performances have always been a leading political instrument for Wilhelm II. They can be understood as part of an implicit or, as in the case of *Sardanapal*, an explicit governing strategy of the ruling elite.[50] The emperor's artistic preference for historic currents

46. On the formation of new artist associations at the turn of the century, see, e.g., Krahmer 2009 and Landwehr 2012; for the cultural policy of emperor Wilhelm II and his anti-modern and anti-naturalistic course in the arts, see Fähnders 1998, 66–68; see also Düwell 1983.

47. For the emperor Wilhelm II and his political ambitions, see, e.g., Beigel and Mangold-Will 2017; Röhl 1993–2008.

48. "I was convinced and set the firm resolution that the Royal Theatre was meant to be an instrument of the monarch, akin to the school and the university, whose task is to foster the younger generation and to prepare them for work to preserve the highest intellectual goods of our glorious German nation. Likewise, the theatre shall make a contribution to the education of mind and character, and to the refinement the moral views. *The theatre, too, is one of my weapons*," quoted in Johann 1966, 77–79.

49. Freydank 2011, 141–42, with reference to Schiller's speech entitled *The Theatre Stage Seen as a Moral Institution* which he gave in 1784 as part of a public meeting of German Electors Association in Mannheim.

50. S. Müller 2011, 173, with further relevant literature.

were deemed by him as the key to societal *Leitdisziplin*—the model discipline for all citizens. He could not have made this clearer than in his speech *True Art*, which he gave on the occasion of the completion of *Siegesallee* in Berlin on 18 December 1901. The marble ancestor gallery, to him, was a first-rate historical project that had committed itself fully to the principles of antique harmony and aesthetics and was thus an expression of "true art." His rejection of modern art forms culminated in the statement, "Art which disobeys the laws and barriers I have defined is no longer art."[51] The only model for art that Wilhelm II accepted was indeed historicism, which exercised an educational influence on his subjects and at the same time served as a political instrument to glorify Wilhelm's notion of empire.[52] The derogatory term *Rinnsteinkunst*, which he coined for modernism, as well as the sculptures he financed, became the cause of public scorn and derision.[53] He misjudged the developments of modern art of his time and the criticism of the style of historicism by both art critics and historians. Even since the late nineteenth century, critics saw the pluralism and eclecticism of historicism more as an expression of escapism than as the edification of a style perceived as to be higher.[54]

The opposition to the emperor's conservative taste was most unmistakably revealed in the reaction to the *Sardanapal* pantomime. Most critics experienced the show as burdensome on account of its exaggerated intellectualism and didacticism.[55] For instance, the *Berliner Tageblatt* wrote:

> The author of the new *Sardanapal* was misguided into stating that arts could "consider themself fortunate to be taken into service for academic science." One can certainly not be more confused about the essence and purpose of art than is expressed in these words.[56]

51. Quoted in Johann 1966, 99–103.

52. "Art should help to influence the people in educational ways; it should also give those of lower standing after their hard work and toil the possibility to rise again and stand tall by their ideals. To us, the German People, the great ideals have become permanent goods, while to other people they have more or less been lost. None are left but the German People, which before all is called upon to preserve, to nurture, and to perpetuate these great ideas; and what comes along with these ideals is that we give the working, toiling classes the possibility to lift themselves up by the beautiful, and to labour their way out of their other spheres of thought." Wilhelm II quoted in Johann 1966, 102.

53. The dismissal of historicism and the derision about the Emperor's attitude is exemplified in the cover-page caricature on the journal *Simplicissimus* of 14.01.1902 (No. 43). The caricaturist Thomas Heine depicted "German Art" as being carried away in a coffin to be buried by two Imperial soldiers. In public, the Hohenzollern Gallery soon came to be called the "Dolls Gallery."

54. Regarding this crisis of historicism in the mirror of critics see Heinßen 2003; Oexle 2007; Maurer 2013.

55. For two years, there even were fortnightly shows specifically directed at pupils and students in academia; Iden 1997, 244.

56. *Berliner Tageblatt*, 02.08.1908, No. 446 (morning issue).

Theater, the pantomime as a genre, and art in general had already emancipated themselves from the rigid dogmatism of historicism, taking it now to be "very real, but boring."[57] Since this kind of outright criticism directed at the emperor was naturally unthinkable, it was Delitzsch who became the target for the critics:

> What was meant to be achieved through Friedrich Delitzsch's collaboration, lifting the old Taglioni ballet to an academic status, resulted in failure, was bound to result in failure. One cannot dance in the drawers of a museum, and one must not turn the stage into a museum of ethnic studies without becoming uninteresting.[58]

The *Berliner Volkszeitung* even spoke of a grandiose failure:

> The amalgamation of these two completely opposing elements resulted in a cross-breeding reminiscent of the pug-poodle-dachshund-pincher; a little bit of everything and altogether disfigured.[59]

The production became infamous for being a museum theater of historicism, and its visual communication, full of pathos and affection, underscored this criticism even more.[60] Both the Berlin journal *Die Woche* and the *Illustrated London News* each dedicated an article to the production which featured an abundance of accompanying photographs.[61] The *Illustrated London News* focused on the essential, "The critics object that there is too much science and too little drama and dancing, but as a spectacle the thing is tremendous."[62] The photographs of the show were left to speak for themselves, filling the entire page and thus reflecting—just as the Berlin journal—"the priority of visual components of the theatrical performance." The "Saviors of Sardanapal," Friedrich Delitzsch and Wilhelm II, had deprived the original piece of its narrative potential and thus

57. *Berliner Tageblatt*, 02.08.1908, No. 446 (morning issue). Also, *Berliner Volkszeitung*, 02.09.1908, No. 412 (evening issue) wrote, "The show was among the most boring ever seen at the opera, and it was only the anticipation of the great palace fire at the end, which indeed is superb stage work, and the presence of the Court that kept the audience of the thèatre parè together. There was, however, ample yawning."

58. *Berliner Tageblatt*, 02.08.1908, No. 446 (morning issue).

59. *Berliner Volkszeitung*, 02.09.1908, No. 412 (evening issue).

60. The production's flopping not only with the critics, but also with general audiences is visible in the production dates recorded in the collections of the theater programs at the State Library in Berlin. The number of productions went from twenty-two in 1908 (although three were organized for special occasions) down to a mere six for the years 1909 and 1910 combined. Of these, four were performed by the emperor's "highest order."

61. *Die Woche*, No. 36, Berlin 1908, 1554–55, double page with photographs of the entire scene, of the stage curtain, and three single shots of the actors.

62. "Assyriology according to the Kaiser: His Majesty's Ballet Sardanapalus" in *The Illustrated London News*, 12.09.1908, 367.

of all of its force. The voluptuousness of the Assyrian king, who as an archetype of the morally deranged Oriental monarch brings down the army's morals and finally causes the doom of the empire is replaced with nothing but an empty space. The Wilhelm/Delitzsch version of the play had even removed the component of "error" altogether. A character development of the figure of Sardanapal, the transformation to tragic hero, was no longer possible. The only original element that the 1908 production held onto was the pyre scene as a melodramatic grand spectacle. However, even this scene, which had been highly praised as impressive stage work, did not manage to come to the rescue of the show. In the reflections on his life, Walter Andrae gives an ironic account of the whole situation:

> It was as though a fateful voice was trying to urge him (Wilhelm II) on and into the future. But whatever it was that was speaking to him seemed to have no internal effect on his sentiment. The play told of a dangerous coalition between the enemies of the Assyrians and the doom of the Empire and the dynasty, and precisely the one who brought about such fate for his own Empire and his own dynasty was the one directing the prophetic theatrical performance! (Andrae 1961, 182)

The ruler figure of Sardanapal, who was engraved in collective memory as the one who cast himself and his empire down into the abyss and who was seen as the most boundless ruler, became the mirror image of the self-proclaimed "Savior of Sardanapal"—Wilhelm II.

Bibliography

Blum, R., G. C. R. Herlosssohn, and H. Marggraff, eds. 1839–1846. *Allgemeines Theater-Lexikon oder Encyklopädie alles Wissenswerthen* für Bühnenkünstler, Dilettanten und Theaterfreunde. Altenburg and Leipzig: Pierer and Heymann.

Andrae, W. 1961. *Lebenserinnerungen eines Ausgräbers.* Berlin: de Gruyter.

Beigel, T., And S. Mangold-Will. 2017. *Wilhelm II: Archäolgoie und Politik um 1900.* Stuttgart: Steiner.

Bernhardt, R. 2009. "Sardanapal: Urbild des lasterhaften orientalischen Despoten; Entstehung, Bedeutung für die griechisch-römische Welt und Nachwirkung." *Tyche: Beiträge zur Alten Geschichte, Papyrologie und Epigraphik* 24:1–25.

Boetzkes, M. 1980. "Quaglio." In *New Grove Dictionary of Music and Musicians,* 15:492–94.

Bohrer, F. 2003. *Orientalism and Visual Culture: Imagining Mesopotamia in Nineteenth-Century Europe.* Cambridge: Cambridge University Press.

Botta, P. E., and E. Flandin. 1849–1850. *Monument de Ninive,* 5 vols. Paris: Impr. Nationale.

Byron, G. G. 1901. *The Works of Lord Byron: A New, Revised and Enlarged Edition with Illustrations; Poetry,* Volume 5, edited by E. H. Coleridge. London: Murray.

———. 1922. *The Works of Lord Byron: Letters and Journals,* Volume 5, edited by P. Rowland. London: Murray.

Delitzsch, F. 1909. "Asurbanipal und die assyrische Kultur seiner Zeit." *Der Alte Orient* 11:1–44.

Düringer, P. J. 1841. *Theater-Lexikon: Theoretisch-practisches Handbuch für Vorstände, Mitglieder und Freunde des deutschen Theaters.* Leipzig: Wigand.

Düwell, K. 1983. "Geistesleben und Kulturpolitik des Deutschen Kaiserreichs." In E. Mai and S. Waetzoldt (eds.), *Ideengeschichte und Kunstwissenschaft: Philosophie und bildende Kunst im Kaiserreich*, 3:15–30. Berlin: Gebr. Mann.

Fähnders, W. 1998. *Avantgarde und Moderne 1890–1933*. Weimar: Metzler.

Fischer-Lichte, E. 1983. *Semiotik des Theaters: Eine Einführung*. System der theatralischen Zeichen. Tübingen: Narr.

Freydank, R. 2011. "'Sardanapal' oder 'Das Theater ist auch eine Meiner Waffen': Geschichte einer Festaufführung im Königlichen Opernhaus." *Mitteilungen der Deutschen Orient-gesellschaft* 143:141–67.

Groth, H. 2013. "Panoramic Byron: Reading, History and Pre-cinematic Spectacle." In K. Mitchell and N. Parsons (eds.), *Reading Historical Fiction: The Revenant and Remembered Past*, 85–100. Basingstoke and New York: Palgrave.

Heinßen, J. 2003. *Historismus und Kulturkritik: Studien zur deutschen Geschichtskultur im späten 19. Jahrhundert*. Göttingen: Vandenhoeck & Ruprecht.

Iden, R. 1997. "Taglioni: Sardanapal." In *Pipers Enzyklopädie des Musiktheaters*, 6:242–44.

Jahrmärker, M. 2006. *Comprendre par les yeux: Zur Werkskonzeption und Werksrezeption in der Epoche der Grand opéra*. Laaber: Laaber.

Johann, E. 1966. *Reden des Kaisers: Ansprachen, Predigten und Trinksprüche Wilhelms II*. Munich: Deutscher Taschenbüch Verlag.

Kohlmeyer, K., H. Schmid, and E. Strommenger. 1991. *Wiedererstehendes Babylon: Eine antike Weltstadt im Blick der Forschung*. Berlin: Museum für Vor- und Frühgeschichte.

Krahmer, C. 2009. "Kunstanschauung – Weltanschauung: Das Ringen um die Kunst in Deutschland um 1900." Études *Germaniques* 4(256):765–98.

Kreidt, D. 1987. *Exotische Figuren und Motive im Europäischen Theater*. Stuttgart: Cantz.

Krengel-Strudthoff, I. 1981. "Archäologie auf der Bühne und das wiedererstandene Ninive: Charles Keans Ausstattung zu 'Sardanapalus' von Lord Byron." *Kleine Schriften der Gesellschaft für Theatergeschichte* 31:3–68.

Landwehr, E. 2012. *Kunst des Historismus*. Cologne: Böhlau.

Layard, A. H. 1849a. *The Monuments of Nineveh: From Drawings Made on the Spot*. London: J. Murray.

———. 1849b. *Nineveh and Its Remains*, 2 vols., London: PUBLISHER.

———. 1853. *A Second Series of the Monuments of Nineveh*. London: J. Murray.

Löhlein, W. 2010. "Mit Zepter und Spaten: Kaiser Wilhelm II. und die Archäologie." In C. Trümpler (ed.), *Das Große Spiel: Archäologie und Politik zur Zeit des Kolonialismus (1860–1940)*, 391–97. Cologne: DuMont.

Malley, S. 2012. *From Archaeology to Spectacle in Victorian Britain: The Case of Assyria, 1845–1854*. Cornwall: Routledge.

Maurer, K. 2013. *Visualizing the Past: The Power of the Image in German Historicism*. Berlin: de Gruyter.

Marchand, S. 2009. *German Orientalism in the Age of Empire: Religion, Race and Scholarship*. Cambridge: Cambridge University Press.

McCall, H. 1998. "Rediscovery and Aftermath." In S. Dalley (ed.), *The Legacy of Mesopotamia*, 183–213. Oxford: Oxford University Press.

Müller, C. 2001. "Pompeius Trogus." In *Der Neue Pauly*, 10:115–17.

Müller, S. 2011. "Cultural Nationalism and Beyond: Musical Performances in Imperial Germany." In S. Müller and C. Torp (eds.), *Imperial Germany Revisited: Continuing Debates and New Perspectives*, 173–85. New York and Oxford: Berghahn.

Oberzaucher-Schüller, G. 2011. "One Out of Many? Bournonville, Paul Taglioni, and the Ballet of the Mid-Nineteenth Century." *Dance Chronicle* 29(3):471–83.

Oexle, O., ed. 2007. *Krise des Historismus – Krise der Wirklichkeit: Wissenschaft, Kunst und Literatur 1880–1932*. Göttingen: Vandenhoeck & Ruprecht.

Oppel, H. 1976. "George Gordon Lord Byron: Sardanapalus." In H. Kosok (ed.), *Das englische Drama im 18. und 19. Jahrhundert: Interpretationen*, 170–83. Berlin: Schmidt.

Piffaut, L. 2015. "Le Sardanapalo (1678) de Freschi: pratiques théâtrales et musicales du contraste dans l'opéra vénitien du XVIIe siècle." *Chroniques italiennes, revue en ligne de l'université de Paris III Sorbonne Nouvelle* 30(2):47–68.

Place, V. 1867. *Ninive et l'Assyrie*, vol. 3. Paris: Impr. Impériale.

Renger, J. 1979. "Die Geschichte der Altorientalistik und der vorderasiatischen Archäologie in Berlin von 1875 bis 1945." In W. Arenhöfen and C. Schreiber (eds.), *Berlin und die Antike*, 2:151–92. Berlin: Deutsches Archäologisches Institut.

———. 2015. "Sardanapal." in *Der Neue Pauly* 11:54.

Reischert, A. 2001. "Sardanapalos." In *Kompendium der musikalischen Sujets: Ein Werkkatalog*, 1:867–68.

Richardson, A. 2004. "Byron and the Theatre." In D. Bone (ed.), *The Cambridge Companion to Byron*, 133–50. Cambridge: Cambridge University Press.

Röhl, J. 1993–2008. *Wilhelm II*, 3 vols. Munich: Beck.

Rölling, W. 2009. "Sardanapal(l)os." In *Reallexikon der Assyriologie*, 12:36–37.

Stauffer, A. 2011. "Sardanapalus, Spectacle, and the Empire State." In M. Grenn and P. Pal-Lapinski (eds.), *Byron and the Politics of Freedom and Terror*, 33–46. Basingstoke, UK: Palgrave.

Stieger, F. 1975. "Sardanapal." In *Opernlexikon: Titelkatalog*, 3:1084.

Svane, M-L. 2015. "Der Orient auf der Bühne: Byrons *Sardanapal* als romantisches Drama und als Melodrama." In H. Hühn and J. Schiedermair (eds.), *Europäische Romantik: Interdisziplinäre Perspektiven der Forschung*, 215–28. Berlin: de Gruyter.

Wilhelm II. 1922. *Ereignisse und Gestalten aus den Jahren 1878–1918*. Leipzig: Koehler.

Ye Go to Thy Abzu

How Norwegian Black Metal Used Mesopotamian References, Where It Took Them From, and How It Usually Got Them Wrong

Daniele Federico Rosa

What do you remember from that time [when you were living in Iraq as a kid]?

A lot of things. I visited Babylon, the ruins of Babylon, and a lot of mythological sites. There were a lot of dangerous things that happened, like being chased by dogs with rabies.

Interview with Varg Vikernes, leader of Burzum (Moynihan and Søderling 2003, 155)

1. As Wolfs among Sheep We Have Wandered: Arsons, a Killing, and the Birth of Black Metal

The devil, they say, always has the best tunes.[1] I have always believed that, if this is the case, Satan must have a devilish taste for music: since he met Robert Johnson at a crossroad near Dockery Plantation, Mississippi, he always showed an inclination for the best musicians around.[2] Something bad must then have happened to him in the late 1980s when he moved to Norway and turned this country into the homeland of

1. "As wolfs among sheep we have wandered" is a literal—typo-included—quote from the back of a popular 1990s Darkthrone t-shirt.

2. Robert Johnson (1911–1938) is celebrated for being, if not the best, then certainly the most famous "Delta blues" musician. This is due not only to the greatness of his music, but also because he was rumored to have sold his soul to the devil to achieve musical success. Robert Johnson's story has been told in many excellent books. Most recently, see Conforth and Wardlow 2019, esp. chapter 9 on the devil.

the unholy, cacophonous rock music style that was destined to become known as the second wave of black metal or "true Norwegian black metal."

Officially born in Britain in the early 1980s, black metal[3] is the subgenre of a subgenre (the "new wave of British heavy metal") of a subgenre ("heavy metal") of rock music. Characterized by sinister lyrical themes (such as devil worshipping, occultism, political extremism, and violence) and (proudly) limited technical skills, black metal only emerged as a proper "scene" when the genre reached Scandinavia, namely, Norway. Here a bunch of teenagers and post-teenagers, who mostly gathered around the Oslo music shop *Helvete* (hell), developed the style and imaginary of early Norwegian black metal—something that would have had an enormous influence on extreme music and on pop culture in general to this day.

The early days of Norwegian black metal recount not only a story of music and youth culture but also of criminality. A few members of the black metal "inner circle" decided to show their bitter opposition to Christianity by setting fire to the *stavkirke*, the medieval wooden churches once common in northwestern Europe. The Fantoft church, originally built around 1150, was completely destroyed by arson on 6 June 1992. About fifty more attacks followed from 1992 to 1996. In every case that was solved, members of the black metal scene were found guilty. There was only one case in which someone inadvertently revealed his own guilt: Taking pride in the Fantoft arson, Varg Vikernes, the founder and only member of Burzum, put a picture of the burnt church on the cover of his band's EP, *Aske* (ashes).[4]

Varg Vikernes, ironically born Kristian (Bergen, Norway, 1973) and now legally known as Louis Cachet, was arrested in 1994 for the killing of Øystein Aarseth (1968–1993), also known as *Euronymous*, a former friend of his and founding member of the band *Mayhem* (whose singer, Per Ohlin, known with his stage-name "Dead," committed suicide two years before, somehow inaugurating the black metal sinister "blood season"). Vikernes was convicted for murder and arson and subsequently served more than fourteen years in prison. His one-man project, Burzum, probably remains to this day one of the most influential heavy metal acts ever. Vikernes, a *sui generis* scholar of folklore and mythology (see his masterpiece, Vikernes 2011), is also probably the

---

3. The term "black metal" was coined with Venom's second LP (Black Metal, Neat Records, Newcastle 1982). Venom is in fact considered the first, true black metal band, even though their leader Conrad Lant, aka Cronos, would have later declared that their intent was not as serious as that of their Norwegian followers: "Coming up with a term like black metal or thrash metal, it was great when bands came along and used those titles. The Norwegians used the term black metal ten years later 'cos they knew they would automatically be put into a category they wanted to be in. They were like, 'This is dirty, this is nasty, this is Satanic, we're gonna put fucking corpsepaint on, sing about Satan'... they knew the black metal tag would give them an identity." See Patterson 2009, 59–61.

4. A history of the early black metal scene is found in Moynihan and Søderling 2003. See also Patterson 2014 (chapter 22 on Burzum).

culprit for taking "serious" Mesopotamian references into the black metal and extreme music lyrical imaginary.

His song "Ea, Lord of the Depths," from Burzum's first self-titled album (Burzum 1992), is probably the first "Mesopotamian" song in black metal. The lyrics, shortened and including a couple of funny misreadings, are taken from R. C. Thompson's 1903 book, *The Devils and Evil Spirits of Babylonia* (1903–1904, 2:149):

> The head is the head of a serpent
> From its nostrils mucus trickles
> The ears are those of a basilisk
> His horns are twisted into three curls
> Ah! Ea, lord of the depths!
> The body is a sun[5] fish, full of stars
> The base of his feet are claws
> His name is Sassu Wunnu[6]
> A sea monster, a form of Ea
> Ah! Ea, lord of the depths!

2. *Fake Old News*

There is virtually no other direct reason why more-or-less correct references to Mesopotamia made their way into black metal's lyrical themes, except that one of the most famous exponents of the scene used them in one of his early songs. References to Mesopotamian mythology, however, had already been used by non-Norwegian extreme metal bands, starting from their very *noms de plume,* such as Absu (formed in Texas, US, in 1989), Marduk (Sweden, 1991), and Behemoth's lead singer Nergal (Poland, 1991). The ancient Near East, perceived as something intrinsically "evil" and diabolical, probably reached these bands as the legacy of H. P. Lovecraft's fictional myth-making.

Lovecraft (1890–1937) was the well-known American writer who invented, among many other things, what is probably the most famous fictional book in history, the *Necronomicon*. The *Necronomicon*, the name of which was probably inspired by Marcus Manilius's poem *Astronomica* (first century CE), made its first appearance in a short story called "The Hound," written in 1922 and published two years later in the *Weird Tales* magazine.[7] The book and his fictional author, the "mad Arab" Abdul Alhazred, were then mentioned in "The Festival" (published 1925), then here and there in several

5. The Thompson text reads SUH-maš and is translated "SUH-fish" (for *suḫurmāšu*), which was probably assumed as a typo by Vikernes, who corrected it into "Sun."

6. For Thompson's *sassu-urinnu*(?). The "wunnu" in Burzum's lyrics is not easily explained. Curiously enough, Sassu Wunnu is also the title of another instrumental Burzum song, which appears on the 2011 album, From the Depths of Darkness (Byelobog Productions, s.l.) and serves as an introduction to a newly recorded version of Ea.

7. On the development of the Necronomicon, see Harms and Wisdom Gonce 2003, 8–28.

other stories until, in 1927, Lovecraft decided to write a short history of the book itself: actually a tenth-century Greek translation of a lost Arab manuscript, the *Al Azif*, the *Necronomicon* was written in the eighth century by a mad Yemeni poet, the aforementioned Alhazred, his wisdom "accrued through his visits to the ruins of Babylon, the subterranean chambers of Memphis, and a solitary spiritual sojourn in the Arab desert."[8] None of this ever really happened; nonetheless, the *Necronomicon*'s story was so powerful that, like Lovecraft himself predicted in a letter to a friend, people ended up believing in it (Quoted in Harms and Wisdom Gonce 2003, 28).

Over the decades, several authors have claimed to have actually discovered the "true" *Necronomicon* manuscript. The most famous case is that of *Simon's Necronomicon*, a modern-day grimoire that a fictional Eastern Orthodox bishop called Simon brought to the US in the 1970s after discovering it and translating it from Greek. Although clearly a fake, or better, a well-constructed hoax (most probably the real author was the American writer and historian of occultism Peter Levenda, who confirmed the *editing*, and not the writing, of the text), this book—originally published in a very limited edition of 666 (Simon 1977)—had a huge influence on occultism and pop culture dealing with occultism, similarly to other famous modern "magical" books such as *The Book of Shadows* or Anton Szandor LaVey's *Satanic Bible*.[9]

It also had an enormous influence on black metal bands, who greedily read it and took inspiration and quotations from it.

What is of particular interest here is that, probably in order to create a sense of eeriness (quite similarly to the *voces mysticae* of the Roman and Greek curse tablets; see Gager 1992), the book makes use of a great number of Sumerian and Akkadian words and names—and of *fake* Sumerian and Akkadian words and names too.[10] *Simon's Necronomicon* is indeed presented as a work of "Sumerian Magick" (where *magick* is a reference to Aleister Crowley, 1875–1947, the infamous British occultist known as "the wickedest man in the world," who used to spell that word this way and considered it a third way between religion and science). In it, real texts and terms are mashed-up with fictional ones, also aiming at giving an ancient background to Lovecraft's stories and creatures. The name of the god *Kutulu* (not mentioned anywhere else) directly reminds one of the Chtulhu of Lovecraft's tales; *Azag-Thot* clearly refers to Azathoth; and so on.

8. Lovecraft's Orientalism and racism have been noted by a number of critics and scholars. As observed by his most famous biographer, the French novelist Michel Houellebecq, "Lovecraft's character is fascinating in part because his values were so entirely opposite to ours. He was fundamentally racist, openly reactionary, he glorified puritanical inhibitions." This is something that could be said about black metal as well (see Houellebecq 1991).

9. On modern magic books, see Davies 2009, 262–77.

10. To see what I mean, check this excerpt from the Invocation of the Nergal Gate: "By the Name which I was given on the Sphere of SHAMMASH, I ask Thee, Open! IA NERGAL-YA! IA ZI ANNGA KANPA! IA NNGA! IA NNGR-YA! IA! NNGYA! IA ZI DINGIR NEENYA KANPA! IA KANTALAMAKKYA TARRA! KANPA!" (capitals in the original text).

In this sense, *Simon's Necronomicon* is the most important Western "pop" artifact that directly connected ancient Mesopotamia and evil; although, not the only one: William Peter Blatty's novel *The Exorcist* (1971) and the movie it inspired a couple of years later famously turned the little known demon Pazuzu into a Satanism superstar worldwide. Readers old enough to have seen the *Ghostbusters* movie might remember about the "Sumerian ghost" appearing on a ziggurat in Sigourney Weaver's refrigerator. That ghost later in the movie is referred to as Zuul, the Gatekeeper. Well, Zuul is no one else but Xul, one of the fictional deities most frequently attested in *Simon's Necronomicon,* where a lot of references to gates—probably resembling the ones Inanna met in her descent—are made.

Early black metal bands undoubtedly took their names from *Simon's Necronomicon,* most notably from the *Book of Calling,* one of the most sinister "books" included. In addition to Kutulu and Azag-Thot, Absu and Marduk are mentioned here.

Although not even Assyriology undergraduates could believe a word of Simon's grimoire, the book has in fact a certain sinister charm, and was put on the same level as any other literary or historical sources by black metal bands using it.

Here are the typical Necronomicon-Lovecraftian-Assyriological lyrics to a black metal song, namely, "Apzu" by Absu (!) from the 1995 album *The Sun of Tipharet:*

> Sea of Uruk, I taste the salt of you
> I hunt through sands of Roba el-Khaliyeh[11]
> Dumuzi Apzu
> Your allure is so very pure
> ZI DINGIR ANNA KANPA![12]
> You shall drown the fearless one!
> The sword of Lapis Lazuli Diadem
> Your fullness and strength is my delight
> EDIN NA ZU, EDIN NA ZU
> Oh mountains of Mashu
> Please help me find the grey stone
> I am in search of the Northern Nineveh
> It's beyond the hills of Zagros
> I thrust my sword onto the veil
> and then in the earth
> reversed lightning strikes Sumerian sands
> They glance at me with eyes of Sunkun Varlooni
> Ye go to thy Apzu, the impious axis of Enidu
> ...
> I have seen Ngaa, God of Heathens

11. The Rub' al-Khali desert where, according to Lovecraft, Alhazred composed the *Necronomicon.*

12. A *Simon's Necronomicon* incantation. EDIN NA ZU, the mountains of Mashu, Sunkun Varlooni, and Ngaa are all others of Simon's quotations.

The cosmos shall be greeted from the blood of the serpent
A serpent well known as Tehom, Mummu, Tiamat[13]
...
Zagros, Avagon, Ngaa, Shabatu![14]

It is barely necessary to note here that such an impious lyrical imagery was not only influent on black metal, but also on its "different twin," death metal. Here are a few excerpts from Sinister's "Awaiting the Absu," a song from their 1995 *Hate* LP:

Necromantic art from the kingdom of Woe
Cthulhu sleeps and dreams the burning pain
Pazuzu plague gods, shaped from the blood of Kingu
Calling of the spirits who dwell in the lost
Dark shining world of the ancient horde
Covered with blood
Embraced by fire, Annu spawned
Screaming demons
Children of the serpent god
Vengeance is sworn!
Wreak vengeance upon them
Secret covenant will have revenge
From the depths the nameless will rise
The seven lords reborn in Ur
The cold burning sword beholds the wrath
Suffer—in pain
Suffer—bleeding
Suffer—to dream
Awaiting the Absu!

And this is "Lord of All Fevers and Plague," a song that the band Morbid Angel (led by guitarist Trey Azagthoth) included in their debut album, significantly entitled *Altars of Madness* (1989):

Ninnghizhidda—open my eyes
Ninnghizhidda—hear my cries
...
I call forth the god Pazuzu
I call forth the lord of plague
...

13. This line is a mix of the Torah and the Enuma Elish.

14. A final invocation that mixes up the Zagros hills, a *Simon's Necronomicon* fictional name, a month name (Shabatu), plus a fourth word that I was unable to track (even though it sounds a lot like Tolkien to me).

Ia iak sakkakh iak sakkakth Ia shaxul!
Ia iak sakkakh iak sakkakth!
Ia shaxul Ia kingu ia cthulu ia azbul Ia azabua!

and so on. This would be funny if it was not so horrible. Mixing up things only because they sound so eerie this way is what black metal bands have done over and over again: Namtar is the hyle of plague according, again, to Absu, in their song "Sceptre Command," while in "Ye Uttuku Spells" they urge Ugallu to "obey the Magus' spell" (where Magus is another reference to Crowley). Poor Ishtar stinks, according to the band Unholy who seem to think of her as a sort of demon ("Stench of Ishtar"), while the band Morturial Eclipse tells us about vampirism in Neo-Babylonian times (as they sing in "At the Gates of Marduk's Shrine," "A new procession is heading to the great shrine of Esagila / Ready to drink the purified blood / Ready to follow the steps of Nebuchadnezzar"). In their "Ode to Pazuzu," Black Funeral tells us the moving story of Pazuzu's Louvre statuette that is secretly thinking about revenge:

Lord of plagues, river of the northern winds, you stare at humanity through your glass cage
Brought from Assyria to the city of Lights
Your energy radiating from the Louvre pyramid
A pestilence set out to destroy human life
In a world made of glass and concrete
The flesh is so weak, so easy to corrupt
Ripped by your infected fangs and claws
Lord Pazuzu, spread sickness in the heart of men
Spread fear and terror in the soul of Jehovah's chosen ones

A lot of other examples could be made, but they can easily be found by reading the lyrics on the internet but not so easily caught by listening to the songs: people unfamiliar with black metal songs will be surprised to discover that all words, when sung in a black metal style, sound exactly the same. Since the early 1990s, black metal has spread from Norway to the world, has evolved into a third wave, then many other waves, and its original antisocial drive has disappeared, to the point that black metal elements have appeared in much less extreme rock music. Something like black metal theory is even currently studied in universities.[15] Black metal seems to have finally been accepted by society. Mesopotamia seems in its turn to have disappeared from black metal imaginary: Ea, Pazuzu, and Xul never liked it easy.

15. Strange as it may sound, black metal theory can also be read in curious academic books such as VV.AA. 2012 or Masciandaro 2010.

3. *What the Hell! Why Did They Choose Evil at All? And What's So Evil about the Ancient Near East, in the End?*

I confess this is going to be the most slippery section of this essay. The writer is not a sociologist, and the help of sociology is the one we should be summoning here. Still, while the black metal self-narrative may be interesting, or even perversely fun in a way,[16] but not very helpful in understanding, even "official" sociology is somehow missing the point when it simply analyzes black metal by putting it in the heavy metal cauldron (see, e.g., Weinstein 2000). It is at least in part true that faster, more extreme subgenres of heavy metal emerged from the 1980s on as a fundamentalist reaction to the 1970s "corrupting" extravagances engendered by the increasing commercial success of early heavy metal bands (and thus an attempt to take a rebellious, anti-mainstream, all masculine musical movement back to the pureness of its origins; see Weinstein 2000, 48–50; Kahn-Harris 2004, 95–111). But distinctions must be made. While certain features can, in fact, be found in a number of extreme heavy-metal styles, no other subgenre so openly embraces pure evil as black metal doe; the only possible exception is the somehow stylistically similar *death-metal* genre[17] (with Sweden, quite strikingly, as one of the prominent scenes), which nonetheless often shows a subtle, yet clear, sort of tongue-in-cheek taste for macabre, occult, or other "antisocial" themes. Moreover, black metal, at least partly, emerged as a reaction to the growing success of death metal, thus becoming a fundamentalist reaction to a fundamentalist reaction, and a reaction that implied that violence and horror—only sung about in death metal songs—became real, and a means to an end. While black metal shares a few formal features with other extreme subgenres, such as fast or distorted and/or screamed vocals, others—such as good skills in playing, or any open interest for the show business—are completely rejected. Moreover, the intent is completely different: there is no positive political message, not even in a rough or naïve form as is the case of some of the most well-known speed/thrash metal acts, such as Metallica, Megadeth, or Pantera. (Rather, there is a distorted political message, delivered in particular by the "national-socialist black metal" movement, which fully embraces Nazism and its occult roots as an element of pure evil and a symbol of anti-Western "liberal" attitudes[18]). There is no irony, no fun, no "guy's vaca-

16. The best reference is still Gorgoroth's lead singer Gaahl talking about what inspires his band's music the most, in the *Metal: A Headbanger's Journey* documentary, directed by Sam Dunn with Scot McFadyen and Jessica Wise (2005). A clip can easily be found by searching "Gaahl's epic answer" on any internet-based video-sharing platform.

17. Death and black metallers generally regard each other as fierce enemies. To make things even less clear for the non-metalhead reader, however, please consider that there have been bands that switched from one style to the other (most notably Darkthrone, a leading "true Norwegian black metal band," which started as a death metal one), and even groups playing a hybrid genre between the two that is sometimes referred to as "blackened death metal" (e.g., the music of Behemoth and Emperor).

18. See Goodrick-Clarke 2002. On national-socialist black metal in general, see also Dornbusch and Killguss 2005 and Maspero and Ribaric 2015.

tion" feeling at all in black metal. There is only evil, darkness, cold, and anything that human beings normally try to avoid.

Explaining the reasons and the scope of such a movement is far beyond the aim of this essay. Let us just limit ourselves to observing that this antiquity has often been associated with far-right politics, of which many members of the Norwegian scene were proponents, not only for nationalist reasons. Ancient myths and traditions, often maliciously misread, are used to give foundation and dignity to certain goals or behaviors (e.g., racism and homophobia).

Black metal has variously been interpreted, not only by sociologists or cultural historians dealing with youth culture and extreme political movements, but also by philosophers and religious studies scholars (see, e.g., Forster 2006). Black metal has also evolved into a small but independent field of research, the "Black Metal Theory," and into a sort of philosophical movement/musical-mystical praxis, the "transcendental black metal," which claims, among other things, that "the murder of Euronymous by Varg Vikernes appears as the founding gesture of black metal" but in fact "it is a mere origin myth ... the real gesture ... is the suicide of Dead,"[19] something that, be it true or not (if ever adjectives like "true" or "untrue" suit such a statement) perfectly captures the spirit of black metal. What is of interest here is how the early black metal scene soon crystallized in a movement that had antisocial, anti-Christian features at its core, and went looking for a sort of historical antecedent of foundation of itself. Antiquity and ancient mythology and folklore, most notably those from Scandinavia and others outside the Judeo-Christian and Greco-Roman canons, including the ancient Near East, were widely used with the scope of rejecting the European and Western culture,[20] and were linked to the present by using occultism and horror literature as a sort of bridge between the ancient texts and modern pop culture.

Bibliography

Burzum. 1992. [Record] *Burzum*. Oslo: Deathlike Silence Productions.

---

19. The transcendental black metal was "launched" by a philosophical treatise written by Hunter Hunt-Hendrix, vocalist and leader of the Brooklyn band Liturgy, now included in Masciandaro 2010, 53–65. The quoted lines on the founding gestures of black metal are on p. 65.

20. Note that references taken from Greek and Roman history and mythology are seldom used in lyrics and artworks by black metal bands, especially those from Greece and Italy, or elsewhere (but the band Diocletian from New Zealand was named after the Roman "emperor" known to be a bloodthirsty tyrant). In such cases, classical antiquity is used to reject "modernity" as it is strictly connected with Christianity and the Catholic and Orthodox churches. See, e.g., the "pagan hellenic black metal" bands Kawir and Nocternity from Greece; Rome is the "divine city" waiting for the Antichrist in "Roma Divina Urbs" by the Roman band Aborym; the god Bacchus and ancient Rome make their way to the lyrical world of Raspail, also from Rome, via an Aleister Crowley quote (see especially the "Ver Sacrum" song).

Conforth, B., and G. D. Wardlow. 2019. *Up Jumped the Devil: The Real Life of Robert Johnson*. Chicago: Chicago Review Press.

Davies, O. 2009. *Grimoires: A History of Magic Books*. Oxford: Oxford University Press.

Dornbusch, C., and H. Killguss. 2005. *Unheilige Allianzen: Black Metal zwischen Satanismus, Heidentum und Neonazismus*. Münster: Unrast Verlag.

Forster, J. 2006. *Commodified Evil's Wayward Children: Black Metal and Death Metal as Purveyors of an Alternative Form of Modern Escapism*. MA thesis, University of Canterbury.

Gager, J. 1992. *Curse Tablets and Binding Spells From the Ancient World*. New York: Oxford University Press.

Goodrick-Clarke, N. 2002. "White Noise and Black Metal." In N. Goodrick-Clarke (ed.), *Black Sun: Aryan Cults, Esoteric Nazism and the Politics of Identity*, 193–213. New York: New York University Press.

Harms, D., and J. Wisdom Gonce, III. 2003. *The Necronomicon Files: The Truth Behind the Legend*, 2nd ed. Boston: Red Wheel.

Houellebecq, M. 1991. *H. P. Lovecraft: Contre le monde, contre la vie*. Monaco: Éditions du Rocher.

Kahn-Harris, K. 2004. "The 'Failure' of Youth Culture: Reflexivity, Music and Politics in the Black Metal Scene." *European Journal of Cultural Studies* 7:95–111.

Masciandaro, N. (ed.). 2010. *Hideous Gnosis: Black Metal Theory Symposium* I. Self-released.

Maspero, D., and M. Ribaric. 2015. *Wolves among Sheep: History and Ideology of National-Socialist Black Metal*. Milan: Tsunami.

Moynihan, M., and D. Søderling. 2003. *Lords of Chaos: The Bloody Rise of the Satanic Metal Underground*. 2nd ed. Port Townsend, WA: Feral House.

Patterson, D. 2009. *Black Metal: Evolution of the Cult*. Port Townsend, WA: Feral House.

Simon. 1977. *Necronomicon*. New York City: Schlangekraft.

Thompson, R. C. 1903–1904. *The Devils and Evil Spirits of Babylonia*. 2 vols. London: Luzac.

Vikernes, V. 2011. *Sorcery and Religion in Ancient Scandinavia*. Oxford: Abstract Sounds.

VV.AA. 2012. *Black Metal: Beyond the Darkness*. London: Black Dog.

Weinstein, D. 2000. *Heavy Metal: The Music and Its Culture*. Revised ed. New York: Da Capo.

Further Listening

As any music fan knows, there is a record list for each listener. Mine is incomplete, arbitrary and wrong like everyone else, and should not be intended as "black metal best records" or as an exhaustive list: the purpose of this section is to provide black metal-illiterate readers with a bunch of records they can access to get an idea of how this paper should sound like—without losing their hearing. It concentrates on the period from 1981 (the "forerunners era") to 1997, more or less when black metal had became a fully integrated mainstream business—something to which Ulver, a band that closes my list, responded by publishing a raw four-track record that, some say, was recorded in the woods (it certainly sounds like it was; their major label fired them). In the age of streaming music, I think providing details of the precise first editions of these records is totally useless. I will limit myself to indicating the year of the original release, plus—in a couple of relevant cases—the year in which the album was recorded.

Venom, "Welcome to Hell" (England, 1981)
Venom, "Black metal" (England, 1982)

Hellhammer, "Apocalyptic Raids" (Switzerland, 1984)
Bathory, "Bathory" (Sweden, 1984)
Celtic Frost, "To Mega Therion" (Switzerland, 1985)
Bathory, "Under the Sign of the Black Mark" (Sweden, 1987)
Mayhem, "Live in Leipzig" (Norway, 1996, recorded 1990)
Von, "Satanic Blood" (USA, 1992)
Burzum, "Burzum" (Norway, 1992) [often printed together with the "Aske" EP, 1993]
Darkthrone, "A Blaze in the Northern Sky" (Norway, 1992)
Beherit, "Drowing Down the Moon" (Finland, 1993)
Rotting Christ, "Thy Mighty Contract" (Greece, 1993)
Absu, "Barathrum: V.I.T.R.I.O.L." (USA, 1993)
Mayhem, "De Mysteriis Dom Sathanas" (Norway 1994, recorded 1993)
Emperor, "In the Nightside Eclipse" (Norway, 1994)
Darkthrone, "A Blaze in the Northern Sky" (Norway, 1994)
Cradle of Filth, "The Principle of Evil Made Flesh" (England, 1994)
Immortal, "Battles in the North" (Norway, 1995)
Burzum, "Filosofem" (Norway 1996)
Ulver, "Nattens Madrigal" (Norway 1997)

"Babylon's Last Bacchanal"

Mesopotamia and the Near East in Epic Biblical Cinema

Kevin McGeough

Ancient Babylon is recreated in cinema in order to be destroyed.[1] The audience who pays to watch the ancient city ruined on screen knows the eventual fate of Babylon. They witness historical-seeming figures through the lens of dramatic irony provided by a modern (and perhaps modernist) perspective, well aware that what they are viewing is a recreation of those characters' last days. The audience watches those characters make choices that will topple empires and usher out the great eras of the ancient Near East. Entangled with that perspective of dramatic irony is the experience of these films in relation to the reception history of Mesopotamia. Babylon, Nineveh, and other cities of the ancient Near East stand as metaphors for all that is wrong with urbanism, wealth, and decadence. These metaphors articulated in the Bible and classical literature have been perpetuated through two thousand years of reimagining. Archaeological discoveries of Mesopotamia may have changed the aesthetics of this reception history, but in popular culture presentations, archaeology seems to have actually reified this older metaphor.[2] The destruction of these cities was in biblical, classical, and later tradition taken as historical evidence for how immoral behavior can act as a poison that corrupts and destroys an empire. The diegesis (the narrative elements of the story actually taking place on screen) surrounding Mesopotamia on film is, for the most part, reliant on the older reception and tropes that were adapted for new dramatic genres of the nineteenth century and then modified for cinema during the silent film era. Despite our profound knowledge of the history and myths of Mesopotamia, most of what is seen on the silver screen is channeled through the lenses of biblical and classical reception.

---

1. The author would like to thank Christopher Epplett for his assistance in locating some of the films under discussion and thank Agnès Garcia-Ventura and Lorenzo Verderame for their kind invitation to contribute to this volume.

2. See the different approach, and failure, of the Sardanapalus drama supervised by Delitzsch and Andrae; Hartmann in this volume.

We see a Mesopotamia in which prophets wander through the streets, not to advise the king on the results of divination (as is well attested for Neo-Assyrian times) but to forecast the destruction of the cities, in the manner of biblical Jonah. The main character of many of these films is not Esarhaddon or Nebuchadnezzar but Sardanapalus, the final king of Nineveh whose story is not preserved in Assyrian annals but in the classical tradition and who was made famous through Lord Byron's (1821) play in blank verse.

As is typical of historical epic cinema, what is authentic is mostly the sets, props, and costumes. Just as in literary historical fiction, the characters themselves rarely behave in a manner that would convince an historian.[3] The experiment of historical imagination stops with the material; what one witnesses on the screen are characters with motivations like those of the present operating within contemporary ideological frameworks, yet dressed in alien garb. By setting a contemporary message in a realistic seeming ancient world, filmmakers offer profoundly powerful arguments about the present. For by making today's values and struggles seem normative throughout history and treating the past as typological, the status quo becomes profoundly normalized. The colossal monuments discovered by Botta, Layard, and others seemed to confirm biblical and classical readings of a powerful ancient civilization ruled by oriental despots devoted to mysterious monstrous gods. The orthostats bearing reliefs of heroic kings and winged gods, the lamassus who guarded palace entrances, and the scenes of daily life infused by militarism were immensely popular with the public and offered opportunity for dramatic, physical recreation in cinematic form. The reliefs especially allowed producers and directors to make claims of historical verism by dressing their actors in authentic-seeming period costumes and constructing sets on a massive scale based on actual Mesopotamian cities. Archaeology offered an aesthetic that convinced audiences of the reality of the reconstruction.

1. Before Cinema: Dramatizing Mesopotamia in the Nineteenth Century

Nineteenth-century stage treatments of Mesopotamia have been addressed elsewhere, so only a cursory discussion of those elements that influenced later film is needed here (see Bohrer 2003; Malley 2012; McGeough 2015c; Ziter 2003). Arguably the most influential productions were those based on Lord Byron's 1821 play *Sardanapalus*. Byron retells Diodorus's story of the last king of Nineveh, Sardanapalus, a king who is otherwise unattested in Assyrian records.[4] Byron had never intended this play to be staged, but after his death, the technology and commercial viability of this kind of his-

3. For one such approach, see Hartmann in this volume.

4. Varying suggestions have been made about who this king could be, if he is based on an historical figure. Sardanapalus may be a Greek rendering of Ashurbanipal, although Diodorus's king bears little resemblance to him. Ashur-Uballit II is more commonly taken as the last king of the Neo-Assyrian Empire, although again, there is little resemblance between him and the Sardanapalus of Byron. For more on this, see McGeough 2015a, 69–70.

Figure 1. Design for scenery for *Sardanapalus* by F. Lloyds, ca. 1853. © Victoria and Albert Museum, London.

torical stage spectacle made it an attractive piece. It was performed in numerous forms throughout the nineteenth century, perhaps most notably in a production by Charles Kean (1811–1868). Kean took the classically inspired story but placed it in a set modeled after Austen Henry Layard's own reconstructions of Nineveh, with costumes and props inspired by Assyrian reliefs (figs. 1 and 2; Kean 1853, 4).[5] Kean's work was not so different from other Victorian historical productions (Meisel 1983, 229–30), where designers attempted to actually reconstruct the material culture of an era, yet made little effort to create veristic characterizations or plots. For Mesopotamian dramatic reception, Kean's production was particularly important since he established the visual tropes and basic staging elements that would later be fundamental to cinematic Mesopotamia.

Kean's show was not the only production that would later influence cinematic visions of Mesopotamia. Towards the end of the nineteenth century, *Sardanapalus* was performed by travelling theaters in Britain and the United States. Long (2006) discusses a circus horse show that used the loose premise of the destruction of Nineveh as the basis for the spectacle. Beyond *Sardanapalus*, operatic productions of Near Eastern

5. For more on Kean's productions, see Malley 2007, 141–42; McGeough 2015c, 113–18; and Ziter 2003, 160.

Figure 2. *Belshazzar's Feast*, John Martin. Yale Center for British Art, Paul Mellon Collection.

and quasi-biblical stories established some of the narrative devices and plot points that were later adapted to cinematic epic. Operas set in the ancient world typically involved star-cross'd lovers who must sacrifice their own romantic lives for the good of the state (McGeough 2015c, 136–87). This type of celebration of personal romantic sacrifice for nationalist purposes was adopted wholesale by "sword and sandal" filmmakers after World War II. Paintings and other visual art of the nineteenth century (such as that produced by John Martin, Eugene Delacroix, and other orientalist painters) would also influence later visions of Mesopotamia (McGeough 2015c, 24–29, 65–78).

2. *Adapting the Stage to the Screen: D. W. Griffith's Intolerance*

These presentations of the destruction of Mesopotamia on the stage and on the canvas all attempted to explore issues of their artist's era by recontextualizing those subjects in ancient times.[6] With the emergence of the cinema, filmmakers took a more direct approach to signaling this parallelism to the viewers. Rather than presuming that audiences would identify an implicit commentary on the present in a film about the past, filmmakers juxtaposed narratives of ancient and contemporary life in the same film.

6. Giovanni Pastore's *Cabiria* (1914) is another epic film that uses ancient events as a means of commenting on the past. In this film, the ancient Romans (paralleling the rising Italian empire of the twentieth century) attack the Carthaginians and their North African empire (paralleling the events of the Italo-Turkish war [1911–1912]).

Sometimes the modern story was set as a framing narrative or vice versa. Other times, like in Cecil B. DeMille's first attempt at *The Ten Commandments* (1923), the ancient story was offered as a prelude to instruct the main narrative. D. W. Griffith's *Intolerance* (1916) was one of the pioneering films that used this approach, although upon its initial release, audiences found it overly long and confusing. The movie features four parallel stories from different time periods: the last days of the Neo-Assyrian empire, Jesus's ministry and crucifixion, the St. Bartholomew's Day Massacre, and contemporary times (1916). Most of the ahistorical characters are not given names, implying that these are typological figures that recur in various places and times. The driving force of historical change is, as the title of the film implies, intolerance. Historical figures, in Griffith's vision of history, can also be typological; David Shepherd (2013, 180–81) has shown that the Babylonian king, Belshazzar, is an explicit character parallel for Christ, perhaps a pre-Christian "worthy."

Part of the financial difficulty that the studio experienced with *Intolerance* was in the huge production costs, and the Babylon set was by far the most lavish, making the movie the most expensive produced up until that time (fig. 3). Griffith had the "Great Wall of Babylon" constructed at life-size scale and this is apparent in the scenes of masses of extras playing Babylonians swarming the stage. Even though the city is Babylon narratively, the research team that designed the set relied mostly on Neo-Assyrian materials for historical models (Seymour 2015, 23; Shepherd 2013, 179). Massive columns topped by colossal rearing elephants flank a staircase that leads up to an enormous gateway. Figures copied from the Neo-Assyrian reliefs decorate the empty spaces of the gate complex although here the figures are taken out of context, depicted as isolated or symmetrical presences, not part of a larger relief narrative.[7] What is truly striking about the images is their monumentality; these decorative figures stand out in stark contrast to what appear to be minuscule people inhabiting the space. Griffith's reliefs have captured and even exaggerated the monumentality of the originals, although moving them from restricted palatial space to the public space of the city-gate. The emotional impact that is intended is similar though. The viewer is awed by the spectacle of a Mesopotamian kingdom. That intolerant practices could bring down such a magnificent and splendid kingdom, Griffith's film seemed to argue, suggested that the same could happen to the United States or Europe.

Yet the reconstruction of Babylon is also signified as such in the film. The intertitle that introduces the set in the film reads: "Note: Replica of Babylon's encircling walls 30 feet in height and broad enough for the passing of chariots." Shepherd (2013, 178) rightly comments that this note takes the viewer out of the "illusion of reality" but makes certain that the audience is aware of Griffith's skill in reconstructing the city. Here is the origin of what becomes a central focus of the historical epic, not historical

7. Jon Solomon (2001, 241) notes that the human-headed winged-bull statues became, because of *Intolerance* and another film, *Judith of Bethulia*, "a necessary detail of any film about Babylon."

Figure 3. The "Babylonian Palace" from *Intolerance*.

veritas itself but a demonstration to the viewer of the filmmakers' abilities to recreate an historically accurate scene on a colossal scale. In seeing that the seeming reality is only illusion, the viewer's willing suspension of disbelief is purposefully broken in order to point to how authentic the inauthentic actually is. The reconstruction of Neo-Assyrian architecture becomes a signifier of a kind of technocratic teleology, in which the wonders of the ancient world can easily be rendered in modern forms. The filmmaker demonstrates that he can build his own versions of the wonders of the past and by so doing, establishes that the past is subordinate to the modern.

Griffith had a research team that compiled a massive scrapbook of what was known of Mesopotamian visual culture at the time and earlier attempts at artistic reconstructions of Babylon (Seymour 2015, 23). Seymour (2015, 25–26) identifies the works of the nineteenth-century painters John Martin and Georges Rochegrosse as particularly influential. Edwin Long's *Babylonian Marriage Market*, based on Herodotus's account, is specifically referenced, according to Seymour (2015, 25), in a pivotal scene at the beginning of the film. Scholars of the era lauded Griffith's efforts: both A. H. Sayce and Morris Jastrow commended the director for his accuracy and attention to detail (Seymour 2015, 28), despite the fact that many of the influences for the set, costume, and prop design came from beyond Babylon and even Mesopotamia. The promotional use of Sayce and Jastrow as guarantors of academic authenticity imitates Charles Kean's use of Austen Henry Layard in his Victorian era promotional material and prefigures how films will come to rely on historical consultants, not so much for production advice as for advertising authenticity.

The archaeological history of Babylon is alluded to in Griffith's film in a scene where Belshazzar reports on his father's discoveries. The title card reads: "Belshazzar's father has a red-letter day. He excavates a foundation brick of the Temple of Naram-Sin, builded 2,300 years before." Babington and Evans (1993, 61) see this

> as a statement of the burgeoning ancient world epic's archaeological interests, its powerful (if limited) commitment to (at least external) historical authenticity, with royal amateur first watched by a film audience whose knowledge of the ancient world was primarily constituted through the way those categories of history analysed by Nietzsche, the "monumental," the "antiquarian," and the "ethical," interpreted the great mid-century archaeological discoveries at Nineveh, Mycenae, Nimrud, etc.

Griffith offers an almost post-modern nod to the source of his own knowledge about Mesopotamia, and the archaeological aesthetic will become one of the primary means for signaling both authenticity and spectacle to cinematic audiences.

Figure 4. Poster from *Cabiria* featuring the elephant-like architecture from the film. Library of Congress Prints and Photographs Division; Digital ID cph 3g13505.

Beyond the conflation of Babylonian and Assyrian material culture, Griffith's sets offer a hybridized generic Orientalist vision, with prominent elephant statues being the most explicit sign that material culture influences from beyond the Middle East were inspirational. David Shepherd (2013, 177–78) argues that the elephant statues in the Babylon of *Intolerance* were influenced by similar architectural features in Giovanni Pastrone's vision of Carthage in *Cabiria* (1914; fig. 4). Michael Seymour (2015, 33, n. 31) agrees, but quotes one of Griffith's researchers who remembers the director having demanded that his team find some kind of historical precedent to justify including elephants (despite the fact that elephants are not depicted in Babylonian art). The inclusion of elephants and other Asian flourishes situates Griffith's Babylon within a much older reception tradition, exemplified by Gustave Moreau's dream-like version of the ancient Near East, where classical and South Asian design was merged with what was known in his era of Egyptian and Near Eastern styles. For painters like Moreau, not enough material culture had yet been recovered from Mesopotamia to function as models for the types of scenes that they were interested in exploring. To fill in the gaps, they operated under the wider Orientalist assumption of the era that the cultures of the east were fundamentally monolithic. So even if painters knew that medieval India had a different visual culture than Mesopotamia, it still provided better models for an historicizing aesthetic than anything else.

Recourse to such eclecticism is not an uncommon solution in artistic situations where authentic visual culture is either not known or not iconic enough for the intended audience (Morcillo and Hanesworth 2015, 7). This Victorian Orientalist visual culture of the Near East shifts westward over the course of the twentieth century, at least in film. A cinematic mélange of the eastern Mediterranean and Near East emerged in Hollywood from the 1950s onward, inspired by Egyptian and Mesopotamian materials, as well as Minoan, Greek, and Roman styles. In the epic films of the 1960s, one can see Minoan frescoes, flanked by colossal bulls, with Egyptian and Greek columns. These design elements, all rooted in archaeologically attested exemplars but combined inaccurately, signified for viewers an aesthetic of historical verisimilitude. Films like *The Story of Ruth* (1960) offer a vision of an hybridized, generic preclassical and non-Egyptian ancient world where elements of Near Eastern and eastern Mediterranean culture are merged.

Griffith's eclectic architectural design had a longer afterlife beyond celluloid. After filming on *Intolerance* was completed, the set was moved to the corner of Sunset and Hollywood Boulevard in Los Angeles where it stood until 1919. Griffith had been unable to afford the demolition of the set himself but the Los Angeles Fire Department had declared it a hazard and by 1919 it had deteriorated substantially. Now Griffith's Assyrian and South Asian Babylon lives on in a shopping mall next to the Kodak Theatre in Hollywood. The Hollywood and Highland Center has a multistoried courtyard that intentionally evokes Griffith's vision of Babylon, with rearing gigantic elephants and the Assyrian-inspired façade built on a colossal scale (fig. 5). Egyptian design had come to be commonly invoked in entertainment and shopping complexes in the Victorian era, through a design schema that Carrott (1978, 34–35) has called the consumer picturesque, usually associated with some kind of architectural advertising. Mesopotamian themes are far less common in these settings than Egyptian, and are most notable in the Hollywood and Highland Center. When they are invoked, they tend to carry similar connotations as the Egyptian styles, although Mesopotamia is less often used

Figure 5. The Griffith-inspired Hollywood & Highland Center Shopping Mall. Adapted from an image by jpellgen (@1179_jp) flickr.

to signify monumentality and more often implies frivolity. Here is a modernist reaction to neoclassicism, where antiquity is still evoked, but an antiquity that departs from the architectural traditions of Greece and Rome. Near Eastern styles look interesting but the facades can be manufactured relatively cheaply and easily fit into existing architectural forms.

For many new types of structures of the late-nineteenth and early-twentieth centuries (like shopping malls and movie theaters), there were no set tropes for what these buildings should look like. The exotic signifies the liminality of the space and its public orientation, and as MacKenzie has argued (1995, 89), was part of a larger language of "pleasure and relaxation." The invocation of Mesopotamia tells the user of the space that this is a location where it is acceptable to ignore the norms of everyday life; it provides a kind of permission for hedonism because of Babylon's association with self-indulgence. The mall is a place where, the logic suggests, all of one's material fantasies can be enacted (and should be enacted) just as the movie theater allows vicarious daydreams to be experienced. This pleasure and relaxation is tied into cinema-going and shopping, both of which were intricately connected to ideas of progress (McGeough 2015b, 109, 242–43). Within this logic of design, the very ancient is claimed as a means of signifying that which is brand new and exciting. It provides a point of comparison (the beginnings of social complexity) marked through iconography that viewers can use to orient themselves and see their participation in shopping or film-going as a culmination of centuries of evolution. Mesopotamia, then, acts as both as an ancient juxtaposition against the most modern of activities (shopping and cinematic entertainment) as well as a signifier of the technocratic teleology in which shoppers and film-goers are participants.

3. *Italian "Sword and Sandal": Mesopotamia in the Post-War Epic*

From Griffith's era onwards, ancient epics became a staple of Hollywood cinema. However, a golden age of ancient epics is often thought to have been inaugurated by Cecil B. DeMille's *Samson and Delilah* (1949). That film, which is more an adaptation of nineteenth-century opera than the biblical book of Judges, offers a specifically postwar framing for ancient narratives. The films that followed based on biblical, classical, and even Egyptian stories, took the nineteenth-century operatic stories of lovers sacrificing themselves for nationalist purposes and reframed them for audiences who had just experienced similar sacrifices in World War II. DeMille made no attempt to hide that this was the purpose of his epic films. His reimagining of biblical stories into mid-twentieth century movies offered a kind of biblical interpretation that Hans Frei (1974) might categorize as premodern, for DeMille felt that biblical times were typological (Forshey 1992, 9). That is to say, events like the Exodus, in DeMille's view, were not only historical but were instructive for all later generations. That they were preserved in the Bible was explicitly so that later generations could continue to learn from those events. DeMille believed that the political history of the United States was part of God's divine plan and so by retelling the story of the Hebrews, he was also telling a story about the United States.[8]

Mesopotamia is not a particularly common setting in the Hollywood epic films of this era. It is really the Italian film industry that embraces Mesopotamian settings and sets epic cinema in Babylon and Nineveh. These films are often referred to as "sword and sandal" films and some film scholars will categorize the Mesopotamian films as "peplum" movies, although some hold that this designation needs to be reserved for Italian films about ancient Rome made from 1958 to 1968 (see Paul 2013, 22). The designation of films as such was initially derogatory, but this cinema has later come to be appreciated in its own right and not simply as a cheaper form of Hollywood epic filmmaking. The dubbing of the actors' voices, the use of the Italian countryside as a stand-in for any part of the ancient world, and the reuse of sets, props, and costumes, gave these movies a feeling of low production values. Despite budgetary constraints (and possibly because of them), these films offer an interesting fusing of the action and epic genres. For while the narratives often invoke the epic scope of the Hollywood films about antiquity, it is within this context that the "muscleman" film emerges, in which a muscle-bound protagonist engages in feats of action daring against armies of foes.

8. For more on this typological and metaphorical use of the Bible in American films of this era, see Reinhartz 2013, 36.

The 1962 Italian film *War Gods of Babylon* (*Le sette folgori di Assur*), directed by Silvio Amadio well represents the very particular Italian approach to ancient epic filmmaking of the era. As is expected for the genre, the Italian countryside stands in, as it often does, for the Mesopotamian floodplain and actors with dubbed voices engage in an operatic romantic plot intertwined with major historical events. In this case, it is two brothers (King Sardanapalus and Sammash) who find themselves lusting after the same woman, Mirra. She is a peasant girl whose entire village was recently destroyed and who is brought to Babylon by the prophet Zoroastro (Arnoldo Foà). The love triangle leads to war and Sammash is killed. Yet it is a flash flood that seals the doom of Assyria and the city of Nineveh is utterly destroyed by flooding, as is Sardanapalus and his court.

The final scene of the film shows the cult statue of Ashur being overwhelmed by water. The implication here is ambiguous. Are the filmmakers implying that this was the doom foreshadowed by the god through his prophet Zoroastro? Or, does this imply the end of Assyria and the worship of Ashur, a sort of teleological comment on the end of pagan times, as is typical of biblical films of the era (many foreshadow the later triumph of Christianity in their final sequences; see, e.g., *The Robe* [1953]). Have all of the romantic missteps been tied up in the destruction of the city? Or, are the events of the humans nothing compared to the fury of nature or the divine powers? The film is unusually ambiguous for the genre.

What is clear, however, is that the point of the film is to watch Nineveh get destroyed. The last half hour of the ninety minute film consists entirely of battle sequences and flood sequences. The battles are typical of the "sword and sandal" genre, where various archers, swordsman, cavalry, and chariots do battle with one another in sequences set in the countryside. The flood sequence here is more innovative for the genre. We first see the rains overwhelming the city's water system, eventually smashing through the city's fortifications. Sequence after sequence shows different ways that people in the city are able to die from flooding. This is the real appeal of the film; it builds on the same impulses that can be found in John Martin's paintings of Babylon's destruction and provides an early version of what will come to be a staple cinematic genre in the 1970s, the disaster film.

The filmmakers offer many nods to verism yet the confusion of times and historical figures is evident here. Zoroastro is not a Zoroastrian prophet but the name probably seemed ancient enough to the filmmakers. Sammash may be a rendering of the deity name Shammash but here is a human. The Babylonian envoy to Assyria is named Hammurabi, but he is not supposed to be the historical Amorite king. Myrrha is the name of the Greek slave in Byron's *Sardanapalus*, and so the character name here is likely not coincidental. Neo-Assyrian reliefs have clearly inspired much of the set and costume design. The soldiers wear the hats typical of the Iron Age soldiers depicted in Assyrian orthostats but also bear the leather armor that was likely previously used in a film set in ancient Rome. The walls of the city are also evocative of images in the reliefs.

Yet, the ornamentation of the architecture blends design from all periods. Babylonian baked bricks are interspersed with Moorish trim. One of the major episodes in the film is a royal lion hunt, obviously inspired by the royal lion hunt sequences in Assyrian art but reimagined to allow real danger for the protagonists.

Other elements refer to things Mesopotamian but again bear little resemblance to known historical behaviors. For example, Sammash lovingly states to Mirra, "Your eyes are like the eyes of Ishtar," a pick-up line that resembles what one might imagine hearing in the 1960s but adapted for historical fiction with a reference to a Mesopotamian divinity. Throughout, the film also presumes the Orientalism expected in representations of Mesopotamia. As is typical, all Eastern practices, through different times and places, are treated as the same. For example, Sammash must go through an ordeal in order to gain the kingship of Babylon and the ordeal chosen is for him to walk over hot coals, a type of ordeal that is typical of representations of South Asia, but is not attested in the investiture ceremonies of Neo-Assyrian times.

Following classical and dramatic traditions, Sardanapalus is associated with the final days of Nineveh. This poses some problems for the filmmakers, for the genre of the biblical epic requires the heroes to be noble and heroic yet many traditions surrounding Sardanapalus suggest that he was anything but.[9] For most of the film Sardanapalus plays a morally upright king. He does not commit adultery with his brother's wife, despite his desires. He is willing to listen to the prophet, rather than have him jailed or killed. Yet when he realizes that his city is to be lost in the flood, his character changes. He proclaims: "Those that belong to the king will perish with him." He forbids his subjects from fleeing the court and instead insists on a final Bacchanalian banquet. As his subjects gorge themselves on food while seeming to scream with fear, the king sets his palace on fire and takes his love, Mirra in his arms. Now that his brother is dead and his kingdom is falling, the two spend their last moments together in an embrace, a romantic and operatic death sequence in which the two lovers separated in life can spend their final moments together. Of course, none of this behavior makes sense given the story that leads up to this point, but it allows for a faithful presentation of the typical reception of Sardanapalus's Assyria, which in earlier art is destroyed by fire while the king and his court satiate themselves with decadent behavior.

The biblical epics of the 1960s often cast Mesopotamia, Egypt, and Rome as authoritarian empires. Which authoritarian empire varies, but usually the ideological presentation is vague enough that these ancient empires can represent Nazi Germany and Cold War era Soviet Union simultaneously. That viewers are expected to take the Assyria of *War Gods of Babylon* similarly is implied by the triumphal sequences that imitate those usually reserved for the Romans. In one of the early sequences, the Assyrian army marches into Nineveh in a parade-like fashion, with a triumphal militaristic soundtrack in the background. *War Gods*, however, spends little time on overt ideology.

---

9. However, see some exceptions noted by Hartmann in this volume.

Ideological divisions within Italy in the postwar years prevented filmmakers from making the kinds of clear political statements offered in American cinema of the era. What commentary is offered is through the prophecy of Zoroastro who argues for progressive governance, where the leaders of the state serve the people and not the other way around. King Sardanapalus is not necessarily against this but he is king in too early of a time and so Zoroastro's comments stand as Whiggish markers of progress yet to come.

Sardanapalus is not the only Mesopotamian character known from classical literature depicted on the silver screen. Semiramis, the legendary queen of Nineveh is the lead character in 1963's *Io Semiramide* (*Slave Queen of Babylon*), played by Yvonne Furneaux. This Italian film deviates greatly from the tale of the queen told by Diodorus, yet still retains some of the key literary elements. There is a sequence in which she disguises herself and sneaks out of the city of Nineveh to meet her love interest. She is credited with building Babylon, although Diodorus does not credit her with constructing the hanging gardens as is implied in this film.

As with *War Gods*, *Io Semiramide* spends little time reflecting overtly on contemporary ideology, at least in comparison to the typical "sword and sandal" epic of the era. However, a vision of Mesopotamian despotism that is typical of other films of the era is offered. Semiramis is the typical Oriental queen; she is completely immoral, unable to control her lust for men and power, and sexually irresistible to the men whom she encounters. She uses slaves in her various efforts, like the other leaders in the film; in this case, slaves are put to work to build the city of Babylon for her own edification. Semiramis does come to realize that slavery is wrong by the end of the film, but by that point her immoral plotting has sealed her fate. The kings with whom she interacts are even more depraved. They willingly execute their subjects for the mildest of offenses (like spilling wine at a banquet) and use horrific types of torture as their means of execution (such as setting men ablaze after dipping their extremities in oil, or slowly drowning them by fixing them to a moving water wheel). As with all of these films, there is a banquet sequence in which the elites recline like Romans and watch a scantily clad woman perform a belly dance with exotic music playing in the background. Most exemplary of cinematic oriental despotism, however, is the consistent infighting amongst the rulers. The plot of *Io Semiramide* is difficult to keep straight since the various lead characters make and break alliances with one another seemingly at random, with little motivation. All of this, however, adds up to a general view of ancient Near Eastern leadership as violent, depraved, unstable, and immoral, contributing to the "otherness" that cinematic epics present as a foil for contemporary life.

Yvonne Furneaux was not the first actress to portray Semiramis. The legendary queen was also played by Rhonda Fleming in 1954's *Queen of Babylon* (*La cortigiana di Babilonia*), another Italian film, which also starred Ricardo Montalban as the Chaldean king Ahmal. Semiramis here is not the queen who built Babylon, but rather a shepherdess who helps Ahmal fight against King Assur, conqueror of Babylon. Through the course of the film, Semiramis becomes part of Assur's harem and eventually becomes the queen of Babylon. Here the film follows a typical operatic style plot and the film presents a Mesopotamia that is visually much in keeping with that of the other Italian cinematic representations of the Near East. In these operatic plots, the lead characters love each other but are kept apart by the politics of the day. At one point Semiramis must agree to marry in order to keep Ahmal safe. Of course, Ahmal, not realizing the goal of her sacrifice takes Semiramis's betrothal as a sign that she does not love him. For postwar viewers of such films, the subordination of one's own romantic life for the good of the state must have reflected and celebrated their own recent sacrifices. Whereas the nineteenth-century opera of Italy, France, and Germany helped celebrate the new (or newly reconstituted nation-states), the same types of plots could be easily repurposed for the generation who had just suffered through World War II.

Related to the Italian "sword and sandal" films of the 1960s were the various Hercules films where the demigod as muscleman engaged in bare-chested battles with foes of different types. The first of these was Pietro Francisci's 1958 *Hercules* (*Le fatiche di Ercole*), which, as Derek Elley has argued, offered the same kinds of confusions about the mythological character in cinematic form as are found in the classical sources (Elley 1984, 55). Given the film's financial success, in part based on its low budget and reuse of sets, costumes, and props from bigger budget "sword and sandal" films, the 1960s saw a yearly output of Hercules films, made with different directors and different actors (Solomon 2001, 15). The demigod encountered Mesopotamian civilization in 1964's *Hercules and the Tyrants of Babylon* (*Ercole contro i tiranni di Babilonia*), directed by Domenico Paolella and starring Peter Lupus (credited as Rock Stevens) in the lead role (fig. 6). Far from the most successful entry in the franchise, this was the only Hercules film that Peter Lupus would star in, although he did play Goliath in 1965's *Goliath at the Conquest of Damascus* and Spartacus in that same year's *Challenge of the Gladiators*. *Hercules and the Tyrants of Babylon* was never given a theatrical release in the United States; it was distributed directly as a television movie, where it became a staple of Saturday afternoon cinema.

As with other films featuring Babylon, the ancient city is rebuilt on screen only to be destroyed. The final sequences of this film feature the systematic destruction of the city, and the film concludes when the city and its people are no more. This destruction, however, is particularly well-suited for a Hercules film and the demigod himself is the main force behind its destruction. He does so by rotating a gigantic wheel that lies beneath the city, within its catacombs, reflecting Cold War anxieties about the potential for wide-scale destruction offered by human made devices. This is a device built by Daedalus, the same Daedalus who built the Labyrinth on Crete, we are told. Babylon, in this film, is a city built entirely on a foundation of sand. By spinning this contraption, Hercules undermines these foundations and the city's buildings crumble into the ground. As they do, fires start throughout the city, and people sink into the ground or are crushed by falling structures. The city is finished off by an invading army, in this case by the horse-based cavalry of the Assyrians.

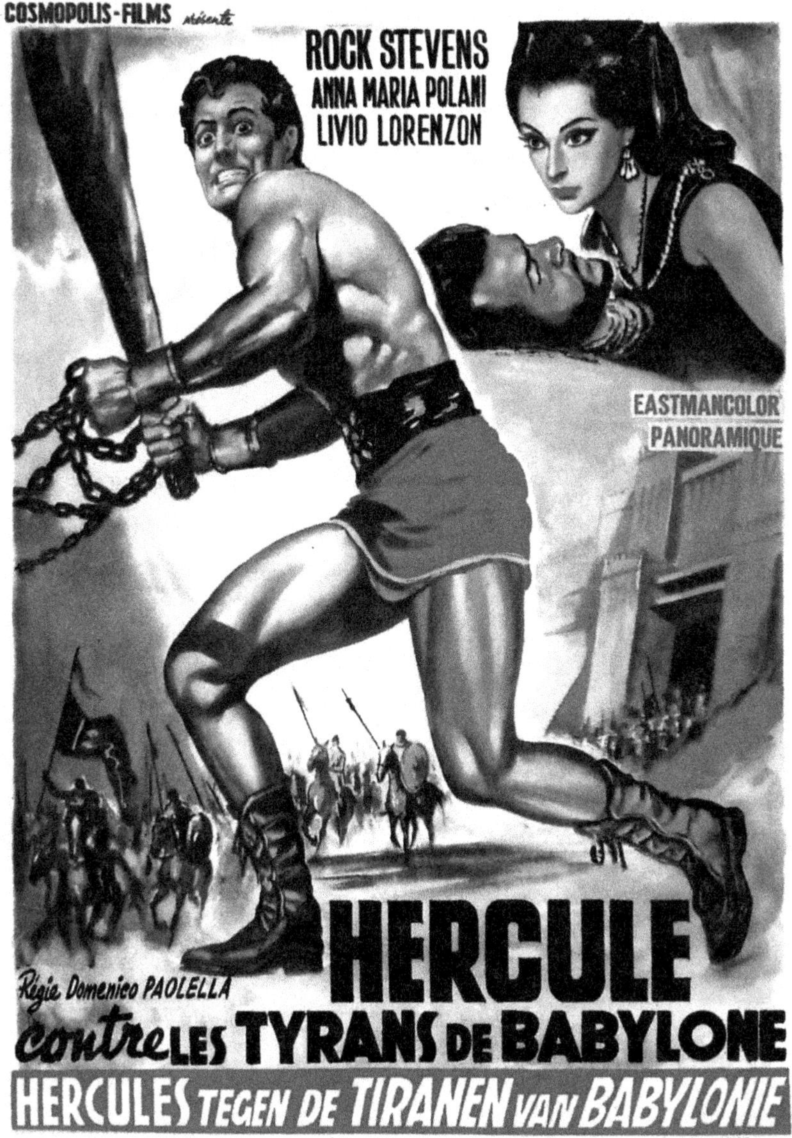

Figure 6. Poster from *Hercules and the Tyrants of Babylon* (1964).

Hercules spins this wheel because he has been tricked by the evil queen of Babylon, Taneal (Helga Liné), who rules the city with her two siblings but wants to be sole ruler of Mesopotamia. She tells Hercules that the wheel just opens a bronze door, behind which lies the treasure of Babylon and he, aware that she desires personal gain, finds this plausible. However, her plans are more complex. Taneal thinks that by destroying the city, she will kill her siblings, and then take over leadership of the region from the rival city of Nineveh. The rulers of Babylon are despots, competing for power and the fact that each of these siblings wants to be sole ruler, plotting and scheming against the others, is what seals Babylon's doom. Each sibling represents a different stereotype of the despotic eastern ruler. Taneal is the sexually provocative, exotically beautiful, but morally corrupt eastern temptress. Salmanassar (Livio Lorenzon) is the bold warrior who wants to fight his way to power. Assur (Tullio Altamura) is the oldest and most conservative of the three, who wants to build an empire through careful plotting. All three find themselves at odds with the King of Assyria, Malik (Mario Petri), whose leadership is centered in Nineveh.[10] The immorality of the tyrannical rulers and competition with other Mesopotamian polities are the real reasons for Babylon's downfall, which is consistent with other cinematic and dramatic receptions of the end of Mesopotamian cities.

The aesthetic presentation of Babylon in this film also evokes some of the typical visual tropes. There are references to Neo-Assyrian style, most explicitly in the winged sphinxes that flank the thrones of the leaders of Babylon. A more curious element of the palace set is the stained glass window, bearing a lamassu. Here the Assyrian is fused with a media typical of later Christian churches, referencing the biblical context but marking Assyria as different. The exterior shots of the buildings are also somewhat like earlier interpretations of Assyrian structures, with architectural ornamentation that reflects that found on Neo-Assyrian reliefs. However, the actual structures seem more reminiscent of Pieter Bruegel the Elder's 1563 and Lucas van Valckenborch's 1594 imaginings of the Tower of Babel. The tiered structures and circular frames of the buildings in the film seem rooted in that stream of Babylonian reception.

Also unsurprising are the Orientalist tropes that are present in both the aesthetics and plot of the film. The Assyrian army looks like it is right out of David Lean's 1962 *Lawrence of Arabia*; this is a cavalry-based military, all in flowing black robes and keffiyahs. Babylon is filled with Oriental markets where various venders in elaborate headscarves attempt to sell their wares. The Oriental banquet scene, however, is uniquely adapted to suit a Hercules film. The feast is presented as is typical of such films but the entertainment is not dancing girls. Rather, it features Hercules fighting various champions from around the world and plays out like wrestling entertainment of the twentieth century.

Hercules and the Tyrants of Babylon is also filled with classical references as one would imagine, given the hybridized subject matter. In plot, the initial framing of the story seems to reflect the Roman story of the rape of the Sabines. The Assyrians have kidnapped a number of women (including Queen Asperia of the Hellenes) as slaves. They plan to repopulate Babylonia by taking these Greek slave women as their wives. Beyond other plot points that one might associate with Hercules, there is a larger hy-

10. The actual names of the characters vary in the dubbed English-language version, making for some confusing moments in the film.

brid aesthetic that is typical of the films of this era, in which Near Eastern styles are fused with those of the Mediterranean. Some of this may reflect the reuse of costumes from other films; the Babylonian army wears what are essentially Roman legionnaire outfits except for Assyrian style helmets. Yet there are also subtle references to Minoan, Greek, and Roman architecture intended as veristic elements for the antique settings. This tendency is more pronounced in the Hollywood films of the era, for which we can perhaps speak of a generalized preclassical cinematic material culture.

Much of what has already been noted about *Hercules and the Tyrants of Babylon* holds true for the earlier *Goliath and the Sins of Babylon* (1963). There is little of the Bible in *Goliath and the Sins of Babylon* despite the name; much of the film, however, reflects the same kinds of classical reception of Babylon that have already been mentioned. The film offers a hybridistic view of the ancient Near East, the classical world, and even medieval times, all refracted through a strongman lens. Goliath in this film is not a Philistine villain but an itinerant hero who in this case helps a city rebel against a tyrannical Babylon.

It is to classical literature that most of the film refers. The marriage of ancient story and strongman narrative is readily accomplished through gladiatorial combat and this Roman institution makes its way into the film. Strangely, Goliath stumbles upon a group of insurgents pretending to train as gladiators but really training for armed rebellion. The conceit allows for a combat sequence well in keeping with the style of the genre. Similarly, the naval battles take place on a supposedly Phoenician trireme, no doubt the leftover sets from another peplum film. Perhaps most directly based on classical literature is the subplot through which Goliath (Mark Forest) is made king of a city under the subjugation of Babylonians by winning a chariot race. By winning the race, he wins the hand of Regia/Chelima (José Greci), reminiscent of how Pelops won the hand of Hippodamia in classical myth. Even the Orientalist stylings are in some ways referenced through the Greco-Roman world for the king of Babylon wears a costume inspired by Darius's, as depicted in the Alexander mosaic from the House of the Faun at Pompeii.

That being said, there are also typical Orientalist trappings in this film. There are banquet scenes although these are far tamer than the promotional material for the film implies. The poster for the American release shows women dressed in belly-dancing garb chained to cages in bondage (fig. 7). The poster bears two slogans: "See the Thousand and One Orgies of Torture" and "The Nights of Pleasure ... The Days of Terror." Both imply the kind of carnal excitement imagined in Orientalist fantasy; the film is far tamer. Clearly the name of the film and the poster all hoped to draw in viewers for the kind of erotic Orientalism that this film really does not offer. Therein lies the urgency to reference Babylon, which by the 1960s bore connotations of unbounded sex and violence for American B-cinema audiences.

The villainous leaders of Babylon are more explicitly drawn from nineteenth-century Orientalism. The rulers are cruel and vicious sadomasochists who torture for their

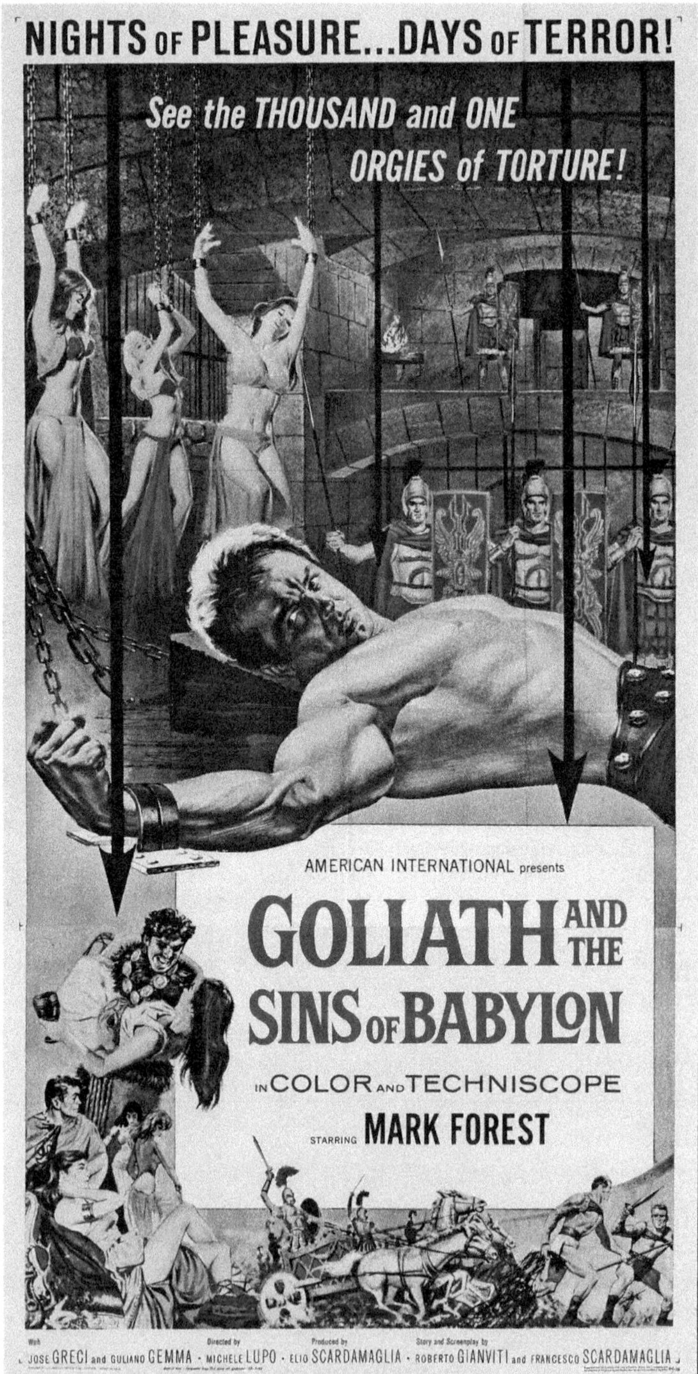

Figure 7. Poster for *Goliath and the Sins of Babylon*.

own amusement. They are corrupt and fight amongst themselves, plotting to murder one another and usurp the power of the king. The city that Goliath fights on behalf of was forced to agree to a peace treaty with the Babylonians. The only term that is explicated in the film is that every year thirty virgins must be sent to the Babylonian king, so that he could kill them for his own amusement. The power of the Oriental king to kill for entertainment is a well-established Orientalist trope and while there is little evidence for a Babylonian king acting in such a fashion, audiences would have little trouble accepting that such behavior was engaged in by the historical Other.

The torture devices used by the Babylonians to test Goliath's strength likewise reference Orientalist tyranny but in this case bear more of a resemblance to medieval torture devices. Using leftover sets and costumes from other films enhances the hybridistic elements of the film. The sets are mostly medieval in appearance, with dungeons, cast-iron portcullis doors, and torches fixed to the walls of the structures. Here are sets that are obviously being reused but this is more meaningful than just the economics of the Italian film industry, for the consistent reuse of sets and costumes from different periods perpetuates a more generic premodern aesthetic that could not help but influence viewers, even though this particular film made no claims to verism. There are some efforts to situate the film within an archaeological Babylon. The Babylonian soldiers bear the helmets known from Assyrian reliefs although the spike on top seems more akin to World War I era Germany than Mesopotamian. Scenes from the Assyrian reliefs are painted as giant frescoes in the architecture of the Babylonian palace. These are unconvincing archaeologically; the ornamentation seems to be directly copied from Giulia Ferrari's encyclopedia of historical design, *Gli stili nella forma e nel colore dalle origini al rinascimento* (1925) with little effort to place the forms in a veristic material context.

And of course, Babylon is destroyed at the end of *Goliath and the Sins of Babylon*. In this case a cavalry torches the city and the viewer watches individual buildings consumed by fire. As it burns, the king proclaims that the city was destined to be burnt and then his corrupt advisor murders him. Here the film ventures into the mildly political, for Babylon's predestined doom is juxtaposed with Goliath's own western sense of governance. For at the end of the film Goliath refuses to take on the role of king, even though he has rightly won it through his chariot skills. He explains that he was not chosen by the people and therefore his leadership is not legitimate. That the hero of the film should anachronistically espouse democratic values is not novel to *Goliath*; this is usually far more overt in biblical and classical epics of the era.[11] That they would manifest in a B-film such as this points to how dependent the genre of the historical epic is upon teleological visions of democracy emerging from the tyranny of Egypt, Mesopotamia, and Rome.

11. For more on the relationship between epic filmmaking and arguments related to democracy, see Elley 1984, 6; and Reinhartz 2013, 97.

4. *Writing on the Walls: Babylon in Twenty-First-Century Christian Cinema*

Whereas the older epics were aimed at wide audiences, the emergence of a distinctly evangelical Christian audience in the 2000s led to the presentation of Babylon through less of a classical lens and more of a biblical one. The classical stories of Babylon and the characters known from Greek sources, such as Sardanapalus and Semiramis were replaced by kings like Belshazzar and characters like the biblical prophet Daniel. As part of its "movie ministry," Pure Flix Entertainment produced its own version of *The Book of Daniel* (2013), featuring Robert Miano as an older Daniel telling of his exploits in Babylon to the Persian King Cyrus (Lance Henrikson). This was a direct-to-video and streaming service film targeted at conservative American Christian communities. That it would likely be seen in a ministry setting is made apparent by the notice at the beginning of the DVD describing the licensing rights within that context. Given the intended audience of *The Book of Daniel*, a veristic ethos was not necessary. There was no need to convince the audience of the historicity of the narrative nor would the audience be concerned with archaeological accuracy. Rather, films such as *The Book of Daniel* are intended as narrative reimaginings of scripture. This may seem counterintuitive, given the emphasis on the literality of scripture by this community in political discourse, but these films are not part of that public conversation. Unlike the biblical epics of the 1960s, in which the plausibility of scriptural miracles was made apparent to mainstream audiences by the special effects of DeMille and others, the evangelical film industry need not be concerned with such argumentation, and audiences, more sophisticated in their knowledge of special effects, are less likely to be convinced by such logic anyways (McGeough 2017). The filmmakers need to find a balance between biblical accuracy, cinematic presentation, and adapting the values of the Old Testament originals to better reflect the values of the contemporary community.

There are some "Assyrian" elements, however. The soldiers wear pointed helmets, reminiscent of those from the older biblical epics. The film opens with a still photograph of an Assyrian relief. In the actual film, however, these reliefs are painted frescoes, much like those found in *Goliath and the Sins of Babylon*. The overarching aesthetic is a merger of the renaissance and the orientalist. Much of the *mis en scène* reflects the recreation of biblical scenes in the paintings of the renaissance through the end of the eighteenth century. The kings wear crowns reminiscent of European monarchs; the dungeon that Daniel finds himself in is that of a European-style castle. Characters wear brightly colored robes, typical of the art of that era. The props and sets likewise reflect this era of biblical reception. Perhaps this is due to the low budget of such films, and like the older Italian peplum films, the props, sets, and costumes here are merely reused. Regardless, by filming ancient Babylon as a medieval European-style setting, the filmmakers are offering a vision of the biblical world that will look comfortably familiar to its audience, who will have a varying but at least passing familiarity of this kind of biblical reception.

The Orientalist trappings are arguably more problematic. As I have argued elsewhere (McGeough 2017), the ancient Near East as portrayed in these films aimed at American protestants offer disturbingly static visions of the Middle East. In *The Book of Daniel*, there is little effort to distinguish between Assyria, Babylonia, Persia, the Ottoman Empire, or the contemporary Middle East. This film offers the typical Orientalist clichés like tyrannical despots, and lavish banquet and harem scenes, although made chaste to suit the tastes of this particular audience. The Judeans, as is common in biblical reception, are dressed as nineteenth-century Bedouin, and inhabit tents much like those found in tourist traps in Israel, Jordan, and Egypt today. Derek Gregory (2004) has shown that this understanding of the region in static terms has had significant implications for American foreign policy in the region. The audiences who will appreciate this film may not be thinking explicitly about the contemporary Middle East but it is highly likely that they will internalize Orientalist messages about the Middle East, which are seemingly sanctioned by the biblical context and authority of such a film.[12]

Perhaps most problematic about *The Book of Daniel* is that the narrative is structured around Daniel's religious conversion of four kings. Daniel's religion is not really presented as Judaism in this film; it is really a kind of cinematic proto-Christianity. The biblical book of Daniel consists of six individual stories about the exploits of Daniel and others in exilic Babylon followed by a description of his apocalyptic vision. This film, which has a title that is meant to frame the film as literarily accurate, restructures the narrative so that Daniel tells these biblical stories so that each of them culminates with the conversion of a pagan king. Here then, the prophet Daniel plays a different role than in the Bible but following earlier traditions is taken as a pre-Christian "worthy." In this film he works as a missionary, converting foreign, non-Christian tyrants to the worship of God. Thus Babylon stands in for the contemporary Middle East and unlike in other cinematic receptions of Babylon, the ancient city is not destroyed but is saved through Daniel's missionary efforts. Christianity is presented as the cure for the ills of the Middle East and historical/biblical precedent is offered as evidence.

Similar trends are recognizable in Mark Burnett's miniseries *The Bible*. Babylon features prominently in episode 5, which depicts the Judean exile to that city. In that series, with its larger budget and greater production values, the filmmakers are better

12. This is not unique to *The Book of Daniel*. Alexander the Great (1956), while obviously dealing with the Babylon of the Persian era, exemplifies the representations of Mesopotamia in the cinema of this period. It is treated as a destroyed empire, one of the many from the region that appear in palimpsest form amongst the material culture of more recent times. The discoveries of Layard make an appearance in this film, such as a golden three-dimensional version of the relief of the being Layard designated as Nisroch. When in Babylon, Darius sits on a throne surrounded by colorful reliefs and sculptures that replicate those from Neo-Assyrian art. Partially this reflects the conflation of Persian and Mesopotamian material culture that is common in nonspecialist treatments. Yet the palimpsest-like treatment also offers a reading of the Middle East that it and its peoples have remained relatively static from antiquity to the present.

able to attempt a veristic archaeological aesthetic. Yet despite the ability to do so, the filmmakers make little effort to recreate a recognizable Mesopotamian visual culture beyond the use of those signifiers that have been in use since the 1960s. The Babylonian soldiers wear pointed helmets and the CGI recreation of Babylon features the Ishtar Gate prominently. Yet there is also the typical blending of classical, Orientalist, and medieval props, sets, and costumes that conveys a generic ancient place rather than an historically specific one. In this series, though, Babylon is not destroyed. Cyrus's troops are shown riding to the gates of the city, but they are let in without a fight.

The Bible departs from other cinematic depictions of the ancient Near East by the explicit, purposeful multiracial casting. Judeans are sometimes dressed, as is typical of cinematic representations, like nineteenth-century Bedouin. Yet some of the actors, especially the women, wear garb that reflects the fashions of the contemporary Middle East. African-American and East Asian actors play the roles of Judeans and Mesopotamians. Here *The Bible* makes the Bible into a story that reflects the diversity of American Protestantism yet still situates the stories within an historical context. The depiction of Nebuchadnezzar is interesting, for the filmmakers have to balance the historical realist aesthetic of the series with the portrayal of the king's madness in Daniel. He is made to look like a menacing "other"; he and Cyrus both wear heavy amounts of eye makeup to give an appearance of exotic difference, a kind of feminization that is typical of orientalist depictions that still allows for the characters to be violent in countenance. Nebuchadnezzar also sports a "unibrow," a seeming nod to Sumerian depictions of individuals.

5. *Conclusions*

Monty Python's 1979 *Life of Brian* featured little of Mesopotamian culture except for the opening credit sequence. There, English words were rendered in a kind of cuneiform font and Neo-Assyrian sculptures were shown briefly in a subtle history of the Near East montage. There, the impression of Babylon as a collapsed culture was reified. Mesopotamia is presented as part of a palimpsest of preclassical civilizations, signifying the rise and fall of ancient empires. That this is done only in passing is meaningful for it shows how powerfully entrenched this reading of Mesopotamia has become. In most of the films surveyed here, Babylon exists to be destroyed. A combination of natural disasters, immoral/corrupt leadership, and non-Christian behavior lead to the destruction of these Mesopotamian cities, cinematically. The presentation is almost typological for we see characters with the values of our own time interacting with these ancients and we see that destruction of Mesopotamia was inevitable. Here the premodern interpretations of Mesopotamia are lifted directly from nineteenth-century reception; even the material culture that works as set dressing and argument for authenticity changes little from the days of Kean's spectaculars. Yet the messages about contemporary life that are embedded within the diegesis do change and are historically specific to the age of the artists who create them. Audiences witness social and political structures that they find disagreeable obliterated with Babylon and the triumph of the values of their own time (i.e., liberal democracy in the 1950s, American Evangelical Christianity in the 2000s) is prefigured through these ancient catastrophes.

What is problematic here is not just the mimetic/solipsistic interaction with the past that is facilitated through these viewing experiences. It is disconcerting because ruminations on the present are mistaken by audiences for actual experiences of historical otherness. There may be more disturbing implications though, especially in a period of history when nativism and fear of the other seems to be on the rise, and academic beliefs of the Victorian era are mistaken as fundamental truths. One of the key features of nineteenth-century Orientalist visions of the region is the timelessness of cultural practices and behaviors. By recreating an ancient Mesopotamia that is doomed to destruction and fetishizing those moments of the obliteration of the city, are filmmakers arguing that these kind of destructive cycles are natural to the regions? Perhaps not explicitly, but the narrative cinematic culture cannot help but be influenced by and reify other media representations of the region. Celebrating Babylon's inevitable-seeming destruction in cinema may have actual real-life implications for the policy decisions made about the region today.

Bibliography

Babington, B., and P. W. Evans. 1993. *Biblical Epics: Sacred Narrative in the Hollywood Cinema*. Manchester: Manchester University Press.

Bohrer, F. 2003. *Orientalism and Visual Culture: Imagining Mesopotamia in Nineteenth-Century Europe*. Cambridge: Cambridge University Press.

Carrott, R. G. 1978. *The Egyptian Revival: Its Sources, Monuments, and Meanings*. Berkeley: University of California Press.

Elley, D. 1984. *The Epic Film: Myth and History*. London: Routledge & Kegan Paul.

Forsehy, G. E. 1992. *American Religious and Biblical Spectaculars*. Media and Society Series. Westport, CT: Praeger.

Frei, H. 1974. *The Eclipse of Biblical Narrative: A Study of Eighteenth and Nineteenth Century Hermeneutics*. New Haven: Yale University Press.

Gregory, D. 2004. *The Colonial Present: Afghanistan, Palestine, Iraq*. New York: Blackwell.

Kean, C. 1853. *Sardanapalus, King of Assyria: A Tragedy, by Lord Byron, Adapted for Representation by Charles Kean*. London: T.H. Lacy.

Long, B. O. 2006. "The Circus." In J. Sawyer (ed.), *The Blackwell Companion to the Bible and Culture*. Blackwell Reference Online. New York: Blackwell.

MacKenzie, J. M. 1995. *Orientalism: History, Theatre, and the Arts*. Manchester: Manchester University Press.

Malley, S. 2007. "Theater/Archaeology: Performing Material History in Charles Kean's Adaptation of *Sardanapalus*." *Nineteenth-Century Studies* 21:139–61.

———. 2012. *From Archaeology to Spectacle in Victorian Britain*. Surrey: Ashgate.

McGeough, K. M. 2015a. *The Ancient Near East in the Nineteenth Century: Appreciations and Appropriations; I. Claiming and Conquering*. Hebrew Bible Monographs 67. Sheffield: Sheffield Phoenix.

———. 2015b. *The Ancient Near East in the Nineteenth Century: Appreciations and Appropriations;*

II. Collecting, Constructing, and Curating. Hebrew Bible Monographs 68. Sheffield: Sheffield Phoenix.

———. 2015c. *The Ancient Near East in the Nineteenth Century, Appreciations and Appropriations; III. Fantasy and Alternative Histories*. Hebrew Bible Monographs 69. Sheffield: Sheffield Phoenix.

———. 2017. "Celluloid Esther: The Literary Carnivalesque as Transformed Through the Lens of the Cinematic Epic." *Journal of the Bible and Its Reception* 4:91–123.

Meisel, M. 1983. *Realizations: Narrative, Pictorial, and Theatrical Arts in Nineteenth- Century England*. Princeton: Princeton University Press.

Morcillo, M., and P. Hanesworth. 2015. "Introduction: Cinematic Cityscapes and the Ancient Past." In M. Morcillo, P. Hanesworth, and Ó. Marchena (eds), *Imagining Ancient Cities in Film: From Babylon to Cinecittà*, 1–17. New York: Routledge.

Paul, J. 2013. *Film and the Classical Epic Tradition*. Oxford: Oxford University Press.

Reinhartz, A. 2013. *Bible and Cinema: An Introduction*. New York: Routledge.

Seymour, M. 2015. "The Babylon of D.W. Griffith's *Intolerance*." In M. Morcillo, P. Hanesworth, and Ó. Marchena (eds.), *Imagining Ancient Cities in Film: From Babylon to Cinecittà*, 18–34. New York: Routledge.

Shepherd, D. J. 2013. *The Bible on Silent Film: Spectacle, Story and Scripture in the Early Cinema*. Cambridge: Cambridge University Press.

Solomon, J. 2001. *The Ancient World in the Cinema*, revised and expanded edition. New Haven: Yale University Press.

Ziter, E. 2003. *The Orient on the Victorian Stage*. Cambridge: Cambridge University Press.

Filmography

Alexander the Great. 1956. Directed by Robert Rossen. USA: C.B. Films.

The Bible (TV miniseries). 2013. Produced by Roma Downey and Mark Burnett. USA: Lightworkers Media.

The Book of Daniel. 2013. Directed by Anna Zielinski. USA: Pure Flix Entertainment.

Cabiria. 1914. Directed by Giovanni Pastore. Italy: Itala Film.

Challenge of the Gladiators. 1965. Directed by Domenico Paolella. Italy: Jonia Film.

Goliath and the Sins of Babylon. 1963. Directed by Michele Lupo. Italy: Leone Film.

Goliath at the Conquest of Damascus. 1965. Directed by Domenico Paolella. Italy: Romana Film.

Hercules (*Le fatiche di Ercole*). 1958. Directed by Pietro Francisci. Italy: Embassy Pictures.

Hercules and the Tyrants of Babylon (*Ercole contro i tiranni di Babilonia*). 1964. Directed by Domenico Paolella. Italy: Romana Film.

Intolerance: Love's Struggle Through the Ages. 1916. Directed by D. W. Griffith. USA: Triangle Film Corporation.

Lawrence of Arabia. 1962. Directed by David Lean. UK: Horizon Pictures.

Life of Brian. 1979. Directed by Terry Jones. Handmade Films.

The Queen of Babylon (*La cortigiana di Babilonia*). 1954. Directed by Carlo Ludovico Bragaglia. Italy: Panthéon Productions.

The Robe. 1953. Directed by Henry Koster. USA: Twentieth Century Fox.

Samson and Delilah. 1949. Directed by Cecil B. DeMille. USA: Paramount Pictures.

Slave Queen of Babylon (*Io Semiramide*). 1963. Directed by Primo Zeglio. Italy: APO Film.

The Story of Ruth. 1960. Directed by Henry Koster. USA: Twentieth Century Fox.

The Ten Commandments. 1923. Directed by Cecil B. DeMille. USA: Paramount Pictures.

War Gods of Babylon (*Le sette folgori di Assur*). 1962. Directed by Silvio Amadio. Italy: APO Film.

He Who Saw the Stars

Retelling Gilgamesh in Star Trek: The Next Generation

Eva Miller

This chapter examines one seemingly small example of Mesopotamian penetration into popular culture: an appearance of the Gilgamesh mythos in one episode of *Star Trek: The Next Generation* (hereafter, and in accordance with fan terminology, *TNG*), retold by Captain Jean-Luc Picard in a pivotal moment of his encounter with an alien Other. Although the retelling, in actor Patrick Stewart's ringing theatrical voice, takes only a few minutes, it fundamentally transforms how the episode, the particularly popular and well-regarded "Darmok" (1991), and arguably the wider Star Trek (hereafter ST) universe, should be read. In a larger sense, it is also incredibly revealing of how Gilgamesh myths have been received and creatively reused in modern popular cultures, in this case as part of a "world literature" inheritance in which it is both strange and familiar.

"Darmok" tells the story of an encounter by the U.S.S. Enterprise with an alien race that communicates only in metaphor, through allusions to foundational myths of their own culture, each generating complex meanings indecipherable to those unfamiliar with their cultural touchstones. It is, then, a story of coming to an alien encounter as we all come to the ancient past. As will be explored in greater detail below, the episode finds the hero Picard trapped on a desolate planet through the machinations of this incomprehensible yet, it soon becomes clear, not hostile, Other. To understand and ultimately befriend the alien counterpart with whom he is stranded, to escape the planet, and finally to produce a productive and peaceful "first contact," Picard must reach into Earth's collective memory for a foundational myth of its own: the story of Gilgamesh and Enkidu. The retelling of Gilgamesh here is part of the episode's wider engagement with the question of reception and retelling of ancient and unfamiliar myths, the means by which they are deciphered, and the purposes for which they are reused—topics that I want to explore here.

This chapter examines that episode in detail and conducts from it a case study in how reception of the ancient Near East has been used to generate new meanings in the modern day. This necessarily involves a free-handed engagement with the ancient Gilgamesh—although Gilgamesh has himself always been a composite of so many different retellings across media that there is no violation of one canonical myth involved in this approach.[1] I would like to understand Picard's retelling of Gilgamesh as part of the ongoing life of the character and to think about how such a flexibility has always been part of the mythic figures Gilgamesh and Enkidu.

In this study, I take a cue from Sarah Iles Johnston's recent work on narrative in the Greek "mythic story world" (2015a, 2015b, 2017). Johnston has employed theories of narrative and reader interaction to understand how ancient myths helped to create and sustain belief. Some of the key characteristics of mythic narratives that she argues achieve this are: plurimediality, that is, appearance in multiple media (Johnston 2015b, 206–10; 2017, 151–54);[2] and seriality, the ongoing, usually episodic and often interconnected nature of individual events and narratives within the story-world (Johnston 2015b, 201–6; 2017, 148–50; 2015a, 297–98). These features encourage audience engagement and the development of "parasocial" relationships with the mythic figures (Johnston 2015b, 196–201; 2017, 144–48). These are "one-sided" relationships of one figure to another who knows nothing of them or does not return their thoughts or imagined interactions. Though initially identified in terms of those with unhealthy delusions about such relationships, it was soon recognized that these are normal ways of relating to others (celebrities, politicians, or admired but distant crushes), and more recently that people form equally intense parasocial relationships with fictional characters as with real people, with cognitive processes that function in similar ways (Giles 2010). Such a concept helps us to understand the "reality" of mythic characters like Gilgamesh and Enkidu for ancient Mesopotamians as something we recognize and experience ourselves. Certainly anyone with even a passing familiarity with the ST fan base will know that intense parasocial relationships with the fictional characters of the ST franchise are a defining feature of "Trekkie" fan culture.[3] Johnston's work offers a fruitful paradigm for thinking about why and how we might study the myths and literature of the ancient world in comparison to and in relation with contemporary texts. The concept of a "story world" as she elaborates it (2015a, 285–88; drawing on ideas first formulated by Tolkien 1947), is highly relevant both to Gilgamesh myths and to ST.

---

1. For a wide overview of Gilgamesh in pop culture, particularly film, with a brief discussion of ST as well, see Turri in this volume.

2. This certainly applies to both Gilgamesh and ST. Plurimediality for Gilgamesh: oral and written literature of various types as well as worked objects of various types. For ST: cinematic, televisual, written, and graphic media, and various types of worked objects.

3. As Johnston (2015b, 196–98) makes clear, however, not only mega-fans will recognize the experience of forming such parasocial relationships. In other words, it doesn't take a full Starfleet uniform and excellent spoken Klingon to qualify: anyone who has ever speculated on what a fictional character might do in a particular situation, felt sad about their deaths, or worried for their (fictional) wellbeing can understand this emotional phenomenon.

The Gilgamesh myth has a long and varied history, with the earliest, disconnected and episodic Sumerian "Bilgamesh" stories likely originating in the late third millennium (George 2003, 7–17). The version discussed in "Darmok" is a modified form of the Standard Babylonian version, likely canonized in the late second millennium BCE (George 2003, 28–33). Gilgamesh, Enkidu, and the monsters they fought were also figures with whom individuals interacted as statues, as engravings, on seals, or suddenly encountered in the entrails of animals, and presumably as figures with whom one might have had a very close parasocial relationship, whose stories informed numerous aspects of daily life (George 2003, 91–148; Graff 2013; Lambert 1987; Howard-Carter 1983, 69–71; Steymans 2010). During the reign of Shulgi, at the very beginning of known Bilgamesh/Gilgamesh narratives (Michalowski 2008, 36–37), as at the late Neo-Assyrian court, the Gilgamesh myths were embedded in discourses about royal power and knowledge, with parallels to discrete elements of the mythology discernible in royal narratives, particularly during the reign of Ashurbanipal (Collins 2016, 48–50; Bonatz 2004, 100). The interaction with characters as meaningful exemplars of certain ideals, whose stories can be understood in various ways and used as parallels that operate on multiple levels is not something that "Darmok" brings to Gilgamesh for the first time, but rather an element of the relationship the mythos has had with its receivers for as long as it has existed.[4] Thus, while it could be said that Picard's retelling of the Gilgamesh-Enkidu story is "incorrect" (as will be seen, it conflates or erases elements of the Mesopotamian stories), this designation is not meaningful and would not have been meaningful in ancient contexts.

The ST universe is often spoken of in terms of "mythology" as well. This term is used by fans for the story and world-building of all narrative worlds, mostly applied to "genre" fiction. In this case, it is a particularly useful term for the franchise given the many narrative and contextual properties it shares with myth-worlds. The original *Star Trek* was created by Gene Roddenberry and first broadcast between 1966 and 1969. After its premature cancellation the franchise lived on, in novels, in an animated series, and in fans' imaginations. Eventually six feature films with the original cast would be produced. *TNG*, first aired in 1987 under the guidance of the aging Roddenberry and ending in 1994 (after a series of other executive producers), represented the first revival of the series as a live-action television serial, with a new cast and an updated U.S.S. Enterprise, set some hundred years after the original television adventures. This would be followed by four further television series (one airing now), as well as a series of four films with the *TNG* cast, prequel films with new actors portraying the original series' cast, and numerous other licensed and unlicensed appearances of ST characters and settings in written, visual, and other media, and in fans' imaginations (in fan fiction as

4. For a compelling argument for how this interaction and interpretation worked, and how different ancient understandings of the Gilgamesh mythology could be to modern scholarly studies, see Ataç 2010.

well as nonnarrative discussion and private reflection). Like the story world of ancient myth, ST is the creation of numerous and varied "authors" (and the power of ST fans and actors, often themselves fans of a previous generation of the franchise, to shape the direction and meaning of the ST universe cannot be underestimated). The consumer of the ST mythic story world situates any individual story within this serial world, aware of wider narrative arcs and wider messages and values.

These summaries should make clear why Johnston's definitions of certain narrative qualities are relevant. Johnston's work suggests the devices by which ancient myths themselves work as meaningful narratives, generating continued engagement from their "receivers." For contemporary story worlds that are similar to mythic story worlds (i.e., hyperserial and plurimedial, as ST is), these observations are particularly useful. Johnston's work can also suggest a way of looking at modern interactions with myths not as existing on the other side of one bright line between ancient and modern, but as part of the ongoing life of mythic narratives. The "reception" of Gilgamesh has been an ongoing and formative part of the mythos for over four thousand years. It is a legitimate endeavor to think about the use of Gilgamesh in ST because this is inherently part of that mythic figure's life, as a character with whom new audiences can develop their own parasocial relationships (just as was done in an ancient context by Neo-Assyrian kings or by anyone who interacted with a Humbaba plaque or rolled a cylinder seal with scenes of this combat).[5]

In the case of "Darmok," all these themes are being explored at a meta level, since it is itself a story in which the Gilgamesh story is told (explicitly, as an ancient myth). Thus it explores some of the very themes that Johnston considers. "Darmok" is itself about the cognitive and cultural reception of ancient myths, and the processes by which their meanings can be productive—of dialogue, of friendship, of diplomacy, of life-saving action.

I do not then seek to examine how Gilgamesh can be reinterpreted in light of ST, nor how ST can be better analyzed through an understanding of Gilgamesh. Rather, I look at how "Darmok" serves as a commentary on the process and possibilities of reception itself. In particular, I consider why it uses Gilgamesh in this way and what meanings the myth is understood by ST to convey. I examine how intertextual engagement with Gilgamesh and Enkidu's encounter, reframed here as a "first contact" narrative, allows readings of "Darmok" that complicate who is contacting whom (through who is being read as Gilgamesh and who Enkidu). I look finally at how "Darmok" specifically, and the Star Trek universe world more widely (especially *TNG*) conceptualize cultural reception as a means of keeping peace and assimilating the alien Other (of the "Earth past" or the future galaxy) to the self.

---

5. I also take cues from recent work in biblical studies to read the Bible "as science fiction," considering it to share certain thematic and conceptual qualities such that this reading can illuminate new aspects of the oft-studied text (Uhlenbruch 2017).

1. Past Literature

Two recent notable books solely devoted to the topic of Gilgamesh's reception history have emerged from outside the field of Assyriology. *Gilgamesh Among Us: Modern Encounters with the Ancient Epic* by Theodore Ziolkowski (2011), who comes from the perspective of comparative literature studies and German studies, looks at the history of the reception of Gilgamesh in the academic and nonacademic realms, and examines its treatment in literature, drama, and art. *Discovering Gilgamesh: Geology, Narrative, and the Historical Sublime in Victorian Culture* by Vybarr Cregan-Reid (2013), examines the rediscovery of the Epic from the perspective of Victorian literature, psycho-geography and environmental studies. Ziolkowski does briefly mention the appearance of the Gilgamesh and Enkidu story in *TNG* (2011, 110–11), but does not elaborate on it in any way. Some of Cregan-Reid's observations on the discovery of the epic in relationship to historical "deep time" are relevant in the context of Gilgamesh's deployment in "Darmok," at the very least in illuminating how Gilgamesh has long been understood as speaking to deep antiquity, and to human links with a past more distant than other any other accepted literary pasts.

There is a relatively large body of academic literature on ST, although the nature and value of this literature has been critiqued, for instance, as "naive and fannish" (Csicsery-Ronay 2005, 503, favorably reviewing Shapiro 2004, which similarly argues against the value of previous ST scholarship). "Darmok" specifically has been discussed in several academic contexts, usually with regard to its treatment of language, decipherment, and otherness. Of these academic treatments, some emphasize the role of Gilgamesh in the episode (notably Dimock 2013, 624–31), while others downplay or do not even mention it (Mailloux 2000; Davis 2005; McGurl 2013). This is somewhat surprising, given the central importance that Picard's retelling of Gilgamesh plays in illuminating the episode's meaning.

No academic articles looking at the question of language, rhetoric, and communication have acknowledged the *generic* importance of the central plot. In depicting a failure of the "universal translator" to meaningfully render alien speech, the episode engages with a question that it knows its fans, and science fiction fans in many contexts, are interested in (e.g., "Translator Microbes" 2017; "Mission Log Podcast" 2016). Thus it must be understood that the episode's engagement with communication is taking place in a context of generic meta-examination of a valuable but controversial, often parodied, science-fiction genre convention. In order to ensure that the ST universe is able to host other stories than those about first communication and language barriers, the narrative convention must normally be embraced, despite its obvious traces of the hand of the storyteller.[6]

---

6. In *Doctor Who* the device is the TARDIS's "mild psychic field"; the conceit is famously parodied in Douglas Adams's "babel fish" (1979). A number of science fiction stories of first contact do turn on language acquisition and decipherment, including recently the film *Arrival* (2016) and the novella it

The appearance of Picard's retelling of Gilgamesh in the context of a rare ST episode about the complexity of true decipherment is significant. Even when we can decipher words enough to translate technically, their true meaning can escape us. This feeling should be familiar to any scholar of Akkadian or (particularly) Sumerian. Indeed, the universal translator as a device raises problems immediately apparent to any scholar of the ancient world, or other cultures and languages very different from our own. The episode considers how, in absence of this universalizing science fiction plot device, we can make our own meanings out of the ancient texts we encounter and retell, no less than out of the alien species we encounter.

2. *"Darmok"*

The episode Darmok is the 102nd episode (Season 5, Episode 2) of *TNG*, originally broadcast 30 September 1991, directed by Winrich Kolbe, with a teleplay by Joe Menosky from a story by Menosky and Philip LaZebnik. It had an unusually long development history, having been in progress as a story idea for two years (Gross and Altman 1995, 228). The episode features a memorable guest appearance from Academy Award nominated actor Paul Winfield, as the alien captain Dathon, to whom Picard, played by Patrick Stewart, narrates the story of Gilgamesh and Enkidu, as an example of a foundational myth of "our" Earth culture.

The episode begins with the Enterprise in orbit around the planet El-Adrel; they have come in response to the broadcast of a mathematical signal from an alien ship apparently seeking to make contact, representatives of an "enigmatic" race known as "the Children of Tama." This race has been contacted by Starfleet seven times over the previous century, but no true communication has been established. Though they have apparently peaceful intentions, the race has been described as "incomprehensible" by past Starfleet officers. Picard is optimistic: "In my experience, communication is a matter of patience, imagination. I would like to believe these are qualities we have in sufficient measure." It soon becomes clear why previous Starfleet teams have struggled: the Tamarians, in contact with the Enterprise over their respective ships' view-screens, speak in English, meaning that their words *are* being translated by the universal translator. However, they seem only, as the android Lt. Commander Data explains in his helpless summation, "to be stating the proper names of individuals and locations." Although it is clear from their inflection, their behavior, and the interactions between themselves, witnessed through the view-screen, that their words have a meaningful sense to them, to the Enterprise crew it appears as gibberish. "Rai and Jiri at Lungha," "Shaka, when the walls fell." The individual words ("wall," "at") and the semantic structure have been within the universal translator's powers, but for once it has been no true help.

---

is based on, Ted Chiang's "Story of Your Life" (1998), Mary Doria Russell's *The Sparrow* (1996), and Ian Watson's *The Embedding* (1973).

It is clear that a disagreement takes place between the Tamarian captain, Dathon, and his first officer, which ends in the captain making a decision: "Darmok and Jilad, at Tenagra." The captain Dathon draws two knives from his belt and before the Enterprise crew can act, the Tamarians have successfully beamed Picard and their own captain away from their respective ships onto the surface of the planet El-Adrel. On the Enterprise, First Officer Riker and the crew struggle to determine how to beam Picard back (the Tamarians are blocking transport to or from the planet) and what the meaning of the Tamarian communications they have received thus far could be. It seems logical to conclude that the intent must be to force a violent contest of champions.

On the planet surface, Picard assumes the same, especially as Dathon keeps trying to press a knife into his hands. Picard rejects this gift, refusing to fight. Dathon is frustrated, continually repeating "Darmok and Jilad, at Tenagra." As night falls on the planet, the captains sit at separate fires, within shouting distance. Dathon's is blazing, while Picard cannot get his going. Picard realizes that his companion might not be hostile when he takes pity on Picard and offers him a gift of flame for his own fire, and achieves his first sense of how the Tamarian language might work:

> DATHON: Temba.
> PICARD: Temba? What does that mean? Fire? Does Temba mean fire?
> DATHON: Temba. His arms wide.
> PICARD: Temba is a person? His arms wide. [*thinking*] Because he's holding them apart in, in generosity. In giving. In taking.

Back on the Enterprise, Data and empath Counselor Troi come to a conclusion about the basic structure of the language and its dependence on metaphor. Searching through dozens of meanings in the Starfleet computers for "Darmok" and "Tenagra" they find two that appear to fit together: Darmok ("a mytho-historical hunter on Shantil 3") and Tenagra ("An island-continent on Shantil 3"). Perhaps, they conclude, this is the "mytho-historical" touchstone that underlies this metaphor. They explain their findings to the crew:

> DATA: The Tamarian ego structure does not seem to allow what we normally think of as self-identity. Their ability to abstract is highly unusual. They seem to communicate through narrative imagery by reference to the individuals and places which appear in their mytho-historical accounts.
> ...
>
> TROI: Exactly. Imagery is everything to the Tamarians. It embodies their emotional states, their very thought processes. It's how they communicate, and it's how they think.

Yet without the same cultural touchstones, that imagery is meaningless. "It is necessary for us to learn the narrative from which the Tamarians drawing their imagery," Data diagnoses.

Meanwhile, Picard too realizes the basic structure of the language and its use of metaphor and allusion. He soon comes to realize that his new friend means well with the knife business: the aim is to ensure they work together to defeat a "beast," an amorphous energy creature apparently native to the planet. Dathon, knowing that there was danger on the planet, has brought them here to face this adventure together (fig. 1). As morning dawns, Picard and Dathon are now fast friends, and have been able to communicate enough that they are just able to discuss tactics as they go up against the beast. Picard is flush with triumph, less at the ongoing battle than at his ability to understand Dathon's metaphors. However, Dathon is mortally wounded in combat, as the beast retreats unharmed.

Fig. 1. A scene from "Darmok."

That night, Picard sits by the fire with Dathon and sees him through his final moments. In a touching scene (widely regarded by fans as deeply moving), Picard establishes that he understands and appreciates his new friend's sacrifice. For the sake of making contact with the other, Dathon has risked his own life. Although Dathon is fading quickly, Picard manages to persuade him to outline the basic substance of the "Darmok and Jilad" story. Darmok, on the ocean: the "mytho-historical hunter" alone. "Jilad on the ocean," another mytho-historical figure, a stranger. The two of them come to Tenagra where they encounter, together, "the beast" at Tenagra. They fight together and end "Darmok and Jilad, on the ocean." As Picard parses it: the ocean, aloneness, the fight against the beast, a coming together. The two people, alone and lonely on the ocean (a symbol of isolation) meet to struggle together towards a common goal, and leave together as friends. Picard recognizes that he and Dathon were to play out this process, to meet as strangers, isolated, but to leave as companions. "Picard and Dathon at El-Adrel."

Weak as he is, Dathon asks Picard for a story in return. The entirety of the exchange is worth quoting:

> PICARD: My turn? No, I'm not much of a story teller. Besides, you wouldn't understand. Shaka, when the walls fell. Perhaps that doesn't matter. You want to hear it anyway. There's a story, a very ancient one, from Earth. I'll try and remember it. Gilgamesh, a king. Gilgamesh, a king, at Uruk. He tormented his subjects. He made them angry. They cried out aloud, send us a companion for our king. Spare us from his madness. Enkidu, a wild man from the forest, entered the city. They fought in the temple. They fought in the street. Gilgamesh defeated Enkidu. They became great friends. Gilgamesh and Enkidu at Uruk.

DATHON: At Uruk.
PICARD: The new friends went out into the desert together, where the great bull of heaven was killing men by the hundreds. Enkidu caught the bull by the tail. Gilgamesh struck it with his sword.
DATHON: Gilgamesh.
PICARD: They were victorious. But Enkidu fell to the ground, struck down by the gods. And Gilgamesh wept bitter tears, saying, "he who was my companion through adventure and hardship, is gone forever."

Dathon hears out the end of this tale and soon breathes his last.

As Picard buries his friend, his crew finally succeeds in beaming him away from the planet just as he himself is about to be gored by "the beast." Both the Enterprise and the Tamarian ship can see from their sensor readings that one of the two life signs on the planet has disappeared. Picard is beamed back to the Enterprise just in time: the Tamarians have concluded that the death of their captain was at Picard's hands and are gearing up for a fatal assault on the Enterprise. But Picard has now learned enough of their metaphorical language through his interactions with Dathon that he is able to dissuade them by successfully narrating what happened on the planet, his comradeship with Dathon, and Dathon's unfortunate death at the hands of the beast. More importantly, he is able to show that he has done what Dathon hoped for: the strangers have made contact, Picard can now speak to them and understand the meaning of their metaphor language. He gives them the new phrase, "Picard and Dathon at El-Adrel," to describe a tragic but ultimately meaningful encounter between strangers who become comrades.

The Tamarians leave peacefully, though in sorrow for their captain, and Picard is cautiously optimistic that if not yet friends, they are at least not enemies. The episode closes, as many *TNG* episodes do, with a scene in Picard's ready room. Riker finds Picard with an old leather-bound book (fig. 2).

Fig. 2. Picard reading the Homeric Hymns. From "Darmok."

RIKER: Greek, sir?
PICARD: Oh, the Homeric Hymns. One of the root metaphors of our own culture.
RIKER: For the next time we encounter the Tamarians?
PICARD: More familiarity with our own mythology might help us to relate to theirs. The Tamarian was willing to risk all of us just for the hope of communication, connection. Now the door is open between our peoples. That commitment meant more to him than his own life.

On this note the episode ends: that to die for communication, with the alien, though also through and with the past, was worth dying for, and that ancient myth should be seen as an ongoing tool in the Enterprise's exploration of alien space.

3. *Why Gilgamesh?*

The appearance of the works of Homer in this closing moment emphasizes by contrast how strange a choice it is to feature Gilgamesh at the episode's emotional climax. Although this volume demonstrates that there has been more interaction between popular culture and the ancient Near East than is often recognized, it is nonetheless the case that such interaction with Gilgamesh is rare enough that when it does appear, it raises questions as to why and how such a comparatively obscure myth has found its way into such a mainstream property. Screenwriter Menosky's choice to put the Gilgamesh story in Picard's mouth is an unusual and rare one.

The most likely reason why he chose Gilgamesh in preference to any other "Earth story" is its age. Gilgamesh is frequently seen as the starting point for "world literature"; it is the only work of cuneiform literature to appear in the *Norton Anthology of World Literature* (Puchner 2012; excerpts from *Enuma Elish* and *Enmerkar and the Lord of Aratta* appear in thematic subsections, but not in the primary chronological sequence). It is thus the oldest narrative work to be widely accounted a work of "literature" and a part of the canon in Western world literary studies; given the prominence of the *Norton Anthology* in defining and guiding many university-level literature syllabi, it can be presumed that Gilgamesh is encountered in this way across many higher education institutions.[7] Gilgamesh suggests, then, an ancient, foundational, and primary myth. If the audience of the episode can be expected to recognize the name and the narrative (which surely is expected, in order to appreciate that Picard does not merely invent it), it is probably in this aspect.[8] Such an idea of a canonical and universal progression of literature is in keeping with the ST understanding of the past as an inheritance belonging to the Federation (that is, the United Federation of Planets, the political "us" of the ST universe) and their (white, elite, American) members with whom the audience identifies (discussed further below). The importance of Gilgamesh within the episode has been highlighted by Patrick Stewart and by the series' producers, with Stewart relating the use of Gilgamesh to the episode's legitimacy as "award-worthy" art (*Mission Overview: Year Five* 2002): Gilgamesh lends (obscure) class.

---

7. Cooppan, in an article discussing the pedagogy of world literature, notes that he begins his "World Literature" course at Yale by teaching the Norton "Gilgamesh" (Benjamin R. Foster's translation) paired with "Darmok" (2004, 23–24).

8. In my own American high school, Gilgamesh was also a feature of "World Literature" teaching; I suspect that many American students will have encountered it in this way and it can be assumed to be a plausible touchstone even for those without university/college-level educations.

Beyond its "primacy" in the world literary canon, the story was also likely chosen because of the way that Gilgamesh and Enkidu's story can be easily read as a first contact narrative, discussed in the next section. The episode does not trace the story of Gilgamesh beyond the story of Gilgamesh and Enkidu's friendship. It thus remakes the central meaning of the epic, ignoring the central importance of its engagement with death and mortality (see Dimock 2013, 626–27, on the episode's modification of this theme). This sort of remaking is easily facilitated by the form and function of epics, in which individual episodes are easily extracted (Johnston 2015b, 203–4). Whatever the meaning of Gilgamesh as understood by any one ancient editor or author, it is not the only meaning that Gilgamesh has had, nor the most valid. "Darmok" participates in that tradition by again restructuring and therefore refiguring the myth's elements. This happens on two levels: the episode's writer, Menosky, reconfigures the events of the epic for his own purposes (to offer a parallel between the story that he is telling and this much greater, much older story that will be familiar to the audience as great "world literature"); within the episode's narrative Picard does the same for his own in-story purposes (to comfort a dying friend and to forge a deeper understanding with the alien, preventing violence).

4. Intertextual Engagement: Rereading Gilgamesh and Enkidu as First Contact Narrative

The Gilgamesh-Enkidu story, as told by Picard, does not offer an exact parallel to his own situation with Dathon (or, on another level, the episode as written by Menosky does not present an exact parallel).[9] In fact, the relationship is tenuous, and Picard's rendition of Gilgamesh and Enkidu's adventures changes and elides elements of the standard Babylonian version from which it derives: for instance, ignoring the role of Shamhat in Enkidu's journey to civilization, eliding the killing of Humbaba (a parallel closer to what Picard and Dathon do in this episode) with the Bull of Heaven incident, leaving out the reason that the Bull of Heaven was sent to Uruk, and ignoring the importance of the gods at every level.

---

9. Although I will not discuss this aspect at length here, it is worth emphasizing that the episode relies on our ability to grasp a whole web of parallels, operating at different levels, among both real and fictional myths. Gilgamesh and Enkidu are a good parallel to the (fictional) heroes Darmok and Jilad; their stories are mutually comprehensible to Picard and Dathon—and immediately comprehensible to the viewer, with only brief retellings. I would argue that this presentation of myth, and certainly its assumptions that its audiences will easily grasp parallels among myths, and between myths and modern stories, should be seen as essentially rooted in science fiction's love affair with the theories of Joseph Campbell's *The Hero with a Thousand Faces* (1949). This work of comparative mythology has been incredibly influential within genre fictions, most famously as a foundational text in George Lucas's creation of the Star Wars series. Its continued prominence in popular culture has long outlived its popularity in academic discussions of myth and narrative.

Instead, I would suggest that the episode invites the viewer to understand the story of Gilgamesh and Enkidu as essentially a story of first contact. "First contact" is a topos of central importance to the ST universe, and within science fiction more broadly. The concept gave its name to a film with the *TNG* cast, widely regarded as one of the best of the franchise, and also to an episode of the *TNG* television series. Because of the obvious scope for different dramatic storytelling possibilities, a number of episodes of *TNG* feature the topos of either intentional or accidental first contact with an alien Other. Retelling the Gilgamesh-Enkidu story in parallel to such a trope reframes it for a modern audience as a story that viewers of ST would be familiar with. Seeing the relationship through a familiar topos may render it more meaningful to modern audiences, a transformation that remakes the story to correspond to our own cultural expectations.

Dathon, as the incomprehensible alien Other who is gradually brought into comprehensibility through Picard's good faith and ingenuity at decipherment—of culture no less than language—can be read as an Enkidu parallel. That he is humanoid but not human in appearance equates too to the description of Enkidu as fantastically wilder than an ordinary man (Tablet I, 105–14). It is significant that Dathon is played, albeit under heavy prosthetic make-up, by Winfield, a black American actor. Thus the episode inescapably calls to mind parallels to American racial division and communication across that division. The choice to cast a black actor as Dathon is likely not accidental or incidental. In ST, black actors are cast as aliens with overwhelming frequency, often in make-up that deliberately obscures their human features and renders them, essentially, "crypto" racial minorities, with racial stereotypes displaced onto their status as literal alien.[10] On *TNG* the most prominent example of this is Worf, the Klingon Starfleet officer played by black American actor Michael Dohrn. Further, with the alien-human dichotomy reinforced by the black-white racial dichotomy, "Darmok" participates in a long-held ST tradition, dating back to the original series in the 1960s, of (often highly clumsy) engagement with American racial issues through the lens of science fiction allegory (Golumbia 1995, 80–91, on a particularly notorious original series example). Thus the episode becomes a comment on communication or miscommunication across racial divides, as well as a more general story of encountering and coming to know the alien Other, in which Gilgamesh's forging of a relationship with Enkidu becomes equated to the Enterprise's mission to seek out and know the alien Other, and this in turn with the need for black and white humans to engage in dialogue, in keeping with ST's liberal humanist principles in which dialogue alone is considered the ultimate social good. The application of an allegory derived from an ancient Near

10. Black actors, from *TNG* onwards, are particularly likely to play Klingons, a warrior race known for their hot heads and outsized concern for honor—the parallel to negative stereotypes of black American masculinity are obvious. A similar dynamic is at work with the Ferengi, an alien race introduced in *TNG*, who have often been noted to embody unflattering and arguably highly anti-Semitic stereotypes of Jews, disguised as alien racial traits, and who are often played by Jewish actors, most prominently Armin Shimerman as Quark in *Star Trek: Deep Space Nine*.

Eastern mythos to such a culturally and temporally specific American societal dynamic is indicative of how widely productive, in unexpected and unintended ways, the reuse of ancient literature can be.

However, reading intertextually, it becomes clear that there is a more salient and arguably more complex parallel at work in the Gilgamesh-Enkidu analogy than one that would equate the alien Other (and by implication, black Americans) with Enkidu, discovered by our hero Gilgamesh-Picard. Over the course of the episode, it is Picard who must learn to speak with the Tamarians, it is Picard who must assimilate to their way of thought. In this sense, Picard is the Enkidu, learning to communicate with a new society whose ways at first are strange to him, moving from (in the Tamarians' eyes) wild unknowingness and incomprehensibility to civilized speech.

That Picard is able to do this accords with the tolerant generosity of the Federation he represents. While other species are often suspicious of and hostile to the alien, Picard is willing to enter into *their* traditions. Indeed, the purportedly peaceful, contact-seeking Tamarians blankly refuse to make communication easier (they are not particularly good at gesture or sign language, something Picard ultimately uses to understand the story of Darmok and Jilad). The Enterprise comes to contact ready to investigate, to study, and to decipher. His crew bring not only the skills of diplomats and scientists, but also of historians, translators, linguists—the skills of academic cultural investigation. The Tamarians, on the other hand, come just as they are and present themselves to be deciphered. In this sense they could be seen again to mirror Enkidu, appearing in the wilderness and passively being made sense of. Yet, despite their status as specimens to be deciphered, it is the Tamarians who engineer the confrontation that creates a lasting companionship between Picard and Dathon, and who seemingly have superior transporter technology to the Enterprise. In different ways then, each side works on the other to bring about the final state of understanding achieved by the end of the episode.

Reading back from this episode through its intertextual engagement with the Gilgamesh-Enkidu mythos, Darmok suggests an understanding of Enkidu's journey from animal world to human world not as a passive process but as an active and intellectual decipherment. If Enkidu is like Picard, he must be understood as an agent-explorer, a heroic decipherer, accommodating himself to Gilgamesh, actively and impressively learning the ways of human society. Whether this was intended in ancient readings is a different question: for our part, however, we can see that such a reading is now possible for a modern receiver of the Gilgamesh mythos. That Enkidu, in the standard Babylonian version, certainly is explicitly created to tame the excesses of Gilgamesh is another reason this parallel might have appealed to Menosky, for the role of the Enterprise as a taming and civilizing force is the primary premise of the show.

The viewer can now experience the Gilgamesh and Enkidu encounter in the light of its integration into the ST universe and a common science fiction topos, where it gains new meaning. Darmok makes an argument for reusing and reiterating elements of ancient myth (and not even the entire myth, but set pieces, type-scenes, or tropes); the episode itself demonstrates the effect of such reuse in its retelling of Gilgamesh, which moves and informs the audience (both the ST viewer and Dathon, as audience to Picard's story) and allows communication and understanding with an alien Other.

5. *"You Will Be Assimilated": Star Trek's Reception of Other Cultures*

This hopeful understanding of the universally applicable power of narrative is of a piece with ST's wider ideology, its own purpose as an ongoing saga, and its optimistic understanding of social and historical journeys. ST is perhaps the leading utopian science fiction series of contemporary culture. It sees history as an upward progression in which people of the future-present learn from the mistakes of their past (including our present). Although many episodes focus on the inevitability of conflict and division recurring (note Picard's caution about whether the Tamarians are yet "friends"), it posits a general upward trend. In ST's Federation there is no money: people work for their own personal betterment. Starfleet is a peaceful exploratory agency, not a military force (although unsurprisingly they are frequently engaged in "defensive" battles). Racism and xenophobia are said to have been widely eliminated from the humans of earth (though, as discussed above, racial "otherness" is often unintentionally or explicitly displaced onto alien species). The crew of the Enterprise are collegiate, good-tempered, kind, and, most significantly here, each engaged in extensive pursuits of personal self-betterment through cultural projects (music, art, martial arts, dance, reading, academic study).

In the future of the *TNG* universe, the values of American elitist, liberal, self-improvement have triumphed. Pursuit of culture for its own sake is considered a fundamental mark of "advancement." *TNG* celebrates its own optimistic sort of multiculturalism, in which any culture, however alien, can be assimilated *to* (white, elite, liberal, human) Federation cultural norms; even before we reach the subject of exploring the (literal) alien, the culture of "Earth" has been unproblematically collapsed into one monoculture, belonging to Picard and his fellow humans in Starfleet (all played by American or European actors). Communication and knowledge-sharing civilizes alien others who can ultimately be allied to or actually join the Federation. In ST, multiculturalism and historical and social progress occur through the assimilation of the alien to this normative identity, where other cultures can be used for self-improvement and diplomatic relationship-building. In a sense then, the Federation ideology is itself a universal translator, not just of language but of history, culture, knowledge, and values, smoothing over context and historical contingencies to render everything into American (or sometimes British-accented) English.

Undoubtedly to displace anxieties about the imperialism and xenophobia inherent in this approach, *TNG* introduced at the end of its second season a primary villain whose method of expansion is designed to contrast to the Federation: the Borg. A collective consciousness with one will, the Borg violently assimilate species, cultures, and planets, their assimilation framed also as reception: "We will add your biological and technological distinctiveness to our own. Resistance is futile" (*Star Trek: First Contact* 1996). That this is exactly what the Federation (and the ST franchise) does to numerous cultures, is at the heart of the moral anxiety the Borg produce; they are repeatedly used to provoke storylines about how humans and the Federation as an entity distinguish themselves from this dark mirror.

The assimilation that the Federation practices, no less than the Borg, includes not only alien and human "Earth" cultures, but also the cultural products, and particularly the narratives, of the human past. In keeping with this understanding of cultural reception, Gilgamesh is "our" Earth culture. The final scene of the episode in which Picard can be seen reading Homer to brush up for future communications is enlightening: the episode suggests that the two myth-worlds are equally prominent representations of ancient Earth culture, and equally "ours." In 1991, when this episode was broadcast, as today, this was not remotely true. Homer is a widely taught, foundational pillar of "Western" literature and an author that American creators and viewers of ST would probably know well; Gilgamesh, despite its status in the world literature canon, is still regarded as non-Western and still relatively obscure. ST imagines a future in which contact with other planets has united (and elided) cultural differences on Earth. This is ST's central theory of contact, or as we might think of it "theory of reception." Contact-reception elides differences and unites different groups, intrasocially and intersocially, by its mere existence. Knowing, learning, and sharing "culture" is productive of peace and social harmony.

Picard initially expresses hesitation in reciting the Gilgamesh and Enkidu tale: he is not in close contact with this element of the past. Indeed, Picard's retelling of Gilgamesh is not strictly "accurate." Nonetheless, his offer of the story is also an offer of a new interpretation to his and Dathon's own experience. In the story that Dathon hoped would explain their meeting, Darmok and Jilad leave together on the ocean, victorious. Dathon's imminent death thus invalidates this comparison. Is this an example of failure then? "Shaka, when the walls fell," in the language of the Tamarians? By introducing Gilgamesh and Enkidu instead as a comparison, Picard suggests an alternate explanation. Beyond expressing his sorrow for his new friend, he repositions Dathon's death as something worthy. Although Picard offers no meaningful "justification" for Enkidu's death, the very existence of a mythic precedent helps Picard and Dathon to understand his death differently; that is, to understand it as something inherently meaningful because it participates in tradition for which there is language.

That Picard would know and care about the ancient Near East is consistent with a primary aspect of the character's back story: Picard once studied archaeology and still maintains a hobbyist's interest in the topic, and in the ancient past more generally. Repeatedly, in episodes that deal with Picard's interest in antiquity, the exploration of the past is equated with the scientific and exploratory mission of the Enterprise in physical space, making explicit the link between contact with the geographical alien and the temporal alien. The archaeology of ST is a fantastical one, in which references to real (historical) Earth archaeology sit alongside those to the archaeology of invented alien worlds. For instance, in "The Chase" (1993), Picard's old archaeology professor tempts him on an adventure by asking: "What if you could have helped Schliemann discover the city of Troy, or been with M'Tell as she first stepped on Ya'Seem? How could anything compare?" In that episode, also written by "Darmok" screenwriter Menosky, Picard finds himself engaged on a search for DNA evidence hidden on planets around the galaxy, in many diverse, seemingly unrelated life-forms. Like "Darmok," this episode posits that the ancient past is still vitally present in human societies (in "Darmok" as language, in "The Chase" as a part of the body) and should be understood as both a mechanism and a reason for connection between diverse cultures.

In both episodes, it is argued that receiving and understanding the ancient past no less than encountering the contemporaneous alien is a means for cultures to come together in peace. This is explicitly stated in "The Chase," in which the shared DNA sequence was seeded by an ancient and dying race in the hope that a biological heritage shared across the universe would someday be discovered and lead to peace. This message of commonality is rejected by all the nonhuman races who have been competing to solve the archaeological puzzle. Picard is disappointed—until he receives a last-minute communication from a Romulan captain who has been thinking it over and been deeply affected (the Romulans are morally gray villains, usually doing the worst but with a better nature the audience lives in hope of seeing win out). Academic investigation of the ancient past, this episode argues, should illuminate the commonality of present people and this biological and historical discovery has a moral imperative: that people in the present should practice peace.

This explicit message echoes the way that Gilgamesh is employed in "Darmok": because Picard, like Dathon, has access to a "mytho-historical" past in which tales of friendship and togetherness through adversity are discussed, he and Dathon can and should make peace. The ancient past both facilitates and morally mandates that peace. In "Darmok," the historical contingencies of the epic, the meaning and role it played in ancient contexts, are unimportant. This is naturally very different from how Gilgamesh is treated within scholarly contexts, though it offers new and contextually appropriate ways of engaging with the historical legacy of ancient Babylonian literature. The Gilgamesh mythos is transformed through its use as a tool of the humanist message (and the soft power) of the Federation, and the ST franchise.

6. *Conclusion*

The retelling and reception of Gilgamesh in "Darmok" works as both a demonstration of and a commentary on the productive, living nature of ancient myth, and its openness to reuse by new receivers. The episode invokes a broader cultural understanding of Gilgamesh as the "original" work of "world literature." The Gilgamesh-Enkidu encounter is presented as a first contact narrative, a lens which allows readings backwards and forwards of both Picard and his alien companion as each of the two mythical heroes. Its assimilation to the ST mythos is part of a wider conceptualization within ST of cultural reception as inherently peace-keeping—and of all "culture" as under its own purview. In its ability to generate new meanings and new relationships between the Gilgamesh mythos and contemporary viewers, ST has indeed remade Gilgamesh in light of its own values and interests, but in a continuation of the process that has always guided the lives of mythical figures.

Bibliography

Adams, D. 1979. *The Hitchhiker's Guide to the Galaxy*. London: Pan Macmillan.

Arrival. 2016. Directed by D. Villeneuve. USA: Paramount Pictures.

Ataç, M-A. 2010. "Representations and Resonances of Gilgamesh in Neo-Assyrian Art." In H. U. Steymans (ed.), *Gilgamesch: Ikonographie eines Helden*, 261–86. Fribourg: Academic Press Fribourg.

Bonatz, D. 2004. "Ashurbanipal's Headhunt: An Anthropological Perspective." *Iraq* 66:93–101.

Campbell, J. 1949. *The Hero with a Thousand Faces*. Bollingen, Switzerland: Bollingen Foundation.

"The Chase." 1993. Season 6, episode 20 of *Star Trek: The Next Generation*. CBS, 24 April.

Chiang, T. 1998. "Story of Your Life." In P. Nielsen Hayden (ed.), *Starlight 2*, 257–314. New York: Tor Books.

Collins, P. 2016. "The Face of the Assyrian Empire: Mythology and the Heroic King." In J. Aruz and M. Seymour (eds.), *Assyria to Iberia: Art and Culture in the Iron Age*, 42–53. New York: Metropolitan Museum of Art.

Cooppan, V. 2004. "Ghosts in the Disciplinary Machine: The Uncanny Life of World Literature." *Comparative Literature Studies* 41:10–36.

Cregan-Reid, V. 2013. *Discovering Gilgamesh: Geology, Narrative and the Historical Sublime in Victorian Culture*. Manchester: Manchester University Press.

Csicsery-Ronay, Jr., I. 2005. "Escaping 'Star Trek.'" Edited by Alan N. Shapiro. *Science Fiction Studies* 32:503–11.

"Darmok." 1991. Season 5, episode 2 of *Star Trek: The Next Generation*. CBS, 28 September.

"Darmok." (n.d.). Podcast Episode 195 of *Mission Log Podcast*. Accessed 25 May 2017. http://www.missionlogpodcast.com/darmok/.

Davis, D. 2005. "Addressing Alterity: Rhetoric, Hermeneutics, and the Nonappropriative Relation." *Philosophy & Rhetoric* 38:191–212.

Dimock, W. C. 2013. "I: Low Epic." *Critical Inquiry* 39:614–31.

George, A. R. 2003. *The Babylonian Gilgamesh Epic: Introduction, Critical Edition and Cuneiform Texts*. Oxford: Oxford University Press.

Giles, D. C. 2010. "Parasocial Relationships." In J. Eder, F. Jannidis and R. Schneider (eds.), *Characters in Fictional Worlds, Understanding Imaginary Beings in Literature, Film, and Other Media*, 442–58. Berlin: de Gruyter.

Golumbia, D. 1995. "Black and White World: Race, Ideology, and Utopia in 'Triton' and 'Star Trek.'" *Cultural Critique* 32:75–95.

Graff, S. B. 2013. "The Head of Humbaba." *Archiv für Religionsgeschichte* 14:129–42.

Gross, E. A., and M. A. Altman. 1995. *Captains' Logs: The Unauthorized Complete Trek Voyages*. London: Little, Brown.

Howard-Carter, T. 1983. "An Interpretation of the Sculptural Decoration of the Second Millennium Temple at Tell Al-Rimah." *Iraq* 45:64–72.

Johnston, S. I. 2015a. "The Greek Mythic Story World." *Arethusa* 48:283–311.

———. 2015b. "Narrating Myths: Story and Belief in Ancient Greece." *Arethusa* 48:173–218.

———. 2017. *Religion: Narrating Religion*. Farmington Hills, MI: Schirmer.

Lambert, W. G. 1987. "Gilgamesh in Literature and Art: The Second and First Millennia." In A. E. Farkas, P. O. Harper, and E. B. Harrison (eds.), *Monsters and Demons in the Ancient and Medieval Worlds: Papers Presented in Honor of Edith Porada*, 37–52. Mainz: von Zabern.

Mailloux, S. 2000. "Making Comparisons: First Contact, Ethnocentrism, and Cross-Cultural Communication." In J. C. Rowe (ed.), *Post-Nationalist American Studies*, 110–28. Berkeley: University of California Press.

McGurl, M. 2013. "II: 'Neither Indeed Could I Forebear Smiling at My Self': A Reply to Wai Chee Dimock." *Critical Inquiry* 39:632–38.

Michalowski, P. 2008. "The Mortal Kings of Ur: A Short Century of Divine Rule in Ancient Mesopotamia." In N. Brisch (ed.), *Religion and Power: Divine Kingship in the Ancient World and Beyond*, 33–45. Chicago: Oriental Institute of the University of Chicago.

Mission Overview: Year Five. 2002. DVD box set extra, *Star Trek: The Next Generation—The Complete Season Five*. Paramount.

Puchner, M. 2012. *The Norton Anthology of World Literature*, 3rd ed. New York: Norton.

Russell, M. D. 1996. *The Sparrow*. New York: Villard Books.

Shapiro, A. N. 2004. *Star Trek: Technologies of Disappearance*. Berlin: Avinus.

Star Trek: First Contact. 1996. Directed by J. Frakes. USA: Paramount Pictures.

Steymans, H. U., ed. 2010. *Gilgamesch: Ikonographie eines Helden*. Fribourg: Academic Press Fribourg.

Tolkien, J. R. R. 1947. "On Fairy-Stories." In C. S. Lewis (ed.), *Essays Presented To Charles Williams*, 38–89. Grand Rapids: Eerdmans.

"Translator Microbes." 2017. Wiki article, *TV Tropes*. Accessed 25 May 2017. http://tvtropes.org/pmwiki/pmwiki.php/Main/TranslatorMicrobes.

Uhlenbruch, F., ed. 2017. *Not in the Spaces We Know: An Exploration of Science Fiction and the Bible*. Piscataway: Gorgias.

Watson, I. 1973. *The Embedding*. New York: Scribner's Sons.

Ziolkowski, T. 2011. *Gilgamesh among Us: Modern Encounters with the Ancient Epic*. Ithaca: Cornell University Press.

Evil from an Ancient Past and the Archaeology of the Beyond

An Analysis of the Movies *The Exorcist* (1973) and *The Evil Dead* (1981)

Lorenzo Verderame

Archaeology is still too incomplete to afford an answer, hence imagination is free to speculate over the whole of Mesopotamia, Persia, India, and kindred regions.
From a letter of H. P. Lovecraft to
R. E. Howard (September 12, 1931)

In this essay I discuss two classic horror movies from the 1970s and 1980s, *The Exorcist* (1973) and *The Evil Dead* (1981). Both movies track the evil's origin, or at least its historical evidence, to ancient Mesopotamia. In both movies, archaeology plays a crucial role, dealing with or evoking this ancient evil. In the main part of the article, I analyze the two movies focusing on ancient Near Eastern motives and the role played by archaeology. Then I discuss how the reference to ancient Mesopotamian demons builds an idea of remoteness and pre-/intra-religious existence of evil. Furthermore, I draw some conclusions on the figure of the archaeologist who has to deal with the world of the beyond, extending my analysis to the Indiana Jones saga. I conclude with a consideration on the ethic of archaeology promoted in Hollywood movies.

1. *Evil from an Ancient Past*

Ancient Mesopotamian demons have had a great impact on popular culture since the very first finds from Assyria arrived in European museums.[1] The display of decorative slabs from ancient Assyrian palaces became one of the main attractions of the British

1. See the introduction to the present volume and the references quoted there, in particular, for the perspective of this article, McGeough 2015a–c; for the rediscovery of the past and antiquarianism in Victorian England, see n. 27.

Museum, and genies and demons were the stars of the Assyrian court in the Crystal Palace in London. The idea of an ancient Mesopotamian demonology rapidly took flight, attracting interest in scientific publications and esoteric groups. Sometimes the connections between the two spheres were evident. In fact, while the library of the British Museum was frequented by the curious and esotericists, early Assyriologists were not unknown in esoteric movements.[2] By the late-nineteenth century, occultism, spiritualism, and other interests in the world beyond were major trends in Great Britain, and archaeologists were involved both personally and professionally. E. A. Wallis Budge, keeper of the Department of Egyptian and Assyrian Antiquities of the British Museum, had to deal daily with people obsessed by mummies, but he was concerned about the spirits of the owner of the mortal remains exhibited in the museum as well (Luckhurst 2012). He was a member of the Ghost Club, one of the first institutions devoted to research on ghosts and hauntings. His translations of ancient Egyptian texts had a great impact on members of occult circles and authors who had rejected Catholicism for a form of neo-paganism.[3] Many works have been dedicated to Budge by people interested in the occult, such as Edith Nesbit's *The Story of the Amulet* (1906) and H. Rider Haggard's *Morning Star* (1910).[4]

On the Assyriological side, the volumes by Leonard W. King, *Babylonian Magic and Sorcery* (1896) and Reginald Campbell Thompson, *The Devils and Evil Spirits of Babylonia* (1903–1904) and *Semitic Magic* (1908), had the same effect, diffusing the idea of a complex demonology that spread from ancient Mesopotamia. Strongly influenced by Robertson Smith's and Frazer's works, quoted in his preface, Thompson (1908, xiv) offers a world of comparative and folkloric interpretation of Mesopotamian incantations, presenting several parallels from other cultures and archetypical figures. In *Semitic Magic*, he says that the Seven Spirits' "predilection for human blood ... is in keeping with all the traditions of the grisly mediaeval Vampires." Thompson notes that these Seven Spirits (Sibitti/Sebettu) reappear later in both Palestinian and Syriac magic spells (Thompson 1908, 52). Thompson's statement about vampires would have been greatly appealing for curious people and adepts of magic, the occult, paganism,

2. A sketch of these relations around the Egyptian antiquities is offered by Luckhurst 2012.

3. One of the most influential works of Wallis Budge still quoted today as a main reference is the volume *Amulets and Superstitions* (1930) whose subtitle reads "the original texts with translations and descriptions of a long series of Egyptian, Sumerian, Assyrian, Hebrew, Christian, Gnostic and Muslim amulets and talismans and magical figures, with chapters on the evil eye, the origin of the amulet, the pentagon, the swastika, the cross (pagan and Christian), the properties of stones, rings, divination, numbers, the Ḳabbālāh , ancient astrology, etc." Budge states that he has consulted several works of the so-called "Occult Sciences" and en passant refers to the usefulness of the works of Waite (Budge 1930, xxxviii–xxxix). The latter is Arthur Edward Waite (2 October 1857—19 May 1942), the famous occultist best known for his role in the Golden Dawn and co-creator of the Rider-Waite tarot deck; he was an assiduous frequenter of the library of the British Museum.

4. For the "aura" of ancient objects and the role of Museum's keepers in Gothic literature see Hoberman 2003.

etc., who would find scholarly support for their theories. It is no wonder that these early works by Thompson and others continue to be the main reference for contemporary authors and artists dealing with Mesopotamian demons. The exhibition of archaeological finds and the scholarly translation of ancient texts had a great appeal for occultists seeking remote knowledge and archaic cults. A direct reference to ancient Mesopotamia was made by the most famous occultist of the past century, Aleister Crowley, who lately identified Aiwass, the "entity" who manifested to him in Cairo between 8 and 10 April 1904, as "the God once held holy in Sumer" and his "own Guardian Angel" (*The Equinox of the Gods*, 1936).

Through the twentieth century, Mesopotamian demons have continued to hold and secure their position in popular culture into modern times. Mesopotamian demons, particularly Pazuzu, are real Mesopotamian stars that can be found almost everywhere. Pazuzu's name and fame spread all across the Western world. Its figure, or its evocative silhouette or name is removed from the original character and can be found in comics and cartoons, music and the arts and, in general, in any form of popular culture.[5] The statue of the demon appears in the adventure of Adèle Blanc-Sec *Le Démon de la Tour Eiffel* by Jacques Tardi (1976). Pazuzu and the powerful weapon known as the "amulet of Pazuzu" are the subject of Howard the Duck's "Bad Girls Don't Cry" (*Howard the Duck* 2002, Vol. 3/3). In Matt Groening's animated sitcoms, Pazuzu is the name of Professor Hubert J. Farnsworth's gargoyle in *Futurama* and he makes his appearance also in a parody of *The Exorcist* included in *The Simpsons* episode "Treehouse of Horror XXVIII." Pazuzu and Oranssi Pazuzu are the names of Austrian and Finnish black metal bands respectively; it is also quoted in the titles and lyrics of black and death metal songs.[6] Hypnopazūzu is the name of a new music project by the eclectic artist David Tibet. The image of Pazuzu appears in artworks and in a video-clip of the band Gorillaz. Pazuzu has been the subject of a series of artworks by the sculptor Roberto Cuoghi. Interestingly, Cuoghi's artwork inspired the name of a fashionable beach bar and restaurant in Corfù.

In film, *The Exorcist* was not the first appearance of Mesopotamian demons on the silver screen. As early as 1922, an image of the statue of Pazuzu appears in Benjamin Christensen's *Häxan*, and in one scene the devil himself has the facial features of the Mesopotamian demon. Many movie monster- or demon-like creatures have been inspired to Pazuzu and other Mesopotamian demons, such as the 1957 British horror

5. It is not in the scope of the present article, nor the competence of the author, to sketch a summary of the various forms Pazuzu and other Mesopotamian demons have taken in role-playing and video games.

6. See Rosa's contribution in this volume. While the evil prerogatives of Pazuzu as lord of "fever and plague" makes him very popular for the dark vision of metal bands, one may wonder what Tony Silvester and The New Ingredient saw in the Mesopotamian demon to entitle the sexy disco track "Pazuzu" (1976): the song has no lyrics and the female moans that accompany the music offer no clues in this direction, if we exclude the erect penis, which is one of Pazuzu's iconographical features.

film *Night of the Demon*. In the same decade the *Evil Dead* trilogy was shot, another blockbuster movie, *Ghostbusters* (1984), referred *en passant* to Mesopotamian demons and mythology.[7] When the professional cello player Dana Barrett (Sigourney Weaver) finds in her fridge a dog-shaped monster, with horns, fangs, and red eyes that says "Zuul," she calls the Ghostbusters. Dr. Peter Venkman (Bill Murray) explains to Dana that "the name 'Zuul' refers to a demigod worshiped around 6000 BC by the ... what's that word? ... Hittites, Mesopotamians, and Sumerians" and that "Zuul was the minion of Gozer," who "was very big in Sumeria." The clumsy knowledge of Dr. Venkman is noted at the very beginning of the movie and is reinforced consistently throughout the film. In a conversation with the other Ghostbusters, when Winston Zeddemore refers to "some moldy Babylonian god ... going to drop in on Central Park West, and start tearing up the city," Egon Spengler points out "Sumerian, not Babylonian" and Venkman replies "Yeah. Big difference."

2. The Exorcist *(1973)*

The call to prayer of a *muezzin*, a sun rising in a red dawn, an ancient Near Eastern site in the desert landscape, flocks of sheep and camels crossing the site while workers in Arab and Kurd robes dig ... A barefoot boy, the head covered with a red *kufiya*, runs through the site and reaches a kneeling old European man who is cleaning a wall. The boy announces to the old man that something has been found. The slow and uncertain gesture and walk suggest the man is old but also tired. Even the way he receives the news about the discovery is one of resignation rather than excitement. While walking towards the find, a wind starts to blow and disturbs the sand. The old man protects and rubs his eyes until he reaches the pit where the new findings lay. An Iraqi archaeologist in a European outfit, sunglasses, and khaki pith helmet shows the tray of findings to the old man. Among lamps, arrowheads, and coins the old man focuses on a silver medal with the effigy of St. Joseph that is not from the same period of the other findings. With the help of his hand and a pickaxe, the old man searches in the excavated hole. He extracts a clod of earth, from which a silhouette of a stone object emerges. The old man swallows while the cleaned object is revealed as an amulet, a stone head of the demon Pazuzu.

The red sunset and the silhouette of a mosque with the minaret mark the beginning of a new scene. From the isolated archaeological site, we move to the city. Blacksmiths' hammering and people's chattering resound all around. The old man is at a table in a crowded café. When the waiter serves him tea, the old man takes some pills with trembling hands: he is ill. He enters a sort of trance, becoming still and silent while the sounds and activities of the town run over him. He walks the streets until he reaches the

7. In different media, such as the animated series *The Real Ghostbusters* or the video game Ghostbusters (Realistic Versions, 2009), elements of Mesopotamian religion and mythology are developed, such as the figures of Tiamat and Marduk.

forge, where three men are rhythmically beating the anvil. One of them turns towards the old man and reveals a white eye, suffering from glaucoma.

In a parenthetical scene, the old man is now in a room where the archaeological findings are kept. The rhythm and slowness of time is marked by a tickling pendulum-clock on the wall. The local superintendent,[8] who sits at the desk dressed in a finely embroidered white *jellabiya*, is recording the objects. The old man approaches the findings and observes the medal of St. Joseph and the Pazuzu head amulet. The pendulum-clock suddenly stops tickling. The superintendent comments "Evil against evil." The old man stares at the clock and then sits on the sofa. The superintendent asks the old man to remain in Iraq, but the old man replies that he must leave because there is something he must do. The old man goes on with his entranced walk through the lanes of the town until he is awakened from his hallucination by a cart that almost runs him over. The old man is now alone and back on the site. Walking through the ruins, he finds himself in the shadow of a giant statue of Pazuzu. The old man and the demon effigy are face to face, each one standing on two opposing rocks. Whirlwinds, a dog fight, and a red sunset suggest the presence of the evil entity.

This is the unforgettable opening scene of *The Exorcist*, directed by William Friedkin in 1973. The film is based on the bestselling novel by William Peter Blatty (1971), who authored the script as well.[9] The movie tells the story of the possession of a young girl, Regan MacNeil, in Georgetown (USA), and the exorcism performed to save her soul. The movie belongs to the so-called "demonic child" genre, featuring children possessed by demons or incarnations of the Antichrist himself, such as *Rosemary's Baby* (1968) or *The Omen* (1976), productions of major labels that were based on bestsellers and starred top actors. Even on the theme of demonic possessions, *The Exorcist* was neither the first nor the last film to deal with the topic.[10] In 1963, Brunello Rondi shot *Il demonio*, the story of Purificata, a woman who was betrayed by her boyfriend, and puts a spell on him. Believed to be possessed, she is then exorcised in the church.[11] During the exorcism, the actress Daliah Lavi in the role of Purificata performs a spider walk, without special effects, that may have inspired the parallel scene in *The Exorcist*. Besides these connections, however, *The Exorcist* was very innovative at the time (Bowles 1976), and remains one of the classics of the genre.

8. "Curator" according to the script, and "Mosul curator of antiquities" in Blatty 1971.

9. For the passage from the novel to the movie script and the different revised versions see Blatty 1974.

10. Limited to the same decade, it is worth mentioning *Żuławski's Possession* (1981), on love relationships and psychological perspectives, and, in the mainstream, a classic of horror such as *Amityville Horror* (1979). More than 130 movies from the 1970s up to the present day reference exorcism in their titles. Since the 1970s, the last decade has seen the production of movies based on possession and exorcism, in what we could thus call exorcism-exploitation.

11. The topic and the location suggest the direct influence of Ernesto De Martino's research on possession and tarantismo in southern Italy.

The opening is divided into three scenes that are marked by changes of location, sunset/sunrise, and by the inclusion of specific sounds. The first and third scenes take place in the archaeological site. In the first scene the site is crowded and noisy; in the third, deserted and silent. The second scene is in the city, where silent/noise and deserted/crowded alternates. A red sun appears at the beginning and the end of the first scene, and also marks the end of the first part of the movie, before we move to Georgetown. At the beginning, the voice of the *muezzin* and the sunrise place us immediately in the Middle East,[12] and a few seconds after a caption informs us that we are in "northern Iraq." After the *muezzin*'s call, the soundscape is dominated by silence and repetitive rhythmic beating: first, on the site, the continuous chatter and pickaxe of the diggers; then in town, the hammer of the blacksmiths in the forge and the murmur of the shoemakers in the underground bazaar alternate with the silent square where men are in prayer or the deserted streets; finally, the hoof beats of the horse and the squeaking of the wheels of the cart that almost runs over the old man and wakes him from his trance close the scene.

The archaeological site at the beginning of the movie is not identified. It is located generically in "northern Iraq," as the caption suggests. Ancient Nineveh, however, is always directly and indirectly referenced in the book and the movie.[13] In the prologue of the book, the location of the site is vague: to the northwest lays Mosul, to the east Erbil, to the south Baghdad and Kirkuk and "the fiery furnace of Nebuchadnezzar"; however, later in the prologue, when Merrin returns to the site, it is clearly identified as the "fifteen-gated Nineveh." Blatty mentions the Temple of Nabu and the Temple of Ishtar as well as the Palace of Assurbanipal, all three situated on the mound of Kouyunjik. In the movie, the locations are Mosul for the town scenes, and the ancient site of Hatra for the archaeological excavations.[14] The ruins and reliefs of the ancient Parthian city are clearly visible.[15] The site, according to Friedkin, was perfect and lacking only the giant statue of Pazuzu that was the climax of the opening part. A statue "fifteen feet long

12. The voice of the muezzin and a sunrise or sunset over the horizon, possibly with the silhouette of a minaret or date-palms, are the main features of the Middle Eastern soundscape and visual palette in Hollywood movies from the last decades of the past century. For the depiction of Arabs in Hollywood movies of the same period, see Semmerling 2006.

13. Friedkin 2013, 505 (the page references for this source refer to the eBook version), "Merrin's discovery at the dig in Nineveh." In the movie, the cardinal speaking to Georgetown University's president says of Merrin "I think I read he was working on a dig around Nineveh." Blatty (1974, 3) mentions the ruin of Nineveh and Nimrud as the main locations in Iraq, but according to Friedkin there was no shooting at all in Nimrud and, as for Nineveh, only in the modern city of Mosul.

14. See in general Dirven 2013. Friedkin (2013, 499) speaks incorrectly of an "ongoing excavation by a German expedition that had been uncovering ancient Hatra for years." The German architect and archaeologist Walter Andrae visited Hatra at the beginning of the past century while excavating Assur, but from the fifties the site has been systematically dug by Iraqi archaeologists and lately by the Italian mission of Roberta Venco Ricciardi (1987–2002).

15. One is the bas-relief of a face or mask in the temple of Shamash.

by ten feet wide" was created in the Warner Brothers studios in Burbank by Bill Malley, based on pictures of Mesopotamian originals in the British Museum.[16]

The old man in the movie is revealed to be Lankester Merrin, the archaeologist and priest (and exorcist) played by Max von Sidow. The character is inspired by the French Jesuit and paleontologist Pierre Teilhard de Chardin (Blatty 1974, 32 [n. 29], 100 [n. 10]). This detail, as well as other elements in both the book and the script, draws from William Peter Blatty's personal life (Friedkin 2013, 411). The son of a Lebanese woman, Blatty (1928–2017) was a devout Catholic. After obtaining his master's degree in English literature at Georgetown University (a Jesuit institution and location of *The Exorcist*'s story) and several menial jobs, he joined the Policy Branch of the USAF Psychological Warfare Division and, later, the United States Information Agency in Beirut. He worked at Loyola University of Los Angeles (a Jesuit private university, now merged with the Marymount in the Loyola Marymount University) and at the University of Southern California. All these elements find a direct connection with the perspectives in Blatty's book.[17]

The opening scene in Blatty's book is slightly different from the movie. The dig is over. Merrin sits at the café (*chaykhana*) and thinks about the excavation. The mound has been "sifted, stratum by stratum, its entrails examined," and apart from few "poor" findings,[18] a lot of human bones, "the brittle remnants of cosmic torment that once made him wonder if matter was Lucifer upward-groping back to his God." This is a long reflection on decay that Blatty develops in the book through the physical features of the local people Merrin meets and is somehow repulsed by ("glaucoma ... rotted teeth"). These elements are directly and indirectly recalled in the movie through the faces of old and ill men and women.

Being an archaeologist and a priest allows Merrin to perceive what his hidden to most. What appears as an old artifact is a sign of the devil for Merrin, confirmed by the presence of the St. Joseph medal out of context. From the discovery of the amulet[19]

16. The story of the shipping of the statue, of the efforts to make vultures approach the statue and dogs fight, and finally the meeting with the "devil worshippers," the Yazidis, are described in great detail by Friedkin (2013, 500–505). Particularly relevant for ethnographic researches is the mention by Friedkin (2013, 510) of "several thousand feet of film of the Rafa'iyyah ritual" stored in "the vaults at Warner Bros."

17. Blatty's Jesuit instruction and devoutness stands out in the acknowledgements of the book where he thanks several authorities of the order and in general "the Jesuits, for teaching me to think." Blatty's theological and psychological interpretations and perspectives have been the object of criticism in most of the articles, academic and otherwise, about the movie; apart from the very same description of the author's choices in Blatty 1974, see the references in Bowles 1976, 197 n. 5, and Semmerling 2006, 261 n. 5.

18. The list of discoveries ("beds and pendants; glyptics; phalli; ground-stone mortars stained with ochre; burnished pots. Nothing exceptional. An Assyrian ivory toilet box") would not be judged as "nothing exceptional" by a real archaeologist!

19. The excavation scene at the very beginning of the movie is not in the book, where Merrin

through the sound and visual phenomena in the streets, to the final apparition of Pazuzu's statue, all these elements are a slow and increasing revelation of the evil manifestation and future fight Merrin will face in the rest of the story. In fact, when the superintendent expresses his wish that Merrin should stay, he replies that he has something to do, meaning that he has understood. In the final scene, Merrin facing Pazuzu's statue is the premise of the fight between the priest and demon. Merrin's precognition is revealed, later, by his words entering MacNeil's house in Georgetown. In Blatty's book, Merrin's premonition is quoted in the very first lines of the story. After the visit to the curator, Merrin goes back to the site seeking confirmation of his presentiment. Merrin's premonition is based on the fact that he has already met the devil! This was in Africa, "ten maybe twelve years" earlier, during an exorcism that lasted for months and nearly killed him.[20]

This explains why Merrin is tired and ill, but also conscious and resigned. The sufferance of the character is wonderfully played by Max von Sidow, who, besides his talent, was helped by the general conditions of shooting in Iraq.[21] The base of the troupe was in Mosul. Each day, by 11:00 a.m. the temperature was 130°F, necessitating two shooting sessions, from 7:00 to 11:00 and 19:00 to 22:00. Von Sidow would begin his day at 3:00 for several hours of makeup and working throughout the day, when the makeup took a further hour to remove. He took three hours sleep a night and a nap in the afternoon. The temperature added to strong wind, illnesses, and political tension. In 1973, the USA had no embassy in Iraq, which was at the time in bad relationships with most of the other Near Eastern countries as well as with USA and Israel. The Ba'ath Party had taken control of the country and Ahmed Hassan al-Bakr was the president. The troupe was the guest and hostage of the Ba'ath Party and, although they had no personal troubles, they witnessed persecutions and executions. For example, the members of the troupe have been confined for several days without knowing why; days later, they noticed that a tentative *coup-d'état* against al-Bakr had been repressed and many of the participants had been hanged, except for the head of the conspiracy, Nazir Kazzar. The general conditions and a hard daily routine helped Max von Sidow to play his role in that state of sufferance and trance.

Both Blatty and Friedkin considered the opening scene in Iraq fundamental to the construction of the character of Merrin and the entire story. It constitutes a necessary premise for the experience the priest-archaeologist will have, and for the interpretation of the symbolic aspects of the successive events. Both Blatty and Friedkin have

notices Pazuzu's head only in the curator's office. In the book, the episode of the pendulum-clock as well as the medal of St. Joseph are absent (see below).

20. The story is developed in the "apocryphal" sequel of the movie, *Exorcist II: The Heretic* (1977). This movie was only inspired by *The Exorcist* and neither Friedkin nor Blatty were involved. Pazuzu and his hypostasis, a swarm of locusts, are the main characters of this movie.

21. This and other events are described in detail in the chapter "The Devil in the Details" by Friedkin 2013.

confirmed the relevance of this part, as well as the difficulties faced while shooting in Iraq. Interestingly, besides the author and director's concerns, this opening part, and in some cases even the character of Lankester Merrin, has been opposed by producers and eventually omitted in the different theatrical remakes and radio dramas (see *passim* in Blatty 1974 and Friedkin 2013).

The crucial moment in the opening of the movie is the discovery of the St. Joseph medal and the Pazuzu head. This specific scene, as well as the presence of the medal in the site, does not appear in the book and were Friedkin's ideas.[22] The medal is among the finds dug up during the final day of excavation. The medal bears an image of St. Joseph sat with Baby Jesus on his arm. The Latin inscription reads "Sancte Joseph ora pro nobis." While he observes the object, Merrin comments "This is strange!" and the Iraqi archaeologist replies "Not of the same period."[23] I would comment that the anachronism of the object out of context adds a kind of atemporal dimension to the fight between good and evil, although, according to Blatty, there was not such intention when the scene was shot.[24] The head of Pazuzu is a pendant to be worn as a necklace. In the book, it is added that the owner "had worn it as a shield." This idea is confirmed by the words of the curator when, approaching Merrin who is in trance, he says "evil against evil." This assumption, which is at the base of Mesopotamian protective amulets,[25] is not properly developed in the plot, if not perhaps on the psychological level. Both objects are thus pendants that work as protective amulets. One recalls the good to fight the evil (St. Joseph's medal), the other the evil to fight the evil (Pazuzu's head).

Even though there is not an intentional temporal connection between the St. Joseph medal and Pazuzu's head, it is relevant. Blatty's background is clearly inspired by the biblical narrative, but the relevance paid to ancient Mesopotamia goes beyond the Bible. It points to the antiquity of such a culture, which treasures the oldest written tradition. This perspective is clearly exposed by Friedkin, who states, "Historically and biblically, there is no more important country on earth than what was once called Mesopotamia" (Friedkin 2013, 493). If, on the one hand, the biblical text underlies most of Blatty's references, such as "the fiery furnace of Nebuchadnezzar" (Dan 3), on the other hand, the amulet of the ancient demon Pazuzu who will reveal himself to be

22. See n. 19. Blatty 1974, 102; Friedkin 2013, 468. According to Blatty (1974, 103), Friedkin wanted to create an effect of the stone stele in the opening of *2001: A Space Odyssey* (1968). Indeed, many hypotheses can be found on fan pages about the medal, and in particular on the relationship of this medal to that, apparently the same, that Damien Karras is wearing. Blatty 1974, 103, writes that Friedkin's original idea was to "add resonances" to the film and a better question would be how a Christian medal ended up in a pre-Christian level.

23. The dialogues of the opening of the movie are in Arabic. In the movie the reply of the Iraqi archaeologist has not been translated in the English subtitles; Blatty 1974, 288.

24. See nn. 19 and 22.

25. Pazuzu (the entire body or only the head) and the Seven demons (Sebettu) appear on the Lamashtu amulets and are used to drive her away. "Demon" here is a generic term for noxious and dangerous entities.

the entity possessing the young girl in Georgetown, points to the pre-Christian nature of evil. Referring to the most ancient written demonological tradition,[26] the narrative is grounding an idea of the primordial origin of evil.

As the heir of antiquarianism in Gothic tales,[27] archaeology is common in horror movies and becomes more prominent in the 1970s. The reasons for this increasing success may lie in functional aspects of archaeology in the development of the narrative. First, it allows the understanding of modern events through the past. Second, the archaeologist has direct access to hidden, forgotten, or "symbolic" knowledge, and to powerful objects. He becomes the main character or the mediator with the world of the beyond, dominated by demons or God.

In *The Omen* (1976), Robert Thorn (Gregory Peck) lost his son at birth and he accepts in substitution a baby whose mother has died in childbirth. When he becomes convinced of the evil nature of the boy, Damien,[28] he decides to visit the cemetery where his real son and the boy's mother are buried. He finds the tomb of his biological son empty and, in the mother's grave, the skeleton of a jackal. The cemetery that Thorn and the photographer Jennings visit is the Etruscan necropolis of the Banditaccia next

---

26. This statement is not completely correct in many points. In particular, the terms "demon" and "demonology" are conventional modern terms not appropriate to ancient cultures such as ancient Mesopotamia; see Capomacchia and Verderame 2011.

27. Horror movies have their roots in Gothic literature, which is closely related to antiquarianism; for the rediscovery of the past and antiquarianism in Victorian England, see, for instance, the monograph of Levine 2003 and the collection of essays edited by Pearson (2006); the recent volume *The Gothic World* collects several overviews with the discussion of previous studies and bibliography, among which one on antiquarianism by Sweet (2014) and two on the relation of horror movies and Gothic literature by Morgart (2014) and Aldana Reyes (2014). Antiquarians are often characters or even the main protagonists of Gothic stories, as in the works of M. R. James (*Ghost Stories of an Antiquary*, 1904; *More Ghost Stories of an Antiquary*, 1911), who was an antiquarian himself; see Moshenska 2012. Archaeologists of horror movies have maintained the main trait of antiquarians, that is, amateurship and a connection with the beyond (see the discussion below).

28. Interestingly, Damien is the name of the main character of *The Exorcist*, Damien Karras: he is the one that lets the demon possess him and then kills himself at the end of the movie. Damien is the English form of Damianós. He and his twin brother Cosmas were physicians from Syria (third century CE) who were martyred. In popular religion, they are particularly linked to therapy and protection. In his book, however, Blatty proposes another origin for Karras's name. It is not related to St. Damien of Syria but to St. Damien of Molokai, who led a leper colony in Hawaii and finally contracted the illness and died. It would be odd that a Greek priest such as Karras would have a name related to a lesser known saint rather than to a widespread venerated saint of the Mediterranean area. I think that here Blatty, a devout Catholic and Jesuit school student, is adding a further layer to Damien Karras's character, suggesting a connection between the final sacrifice of St. Damien of Molokai contracting leprosy and Damien Karras inviting the demon to possess him. It should be noted that the birth name of St. Damien of Molokai was Jozef De Veuster and he chose the name Damien (or better the Flemish form Damiaan) from St. Damien in view of his missionary assistance to lepers.

to Cerveteri.[29] Furthermore, when convinced that his "son" Damien is the Antichrist, Robert Thorn visits Carl Bugenhagen, an archaeologist excavating the ancient site of Megiddo in Israel. Bugenhagen gives Thorn seven ancient daggers that can kill the Antichrist.[30] The character of Bugenhagen in *The Omen* recalls that of Merrin in *The Exorcist*. Both archaeologists are digging in the ancient Near East in sites with connection to the biblical narrative (Megiddo and Nineveh), and unearth highly iconic artifacts (Pazuzu's amulet and St. Joseph medal in *The Exorcist*) or powerful objects (the seven daggers in *The Omen*), which have a connection to the world of the beyond. Furthermore, their experience with evil allows them to forewarn it,[31] but their lives are nevertheless doomed.

3. The Evil Dead *(1981)*

Halfway between horror and comedy is Sam Raimy's trilogy:[32] *The Evil Dead* (1981), *Evil Dead II* (1987), and *Army of Darkness* (1992).[33] The first title of the trilogy is properly a horror movie,[34] while the sequels are horror comedies or parodies.[35]

---

29. The same location has been used for another movie focusing on archaeology, the thriller *L'etrusco uccide ancora* (1972).

30. In the sequel (*Damien: Omen II*, 1978), after Robert Thorn's death, Carl Bugenhagen receives back the seven daggers and while digging a wall in Megiddo he finds an image of the Antichrist that is identical to Damien Thorn; eventually Bugenhagen will die along with his colleague archaeologist Michael Morgan, buried alive under a collapsing wall. Yigael's walls, as it is called in the movie, bears several images that Yigael drew in the thirteenth century CE after receiving a vision of the future coming of the Antichrist (Damien Thorn). The script authors' inspiration for the name of Yigael may have come from the famous Israeli archaeologist Yigael Yadin, who directed the excavations in Megiddo in the 1960s and early 1970s.

31. It is not specified if Bugenhagen is a priest as well.

32. In 1978, Sam Raimi shot the short film *Within the Woods*, which can be considered a forerunner of the *The Evil Dead*; see n. 51. Recently, the television series *Ash vs Evil Dead*, produced by the same executive producers of the *Evil Dead*'s trilogy, stars the protagonist, Ash Williams (Bruce Campbell), obliged to face the Evil Dead thirty years after *Evil Dead*'s trilogy events (three seasons 2015–2018). In 2013 the director Fede Alvarez realized a remake of *The Evil Dead*, produced by Sam Raimi, Bruce Campbell, and Robert Tapert; while the main plot (the cabin, the party of friends, the possession) is left unchanged, and many scenes are ingenious remakes of the original ones, the story of the Book of the Dead has been omitted in favor of witches and exorcisms so (possibly too) popular in horror movies of the last decades; see n. 10.

33. The first two movies, *The Evil Dead* and *Evil Dead II*, have been released in Italy as *La casa* (*The House* 1981) and *La casa II* (1987). The success of Raimi's movies led to the exploitation of *La casa* for a series of movies unrelated to the *Evil Dead* trilogy. The common element of these movies was haunted houses. They were shot in the USA by American troupes and actors. As were many teenagers of the time, I was disappointed in attending such movies in great expectation of *Evil Dead*'s sequels until *Army of Darkness*, released in Italy as a translation of the original title (*L'armata delle tenebre*).

34. For an analysis of the movie and its position within the horror films' evolution see Hoxter 1996 and Egan 2011, 55–92.

35. Hoxter (1996) adopts the term "splatshtick" to describe the type of humour developed in *The Evil Dead*'s trilogy.

In *The Evil Dead*, a cheerful party of young people spends the weekend in a cabin in the woods of Tennessee.[36] A haunting presence, never shown[37] and mostly evoked only by sound effects, lives in the woods around the cabin. It manifests itself at the very beginning of the movie[38] and tries to cause a car accident between the car[39] belonging to the party and a red pickup just after crossing the border with Tennessee. However, the presence is only later noticed by the protagonists, having arrived at the cabin after sunset. The party of friends comprises two couples, Ash[40] and Linda, and Scotty and Shelly, plus Ash's sister Cheryl. After crossing an unsafe bridge,[41] the friends arrive at the cabin. The classic empty rocking swing that suddenly stops when Scotty approaches the door of the cabin should have warned the oblivious visitors, but, as the horror movies rules require, it is ignored. The presence first manifests itself to Cheryl. The girl is drawing a pendulum clock that is in the room. When the ticking stops, it chimes eight times.[42] From the open window the wind moves the curtains. Cheryl's hands shake and are compelled to draw a figure with a face.[43] The wind drops. Cheryl stares at the figure she has drawn and suddenly a trapdoor on the floor begins to tremble. Apparently, Cheryl tells no one what happened.[44] It is only during the toast at the beginning of dinner that the trapdoor bursts open and everyone notices it. After some words around the opened trapdoor leading to a dark cellar, Scotty finally decides to go down the stairs. His prolonged absence and lack of reply to the friends' calls cause anxiety and Ash decides to

36. The origin of the party as well as the actual location where the scenes were shot is Michigan.

37. "There are many scenes shot from the point of view of the evil force ... the Force POV" (Warren 2000, 180).

38. The movie begins with the point of view shot of the presence flying over the waters of a swamp and then through the woods.

39. The car is a 1973 Oldsmobile Delta 88 Royale; it belongs to Sam Raimi and appears in almost all his films. In *Army of Darkness*, Ash is sucked in a time portal together with his car and thrown back in the fourteenth century; the car, decorated with medieval insignia and armed as a scythed chariot with a giant rotating propeller on the bonnet, will be used by Ash finally to rout the army of the dead.

40. Ash (Ashley Joanna) Williams is the main protagonist of the entire trilogy. The shortened name Ash recalls *The Evil Dead*'s last sentence "that's all that was going to be left of him in the end"; see Warren 2000, 181.

41. The bridge, the sole connection with the rest of the world, will be destroyed—not fallen to pieces, but uprooted by the evil presence—leaving no way of escape to the protagonists; see, however, n. 49.

42. The pendulum clock showing the wrong hour, stopping, or running is a classic manifestation of evil in horror literature and movies; in *The Exorcist* it stops when Merrin takes the Pazuzu's head in the Iraqi curator office (see above).

43. The drawing is a parallelepiped with eyes, nose, and mouth roughly sketched in the middle. It is a depiction of the Book of the Dead, which will later be found in the cellar of the cabin. In the original script the drawing is a sketch of a book with ancient writing on the cover (see n. 46).

44. In the original script the trapdoor is noticed as soon as the party enters the cabin. Scotty uses the keys of the cabin to unlock the chain that secures the trapdoor, but he is unable to open the hatch. After the scene of Cheryl's drawing, Ash and Linda enter the room and ask Cheryl if the drawing is that of a Bible.

go after his friend. He finds him in a room at the end of the cellar. In one corner of the room is a table. A torn poster of *The Hills Have Eyes* movie hangs on the wall.[45] Scotty has found a rifle with ammunition on the table. Ash, instead, focuses on some notes and a strange leather-bound book with a face on the cover.[46] He begins to leaf through the book whose pages are covered with mysterious writing and drawings of skeletons, demons, etc. Scotty notices also a dagger with a hilt decorated with skulls and bones.[47] On the small table there is also a reel to reel tape recorder, which is carried upstairs by Ash and Scotty together with all the other items. The party is gathered in front of the fireplace when Ash turns the tape recorder on. The voice of an old man is heard. He will be identified later as Professor Raymond Knowby, who retired to the cabin in the woods together with his wife, Henrietta Knowby, to continue his research undisturbed from the distractions of modern civilization and academia. He found a book about the ruin of Kandar, somewhere in Egypt or the ancient Near East, which contains Sumerian burial practices and rituals. The book entitled *Naturan Demanto* (or *Naturom Demonto*) translated by Knowby as *Book of the Dead*, is bound in human flesh and inked with human blood. It deals with resurrection and demonic evocation. Some incantations allow the demons to possess the living, who then become "Deadites." The voice of Knowby reciting the incantation from the recorder activates the evil entities living in the woods, which until then had only lurked around and now start possessing one after another of the five friends. What follows is one hour of escapes, fighting Deadites, splatter, etc., ending with only one survivor, Ash. However, while he feels safe when the sun rises, the movie ends with his terrified face as he is attacked by the presence.

Evil Dead II (1987) is a remake, rather than a sequel, of *The Evil Dead*. The location (the cabin in the woods), the basic idea (demonic presences), and the main objects (the *Book of the Dead* and the "kandarian" dagger) are the same. Some characters are omitted, and new ones introduced. The party of young people disappears,[48] and only Linda makes a very short appearance. The protagonist is the iconic Ash and most of the film focuses on him. The story of the encounter of the book and of its discoverers underlies the events that occur in the cabin. Professor Knowby is now joined by his wife Henrietta, the first victim of Knowby's evocations. Having become a Deadite, she

45. This is an intertextual reference to Wes Craven, director of *The Hill Have Eyes* (1977), who in turn has referred to Steven Spielberg's *Jaws* (1975) in a sequence in *The Hills Have Eyes* and, successively, to the same *The Evil Dead* in *A Nightmare in Elm Street* (1984) in response to Raimi; see Egan 2011, 110 n. 36.

46. In the script, the book has ancient writing on the cover; see n. 43.

47. This is known as the "kandarian dagger" (Sumarian dagger in the script), as it was found together with the Book of the Dead in the ruins of Kandar by Professor Knowby. It can "terminate" Deadites. In *The Evil Death*, the blood or, better, the putrid fluid of the stabbed Deadite flows through the mouth of the skull on the hilt.

48. However, the combination of the two couples will be fulfilled in the second part of the movie; see n. 49.

has been jailed in the cellar. Their daughter, Annie, and Ed Getley, Knowby's assistant and Annie's boyfriend, reach the cabin together with a local couple, Jake and his girlfriend Bobby Joe,[49] and take part in the possessions and demonic fighting. The story of the *Book of the Dead* as well as its "mythology" is more developed with minor changes from *The Evil Dead.* We learn, for example, that the original name of the book is *Necronomicon ex mortis* (*Necronomicon ex mortes* in the original script) and was written by the Dark Ones[50] when the Earth was ruled by spirits and "the seas ran red with blood," the very same blood used to ink the book. Any reference to Egypt or the ancient Near East from the previous movie is omitted. We learn, instead, that Kandar is a medieval castle where Knowby and his group (wife, daughter, and assistant) found the *Book of the Dead* and where Ash is transported by a temporal portal that brings him back to 1300 CE at the end of the movie.

Army of Darkness (1992) is a sequel to *Evil Dead II.* Having landed in 1300 CE in Kandar, apparently somewhere in Great Britain, Ash commits himself to the quest of the *Book of the Dead,* whose incantations will free the country from evil presences and allow him to go back to his own time. The quest ends successfully, but a spell incorrectly pronounced by Ash when handling the book has a terrible consequence: he invokes the army of the dead, led by a double of Ash himself created by accident during the quest. The book is recovered, but an army of skeletons menaces the castle. Uncertain about whether to go back to his own time or to support the besieged people, Ash finally leads the vanquishing battle against the army of the dead.

Considering that *Evil Dead II* is a remake of *The Evil Dead* that is in turn based on the main plot of *Within the Woods,*[51] we can regard the three movies as being based on the same idea and motives. Raimi is the author and director of all three.[52] The changes are thus part of a mythopoetic process in which the main character, the (anti)hero Ash, is molded and the "historical" and "mythological" background of the evil presences are created. Small wonder some elements are thus extended, developed, or added, and that others are diminished or cut, creating inconsistencies that do not affect the de-

---

49. Annie Knowby and Ed Getley try to reach the cabin, but find themselves cut off by the collapsed bridge (see n. 41). The local people offer to take them to the cabin through a path through the woods. This incident grants the reassembly of two couples in the cabin as in *The Evil Dead.* Ash together with Lynda composed one of the two couples in *The Evil Dead,* and in *Evil Dead II* he plays an external role, a kind of guide or expert of the evil manifestations in the cabin and again only survivor of the party.

50. Who these Dark Ones are is never fully explained. They recall the Ancient Ones of Lovecraft's mythology, a race of alien beings erroneously worshipped as gods; see McGeough 2015c, 375–77. For the Necronomicon see the contribution of Daniele Rosa in this volume.

51. In this short movie, the plot and most of the elements of the future *The Evil Dead* are established: the cabin, the two couples, the possession; the "object" causing the evocation is not a book, but a dagger (the forerunner of the kandarian dagger) found on a Indian burial ground.

52. Raimi is the only author of *Within the Woods* and *The Evil Dead* and wrote *Evil Dead II* with Scott Spiegel and *Army of Darkness* with Ivan Raimi; see in general Warren 2000.

velopment of the two stories, *The Evil Dead* and *Evil Dead II,* and its sequel *Army of Darkness.*[53] In historic-religious terms, we have an evolving mythopoesis rather than an established mythology.

The book is called *Naturom Demonto* (or *Naturan Demanto* according to the script), translated as *Book of the Dead* in *The Evil Dead.* Besides being clearly inspired, along with many other elements, by Lovecraft and Cthulhu's myths, the book is identified with Lovecraft's *Necronomicon* (or better *Necronomicon ex mortis* or, according to the script, *Necronomicon ex mortes*) only at the beginning of *Evil Dead II,* the original name (*Naturom Demonto* or *Naturan Demanto*) disappearing. From one copy with some key pages fortuitously torn out and hidden (*Evil Dead II*), in *Army of Darkness* two more copies of the book surface.[54] Bound in human flesh and inked with human blood, it contains ancient Sumerian burial practices and funerary incantations (*The Evil Dead*); successively, the book is said to "serve as a passage way to evil world beyond" and written with the blood filling the oceans in ancient times. Even its authorship is debated. Possibly created in Egypt[55] or at least originally kept there,[56] in *Evil Dead II* the book was written by the same Dark Ones.

The site where the *Book of Dead* was discovered changes from one movie to the next. In *The Evil Dead,* the archaeological expedition is carried on at the ruins of Kandar. The references to ancient Egypt and Mesopotamia suggest the site is located somewhere in the Near East. The name Kandar is Raimi's creation,[57] possibly inspired by the Persian *kandar* "town, village" present in some modern Persian toponyms, or as an alternate spelling of Kandahar (Qandahār).[58] However, in *Evil Dead II* and *Army of Darkness,* Kandar becomes a castle in Great Britain where the *Book of the Dead* was hidden in the fourteenth century CE.

In *The Evil Dead,* Knowby describes the *Book of the Dead* as dealing with Sumerian ("Sumarian" in the script) "burial practices and rites," practically a handbook to manage the deceased. In *Evil Dead II* the book serves as a passageway to the evil world beyond; Sumerians are not mentioned, and the antiquity of the book is now taken back to

---

53. On the contrary, these inconsistencies affect the fans, who are eager for a coherent mythology. In Wiki and fan pages, the exegetical effort of the fan creates different and even new theses and hypotheses, filling the gaps and dissolving the incongruities.

54. In *The Evil Dead*'s script, the book is the first of six volumes, now lost.

55. In the comic book *Army of Darkness: Ashes 2 Ashes* (Dynamite Entertainment, 2004).

56. Only the high priests of the Ca'n Dar tribe could possess these books, according to *The Evil Dead*'s script; see below.

57. In the script the name is Ca'n Dar, which is also the name of the tribe that possesses the book.

58. Some fans argue that it is part of Lovecraft's mythology, but I have not found a reference to any such name in Lovecraft's works. The name is always written in the script and spelled as Kandar and it is possible to find it transcribed on the internet as Kandahar. Similarly, fans often mention the Kandar castle in *Equinox* (1970). *Equinox* presents several similes to *The Evil Dead* (the party of friends in the woods, the cabin, the book and a professor translating it, etc.) and has been a source of inspiration for Raimi, but the name of the castle is never mentioned in the movie.

the beginning of the world, when "the seas ran red with blood." In the *Army of Darkness*, the book is described as in *The Evil Dead*. It is an ancient Sumerian ("Sumarrian" in the script) text, containing "bizarre burial rites, prophecies ... and instruction for demon resurrection." The name "Dark Ones," those who have written the book, may recall the expression "Black headed (people)," the term the Sumerians used to call themselves, but it is clearly inspired by Lovecraft's "Ancient Ones," as the *Book of the Dead* is lately identified with Lovecraft's *Necronomicon*. References to the Sumerian(s) in Raimi's works are, however, a form of exoticism. There are no further mentions of Sumerian, nor is there any relationship between the Sumerian spells and the rest of the story. In fact, even the language of the spells is inspired by Lovecraft's language in the Egyptian "style" and sounds nothing like Sumerian at all. Oddly, in the Italian dubbing, Scotty's exclamation during Knowby's reciting ("No big deal!") has been rendered as "Senti com'è divertente il sumero!" ("How funny Sumerian sounds!"). A relationship with ancient Sumer is taken back in the television series *Ash vs Evil Dead* (season 3), where the Knights of Sumeria are an ancient order who protect the world from Deadites. The acronym KOS is engraved on the rings of the members of the order. This "resurrection" of the Sumerian origin is fictitious. The topic is not fully developed and leaves viewers with disappointment and much guesswork, according to fan comments on the webpages.

4. *Evil and the Archaeology of the Beyond*

Vague or precise, conscious or not, mere inspiration or direct reference, the use of Mesopotamian demons in popular culture highlights their antiquity, cultural remoteness, and primordiality, being that Mesopotamia was the first culture to produce written records. Thus, we can speak of a general exoticism. Elsewhere, however, the use of Mesopotamian motives is more precise and central to the narrative development. In the two movies discussed here, it underpins the idea that evil is ancient and constantly lurking. It is remote and has already been fought in the past. Evil lives in a different dimension; time stops when it reveals itself[59] and time periods overlap. In *The Exorcist*, Merrin finds the amulet of Pazuzu together with pieces from other periods, including the medal of St. Joseph. In the *Evil Dead* trilogy, the *Book of the Dead* was found and hidden several times, lastly in the medieval castle of Kandar.[60] From this perspective, evil is original, primordial, and, thus, interreligious, in the sense that different religions and beliefs fight an evil that always manifests itself in the same manner. This is the case of Pazuzu in *The Exorcist* or the Dark Ones in *The Evil Dead*.

Archaeology plays a limited but crucial role in both movies.[61] It is the archaeologist who unearths powerful objects, symbolic like the Pazuzu amulet (*The Exorcist*), or

59. For the topic of the pendulum-clock that stops tickling or runs backward see n. 42.

60. See also n. 30 for Yigael's vision of the Antichrist in *Damien: The Omen II*.

61. The "archaeologists" of these movies share common traits with the Gothic novels' antiquar-

effective like *The Book of the Dead* (*The Evil Dead*) or the seven daggers of Megiddo that can kill the Antichrist in *The Omen*. They may encounter them by chance or seek them intentionally. In *The Evil Dead*, most of the information about what happened before the arrival of Ash and his friends at the cabin, as well as of the origins of *Book of the Dead* and the demons, is provided by the direct voice of Professor Raymond Knowby in the tape recorder. It is he who leads the excavation at the Kandar ruins and unearths the *Book of the Dead* and the kandarian dagger. In the original script his name is Julian and he introduces himself as professor of ancient Egyptian mythology at Dextin University at the beginning of the recording.

Different from *The Exorcist*, where the excavation and events in Iraq are a necessary premise to the experience Merrin will face, in *The Evil Dead* the archaeologists play the classical role in unearthing hidden and dangerous "things" and invoking, consciously or unconsciously, evil and dangerous powers of the past. Usually the archaeologist is also a victim of his misdeeds. In *Evil Dead II*, Knowby discovers the *Book of the Dead* and begins its translation[62] but does not restrain himself from reciting the invoking incantations.[63] His wife is then possessed and tries to kill Knowby, their daughter Annie, and Ed Getley, who has joined the professor at the cabin with new pages of the book. Ed Getley is possessed and is "terminated" by the hand, or better the ax, of Ash. Annie dies stabbed with the kandarian dagger wielded by Ash's possessed severed hand. The

---

ians (see n. 27). They are not amateurs, but, besides their academic background and affiliation they show naïve features that have their roots in antiquarianism. Their approach to relics of the past and the contact with the beyond will be discussed below. Here it is worth noting the scholarly skills they possess go from archaeology to epigraphy, from history to religion, covering different cultures These skills, however, operate at a superficial, functional level that is subordinated to their purposes, that is, to find treasures and unveil mysteries. Enlightening is the mastering of ancient languages. Epigraphy has no mysteries for them. They can easily read ancient writings and fluently and correctly reproduce dead languages. In this sense, Indiana Jones is a real "omniglot," for he has to master the writing and language of all the ancient cultures that are the scenario of his different adventures. However, their mastering of ancient languages may go further and imply the skill to speak and understanding dead languages, if necessary. In *Stargate* (1994), Dr. Daniel Jackson (James Spader), after initial difficulty ("I can't make it out, sounds familiar. Bit like Berber, maybe Chadic or Omotic"), he is able to communicate with the descendant of the ancient Egyptians deported in the alien planet ruled by Ra. More surprising is the auditive ability of Dr. Awolowa Odusami (Hakeem Kae-Kazim) in *The Fourth Kind* (2009), who is able to identify the alien speech as Sumerian after hearing a disturbed recorded communication on the telephone.

62. In *Equinox*, the university professor ("odd" according to the police officer) Arthur Waterman is a geologist and, as a scientist, starts experimenting with the rituals of the book because he does not believe they will work. He will die. In the movie, Professor Waterman is played by the American fantasy, horror, and science fiction writer Fritz Leiber.

63. Even worse, by recording it he causes a new invocation each time the recorder is played. This is an evolution of the classical invocation curse, which is widened by recording on new technological media, such as a tape or video recorder. The best-known example is the cursed videotape of *Ringu* (1998) that evokes Sadako and causes the death of everyone who plays the tape.

fate of Knowby is not known. He certainly dies, for he appears as a spirit, pledging his daughter to recite the incantation and destroy the "evil presence" (*Evil Dead II*).

The archaeologist motivated by lust for knowledge and personal power, who eventually becomes a victim of his misdeed, is also well sketched in the genre of archaeological treasures seekers. These may be amateur diggers,[64] but in the Indiana Jones saga we are dealing with professional and academic archaeologists, as with Professor Knowby in *The Evil Dead*. In the Indiana Jones movies, the division and differences between the hero and his antagonists become relevant. René (Emile) Belloq, who literally steals Jones's discoveries, supports the Nazi quest for esoteric relics, and uses their power for his research (*Raiders of the Lost Ark*, 1981). Elsa Schneider first assists Professor Henry Jones and then his son Indiana in the quest for the Holy Grail, but she is secretly a Nazi supporter who seeks to fulfill her personal purposes (*Indiana Jones and the Last Crusade*, 1989). They both act ruthlessly to achieve their aims, which lie between scientific and personal achievement. Indiana Jones himself is often attracted and tempted by this obscure power. In his eyes, he has the same ardor of his antagonists when he looks the Peruvian golden idol, the lost Ark, and the Holy Grail, but in that very moment he restrains himself, while his antagonists do not and are doomed by their lust. Both antagonists die because of their lack of limits, Belloq summoning the spirits of the Ark, and Schneider trying to reach the Grail, which has fallen down a chasm. Their lack of scruples and dubious morality is a feature of such characters, who do not hesitate to sacrifice innocent victims for their purposes. Belloq tries unsuccessfully to seduce Jones's partner, Marion, in exchange for food and a clean dress; Schneider successfully seduces both Jones and his father to obtain information on the Grail. Besides charm and a mundane manner, the French archaeologist Belloq and the attractive Schneider have no scruples in handing Indiana to the Nazi or condemning him to certain death. In *The Evil Dead*, Knowby not only summons the kandarian demon, but in the series *Ash vs Evil Dead* (season 2) he tries to transfer the demon possessing his wife Henrietta to his student Tanya causing Tanya's death.

This image of egotism may be paralleled with that of the mad scientist of the horror and science fiction genres, but I see a slight difference between the two figures. They have many common traits. They are mostly selfish and eager for success, have a blind faith in science and knowledge, or use the two for their own purposes. However, the scientist—who can be mad, acting for the good of humanity, or for personal reasons—often aims at—or even obtains—tangible scientific progress. For archaeologists, it is more of a personal quest for spiritual or metaphysical growth and power. This discrepancy reveals a misunderstanding of the role and aim of the archaeologist (at least as a professional figure), who is perceived as someone following their passion and seeking their own progress.

---

64. See n. 27.

A crucial point regarding the wider public perception and moral valuation of these characters should be brought to the fore. In these movies, the "bad" archaeologist is the one who surpasses certain "metaphysical" limits, that is, who seek to contact the world of the beyond, be it divine, demonic, or alien. This is the case of Knowby with the *Book of the Dead*, Belloq with the Ark, and Schneider with the Holy Grail. There is no judgment on the way the artifacts are managed or trafficked. Indiana Jones has no problem in taking away artifacts from their original places and selling them to the university museum. This is his job. At the beginning of *Indiana Jones and the Last Crusade*, Indiana Jones faces Panama Hat, who has found the Cross of Coronado and reclaims it from Jones as his own property. Jones replies that "It belongs in a museum." After having burst Panama Hat's boat and killed him and his gang, he presents the Cross of Coronado to the museum of his university, adding to Marcus Brody, Jones's friend and curator of the collections, "We can discuss my honorarium over dinner and champagne tonight." Not only everyday goods are destroyed by Indiana Jones, but also ancient artifacts and entire temples in order to secure a "treasure," which is always a gold or precious object.

In Indiana Jones and the Last Crusade, when received by the American businessman Walter Donovan, Jones enters a room with cupboards displaying museum-quality artifacts that Jones observes in admiration. In Donovan's words, he and Jones are not different, since they both have "a passion for antiquities:" it is something "personal" and a "passion." Jones is perfectly comfortable with the context and Donovan's statement; he even gives consensus and credibility to Donovan by adding that he is usually very generous with donations to the museum and by praising his private collection. Donovan is revealed to be a negative character for ruthlessly fulfilling his personal aims and supporting Nazis, as did Belloq and Schneider.

Private collections and their relationship to scholars is one of the main contemporary concerns in academic archaeological debate, but has limited impact on public opinion. In popular culture, archaeologists swing from treasure seekers to researchers of hidden knowledge.[65] The image of archaeologists proposed by popular culture should lead to a serious reflection on the disparity between how "we" perceive our work and how "they" perceive our work, that is, the idea of archaeology outside academic circles (public archaeology) and, in a general sense, the perception the wider public has on how archaeological research is conducted.

Bibliography

Aldana Reyes, X. 2014. "Gothic Horror Film, 1960–Present." In G. Byron and D. Townshend (eds.), *The Gothic World*, 388–98. Cambridge: Cambridge University Press.

Blatty, W. P. 1971. *The Exorcist*. New York: Harper & Row.

———. 1974. *William Peter Blatty on "The Exorcist": From Novel to Screen*. New York: Bantam.

65. For a general overview of archaeologists in popular culture see Moshenska 2017.

Bowles, S. E. 1976. "'The Exorcist' and 'Jaws.'" *Literature/Film Quarterly* 4:196–214.

Boyes, P. 2016. "Science Fiction and Archaeology: Part 2—Grave-Robbers, Explorers and Dilettantes." *Ancient Worlds.* Online: https://ancworlds.wordpress.com/2016/10/11/science-fiction-and-archaeology-part-2-grave-robbers-explorers-and-dilettantes/ (accessed 7 November 2019).

Campbell, B. 2001. *If Chins Could Kill: Confessions of a B Movie Actor.* New York: LA Weekly Book.

Capomacchia, A. M. G., and L. Verderame. 2011. "Some Considerations about Demons in Mesopotamia." *Studi e materiali di storia delle religioni* 77:291–97.

Dirven, L. 2013. *Hatra. Politics, Culture, and Religion between Parthia and Rome.* Oriens et Occidens 21. Stuttgart: Steiner.

Egan, K. 2011. *The Evil Dead.* Cultographies. London: Wallflower.

Evil Dead Wiki. n.d. http://evildead.wikia.com (accessed 7 November 2019).

Friedkin, W. 2013. *The Friedkin Connection: A Memoir.* New York: Harper.

Hoberman, R. 2003. "In Quest of a Museal Aura: Turn of the Century Narratives about Museum-Displayed Objects." *Victorian Literature and Culture* 31:467–82.

Hoxter, J. 1996. "The Evil Dead: Die and Chase: From Slapstick to Splatshtick." *Necronomicon: The Journal of Horror and Erotic Cinema* 1:71–83.

King, L. W. *Babylonian Magic and Sorcery.* London: Luzac.

Levine, P. J. A. 2003. *The Amateur and the Professional: Antiquarians, Historians and Archaeologists in Victorian England 1838–1886.* Cambridge: Cambridge University Press.

Luckhurst, R. 2012. *The Mummy's Curse: The True History of a Dark Fantasy.* Oxford: Oxford University Press.

McGeough, K. 2015a. *The Ancient Near East in the Nineteenth Century: Appreciations and Appropriations; I. Claiming and Conquering.* Hebrew Bible Monographs 67. Sheffield: Sheffield Phoenix.

———. 2015b. *The Ancient Near East in the Nineteenth Century: Appreciations and Appropriations; II. Collecting, Constructing, and Curating.* Hebrew Bible Monographs 68. Sheffield: Sheffield Phoenix.

———. 2015c. *The Ancient Near East in the Nineteenth Century: Appreciations and Appropriations; III. Fantasy and Alternative Histories.* Hebrew Bible Monographs 69. Sheffield: Sheffield Phoenix.

McLaine, R. n.d. *Book of the Dead: The Definitive Evil Dead Website.* Accessed June 2018. http://www.bookofthedead.ws.

Mitchell, C. P. 2001. *The Complete H. P. Lovecraft Filmography.* Westport, CT: Greenwood.

Morgart, J. 2014. "Gothic Horror Film from *The Haunted Castle* (1896) to *Psycho* (1960)." In G. Byron and D. Townshend (eds.), *The Gothic World,* 376–87. Cambridge: Cambridge University Press.

Moshenska, G. 2012. "M. R. James and the Archaeological." *Antiquity* 86:1192–201.

———. 2017. "Archaeologists in Popular Culture." in G. Moshenska (ed.), *Key Concepts in Public Archaeology,* 151–65. London: University College London Press.

Semmerling, T. J. 2006. *'Evil' Arabs in American Popular Film: Orientalist Fear.* Austin: University of Texas Press.

Sweet, R. 2014. "Gothic Antiquarianism in the Eighteenth Century." In G. Byron and D. Townshend (eds.), *The Gothic World,* 15–26. Cambridge: Cambridge University Press.

Thompson, R. C. 1903–1904. *The Devils and Evil Spirits of Babylonia.* London: Luzac.

———. 1908. *Semitic Magic: Its Origins and Development.* London: Luzac.

Wallis Budge, E. A. 1930. *Amulets and Superstitions.* London: Oxford University Press.

Warren, B. 2000. *The Evil Dead Companion.* London: Titan.

Filmography

Amityville Horror. 1979. Directed by Stuart Rosenberg. USA: American International Pictures.
Army of Darkness. 1992. Directed by Sam Raimi. USA: Dino De Laurentiis Communications and Renaissance Pictures.
Ash vs Evil Dead, 2015–2018. Television series. New Zealand: Renaissance Pictures and Starz Originals. Season 1 (2015–2016), 2 (2016), 3 (2018).
Damien: Omen II. 1978. Directed by Don Taylor. USA: Twentieth Century Fox.
Il demonio. 1963. Directed by Brunello Rondi. Italy and France: Titanus.
Equinox. 1970. Directed by Jack Woods (and Denis Muren, uncredited). USA: Tonylyn Productions.
L'etrusco uccide ancora. 1972. Directed by Armando Crispino. Italy, West Germany, Yugoslavia: Inex Film.
The Evil Dead. 1981. Directed by Sam Raimi. USA: Renaissance Pictures.
Evil Dead II: Dead by Dawn. 1987. Directed by Sam Raimi. USA: Rosebud Releasing and Renaissance Pictures.
The Exorcist. 1973. Directed by William Friedkin. USA: Warner Brothers and Hoya Production.
Exorcist II: The Heretic. 1977. Directed by John Boorman. USA: Warner Brothers.
The Fourth Kind. 2009. Directed by Olatunde Osunsanmi. USA: Gold Circle Films.
Häxan. 1922. Directed by Benjamin Christensen. Sweden and Denmark: Svensk Filmindustri.
The Hills Have Eyes. 1977. Directed by Wes Craven. USA: Blood Relations.
Jaws. 1975. Directed by Steven Spielberg. USA: Zanuck/Brown Productions and Universal Pictures.
Night of the Demon. 1957. Directed by Jacques Tourneur. UK: Sabre.
A Nightmare on Elm Street. 1984. Directed by Wes Craven. USA: New Line Cinema.
The Omen. 1976. Directed by Richard Donner. UK and USA: Twentieth Century Fox.
Possession. 1981. Directed by Andrzej Żuławski. France and West Germany: Gaumont.
Ringu. 1998. Directed by Hideo Nakata. Japan: Ringu/Rasen Production.
Rosemary's Baby. 1968. Directed by Roman Polanski. USA: William Castle Productions.
Stargate. 1994. Directed by Roland Emmerich. USA: Metro-Goldwyn-Meyer.
Within the Woods. 1978. Directed by Sam Raimi. 1978. USA: Sam Raimi.

The Ancient Near East in Czech Comics and Popular Culture

The Case of Jáchym and the Printer's Devil

Jana Mynářová and Pavel Kořínek

For the early Czech comics[1]—created, produced, and published in the first half of the twentieth century—the adventure "loci communes" were often the exotic lands of Africa and the polar regions. The heat of "Sub-Saharan" Africa and the freezing loneliness of the Arctic offered a popular background to the heroic and humorous stories of early Czech comic creators. It is worth mentioning that these regions, these "places of adventure," were more often than not depicted in a general, stereotypical way, with nearly no attention to concrete geographical, historical, or political context, as was common in nearly all comic traditions at that time. The "Africa" of the Czech comics of the 1920s and 1930s was usually this imaginary chaotic place, which you could identify by the presence of sand, elephants, giraffes, hippopotami ... and of course, stereotypically depicted black natives, all nearly naked, with bulging eyes, oversized lips and the tendency for cannibalism (and/or wearing the banana girdle).

On the other hand, the representation of Egypt or the Near East was much less common: the commonplace of adventure was a wilderness, a domain of nature, not a cultural (urban, civilizational) space. These regions—with their cultural otherness—are several times mentioned, but, with the sole exception of *Kačák detektiv* (*Drake the Detective*), never fully realized. The detective duck protagonist of that singular comic by

The portion of this paper prepared by Jana Mynářová was written within the framework of the Charles University Progress project Q11: "Complexity and Resilience: The Ancient Egyptian Civilisation in Multidisciplinary and Multicultural Perspective." The portion of this paper prepared by Pavel Kořínek was written within the framework of the long-term development project, research institution 68378068. The authors would like to express their thanks to the anonymous reviewer for his/her valuable comments and suggestions, and to the institutions and individuals that kindly allowed us to use their images.

1. For a recent discussion on the history of Czech comics see esp. Diesing 2011; Kořínek and Prokůpek 2012; Prokůpek, Kořínek, Foret, and Jareš 2014.

Jan J. Holub (script) and René Klapač (art) is investigating the robbery of Mr. Hedgehog's safe deposit, and the various hints lead him finally to the heart of an Egyptian pyramid. The inspirational sources that somehow led to this story, published in 1933–1934, can be easily located in the contemporary press: the decade after the excavation of the tomb of Tutankhamun and the following sensational stories about the associated curse, and the discussions whether this tomb was in fact robbed or not, were still very well rooted in the public conscience.

After the Communist coup of 1948, the situation changed once again. Comics were perceived as something sinister, as an imperialistic menace that threatened to poison the progressive pioneer youth and therefore endanger the bright future of state controlled socialism. After a period of nearly total banning (roughly 1949–1956), comics were slowly returning to the Czech printed media, but the genre differentiation was strictly limited. The ideological critics (led by their notions of what is "appropriate," "suitable," "aesthetic," and "didactically proper") of that time demanded that the new, improved and officially recognized version of sequential pictorial narratives (since the word "comics" was in itself considered extremely dubious) would promote the everydayness of small ordinary lives. There was no place for thrilling epic or for adventure in foreign lands: Czech comics protagonists were to a large degree sentenced to the convenience of well-ordered lives (much like their audience). You want an adventure? Go on a well-organized trip to the mountains! Learn ice-skating! Or immerse yourself in forest mushroom picking!

In light of this, the exotic lands were somehow missing from Czech comics of the second half of the twentieth century. This is true even for the mostly vast serial structures of Czech comics. *Čtyřlístek* (*Four-Leaf Clover*), probably the most famous Czech funny animals comic of all time, created in 1969 as the title series of the eponymous nonperiodical "magazine," had a lot in common with similar genre series from other countries—it can be easily compared with the "Duckburg" stories of Disney (as established mainly by Carl Barks) or with the German comics about two little foxes *Fix und Foxi* by Ralf Kauka. But while in both these series Egypt and the ancient Near East (or its motives: pharaohs or mummies) were occasionally used as a story-background,[2] in *Čtyřlístek* almost no stories were set in this region (at least before the Velvet Revolution of 1989).[3] If the region was in fact used as a dominant story location in one special case—in the episode *Ztracená pyramida* (*The Lost Pyramid*) from the year 1984—it focused its setting the global tourism of modern times.

2. In the Disney Duck comics by Carl Barks and others, the depiction of the ancient Near East or its monuments was quite common. For a detailed analysis see Blum 2005. For Fix und Foxi, see for example, the story "Der magische Staubwedel" (1981).

3. After the Velvet Revolution and the opening of Czech society and the press market, *Čtyřlístek* had to adapt itself if it wanted to survive at the same newsstand as the newly imported Western comics (e.g., Disney). The adventures escalated and the idea of exotics returned to Czech comics. Since then, the quartet of animal friends from *Čtyřlístek* visited the region of the Near East on several occasions.

Similarly, the idea of time travel was also considered "adventure-related" and therefore likewise quite dubious. The only reasoning for it, the only excuse that could somehow justify this "nonsense," was if it was for educational purposes.

If we leave out the occasional depictions of the ancient Near East in didactical tableaus of "Illustrated Schools" (comics-like compositions of didactic illustrated text), the most interesting and the most important depiction of the ancient Near East from Czech comics before 1989 happened in the educational/humoristic series *Jáchym a tiskařský* šotek (*Jáchym and the Printer's Devil*) by Leo Pavlát (script) and Věra Faltová (art). This series was published in *Čtyřlístek* magazine, the only semi-periodical comic book published during normalization-era Czechoslovakia. It was somehow unique: it brought together the "comics-novice" Leo Pavlát, at that time editor of the nonfiction branch of the publishing house Albatros (that focused on books for children), with Věra Faltová, one of the most experienced Czech comics artists of all times. This comic was a sequel of sorts. In 1982 Leo Pavlát published a nonfiction book about the history of writing systems and book history entitled *Tajemství knihy* (*The Secret of a Book*). Four years later he returned to the topic and adapted it for a comic series. Among the altogether thirteen episodes published between 1987 and 1990 (*Čtyřlístek* 148–171) there are four or five closely related to the topic of this paper. This comic series offers a unique opportunity to study representations of the ancient Near Eastern world in the context of popular culture aimed at children.

Episode 1, *Obrázkové písmo* (*Picture Writing*, Pavlát and Faltová 1987a), represents an introduction to the plot. Jáchym, a schoolboy, wins a school reading contest and is awarded with a volume dedicated to the history of books (in a nice metatextual gesture it is Leo Pavlát's above-mentioned book). Upon arrival home, Jáchym and his parents find out that the book is full of misprints. A Printer's Devil suddenly appears to be blamed by Jáchym for spoiling his book. In his reply, the Printer's Devil provides Jáchym with a blue cap, allowing him to time travel, and suggests learning about the history of books by himself. As the title of the Episode 1 suggests, the very first adventure brings Jáchym and the Printer's Devil "a couple of thousand years" back to prehistory, depicted as a rocky landscape inhabited by hairy people clothed in skins and carrying mauls. A reading class is taking place at the moment with a depiction of a stag and a house and the teacher reading the "text" as "me, a stag, a house," clearly referring to a simple way to express the most basic ideas important for early inhabitants of the planet. Throughout the story the teacher proceeds to more complicated expressions including full sentences, though still expressed in ideographic writing.

Episode 1 prefigures well both the content and form of the following episodes for which a number of clichés are typical. The endeictic elements of setting the story into prehistory are above all the rocky landscape filled with wild flora and an "uncivilized" appearance of its inhabitants with long, unkempt hair dressed in animal skins and using "primitive" tools and weapons.

The next episode does not follow a chronological sequence and instead of proceeding to the earliest writings of the ancient Near East and Egypt, the readers are brought to the world of the Phoenician alphabet; a writing system the readers were already familiar with from their own language (episode *Fénické písmo = Phoenician Writing*, Pavlát and Faltová 1987b). Similar to the previous episode, the plot is rather simple with Jáchym and the Printer's Devil discovering the world of the Phoenicians. The characteristics of the Phoenicians can be easily identified as the plot takes place on a typical tub-shaped Phoenician ship with a horse head at its end. The Phoenicians are depicted with dark hair and long, dark beards, wearing knee-length white skirts. Their "primitive" demeanor is illustrated by their ignorance regarding the use of cutlery as opposed to their education, reflected in the use of the alphabet. The owner of the ship differs significantly from his crew with his long purple garb, kempt and frizzed-up hair and beard. Another part of the story is set in a quarry—a scriptorium, located not far from a Phoenician port, where Jáchym is supposed to compete in writing with a Phoenician scribe. Here once more a joust between the modern world—represented by Jáchym, asking for a paper and a pencil, and a Phoenician scribe equipped with a hammer and a stylus—takes place. The supposedly Phoenician text, incised with a stylus on the stone block is clearly depicted, organized into seven horizontal lines with four to five letters per line. While some of the letters can be read easily, there are several cases in which the identification of the original shape of the letter is impossible. As a matter of course, the individual signs cannot be read as a "text" per se, though it provides a lay reader with a relatively good outline of the Phoenician alphabet.

The third episode, entitled *Hliněné tabulky* (*Clay Tablets*, Pavlát and Faltová 1987c), brings Jáchym and the Printer's Devil to Mesopotamia, or more precisely to the world of ancient Sumer. Their adventure starts with a depiction of four cuneiform tablets bearing a single cuneiform sign on each of the rectangular ("portrait format") tablets, and a map of "Sumer" in the fourth to second millennia BCE pictured in a slightly distorted form and mentioning the rivers Euphrates and Tigris, as well as the modern city of Baghdad. Contrary to the identification of the cuneiform tablets to be "Sumerian clay tablets with a cuneiform script" the individual signs resemble mostly the Neo-Assyrian script. This is not surprising since the Neo-Assyrian script or inscriptions are often used to illustrate the cuneiform writing in Czech (or Czechoslovak) nonfiction books aimed at a general readership (see, e.g., Zamarovský 1966, 155; Klíma 1976, 32–33; Bič 1979, 110–11). In this case three out of the four signs can easily be identified as ḪA (upper right tablet, MZL 856, MEA 589),[4] GUD (lower left tablet, MZL 472, MEA 297), and APIN (lower right tablet, MZL 90, MEA 56). The only

4. There are several cuneiform sign lists, with MZL and MEA being the most extensively used. MZL is an abbreviation employed for *Mesopotamisches Zeichenlexikon* (Borger 2003) and MEA for *Manuel d'épigraphie akkadienne* (Labat 2011). In these lists, each cuneiform sign is identified by a number. These numbers—together with the abbreviation of the particular volume—are used for a distinct identification of the signs in Assyriological literature.

exception is the sign on the upper left tablet which consists of a *Winkelhaken* (a basic wedge without a tail created by pressing the point of the stylus into the clay) followed by a vertical wedge. While an interpretation of the sign as IGI (MZL 724, MEA 449) with a final horizontal wedge missing appears a possible explanation, in this case it is probably the sign UD (MZL 596, MEA 381) with two small *Winkelhaken* preceding the vertical that can be seen as the original sign. Such an explanation is based on the fact that all three recognizable cuneiform signs can be identified in a table provided to illustrate shapes of cuneiform signs in a monograph written by the same author as the comics episode and published shortly before the comics series.[5] In this particular table a simplified overview of the development of cuneiform writing from its pictographic forms to Neo-Babylonian signs and provided with logographic and syllabic readings, as well as the most basic meanings of the represented signs is provided.

The nine signs employed to illustrate the phenomena are LU (MZL 812, MEA 537), GUD (MZL 472, MEA 297), ANŠE (identified as ANŠU, MZL 353, MEA 208), ḪA (identified as KU; MZL 856, MEA 589), AN (identified as DINGIR, MZL 10, MEA 13), UD (written as UTU, MZL 596, MEA 381), ŠE (MZL 579, MEA 367), APIN (MZL 90, MEA 56), and É (MZL 495, MEA 324). Since the three signs (GUD, ḪA, APIN) depicted in the comics strongly resemble the signs in the table provided in the monograph, it is highly likely that the problematic fourth sign can be identified in the table as well. With the exception of UD, all other depicted signs are either too complex (LU, ANŠE, ŠE, É) or differ significantly (AN) from the drawing, making the identification with a corrupt writing of the UD sign highly likely.

Sign Name	**Sign Nos.**	**Neo-Assyrian Sign**
LU	MZL 812, MEA 537	𒇻
GUD	MZL 472, MEA 297	𒄞
ANŠE	MZL 353, MEA 208	𒀲
ḪA	MZL 856, MEA 589	𒄩
AN	MZL 10, MEA 13	𒀭
UD	MZL 596, MEA 381	𒌓
ŠE	MZL 579, MEA 367	𒊺
APIN	MZL 90, MEA 56	𒀳
É	MZL 495, MEA 324	𒂍

Upon arrival in Mesopotamia, the background to the story follows the same paradigm, reflecting the most routine and traditional views on the landscape as a hot, joy-

5. Pavlát 1988, 32. The first edition was published in 1982; see Pavlát 1982. According to the author, the table with cuneiform signs was adapted from Zamarovský (1983 [1966], 155), who refers to Wiseman 1958.

Figure 1. Citizens of the ancient Mesopotamian city of Ur (?), Čtyřlístek 150, 14. © Faltová heirs.

less desert under the shining sun with a mud-brick ziggurat (of Ur?) behind a city wall. While both Jáchym and the Printer's Devil are wearing felt skirts, the local man—driving a cart pulled by two oxen and clearly resembling the carts known from the King's Grave (PG 789) at Ur—is dressed in a long cloak of felt, with Gudea's royal turban on his head. The cart is loaded with baskets full of cuneiform tablets and when one of the tablets falls down (the above-mentioned "UD-sign" tablet) Jáchym throws it back, hitting the head of the man. This leads to a cart collision at the gate of the Mesopotamian city. Upon the request of the cart driver both Jáchym and the Printer's Devil are caught, manacled and brought in the presence of the ruler's son to whom the "library of fairy tales" belonged.[6]

In this part of the story the space is filled with local men dressed in long cloaks of felt, sometimes inappropriately supplemented by trousers. Most are sporting long beards with only a single adult man cleanly shaved. Their heads are either covered with various types of hats or caps or they are depicted bareheaded with their long hair kempt (even curled) and parted. Of special interest is a group of men standing at the entrance to the palace. All are standing with their hands folded in a very traditional gesture of greeting and praying (fig. 1). Their composition, as well as their dress and physical appearance with typically dominant bulging eyes resemble strongly the group of Early Dynastic II statues from the square Abu temple in Tell Asmar (ancient Eshnunna; fig. 2). As a punishment for the damage to the prince's library, Jáchym and the Printer's Devil are forced to produce a new library of cuneiform tablets. In order to frighten the two characters, the scene of hearing and the subsequent verdict is set into a room dominated by a monumental statue of a seated lion with robust open maw and shaggy thick mane. Once again, the object can be clearly identified with the actual piece of one

6. It was this library that the cart was transporting when the accident occurred.

Figure 2. Early Dynastic II statues from Tell Asmar/Eshnunna; © University of Chicago, Oriental Institute.

of the Old Babylonian terracotta lion statues originally situated at the entrance to the Dagan temple at the ancient site of Shaduppum (modern Tell Harmal) and kept in the collections of the National Museum of Iraq in Baghdad (IM 52560). In this particular case, there is even a modern-day *postscriptum* to the story. While one of the Shaduppum statues (IM 52559) survived the looting of the Iraqi museum intact, the one depicted in the comics' story (IM 52560) had its head destroyed during museum looting in 2003, in the aftermath of the U.S. invasion in the spring of the same year. The Iraqi American artist Michael Rakowitz recreated the statue as part of his exhibition project *The Invisible Enemy Should Not Exist*, giving the statue (and many other iconic objects destroyed or stolen from the Baghdad Museum) yet another lease on life.[7]

The part of the plot in which Jáchym and the Printer's Devil are preparing the material for the new cuneiform tablets is set at the banks of a river lined with palm trees and muddy soil. The production process is limited to bringing the clay in baskets, turning the clay into the proper shape (the Printer's Devil says: "The tablet must not be either large or small, either thick or thin"; fig. 3) and inscribing the tablets by scribes

7. The objects for the display were selected both based on the information provided by Interpol and the database Lost Treasures from Iraq of the Oriental Institute, University of Chicago; see especially Reichel 2005 and 2008. Photographs of both terracotta statues are available in the database at http://oi-archive.uchicago.edu/OI/IRAQ/dbfiles/objects/2192.htm (IM 52559) and http://oi-archive.uchicago.edu/OI/IRAQ/dbfiles/objects/2193.htm (IM 52560) (accessed 23 September 2019).

Figure 3. Production of clay tablets, Čtyřlístek 150, 15. © Faltová heirs.

Figure 4. Writing a cuneiform tablet, Čtyřlístek 150, 16. © Faltová heirs.

sitting at the river. The scribes are complaining about the time pressure and the accompanying text informs that "the inscribed tablets still must be fired." In spite of the Printer's Devil's endeavors, Jáchym shows his willingness to help the scribes but fails to produce proper cuneiform signs. The little imp clearly mentions: "Oh, come off it! The cuneiform writing must be mastered!" (fig. 4). When the new "library" is brought to the ruler's son, he is sitting in his bed, which is decorated with motifs from the Ishtar Gate at Babylon. An attempt to read from the newly produced tablets fails and one of the scribes can read a series of discontinuous syllables and meaningless words only. In order to mollify the upset son of the ruler Jáchym starts telling him typical Czech fairy-tales and successfully manages to bring everyone in the room to sleep.

Both episodes 4 (*Jak se dělá papyrus* = *How a Papyrus is Made,* Pavlát and Faltová 1988a) and 5 (*Záhrobní svitek* = *A Funerary Roll,* Pavlát and Faltová 1988b) continue the story in ancient Egypt. While in the first episode the production of a papyrus roll is described, it is the second part of the story in which the papyrus roll is inscribed with funerary texts. At the beginning of Episode 4 the Printer's Devil explains the difference between paper (in Czech "papír") and papyrus ("papyrus," in Czech) to a confused Jáchym, who considers the writing "papyrus" to be a grammatical mistake for "papír" written with "í." He brings Jáchym to Egypt to understand the differences between the two writing materials. The Egyptian landscape is filled with monuments (pyramids) and natural elements (the River Nile, papyrus thickets) and Jáchym together with the Printer's Devil are hiding themselves in the shadow of a pyramid observing the theft of papyrus rolls. After the subsequent fight the two are mistakenly considered to be the thieves by the chasers, who are—as representatives of power—wearing hats referring to the Egyptian royal white crown (although one is depicted in yellow). Similar to the previous episode, they are brought in the presence of a ruler sitting on a throne with his face depicted in the characteristic Egyptian side-view with one prominent eye and a black wig. They are sentenced to work on the production of papyrus rolls for free. During the harvest of the papyrus plants in the marshes they are chased by a disturbed crocodile. Trying to bite them to death the crocodile cuts the plants ("like a harvester"). Jáchym and the Printer's Devil bring the pieces of papyrus plants to the land in order to be cut into smaller ones. The crocodile intervenes unintentionally by biting the pieces into small regular stakes suitable for the further production of papyrus rolls. Later Jáchym puts down the cut bands of papyrus while the Printer's Devil runs for water. And again, the crocodile—trying to destroy their work—pestles the prepared papyrus bands with his tail and thus helps them to produce the papyrus roll. The proper process of production is depicted with two Egyptians in the background, providing a contrast to Jáchym's plot. The Egyptians are very much surprised by the successful attempt of Jáchym and the Printer's Devil to make the roll and are astonished when they realize that it was made with the unintentional help of a crocodile.

Episode 5 represents a sequel to the previous episode. Jáchym pretends to write like an Egyptian scribe but the Printer's Devil is surprised by the fact that he is using a felt pen as his writing tool. In front of them a book lies open showing a picture of the seated Old Kingdom statue of the "Louvre scribe" (E 3023), undoubtedly one of the most iconic objects of Egyptian art associated with writing and scribes.[8] Bringing Jáchym to Egypt the little devil describes the individual steps employed for writing on a papyrus. Both the Egyptian scribe and the inhabitants of the Nile Valley are depicted in a way that reflects the traditional ancient Egyptian perception of human figures. When the work on the papyrus roll is finished they can see a depiction of the protective Egyptian goddess Taweret with an *ankh*-symbol in her left hand and an unrecognized object in her right hand, identifying the contents (somehow illogically) to be a funerary papyrus. In a very abbreviated and humorous manner, the Printer's Devil explains to Jáchym the most basic ideas of one's existence in the afterlife. At that moment, they are caught and in order to save themselves they pretend to be scribes. In order to prove this claim, they are asked to write the names of several gods including those of Re, Amun, and Thoth. The Printer's Devil helps Jáchym by instructing him to draw the images of the gods. Their attempt fails but at that moment the news of the Pharaoh's death arrives, and they are asked to dispatch his funerary roll without any delay. Both Jáchym and the Printer's Devil are entrusted to deliver the roll to the Pharaoh's tomb, which would give them a chance to see his treasures. A long queue of treasure bearers trails in front of the entrance to the pyramid with each object enumerated upon its entrance to the tomb. The entrance is observed by a high official. While the ordinary Egyptians are dressed in their short white skirts, his body is fully wrapped in a long blue-gray robe, girdled in yellow (golden?) belts referring to the spread wings of a vulture goddess. His head is again covered by a white crown depicted in orange color and edged with a string of red beads. Observing the pharaoh's treasures, Jáchym is locked up inside the pyramid. When he wants to show himself to the Printer's Devil, he puts on his head a headwear closely resembling the golden mask of Tutankhamun, only to find out that the entrance to the pyramid was blocked in the meantime. The plot continues with another typical Egyptian cliché: the arrival of tomb robbers. While they are trying to break into the royal tomb, Jáchym is scared and tries to find help in the funerary papyrus. When he finally meets the two robbers, they are scared out of their wits and afraid that the Pharaoh has come to life again.[9] Jáchym, on the other hand, considers them to be creatures from the Netherworld. He finally returns back home and while the Printer's Devil sits and pretends to write like an Egyptian scribe, Jáchym realizes that in order to know more about ancient Egypt, it is much better to just read about it.

Comparing the two worlds depicted in the series, namely, the ancient Near East and Egypt, one has to notice that there are several similarities. These are mostly related

8. The very same statue is depicted in the volume of Pavlát (1988, 45).

9. Surprisingly, he is not fully dressed as a mummy, considered largely an icon of horror in nineteenth- and twentieth-century pop culture; see especially Day 2006; 2013, 2015; Halliwell 1986; Lupton 2003; Madison 1980.

to the plot itself being somehow simplified. By disturbing the ancient world Jáchym and the Printer's Devil are forced to closely observe and learn the ancient procedures to produce either a clay tablet or a papyrus roll. But there are also many differences. While in the ancient Near Eastern context the fictive story is set into somewhat realistic scenery, the Egyptian world is full of clichés accompanying depictions of the supposed reality. Thus, the episode most concisely depicting the "real world" is the third episode "Clay Tablets" set to a Mesopotamian background. Here one may even identify with certainty not only the typified objects, characteristic for the culture, but also the respective pieces present as photographs in literature and available to the authors (the ED II statues from Eshnunna, the terracotta lion from Shaduppum, decorative motifs from the Ishtar Gate from Babylon, etc.). From the perspective of historical reality, the Mesopotamian episode is more accurate than the Egyptian ones, which are definitely more schematic. This phenomenon can reflect a different level of understanding of both worlds by the general readership and the authors. Beginning in the early nineteenth century, there has been a strong and continuous wave of "Egyptomania" in Czech culture. This "Egyptomania" took different shapes and forms in architecture, as well as in literature and arts and it led to increased general awareness about visual elements of ancient Egyptian culture (see Navrátilová 2001, 2003, 2006, 2007; Prahl 2007). For this reason, Egypt and its setting is considered as largely known, and therefore the authors do not feel the necessity to "copy" the individual objects and their details (such as the "Louvre Scribe") and they can bring into the story many stereotyped components (pyramids, royal crowns, hairstyles, dresses, etc.). They simply anticipated a certain level of knowledge of ancient Egyptian reality (and realia) among their readers. On the other hand, ancient Mesopotamia, its material and spiritual world, is to a degree insufficiently presented in literature and known among the general public, and more detailed and precise depictions can be interpreted as a result of this. There are two closely related possibilities to explain this interest in exact details. It can be read as an educational gesture aimed to increase the readers' knowledge of the ancient Near East, but at the same time, it can also be a reflection of author's and artist's uncertainty when working with these topics. The higher degree of relevant details can therefore be linked to a lesser degree of knowledge on the part of both the authors and the readers. In accordance with this argument, the cuneiform writing attested in episode three is more than a random set of wedge-shaped impressions on clay; it is actual writing with individual signs clearly recognizable.

Conclusions

With its didactic character, *Jáchym a tiskařský* šotek represents a unique phenomenon in Czech comics of the twentieth century. With respect to the world of ancient Egypt and the ancient Near East it offers two different perspectives probably arising from the assumed knowledge of the readers. Especially in the second half of the twentieth century both Egypt and the Near East were presented to the general audience by means of a series of monographs, authored and translated from foreign languages. However, it was obviously ancient Egypt that drew the attention of the general public more than the ancient Near East and such an enchantment is reflected in the general level of acquaintance with its material and spiritual world. "Egyptomania" of the early days evolved into a society-wide interest in all aspects of ancient Egypt. The work of Czechoslovak and later Czech Egyptologists was widely presented in media, and fictional accounts of the lives of prominent figures of ancient Egypt became bestsellers. *Farao* by Bołeslaw Prus, in Czech *Faraon,* was published for the first time in 1899, shortly after the Polish original, and in between 1950 and 1972 it was reedited no less than five times. Mika Waltari's *Sinuhe egyptiläinen* (*The Egyptian*) had its first Czech edition in 1965 and remains one of the most beloved novels of Czech readers to this day.[10] Entering the world of ancient Mesopotamia, the authors are facing some unfamiliarity with the material on the side of their readership. In order to bridge it as well as to offer the readers an accurate picture of the ancient world they find their inspiration—in an elaborate way—in non-fiction literature. The ED II statues from Eshnunna seem to be among these "iconic" objects presented either as a group (Hrozný 1943, 56; Zamarovský 1966, 231; Brentjes 1973, fig. 96), or as individual statues[11] or even in particular details (Brentjes 1973, figs. 97–98). The city in which the story is set is highly likely to be identified as the city of Ur with the ziggurat dominating its landscape.[12] Among the dominant objects chosen to illustrate the world of ancient Mesopotamia one finds generally better-known motives such as the Ishtar Gate of Babylon (Klíma 1962, pls. XXII–XXIII; Zamarovský 1966, 41; Burian 1973, fig. 29; Hruška et al. 1977, figs. 9, 11; Součková 1979, pls. IX–XI; Moscati 1984, n.p.; Klíma 1985, pls. 10, 12a–b, 13a–b; Hruška 1987, n.p., 120) or, rather surprisingly, one of the Tell Harmal lions, which occupies a prominent position, serving to dominate the royal audience hall (Zamarovský 1966, 225; Klíma 1976, pl. XX; Součková 1979, fig. 97; Hruška 1987, n.p.).

When working on *Jáchym and the Printer's Devil,* Věra Faltová was already an established and highly experienced comics artist. Since 1965 she has published hundreds of pages in more than a dozen series. When composing the content of the panel and efficiently arranging all the figures and objects she employed her deep knowledge and understanding of comic form. Her page compositions are easily decipherable; her main

10. In 2009 Czech Television adapted the British format "The Big Read" as "Kniha mého srdce." This popular multimedia poll wanted to select—as the title says—"The book of our heart." Waltari's *The Egyptian* finished sixth of all books, leaving many Czech classics behind, see https://www.ceskatelevize.cz/porady/10214215895-kniha-meho-srdce/ (accessed 11 April 2019).

11. Usually a statue of a man and a woman, see Burian 1973, pl. I; Součková 1979, fig. 62; Moscati 1984, s.n.

12. Either as a reconstruction, based on Woolley 1939, pl. 86 or a photo of the ziggurat of Ur appears in Hrozný 1943, 80, 81; Klíma 1962, 13; Zamarovský 1966, 96, 97; Hruška et al. 1977, fig. 4; Součková 1979, 83, pl. VII; Hruška 1987, 228, 133.

characters are at the same time easily recognizable and highly stylized. Nevertheless, there is one striking difference between depictions of the ancient Egyptians and people of other geographical and cultural origin. When filling her panels with Chinese people, Romans, or Babylonians, Faltová freely selects how she draws these individuals: in accordance with the imaginary "eye of the camera" she depicts them in portrait, profile, semiprofile, etc. On the other hand, the ancient Egyptians are nearly always drawn in profile. It corresponds with the way the ancient Egyptians depicted themselves in reliefs. Věra Faltová's 1980s artistic style is in this way shaped and corrected by a millennia-old tradition. Popular culture thus depicts ancient history, but at the same it is shaped by it.

Bibliography

Bič, M. 1979. *Stopami dávných věků: Mezi Nilem a Tigridem.* Prague: Vyšehrad.

Blum, G. 2005. "Imagining Egypt." In G. Blum (ed.), *Carl Barks Collection,* Vol. 1, 223–34. Copenhagen: Egmont.

Borger, R. 2003. *Mesopotamisches Zeichenlexikon: Zweite, revidierte und aktualisierte Auflage.* Alter Orient und Altes Testament 305. Münster: Ugarit-Verlag.

Brentjes, B. 1973. *Zlatý věk lidstva.* Translated by J. Součková. Prague: Orbis. Translation of Brentjes, B. 1968. *Von Schanidar bis Akkad.* Leipzig, Jena, Berlin: Urania-Verlag.

Burian, J. 1973. *Cesty starověkých civilizací [Pathways of Ancient Civilizations].* Prague: Práce.

Day, J. 2006. *The Mummy's Curse: Mummymania in the English-speaking World.* London and New York: Routledge.

———. 2013. "The Maid and the Mummy." In R. Dann and K. Exell (eds.), *Egypt: Ancient Histories, Modern Archaeologies,* 193–231. New York: Cambria.

———. 2015. "Repeating Death: The High Priest Character in Mummy Horror Films." In W. Carruthers (ed.), *Histories of Egyptology: Interdisciplinary Measures.*), 215–26. Routledge Studies in Egyptology 2. New York and London: Routledge.

"Der magische Staubwedel." 1981. *Fix und Foxi Sonderheft Zaubern* 13:3–11.

Diesing, H. 2011. *Český komiks 01. poloviny 20. století.* Prague: Verzone.

Halliwell, L. 1986. *The Dead That Walk: Dracula, Frankenstein, the Mummy and Other Favorite Movie Monsters.* New York: Continuum.

Hrozný, B. 1943. *Nejstarší dějiny Přední Asie a Indie [The Earliest History of Near East and India].* 2nd ed. Prague: Melantrich.

———. 1987. *Pod babylónskou věží [Under the Tower of Babylon].* Prague: Práce.

Hruška, B., L. Matouš, J. Prosecký, and J. Součková. 1977. *Mýty staré Mezopotámie: Sumerská, akkadská a chetitská literatura na klínopisných tabulkách [Myths of Ancient Mesopotamia: Sumerian, Akkadian, and Hittite Literature on Cuneiform Tablets].* Prague: Odeon.

———. 1962. *Společnost a kultura starověké Mezopotámie [Society and Culture of Ancient Mesopotamia].* Prague: Nakladatelství Československé akademie věd.

———. 1976. *Lidé Mezopotámie [People of Mesopotamia].* Prague: Orbis.

———. 1985. *Zákony Asýrie a Chaldeje: Pokračovatelé Chammurapiho [Laws of Assyria and Chaldea: Continuators of Hammurabi].* Prague: Academia.

Kořínek, P. 2014. "Komiksová menažérie Věry Faltové." In V. Faltová and V. Steklač (eds.), *Dobrodružství Mořských vlků,* 218–30. Prague: Albatros.

Kořínek, P., M. Foret, and M. Jareš. 2015. *V panelech a bublinách: Kapitoly z teorie komiksu.* Prague: Akropolis.

Kořínek, P. and T. Prokůpek. 2012. *Signals from the Unknown: Czech Comics 1922–2012*. Řevnice, Czech Republic: Arbor Vitae.

Labat, M. 2011. *Manuel d'*épigraphie *akkadienne (Signes, Syllabaire, Idéogrammes)*. 6th ed. Paris: Geuthner.

Lupton, C. 2003. "'Mummymania' for the Masses: Is Egyptology Cursed by the Mummy's Curse?" In S. MacDonald and M. Rice (eds.), *Consuming Ancient Egypt*, 23–46. London: University College London.

Madison, A. 1980. *Mummies in Fact and Fiction*. New York: Franklin Watts Library.

Moscati, S. 1984. Živoucí *minulost* [*Living Past*]. Prague: Panorama. Translation of S. Moscati, *Il passato che vive*, 1979. Milan: Mondadori.

Navrátilová, H. 2001. "Some Egyptianizing Theatre Decorations at the Stage of the National Theatre in Prague, 1883–1900." *Archiv Orientální* 69:419–26.

———. 2003. *Egyptian Revival in Bohemia 1850–1920*. Prague: Set Out.

———. 2006. "The Egyptian and the Egyptianising art inspiration in Bohemia: the case of Ludwig Kohl (1746–1821)." In J. Holaubek, H. Navrátilová, and W.B. Oerter (eds.), *Egypt and Austria II: Proceedings of the Prague Symposium, October 5th to 7th, 2005*, 115–22. Prague: Set Out.

———. 2007. "The Wisdom of Egypt in the Art of František Bílek." In T. Glück and L. Morenz (eds.), *Exotisch, weisheitlich und uralt: europäische Konstruktionen Altägyptens*, 265–80. Münster: LIT.

Pavlát, L. 1982. *Tajemství knihy* [*The Secret of a Book*]. 1st ed. Prague: Albatros.

———. 1988. *Tajemství knihy* [*The Secret of a Book*]. 2nd ed. Prague: Albatros.

Pavlát, L., and V. Faltová. 1987a. "Jáchym a tiskařský šotek: Obrázkové písmo" ["Jáchym and the Printer's Devil: Picture Writing"]. *Čtyřlístek* 148:24–29.

———. 1987b. "Jáchym a tiskařský šotek: Fénické písmo" ["Jáchym and the Printer's Devil: Phoenician Writing"]. *Čtyřlístek* 149:18–23.

———. 1987c. "Jáchym a tiskařský šotek: Hliněné tabulky" ["Jáchym and the Printer's Devil: Clay Tablets"]. *Čtyřlístek* 150:12–17.

———. 1988a. "Jáchym a tiskařský šotek: Jak se dělá papyrus" ["Jáchym and the Printer's Devil: How a Papyrus is Made"]. *Čtyřlístek* 153:18–23.

———. 1988b. "Jáchym a tiskařský šotek: Záhrobní svitek" ["Jáchym and the Printer's Devil: A Funerary Roll"]. *Čtyřlístek* 155:18–23.

Prahl, R. 2007. "Egyptianising Motifs on Tombs in the Czech Lands around 1800: The Periphery of Egyptomania?" In J. Holaubek, H. Navátilová, and W. B. Oerter (eds.), *Egypt and Austria III: The Danube Monarchy and the Orient; Proceedings of the Prague Symposium, September 11th to 14th, 2006*, 191–206. Prague: Set Out.

Prokůpek, T., P. Kořínek, M. Foret, and M. Jareš. 2014. *Dějiny československého komiksu 20. století* [*History of Czechoslovak Comics of the Twentieth century*]. Prague: Akropolis.

Reichel, C. 2005. "Beyond Cataloguing Losses: The Iraq Museum Database Project at the Oriental Institute, University of Chicago." *Visual Resources* 21(1):93–113.

———. 2008. "Cataloging the Losses: The Oriental Institute's Iraq Museum Database Project." in G. Emberling and K. Hanson (eds.), *Catastrophe! The Looting and Destruction of Iraq's Past*, 51–63. Oriental Institute Museum Publications 28. Chicago: The Oriental Institute Museum of the University of Chicago.

Součková, J. 1979. *Starověký Přední východ* [*Ancient Near East*]. Prague: Mladá fronta.

Wiseman, D. J. 1958. *Illustrations from Biblical Archaeology*. Grand Rapids, MI: Eerdmanns.

Woolley, L. 1939. *Ur Excavations*, Vol. 5, *The Ziggurat and Its Surroundings*. Publications of the Joint Expedition of the British Museum and of the University of Pennsylvania, Philadelphia, to Mesopotamia. London and Philadelphia: British Museum and University Museum.

Zamarovský, V. 1966. *Na počátku byl Sumer* [*At the Beginning There Was Sumer*]. 1st ed. Prague: Mladá fronta.

———. 1983. *Na počátku byl Sumer* [*At the Beginning There Was Sumer*]. 2nd ed. Prague: Panorama.

Gilgamesh, The (Super)Hero

Luigi Turri

In the novel *The Time Masters* (1953) by Wilson Tucker, we can read the following dialogue between a certain Shirley and a certain Gilbert Nash:

> "The point is slowly becoming clear. The translator found a Biblical story on the stone tablets." ... "No. He found what was supposed to be a work of pure fiction." ... "And the tablets were supposed to be how old?" "Three or four thousand years. Do you see now why the Victorians suddenly suffered rising blood pressure?" (Tucker 1953; cited from *Startling Stories*, vol. 31, no. 2 [1954], 45–46).

And in fact, at the meeting of the Society of Biblical Archaeology in London, on 3 December 1872, when George Smith, a former banknote engraver and a brilliant self-taught Assyriologist, gave his lecture on the Chaldean account of the deluge, someone must have suffered rising blood pressure: either because of the sensational discovery itself—a text thousands of years old, now known as the eleventh (clay, not stone) tablet of the standard Babylonian epic of Gilgamesh, or because this text, which tells the story of the great flood, was older than the Bible.[1] As George Smith's patron, Sir Henry Rawlinson, explained,

> the tablets found in the ruins of Nineveh dated only from the age of Sardanapalus [i.e., Assurbanipal], in the sixth or seventh century BC, yet they were copies of very more ancient documents.[2]
>
> [They] belonged to the time of a monarch whose name ... Mr. Smith was unable to read phonetically, and therefore called him by the value of the signs of

1. The story of this discovery is related by Smith himself (1875a). A detailed account of these events and the subsequent developments that led to the assemblage of the whole Gilgamesh corpus, is given by Silvia Chiodi in the afterword to Pettinato 2004, 451–503. For the reaction to the discovery, see Ziolkowski 2011, 8–15 and Cregan-Reid 2013.

2. I was able to find the article "The Chaldean Story of the Deluge" in several New Zealand newspapers, dated February or March 1873, the earliest being the *Otago Daily Times*, 22 February 1873, supplement, 6. All of them report that the article comes from the *Liverpool Mercury*, but do not specify the date.

> his name, Izdubar, and he probably lived in the epoch immediately following the flood.[3]

The author was "a heathen, a contemporary of Noah; and it was undeniable that" he "could never have heard of the Bible—since it had not been written at that time" and he "had written the history of the flood in a most unbiased manner, and had not had the advantages of inspiration in the matter from on High. Yet in the discovered stones they had a history of the flood identical with the account given in Genesis." This "corroboration" of the Bible text occurred at a time when "a large number of savants were causing a great turmoil to disprove the authenticity of the Mosaic History of the Deluge."[4] "This discovery is evidently destined to excite a lively controversy.... It is possible that the Chaldean inscription, if genuine, may be regarded as a confirmation of the statement that there are various traditions of the deluge apart from the Biblical one, which are perhaps legendary like the rest."[5]

1. *The Hero Reborn*

After almost two thousand years, this was the first public appearance of Gilgamesh, or Izdubar as he was called then. At that time the press was the only existing mass media, and Gilgamesh got a lot of attention from it worldwide. It is true that at the beginning it was the great flood that attracted everyone's attention and even Smith himself stated that the stories of Izdubar "are principally of interest from their containing the Chaldean account of the Deluge" (Smith 1875b, 166). To reinforce the connections with the Bible, even the characters of these stories were linked to biblical ones and so Izdubar became "the same as the Nimrod of the Bible" (Smith 1875a, 166). But someone had already started to notice Izdubar/Gilgamesh, and in a review of Smith's *Assyrian Discoveries* we can read that two-thirds of the volume are "devoted to translations and discussions of inscriptions newly discovered or made more complete by the new discoveries. The first in order and in interest is the cycle of Izdubar legends," and here the reviewer relates the story, with the deluge as just an episode within it—a story inside the story, told to Izdubar by one of the other characters. The author of the review stresses that "we have here not merely the oldest but so far as we know, the only true epos in the whole range of Semitic literature."[6]

It did not take long before Gilgamesh acquired an audience and became part of popular culture, breaking out of the restricted domain of Assyriology. He was univer-

3. "A Chaldean Story of the Deluge," *Chicago Daily Tribune*, 24 December 1872, 7.

4. "The History of the Flood," *The Colonist*, Nelson, New Zealand, 2 May 1874, 4.

5. "English Notes: Miscellaneous Gossip from the British Capital; Noah's Log," *The New York Times*, 22 December 1872, 1. For Mr. Smith's position on the topic, see Smith 1875b, 284. For a summary of the Babel-Bibel Streit, see Ponchia 2013 with literature.

6. "New Publications: Smith's Assyrian Discoveries," *The New York Times*, 27 February 1875.

sally acclaimed as an authentic hero and the stories of his deeds were compared to the classical epos: *Das Babylonische Nimrodepos* (*The Babylonian Nimrod Epic*; Haupt 1884) was the title of the first complete cuneiform edition of the text, while the subtitle of its first translation was *Eine altbabylonische Heldensage* (*An Old Babylonian Heroic Saga*; Jeremias 1891); this latter book was particularly important because it gave access to the text to a general audience of non-Assyriologists (at least those able to read German).

There was such hype surrounding the rediscovered hero that even the esteemed scholar Theophilus Pinches (1889–1890, 264) started a short seminal note so enthusiastically that the text resembles more a sensational front-page headline than an academic work: "It has been found at last, the long wished-for reading of the name of the well-known hero, and it is neither Gišṭubar, nor Gišdubar, nor Gišdubarra, nor Izdubar, nor finally, Namraṣit, but GILGAMEŠ."[7]

2. *The First Hero*

Soon the so-called Gilgamesh epic[8] was labeled as "the most notable literary product of Babylonia as yet discovered in the mounds of Mesopotamia" (Jastrow and Clay 1920, 9) and still today it is considered, "as matter of fact, the most ancient known epic-heroic poem" (Pettinato 2003, iii). This means that its eponymous hero is also the earliest hero. This primacy was clearly acknowledged in the 1950s by Samuel Noah Kramer, one of the most renowned twentieth-century experts on Sumerian history and language: in a didactic book about the "Firsts" in recorded history (Kramer 1981), Gilgamesh—as man or literary work—features in nine out of thirty-nine of these: for example, he is said to be the first to convoke a bicameral congress ("First" no. 5; Kramer 1981, 30–35)[9] and "the original St. George," the first human to slay a dragon, the monster Huwawa ("First" no. 22; Kramer 1981, 168–80)—and we can add that he could also be the first "man of many devices,"[10] because he defeated the monster with his wit exactly as Odysseus did with the Cyclops Polyphemus. The works analyzed by Kramer were ancient Sumerian poems and not the more recent Babylonian version discovered by Smith, the last part of which, according to the author, "is nothing more than a practically verbatim translation into the Semitic Akkadian ... of the second half of a Sumerian poem"—so the first case of literary borrowing ("First" no. 23, Kramer

---

7. On the name of Gilgamesh, see George 2003, 71–90.

8. In the ancient Near East there was not the custom of giving titles to literary works. In library archives they were called by their first line, in this case: "He who saw everything." See Pettinato 2006, xvi–xxiv.

9. The congress consisted of the assembly of the elders on one side and that of the armed male citizens on the other.

10. This is Murray's 1919 translation of πολύτροπος, the epithet that Homer used to designate Odysseus in the first line of the Odyssey. The word "may be translated versatile or resourceful," according to Snider 1895, 6.

1981, 181–222). In fact various people recounted, handed down, rewrote, extended, and enriched for two thousands years the deeds of the hero. After the Sumerians, there were the Assyrians and the Babylonians, then the Hittites, the Syrians, the Palestinians, the Hurrians and the Elamites—all the people of the ancient Near East.

On this basis, it was natural for Kramer to conclude that the Gilgamesh stories were the product of Man's First Heroic Age ("First" no. 24, Kramer 1981, 223–44). At the beginning of the twentieth century, the Heroic Ages were at the center of H. M. Chadwick's studies on oral poetry and traditional literature. In his view,

> the type of poetry commonly known as heroic is one which makes its appearance in various nations and in various periods of history. No one can fail to observe that certain similar features are to be found in poems of this type which are widely separated from one another both in date and place of origin," and he concludes "that the resemblances in the poems are due primarily to resemblances in the ages to which they relate and to which they ultimately owe their origin.[11]

So according to this early twentieth century view, a Heroic Age is a stage in the development of human societies likely to give rise to legends about heroic deeds, that were handed down in orally transmitted tales and converted into literature centuries later. Kramer adds that,

> while there is little doubt that some of the adventures celebrated in the poems have a historical basis, the poet does not hesitate to introduce unhistorical motifs and conventions, such as exaggerated notions of the heroes powers, ominous dreams, and the presence of divine beings.... The pattern of Sumerian heroic poetry is similar to the pattern of Greek, Indian, and Teutonic epic material

and

> since it is hardly likely that a literary genre so individual in style and technique as narrative poetry was created and developed independently, at different time intervals, in Sumer, Greece, India, and Northern Europe, and since the narrative poetry of the Sumerians is by all odds the oldest of the four, it seems reasonable to conclude that in Sumer may be found the origin of epic poetry.[12]

---

11. Chadwick 1912, vii–viii. Hector M. Chadwick was a scholar who aimed to integrate the philological study of Old English with archaeology and history.

12. Kramer 1981, 226. These are three Indo-European Heroic Ages, which flourished toward the end of the second millennium BCE, and the latter in the mid-first millennium CE; they later evolved, in their written forms, into the Homeric poems, the Mahabarata, and the Nordic saga.

To date we know of ten or so not-so-long Sumerian poems that could be identified as epic tales, half of which revolve around Gilgamesh (see George 2003, 4–17), who according to the *Sumerian King List* was the fifth king of the Dynasty of Uruk.[13] The first historically attested dynasty, between 2800 and 2600 BCE, was the first Dynasty of Ur, which followed that of Uruk. So the Heroic Age of Sumer must be placed earlier, in the fourth millennium, during what for archaeologists is the Uruk period, marked by the emergence of urban life in Mesopotamia.

In the late 1920s Robert Howard, one of the most prolific authors of pulp magazines, started to build his own imaginary Heroic Age, the Hyborian Age (see Howard 1938; Shanks 2012), much older than Gilgamesh and any known Heroic Age, but with which it shares many features: one mighty hero, extraordinary deeds, powerful enemies, vengeful gods, and supernatural beings. The language and style are less impressive, despite the many epithets used, and the absence of any possible historical connections makes the suspension of disbelief easier; reading becomes just a guilty pleasure. So from Heroic Age to the Heroic Fantasy, the new popular literary genre invented by Howard, there is but a short step: it is enough to eliminate the historical basis. The use of distinguished names taken from proper heroic sagas tickles the reader, who knows, maybe unconsciously, that he has heard them before, but does not need to know precisely who they are: in Howard's artificial mythology, Ishtar is one of the most important Hyborian goddesses, and the main hero Conan is a Cimmerian, but they have nothing to do with the goddess that tempted Gilgamesh or the people who—according to Homer—lived at the edge of the world, beyond the Ocean, near the entrance of Hades.

Howard was an avid reader, but he grew up and spent most of his short life in the small town of Cross Plains, Texas, and consequently had limited access to libraries; his main reading material was magazines (Finn 2012, 55). So we can suppose that his knowledge of Mesopotamian culture came mainly from popular books and articles, but that was enough to spark his imagination. As far as I know he never mentions Gilgamesh directly in his works but novelettes such as *Black Colossus* (1933) and *Rogues in the House* (1934) are full of references to Mesopotamian characters and so on. The convergence of heroic epic themes with those of heroic fantasy and the path opened by Howard towards the free use of mysterious ancient characters have influenced later fantasy. It is quite significant that the illustrations of *L'Épopée de Gilgamesh: Le Trône d'Uruk* (2010), a graphic novel by Brion and Blondel very loosely based on the Sumerian poem *Gilgamesh and Agga*, resemble more Howard's Conan than a Sumerian mythical king: the main purpose of this comic is clearly to entertain and amaze the readers with its powerful and spectacular oil painting-like drawings and with the deeds of a hero called Gilgamesh.

---

13. For the Sumerian King List see the classic Jacobsen 1939 and updated bibliography in The Electronic Text Corpus of Sumerian Literature (http://www-etcsl.orient.ox.ac.uk/).

3. *The Universal Hero*

After his great success in antiquity, toward the half of the first millennium BCE, with the fall of Nineveh and Babylon, the hero started to fall into oblivion and the numerous texts that told of his adventures remained buried under the sand, together with the civilizations that had written them,[14] until their nineteenth-century rediscovery. But although the name of Gilgamesh did not survive the fall of the civilizations that created him, the topics, episodes, and suggestions of the epics seem to resurface repeatedly in the Homeric poems, the Bible, the Arabian Nights, and so on, as far as the Romance of Alexander.[15] This is because the themes dealt with are universal and the imagery is shared by the entire world,[16] so it should not be a surprise that some modern versions of Gilgamesh more closely resemble another Heroic Age, that of Homer, more familiar to us, than an ancient Near Eastern one. It is enough to look at a Spanish television production, "En Busca de la Inmortalidad" (2001, episode of the series *Crónicas de la Tierra Encantada*), directed by Jose Ortega, who also wrote the novel *Gilgamesh y la muerte*: his Siduri is by far more similar to Circe or Calypso than to a Sumerian or Babylonian goddess.[17] It might be objected that this could have been due to the production's budget constraints, but it is undeniable that it offers us a more familiar portrayal, which distracts viewers' attention less than an exotic representation and thus facilitates concentration on the aspects that the author wants to emphasize. Since the early twentieth century, then, in treatments of the epic, the philological and historical details have often been downplayed in favor of more personal interpretations of its themes. Besides the precursors from high culture and fine or elite arts (see Ziolkowski 2011), Gilgamesh resurfaces in hundreds of different works of popular art, novels, comics, music, and television.

4. *The Hero in Outer Space*

Gilgamesh seems to have found a privileged place in speculative fiction products,[18] especially in the genre of science fiction, which should not be surprising. Science fiction arose with the transformations wrought by the Industrial Revolution and deals with the

---

14. On the very few mentions of Gilgamesh after the fall of Nineveh, see Tigay 1982, 251–55; George 2003, 60–64; 2007. On the mention in Aelian's Περὶ ζῴων ἰδιότητος (*On the Nature of Animals*), see Henkelman 2006.

15. See, e.g., Lord 1990 (other epics), Dalley 1991 (Arabian Nights) and Henkelman 2010 (Alexander).

16. A forthcoming article will be devoted to Jung, "archaic remnants," "primordial images," and "archetypes." On these topics see Jung 1964, 67–73.

17. On the similarities between Siduri and Circe or Calypso, see Nagler 1996.

18. The Oxford Dictionary defines "speculative fiction" as "a genre of fiction that encompasses works in which the setting is other than the real world, involving supernatural, futuristic, or other imagined elements." On the subject see Heinlein 1947.

impact of science and technology upon society and individuals: its themes include travel in other worlds, alien beings, dystopias, and prophecies, and many of these subjects are present in the Gilgamesh epic—the adventurous trip to the Cedar Forest and the fight with Humbaba, the prophetic dreams, the quest for immortality—with the only difference that instead of science these concerned religion. We have to bear in mind that in the past, religion was used to explain natural phenomena or even as a substitute for medicine, so its function was not too different from that of science today.

The formal consecration of Gilgamesh as a sci-fi character arrived in 1977, when the author and academic scholar James Gunn started to publish the successful (and still in print) anthology series *The Road to Science Fiction,* a sort of textbook that reviews the evolution of science fiction literature. The first of the six volumes is subtitled *From Gilgamesh to Wells,* and although no passage from the epic is present, our hero has the honor of being in the title and an important role in the introduction:

> Gilgamesh's concerns are those of science fiction: social (people need a heroic king, but what do people do when a king rules too heavily?) and personal (can man live forever, or, if not, how does he live with the fact of death?) ... The epic even contains a bit of technology, not only the weapons with which Gilgamesh and Enkidu do battle but the bricks with which the wall of Uruk is built.

Gunn explicitly compares Gilgamesh to "the novels of Edward Elmer Smith, particularly the Lensman series," one of the masterpieces of space opera, a subgenre of science fiction—or its degeneration, as it is considered by the purists—in which interplanetary battles are seasoned with chivalric romance and melodramatic adventure, while science and plausibility—key elements of proper sci-fi—are left aside. The term "space opera" was coined in the 1940s by Wilson Tucker, a prolific sci-fi writer, fanzine publisher, and pioneer critic, nonetheless one of the first to use Gilgamesh in works of this genre. In *The Time Masters* (1953), the main character, Gilbert Nash, seems to have no past—but actually he has one! He is a humanoid alien—the only differences from humans seem to be extreme longevity, telepathic abilities, and a yellow cornea—who hurtled to Earth ten thousand years ago; he has lived through the millennia, guiding humanity toward civilization, and had many identities, one being that of Gilgamesh. Nowadays, in the novel, he is working as a private detective and has to find Carolyn, the missing wife of a scientist involved in the top-secret Ridgerunner Project, which aims to send a spacecraft beyond the solar system for the first time. Then the scientist is found dead, and Nash begins to suspect that the missing wife is the murderer and also the only other surviving alien, considered for centuries a goddess by humans (e.g., the white goddess in south Africa and Palestine, Hathor in ancient Egypt, and the lioness goddess in Crete), who is now trying to find a way back to the stars.

Gilbert Nash comes back in *Time Bomb* (1955). Here, Lieutenant Danforth (soon to be dismissed) is investigating a series of mysterious explosions that are killing members of the Sons of America, a fanatical extremist group that is close to seizing power in the United States. He suspects that—incredibly—the terrorists are operating from the future. Nash stays in the background, observing, and guiding Danforth to the solution.

As should be clear from these quick glances at these two novels' plots, Gilgamesh is just a pretext, a stratagem to create a mysterious and charming character because antiquity is far-off, vague, obscure, and fascinating, just as outer space is. Except for some facetious remarks—such as those at the beginning and end of this text—very little else connects Nash to our hero. On the other hand, the use of Gilgamesh implies that in the 1950s he must have been already rather well known, even to the common reader.

This free use of a hero and his companions' names—as we have seen in heroic fantasy—is rather common in all kind of speculative fiction products: novel, cartoons, even videogames.[19] A Gilgamesh, dressed as a kabuki actor, roams across dimensions thanks to the power of No-thing in the videogame franchise *Final Fantasy*.[20] The smart and skillful warrior, with his gigantic ego, sometimes accompanied by his friend Enkidu, is one of the foremost characters in the long saga started in 1987 and not yet finished. Another Gilgamesh appears in the Japanese visual novel *Fate/stay night* (2004) and related products,[21] as a selfish, arrogant, and sadistic being; he became that way after the death of his only friend Enkidu. Involved in the wars for the conquest of the Holy Grail (!), he is one of seven resurrected souls, the most powerful one, being mankind's oldest hero, the original model on which other heroes are based. Each one of these resurrected souls possesses superhuman characteristics and abilities or artifacts called Noble Phantasms: Gilgamesh's are the "Gate of Babylon," "Enkidu: Chains of Heaven," and "Ea: Sword of Rapture."

When Richard Chandler, director of the low-budget movie *Gilgamesh* (2014), was asked how faithful he remained to the ancient texts, he answered: "Not very faithful. That is where I got the name from, but instead of a king, my version of Gilgamesh is an entity. But does dress similar" (Haberfelner 2011). In another interview, he says, "Just about none of that poem was used. I've been getting calls from all over the world, mainly from guys from the Middle East, asking if we were making the same film.[22] It's getting

---

19. See Couto-Ferreira 2008 for the apocalyptic Japanese animated series "Gilgamesh" (2003, 26 episodes). This "anime" was based on a previous homonymous "manga" (i.e., Japanese comic) by Shotaro Ishinomori, serialized between 1976 and 1978.

20. The official website (http://www.finalfantasy.jp/) is available only in Japanese. See alternatively http://finalfantasy.wikia.com/wiki/Final_Fantasy_Wiki.

21. A visual novel is an interactive game consisting of narration and interactive elements. See Cavallaro 2009, 8 (definition) and 146–60 (Fate/stay night). Several mangas, animes, and novels are derived from the original title.

22. Probably Chandler is talking about Gilgamesh (2011) by Peter Ringgaard, a Bahrain/Denmark production, spoken in Arabic, and the only movie faithfully adapted from the epic, though rather short.

funny. When I tell them this is sci-fi and I just like ancient Sumeria, they become very confused" (Loeffler 2014a). Another context expresses the plot of the movie, which is about

> a military expedition in Siberia gone wrong. The existence of humanity is in peril as Inanna, Sumerian goddess of lust and war has summoned a giant meteor to destroy the planet, after being accidentally set free from her ancient prison. Her captor, and the planet's guardian, Gilgamesh must embark on an epic quest to save the human race from Inanna's wickedness. With the government failing, the economy plummeting, and anarchy running wild, a true tale of good and evil shall be told through the eyes of our savior.[23]

To sum up, according to the webzine *Yell! Magazine*, "*Gilgamesh* is an interesting film that may or may not be about the U.S. and its foreign and domestic policies. You'll have to decide that for yourself" (Loeffler 2014b).

A consistent mix of allusions to well-known characters and stories from the past is typical of many steampunk novels. In *Codex Gilgamesh* by Umberto Ceretoli (2013) the resurrection of the Immortals' Army of our hero is the aim of baron Victor von Frankenstein, who fled from London on a flying ship projected by Leonardo da Vinci and is chased by Eudora, Hunter of Her Majesty Queen Victoria. The extravaganza of the plot hides interesting causes for reflection on the consequences of progress, human limits, and the precariousness of his knowledge. And this somehow creates a link to the themes of the epic.

Motivic analogies are one of the "four basic modes of modernization" identified by Ziolkowski (2011, 47–48), the other being translations, fictionalizations, and postfigurative interpretations. All of them—including translations, as we will see—are used in sci-fi works dealing with Gilgamesh. Fictionalization might vary a lot, from faithful reconstruction to ways to narrate other stories, as in the case of the Doctor Who novel *Timewyrm: Genesys* by John Peel (1991).[24] But analogies seem to be preferred; a vivid example comes from "Darmok," an episode of *Star Trek—The Next Generation*[25] that is considered by fans one of the best and most profound of the entire series (Hoffman 2013). In their effort to make contact with the Tamarian race, the *Enterprise* crew is baffled: their universal translator translates the words of the Tamarians but their sentences make no sense. Dathon, the Tamarian captain, transports himself and Captain Picard onto the nearby planet El-Adrel and creates "a particle scattering field on the planet's

---

23. See https://www.kickstarter.com/projects/1106349481/gilgamesh-motion-picture.

24. Doctor Who is the time and space traveller par excellence; his adventures started in a BBC show in 1963 and still continue, both on television and in novels, audio dramas, and comics.

25. After the original and the animated ones, *The Next Generation* is the third television series of the Star Trek franchise. "Darmok" is its episode 102, the second of the fifth season. On Gilgamesh and Star Trek, see Eva Miller's contribution to this volume.

ionosphere"[26] that prevents both of them from being brought back to their ships. Picard is puzzled: the action seems to be a hostile one, moreover Dathon has handed him a dagger while saying "Darmok and Jalad at Tanagra"—a challenge to duel?—but at the same time he shares his fire with him during the night. On the *Enterprise* they start to deduce that the Tamarian language is entirely based on allegories, but they think that without any knowledge of Tamarian folklore and traditions the language will remain indecipherable. On the other side, the Tamarians can understand only allegories and not the straightforward use of language. In the meantime both captains are assaulted by a monstrous predator, which they fight together. They defeat it, but Dathon is mortally wounded. Picard says:

> You knew there was a dangerous creature on this planet and you knew from the tale of Darmok that a danger shared might sometimes bring two people together. Darmok and Jalad at Tanagra. You and me, here, at El-Adrel ... There's a story, a very ancient one, from Earth. Gilgamesh and Enkidu. At Uruk. The new friends went out into the desert together where the great bull of heaven was killing men by the hundreds. Enkidu caught the bull by the tail. Gilgamesh struck him with his sword. Gilgamesh. They were victorious. But Enkidu fell to the ground, struck down by the gods. And Gilgamesh wept bitter tears, saying: "He who was my companion through adventure and hardship is gone forever."

Picard has now understood, but it is too late: Dathon smiles and dies. The story of the most ancient hero seems to be—literally—universally intelligible. And this is even more true in the year 2000, when a Klingon translation of the epic was published (Cheesbro 2000), the first earthly literary work to be translated into the language of this Star Trek's extraterrestrial humanoid warrior species[27]—actually there are also Klingon versions of *Hamlet* and *Much Ado about Nothing*, but they do not count, since according to the Klingon, Shakespeare (or, better, *Wil'yam Sheq'spir*) was one of them and *Hamlet* is actually about an attempted *coup d'état* in their empire.[28]

The universality of the story emerges also from the stage play *Gilgamesh in Uruk (G.I. in Iraq)* by Blake Bowden, performed in Cincinnati, Ohio, in 2007. It tells the story of two American soldiers in Iraq; one of them is suffering from post-traumatic stress disorder, and while his buddy is trying to calm him with some music they are

---

26. All the quotes are from the episode "Darmok."

27. Klingon is probably the most widespread spoken fictional constructed language after Tolkien's Middle Earth languages. It was first heard in the movie *Star Trek: The Motion Picture* (1979) and was subsequently described by Marc Okrand in the book *The Klingon Dictionary* (1985). In 1992 the Klingon Language Institute (KLI) was founded in Flourtown, Pennsylvania.

28. *Star Trek VI: The Undiscovered Country* (1991). By the way, these claims are not new for Shakespeare and earlier he had been Germanized: see Burt 2008, 442–44 and *"Pimpernel" Smith* (1941), a British anti-Nazi movie directed by and starring Leslie Howard.

both thrown into a mythical world, that of Gilgamesh the King and Enkidu. Their story, the slaying of the monster Humbaba and the return to Uruk, the death of Enkidu as a consequence of their deeds, take on different meanings in their present situation. The buddy concludes that "the best way to connect with others is via stories." "Give me a story," he says. "I soak that right up." What's more, he adds, "Be willing to share stories and hear the stories of others, even if they differ from your own" (Pender 2007). And this illustrates how fictionalization, postfigurative interpretation and motivic analogies can act together.

A commercial fictionalization "drawing 'freely' on both Mesopotamian history and the ancient Gilgamesh epic," is *Gilgamesh the King* by Robert Silverberg, who "offers an earnest, fairly colourful, but rather plodding folkloric/picaresque narrative" (Kirkus Review 1984). We must acknowledge that the book is actually considered one of Silverberg's best by his fans. In the "Afterword" to the novel, Silverberg writes:

> at all times I have attempted to interpret the fanciful and fantastic events of these poems in a realistic way, that is, to tell the story of Gilgamesh as though he were writing his own memoirs, and to that end I have introduced many interpretations of my own devising which for better or for worse are in no way to be ascribed to the scholars. (Silverberg 1984, 319)

The story starts when Gilgamesh is six, with the death of his father Lugalbanda and the start of our hero's obsession with death. A peculiarity of the novel is that there are very few supernatural events in it: Inanna is actually interpreted as the mortal priestess of the goddess and even Ziusudra is not the sole immortal man but just a title borne by the leader of a group of persons, living where the original Ziusudra arrived, escaping from the big flood—that was just that, a natural event that flooded the steppe.[29] And that should not surprise, since when he wrote the novel Silverberg was already a science-fiction veteran and, as mentioned above, the likelihood of the events is fundamental to proper sci-fi.

Silverberg's infatuation with Gilgamesh did not end here. A couple of years later, his "Gilgamesh in the Outback" was published and won the Hugo Award for best novella.[30] Later it was recompiled with two other sequels, "The Fascination of the Abomination" and "Gilgamesh in Uruk," into the novel *To the Land of the Living*. Here the tone and the subject are completely different from the previous book: the story, now told in the third person, is set in the present, and so it has been quite a long time that Gilgamesh has been *living* in the afterworld—a place with no escape where all the dead live again and where the more recently dead have brought their new technologies as well as their somewhat distorted ideas of the ancient heroes. Here, in this dystopian

29. See a summary of the novel in Ziolkowski 2011, 119–23.

30. The prizes are awarded since 1953 and are named after Hugo Gernsback, pioneer founder of the science fiction magazine *Amazing Stories*.

world, Gilgamesh himself embarks on an adventure, an *odyssey*, in search of "his friend, his true brother, his other self" Enkidu, whom he has lost again and a rumored gateway that should exist somewhere and that could lead them back to the land of the living. It is a self-discovery trip, made alongside other well-known persons such as Helen of Troy, Simon Magus, and Picasso:

> The story is interesting for the reason that the theme of Emptiness is juxtaposed with contemporary ideas of the underworld. On the one hand, it is the space action of science fiction novel, on the other, however, it points to the archetypal actuality of the ancient events, making the sterile philological knowledge into elements of the modern field of cultural references. Hell ... takes on the speculative meaning. (Trocha 2016, 24)

5. *The Superhero*

In addition to science fiction, fantasy, alternate history, and dystopia, another speculative fiction genre is superhero, which is mainly to be found in American comics: a superhero is "a heroic character with a selfless, pro-social mission; with superpowers—extraordinary abilities, advanced technology, or highly developed physical, mental, or mystical skills; who has a superhero identity embodied in a codename and iconic costume" (Coogan 2006, 30). The deeds of Gilgamesh, the hero himself, do not match those of the other humans; this is stressed from the very beginning of the classical Babylonian version of his epic: "Surpassing all other kings, hero endowed with a superb physique ... two-thirds of him god and one third human" (I 27 and 48).[31] Gilgamesh is "the first superhero to emerge from anonymity and to have a precise identity, a name and more ... Gilgamesh already possesses many features of the 'classic' superhero, that of the so-called Golden Age of Comics (the 1940s)" (Santi 2013, 31; see also Coogan 2006, 118–21, 68). He has a sidekick, Enkidu—as, for example, Batman has his junior counterpart, Robin—and each cries for the loss of his friend.[32] Just as Gilgamesh starts his quest for transcendent power, immortality, after the death of Enkidu, a youthful Bruce Wayne (the future Batman) decides to fight crime after the killing of his parents, as does Peter Parker after the murder of his beloved Uncle Ben.[33] It is in this circumstance that Peter/Spiderman, who has discovered that thanks to his new powers he could have captured the murderous criminal earlier, realizes that with great power comes great responsibility. And Gilgamesh, the great king, decides not to try the magical plant of youthfulness immediately but to share it with the old folk of his city, Uruk. Most of all, Gilgamesh is divine, not human, but he is also human—we

31. The Gilgamesh epic is quoted in the translation by George 2003.

32. See the reaction of Batman as Jason Todd, the second incarnation of Robin, is killed by the Joker in "A Death in the Family," *Batman* 426–29 (December 1988–January 1989), DC Comics.

33. *Amazing Fantasy* 15 (August 1962).

could say that, as all superheroes, he is beyond-human, exactly as Superman, who was adopted by a Kansas farm couple and raised as a human with the name of Clark Kent but who is actually an alien, born Kal-El on planet Krypton, and launched to Earth just before his planet's destruction.[34] Moreover, like many superheroes, Gilgamesh refuses sexual temptation (note, for example, Batman and Catwoman) and fights against super villains, such as Humbaba or the Bull of Heaven. But can we consider Gilgamesh a proper superhero? Coogan (2006, 259, n. 34) writes:

> The term superhero is often applied to all sorts of characters and people from Beowulf and Luke Skywalker to Tiger Woods and Michael Jordan. These applications come out of a metaphoric use of the term to describe characters and people who seem a step above others in their class, whether epic, science fiction, or sports. This metaphoric use has its base in genre. And that's why George W. Bush could be referred to as a cowboy. The problem is that the superhero genre, unlike the western, is not well defined in scholarly or popular culture.

But an early connection between mythical heroes and modern superheroes is undeniable. One of the earliest comic superheroes, Capitan Marvel,[35] was Billy Batson, a boy who, with the magic acrostic word "Shazam," was able to transform himself into an adult with the powers of Solomon (wisdom), Hercules (strength), Atlas (stamina), Zeus (power), Achilles (courage), and Mercury (speed). He was also labeled *The World's Mightiest Mortal*, because, as with Gilgamesh, superheroes ARE mortal. Probably the most famous death of a superhero was that of Superman,[36] but even Marvel Comics' homonymous Capitan Marvel died, and not because of some super villain or to save earth from some catastrophe, but because of cancer.[37] Even superheroes can die from natural, human causes—as indeed Gilgamesh died of old age. It is true that most of them, sooner or later, are actually brought back from death somehow, and continue to fight for justice, but even Gilgamseh—as we have seen and will see below—has been resurrected several times by modern authors, who cannot accept the death of a hero.[38]

---

34. The first version of Superman's origin appeared in *Action Comics* 1 (June 1938) and was later retold several times. see, e.g., *The Man of Steel* 1 (July 1986).

35. The first story was published by Fawcett Comics in *Whiz Comics* 2 (February 1940), less than one year after Superman. Capitan Marvel was the most popular comic book superhero character of the Golden Age and the first one to be adapted into a movie (*Adventures of Captain Marvel*, 1941), but was at the center of a long fight with DC Comics, which sued Fawcett Comics for copyright infringement. In 1953 Fawcett agreed to cease publication of Captain Marvel permanently. Marvel Comics had taken stock of the situation and started to publish its own Captain Marvel in 1967.

36. "Doomsday!" *Superman*, vol. 2, 75 (January 1993).

37. Jim Starlin, "The Death of Captain Marvel," April 1982, Marvel Comics.

38. Even in mythology most of the heroes die, but their death is often not clearly mentioned. See Santi 2013, 35–36.

Besides these analogies between Gilgamesh and the superheroes, a couple of homonymous comic characters exist, as the one created by Jack Kirby in 1977. Kirby was one of the most influential comic book artists and in a career lasting more than fifty years he has revolutionized their visual language, freeing them from the rigid grid used for newspaper comic strips. Kirby's Gilgamesh first showed up in issue 13 of Marvel Comics' *The Eternals* (1977), a comic book series about a race of super humans, created five million years ago by the alien Celestials and their genetic experiments performed on early proto-humanity. The Eternals have witnessed all human history and are known by several civilizations that have mistaken them for gods or heroes—more or less the same thing that happened to Gilbert Nash and Carolyn in *The Time Masters* (see above).

More closely connected to the epic is the four-issue limited series *Gilgamesh II*, published by DC Comics in 1989, written and drawn by Jim Starlin—already guilty of the above-mentioned death of Capitan Marvel. Gilgamesh is an alien raised on Earth where he arrived as a baby on a capsule—exactly like Superman—after the destruction of his mothership, shelled by the NORAD (North American Aerospace Defense Command), which mistook its presence for a Russian missile attack. The story includes a cold war, biological warfare agents, nuclear bombs, and Enkidu (or Otto as he is called here). Otto is seduced by secret agent Bambi who has to convince him to leave the Colombian rainforest and allow the superpower of the twelve United Corporations, headed by Gilgamesh, to follow their imperialistic interests—and this at a time when the FARC was constantly in the public eye. Gilgamesh and Otto come back to the forest to defeat the Nightshadow and then they fight against a ninja villain sent by one greedy member of the council to punish Gilgamesh, who denied him a favor. With the appropriate adjustments to set it in a near dystopian future—or past, if we consider that the story is set twenty-five years after 1989, its publication date—the plot does not deviate much from the original one but is used to give a satirical and disenchanted vision of the late-1980s world. The most different part is the ending: after the loss of Otto and the vain quest for a means to defeat death, Gilgamesh comes back from his trip—short for him but two thousand years long in Earth time—just to discover that the new inhabitants of the planet, who have replaced humans after a nuclear catastrophe, do not know anything of him—but is it true? After the encounter, he decides to disappear forever in the Void without realizing that he has spoken only to some children of the new race. This is a shock for Gilgamesh fans. It is common idea that even if he died, Gilgamesh reached immortality through the memory of his deeds, but here there is only desolation and "the lone and level sands stretch far away." As in Shelley's sonnet *Ozymandias* (1817), Starlin's message is political.

The grief for the loss and the hopeless quest for a solution to death have always been felt to be the most moving part of the story by modern readers and artists dealing with it. These aspects give humanity to the hero, to the superhuman being, and connect his extraordinary life with our normal ones. Nobel Prize winner Elias Canetti wrote in the second volume of his memoirs, *Die Fackel im Ohr: Lebensgeschichte 1921–1931*

(*The Torch in My Ear: Memoir 1921–1931*): "The question if *I believe* in such a story does not touch me at all; in the face of my most real substance, how can I decide if I believe in it or not? There is no need to repeat parrot-like that so far all the men are dead, we have to decide whether *to accept* death submissively or to rebel against it" (Canetti 1980, 60, translated from the German).

The obsession with death is at the center of an Argentinian comic by Robin Wood, probably one of the world's most prolific comic writers. His career started in 1967, when he was still a factory worker in Buenos Aires and created for his friend Lucho Olivera, almost by chance, *Nippur de Lagash* (Nippur from Lagash),[39] one of the most important Argentine comics, published for more than thirty years and nearly 450 episodes. A couple of years later, the same Olivera started to write and draw another long-lived series, that of *Gilgamesh el Inmortal* (fig. 1). Yes, the "Immortal."

After a first run between 1969 and 1975, *Gilgamesh el Inmortal,* was rebooted by Wood (Olivera remained as artist) in 1980. In this work the modernization of our hero's story acts on a double level, a very loose fictionalization at the beginning followed by several analogies in the second part.[40] In the first episode we discover that Gilgamesh is one of the Guardians of the Universe and that he desires to go back to Earth to go over his whole life again,[41] and so, in the next few episodes, his story as a mortal is retold. It is not the story of Gilgamesh the hero, but that of Gilgamesh the man, the child that encountered death for the first time (as in Siverberg's *Gilgamesh King of Uruk*), the warrior that fought for his homeland and killed enemies, the king that built Uruk, the mighty city, the friend of Nippur (yes, there is a crossover with the other comic). Except the encounters with the diviner Samas and an alien being, Utnapistim, every supernatural element is set aside (another analogy with Silverberg's novel); everything is a sort of philosophical reflection on life and death set in ancient Mesopotamia. The encounter with the alien is the breakthrough: he gives Gilgamesh immortality, but this turns out to be a curse. Immortality scares and disheartens the king's subjects: they are born and die. All their efforts, achievements and desires seem to be worthless compared to the eternity of their king and so they start to neglect their duties. To give them new hope, Gilgamesh needs to die, and so he pretends to be killed. Gilgamesh is now a legend, Uruk revives and human history begins, with the Immortal living incognito through all of it—Assurbanipal's devastations, the crucifixion, the Crusades, the *Conquistadores*, Napoleon's Russian campaign, the Nazi concentration camps, Hiroshima—until the elimination of life on Earth because of a global war. From the very beginning, death is present on almost every page. There is only one hope left for the Immortal, the last

39. The first episode was published in the comic magazine *D'Artagnan* 1967, no. 151.

40. It can be reported that the Italian collected edition (*Eura Editoriale,* 1990–1998) consists of twelve volumes, just as the Babylonian epic is in twelve tablets. But this could be merely a coincidence. The episodes in the series were previously published in a comic magazine, *Skorpio* (VII/49, 1983, first episode).

41. *D'Artagnan* 1980, (N.S.) no. 2.

man on Earth: a secret base in the United States where several children were put into hibernation. But there is an ocean in between and "the crossing is perilous, its way full of hazard" (*Gilgamesh* X 83), especially for one lone man. Somehow Gilgamesh crosses it, reaches the base, flies towards the stars with the children and—after a long, second journey into the unknown—he finds a planet suitable for human life, which he calls Sumer. In the new civilization he creates, one of the first acts is the killing of a youth by his brother: nothing changes, this is human nature.[42] Gilgamesh knows that and is aware that there is no solution; immortality is not for humans, it is a burden bigger than death. But he still fights against death, he is somehow similar to Canetti (1980, 60–61, translated from German):

> The right to the splendour, wealth, misery, and despair of all experience, I have conquered it by rebelling against death. I lived in this endless state of revolt. And though my sorrow for the loved ones I have lost over the years was not less than that of Gilgamesh for his friend Enkidu, in one thing, in only one thing, I have overcome the lion-man: every man's life is dear to me, not just that of my loved ones.[43]

After sixty-six episodes, the Immortal became one of the Guardians of the Universe, and so we go back to the very beginning of his trip. Then, the story continued for several years, but with other writers.

Argentine comics are very different from American ones and reflect the climate of constant economic and political crisis that has characterized the country throughout the second half of the twentieth century, mirroring in them its gloomy reality without apparent solution, as may also be clearly seen in the most famous local humorous comic strip, *Mafalda* (1964–1973) by Quino. Science fiction and fantasy fulfill perfectly these tasks as well, and like *Gilgamesh el Inmortal*, many other Argentinian comics hide a profound political message. In particular, *El Eternauta* (1957–1959), by Héctor Germán Oesterheld and Solano Lopez, became one of the most enduring creations of Argentine culture, a symbol of resistance against political oppression, foreign intrusion and social control, an emblem of liberty—and it cost the writer his life, *desaparecido* in 1977, just a few years before the publication of *Gilgamesh el inmortal* by Wood. And we can suppose that the obsession with death in the comic is connected with the disappearance of thirty thousand civilians between 1976 and 1983 in Argentina, during the military dictatorship led by General Jorge Rafael Videla.

With this dark version of our hero, probably the darkest and most desperate one, we conclude our excursus on Gilgamesh in speculative fiction works. Only a small part

42. Connections between the Bible and Gilgamesh are not so uncommon and something similar also occurs in the anime Gilgamesh (see n. 19).

43. This was more than a lifelong rebellion for the German language Bulgarian-born British citizen Canetti, since his last posthumous book, *Das Buch gegen den Tod* (*The Book against Death*), has been published only recently, in 2014, twenty years after his death.

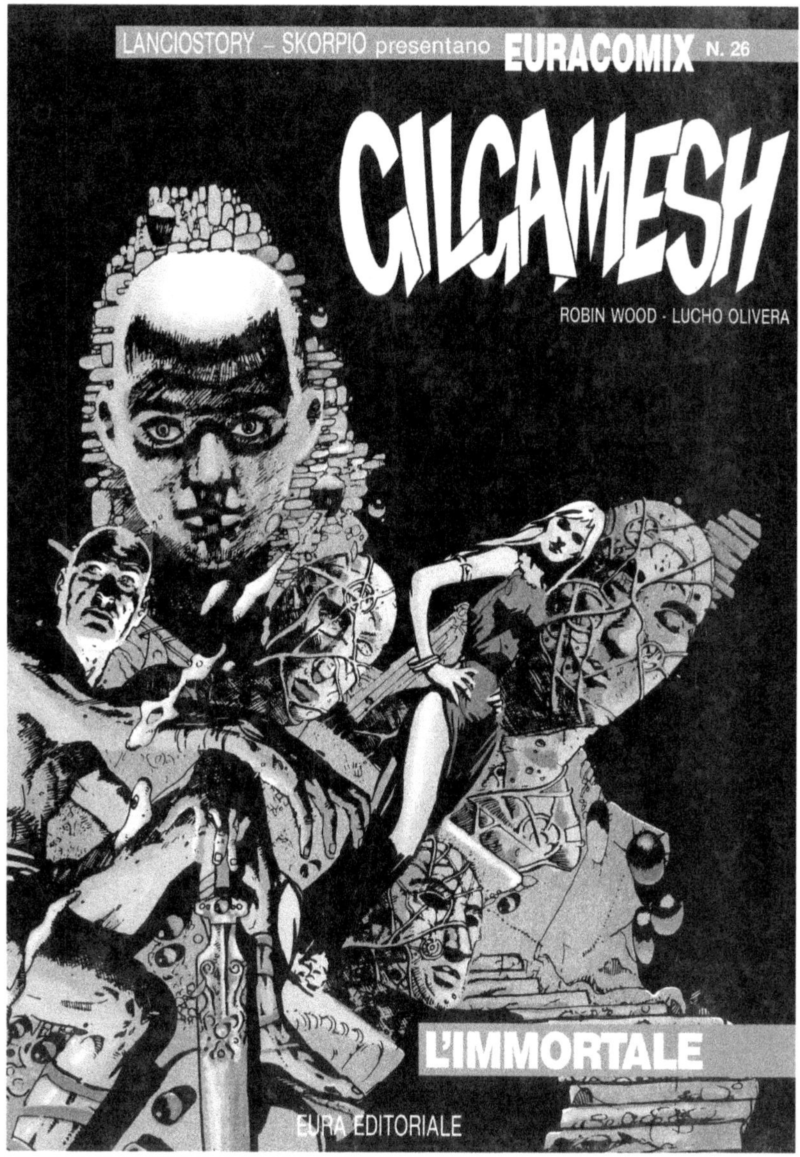

Figure 1. Cover of the first volume of the Italian collected edition of *Gilgamesh* by Robin Wood and Lucho Olivera, published by Eura Editoriale in 1990 (© Editoriale Aurea).

of these products has been mentioned here, to show the different approaches to the epic in popular culture; a longer list, extending beyond the limits of a genre, can be found in Ziolkowski's book, though "no study of reception can reasonably aspire to absolute completeness" (Ziolkowski 2011, xi)—and in fact many works mentioned here are not present there.

6. A Couple of Questions and a Tentative Answer

We just have two last questions. The first is from "Gilgamesh," one of the reviews of fictitious books by fictitious writers, written by the well-known Polish philosopher/science fiction writer Stanisław Lem and published in his book *Doskonała próżnia* (*A Perfect Vacuum*) in 1961. "Gilgamesh" is the *review* of Patrick Hannahan's book of that name, which is supposed to be a 395-page reconstruction of the last thirty-six minutes of G. I. J. Maesh, sentenced to death, followed by 847 pages of exegesis made by Hannahan himself (see Ziolkowski 2011, 97–99). The reviewer has no doubt: just as the epic of Gilgamesh is greater than the *Odyssey*, this book is surely greater than Joyce's *Ulysses*. The question is: with all this rewriting, retelling, reinventing of the myth "where exactly is one to draw the line between the multiplicity of meaning that marks the integration of a genius, and the sort of enriching of a work with meanings that represents the pure schizophrenia of a culture?" (Lem 1979, 39).

We do not know the answer to this, but Gilgamesh himself, incarnated as Gilbert Nash, has answered in *The Time Masters* the second, more important question: "Did this adventurer, this Gilgamesh fellow, find his immortality?" The answer: "He found what he was searching for. But it was much too late to save his life" (Tucker 1953; cited from *Startling Stories*, vol. 31, no. 2 [1954], 46).

This answer could give some hints regarding a response to the first question. Many of the modern works based on Gilgamesh are more aligned with the epic's themes than its plot, themes that have crossed all of mankind's history. Their presence in the first-known written literary works shows modern readers the urgency of these issues to be addressed and conceptualized. The use of the epic to discuss them is an added value, the recognition of their universality and eternity, of a human need since the time man decided to shape the world through written texts. The nineteenth-century discovery of the long-lost epic has clearly shown how some instincts, desires, hopes, griefs, and fears have never changed. On one hand the discovery has made a faraway and mysterious world, that of Mesopotamia, more familiar to modern humanity, and on the other it has shown us that some problems have never really been resolved. This made us feel lost—something like travellers in outer space—and at the same time less alone, in the company of the five thousand years of humanity that came before.

What about the many popular fiction works that merely use the names or some feature of the epic but that do not actually seem to have anything to do with our hero? This is surely a device to bewitch and seduce readers, but in order to do that, it is necessary that they are somehow, at least on an unconscious level, familiar with those ancient, almost atavistic, characters and stories.

Maybe Gilgamesh could not save his life, but through his deeds he created a connection with mankind, a connection that has never really been lost and that emerges in different ways and through different intellectual works, from high literature to video games. Every mention, every story based on the epic, every analogy, is not just an "integration" or a representation of "cultural schizophrenia": above all, they recognize the universality of Gilgamesh.

Bibliography

Canetti, E. 1980. *Die Fackel im Ohr. Lebensgeschichte 1921–1931*. Munich: Carl Hanser. English translation, *The Torch in My Ear*. New York: Farrar, Straus, and Giroux, 1982.

Cavallaro, D. 2009. *Anime and the Visual Novel: Narrative Structure, Design and Play at the Crossroads of Animation and Computer Games*. Jefferson, NC: McFarland.

Chadwick, H. M. 1912. *The Heroic Age*. Cambridge: Cambridge University Press.

Coogan, P. 2006. *Superhero: The Secret Origin of a Genre*. Austin, TX: MonkeyBrain Books.

Couto-Ferreira, M. É. 2008. "Gilgameš in Giappone: Riferimenti ai miti sumero-accadici nell'anime." In B. Bellucci, E. Jucci, A. Rizza and B. M. Tomassini Pieri (eds.), *Traduzione di tradizioni e tradizioni di traduzione: Atti dil quarto incontro "Orientalisti" (Pavia, 19–21 Aprile 2007)*, 39–51, Milan: Qu.A.S.A.R.

Cregan-Reid, V. 2013. *Discovering Gilgamesh: Geology, Narrative and the Historical Sublime in Victorian Culture*. Manchester: Manchester University Press.

Dalley, S. 1991. "Gilgamesh in the Arabian Nights." *Journal of the Royal Asiatic Society* 1:1–17. Reprinted in Maier 1997, 214–33.

Finn, M. 2012. *Blood and Thunder: The Life and Art of Robert E. Howard*. 2nd expanded and corrected ed. Sugar Land, TX: Robert E. Howard Foundation Press.

George, A. R. 2003. *The Babylonian Gilgamesh Epic: Introduction, Critical Edition and Cuneiform Texts*. 2 vols. Oxford: Oxford University Press.

———. 2007. "Gilgamesh and the Literary Traditions of Ancient Mesopotamia." In G. Leick (ed.), *The Babylonian World*, 447–59. London: Routledge.

Gunn, J., ed. 1977. *The Road to Science Fiction*. Volume 1: *From Gilgamesh to Wells*. New York: New American Library.

Haberfelner, M. 2011. "An Interview with Richard Chandler, Director of Gilgamesh." *Search My Trash*, August. http://www.searchmytrash.com/cgi-bin/articlecreditsb.pl?richardchandler(8-11).

Haupt, P. 1884. *Das Babylonische Nimrodepos*. Leipzig: Hinrichs.

Heinlein, R. A. 2011. "On the Writing of Speculative Fiction." In L. A. Eshbach (ed.), *Of Worlds Beyond: The Science of Science-Fiction Writing*, 9–17. Reading, PA: Fantasy Press. Reprinted in 2011. *The Nonfiction of Robert Heinlein: Volume I*, 219–28. Houston: Virginia Edition.

Henkelman, W. F. M. 2006. "The Birth of Gilgameš (Ael. NA XII.21): A Case-Study in Literary Receptivity." In R. Rollinger and B. Truschnegg (eds.), *Altertum und Mittelmeerraum: Die antike Welt diesseits und jenseits der Levante; Festschrift für Peter W. Haider zum 60. Geburtstag*, 807–56. Stuttgart: Steiner.

———. 2010. "Beware of Dim Cooks and Cunning Snakes: Gilgameš, Alexander, and the Loss of Immortality." In R. Rollinger, B. Gufler, M. Lang, and I. Madreiter (eds.), *Interkulturalität in der Alten Welt: Vorderasien, Hellas, Ägypten und die vielfältigen Ebenen des Kontakts*, 323–59. Wiesbaden: Harrassowitz.

Hoffman, J. 2013. "Decifering 'Darmok.'" *Startrek.com*, 20 November. http://www.startrek.com/article/one-trek-mind-deciphering-darmok

Howard, R. E. 1938. *The Hyborian Age*. Los Angeles: Cooperative Publications.

Jacobsen, T. 1939. *The Sumerian King List*. Chicago: University of Chicago Press.

Jastrow, M., and A. T. Clay. 1920. *An Old Babylonian Version of the Gilgamesh Epic on the Basis of Recently Discovered Texts*. New Haven: Yale University Press.

Jeremias, A. 1891. *Izdubar-Nimrod: Eine altbabylonische Heldensage, nach den Keilschriftfragmenten dargestellt.* Leipzig: Teubner.

Jung, C. G. 1964. *Man and his Symbols.* New York: Doubleday.

Kirkus Review of Robert Silverberg, *Gilgamesh the King.* 1984. *Kirkus Reviews,* 15 October. Accessed 25 September 2019. https://www.kirkusreviews.com/book-reviews/robert-silverberg-20/gilgamesh-the-king/.

Kramer, S. N. 1981. *History Begins at Sumer: Thirty-Nine Firsts in Recorded History.* Philadelphia: University of Pennsylvania Press.

Lem, S. 1979. *A Perfect Vacuum. Perfect Reviews of Nonexixtent Books.* New York: Harcourt Brace Jovanovich. Translation of *Doskonała próżnia.* Warszawa: Czytelnik, 1971.

Loeffler, S. 2014a. "Gilgamesh Writer/Director, Richard Chandler, Talks Heavy Metal, Boobs, His New Film and More." *Yell! Magazine,* 18 June. http://www.yellmagazine.com/gilgamesh-writer-director-richard-chandler-talks-heavy-metal-boobs-film-interview/86325/.

———. 2014b. "*Gilgamesh* (2014) Review." *Yell! Magazine,* 15 December. http://www.yellmagazine.com/gilgamesh-2014-review/93644/.

Lord, A. B. 1990. "Gilgamesh and Other Epics." In T. Abusch, J. Huehnergard, and P. Steinkeller (eds.), *Lingering over Words: Studies in Ancient Near Eastern Literature in Honor of William L. Moran,* 371–80. Atlanta: Scholars Press. Reprinted in Maier 1997: 294–306.

Maier, J. R., ed. 1997. *Gilgamesh: A Reader.* Mundelein, IL: Bolchazy-Carducci.

Murray, A. T., trans. 1919. *Homer: The Odyssey.* Loeb Classical Library. Cambridge, MA: Harvard University Press.

Nagler, M. N. 1996. "Dread Goddess Revisited." In S. L. Schein (ed.), *Reading the Odyssey: Selected Interpretive Essays.* Princeton, NJ: Princeton University Press.

Pender, R. 2007. "Onstage: Review: Gilgamesh in Uruk (G.I. in Iraq)." *CityBeat.com,* 3 October. Accessed July 2017. http://www.citybeat.com/arts-culture/theater/article/13025461/onstage-review-gilgamesh-in-uruk-gi-in-iraq.

Pettinato, G. 2004. *La Saga di Gilgameš.* Milan: Mondadori.

Pinches, T. G. 1889–1890. "Exit Gištubar!" *Babylonian and Oriental Records* 4:264.

Ponchia, S. 2013. "Riflessioni a cent'anni dalla polemica Babel-Bibel." *Revue d'assyriologie et d'archéologie orientale* 107:85–99.

Santi, F. 2013. *Aspettando Superman: Storia non convenzionale dei supereroi, da Gilgamesh a Fabrizio Corona.* Rome: Gaffi.

Shanks, J. 2012. "Hyborian Age Archeology: Unearthing Historical and Anthropological Foundations." In J. Prida (ed.), *Conan Meets the Academy: Multidisciplinary Essays on the Enduring Barbarian,* 13–34. Jefferson, NC: McFarland.

Smith, G. 1875a. *Assyrian Discoveries: An Account of Explorations and Discoveries on the Site of Nineveh, during 1873 to 1874.* London: Sampson Low, Marston, Low & Searle.

———. 1875b. *The Chaldean Account of Genesis.* London: Sampson Low, Marston, Low & Searle.

Snider, D. J. 1895. *Homer's Odyssey: A Commentary.* Chicago: Sigma.

Tigay, J. H. 1982. *The Evolution of the Gilgamesh Epic.* Philadelphia: University of Pennsylvania Press.

Trocha, B. 2016. "Between the Clichés and Speculative Re-Narration: Features of Ancient Themes in Popular Literature." In K. Dominas, B. Trocha, and E. Wesołowska (eds.), *Antiquity in Popular Literature and Culture,* 21–36. Newcastle upon Tyne: Cambridge Scholars.

Tucker, W. 1953. *The Time Masters.* New York: Lancer.

Ziolkowski, T. 2011. *Gilgamesh among Us: Modern Encounters with the Ancient Epic.* Ithaca: Cornell University Press.

Mystery Literature and Assyriology

Francesco Pomponio

The whole world recognizes 1841 as the year of the birth of mystery literature. In 1841 Edgar Allan Poe published "The Murders in the Rue Morgue," the first detective story.[1] Mystery literature, following the laws of nature, was born small—that is, in the form of the short story.[2] In 1845, the booklet *Tales* was published in the series *Wiley and Putnam's Library of American Books* (at the price of 50 cents!). In it "The Murders in the Rue Morgue" was followed by the other two tales that had as detective the father of all the amateur sleuths, C. August Dupin ("The Mystery of Marie Rogêt" and "The Purloined Letter"),[3] with the addition of a fourth tale, "The Gold Bug," based on the deciphering of a parchment. A fifth tale "Thou Art the Man" was published in 1844. In all, in these five tales we find the following firsts of the mystery literature: (1) the eccentric amateur detective; (2) the worshipful and dull stooge, who is also the teller of the detective's stories; (3) the crime that baffles the official detectives; (4) the wrongly accused person; (5) the application of the principles of the mystery literature to the solution of a real life case; (6) the use of the psychological deduction; (7) the double bluff; (8) the guilty who is the less-suspected person (or, we shall say better, the less suspected primate); (9) the psychological trick in order to wring a confession from somebody; (10) the employment of the ballistics in the criminal investigation; and (11) the anonymous detective.[4]

The appreciation of Poe's stories is universal. Just to mention a few examples of the adoration of Poe, I note the statuette-caricature (see fig. 1) of "the finest of finest of

1. The present article is the reworking, with a good deal of additions, of Pomponio 2010b.

2. See Thomson 1978, 76. It is the first treatise on the detective story written in the English language (1931).

3. This tale was rated by his author as "the best of my tales of racination" (in a letter to James Russell Lowell of 2 July 1844).

4. See Queen 1969, 78–79. To these firsts he added "the motif of the hermetically sealed room," but, aside from the tale of Daniel and the priests of Bēl in the Bible and that of Pharaoh Rampsimptus's treasure chamber in Herodotus (see Sayers 1928, 51–52 and 58–61), the first story of the sealed room is the tale "Passage in the Secret History of an Irish Countess," published in *The Dublin University Magazine* of November 1838 by J. Sheridan Le Fanu, even if in it a detective does not yet appear (see Greene 1987, 11).

Figure 1. Statuette of Edgar Allan Poe Awards. http://i.huffpost.com/gen/1134706/thumbs/o-EDGAR-AWARDS-2013-facebook.jpg

Figure 2. Japanese novelist Taro Hirai, aka Erdogawa Rampo (1895–1965). Photograph from Wikimedia Commons.

artists," following George Bernard Shaw's definition of Poe, which has been awarded since 1946 to the best productions in the field of the mystery literature by the *Mystery Writers of America* and the pseudonym (Erdogawa Rampo)[5] of Taro Hirai (see fig. 2), one of the first and best Japanese writers of detective stories. But Poe is not without his critics: for instance, there are essayists who have devoted themselves to unveil the implausibility of C. Dupin's investigative methods.[6]

For the other field, that of Assyriology, the date of birth is not established with the same consensus, but in 1842[7] the diplomatic residence of Mosul, the capital of a *vilayet* of the Ottoman Empire, was assigned to Paolo Emilio Botta (fig. 3). Mosul is a few miles away from the Assyrian cities. Botta's excavations at Nineveh started in December of the same year and the first archaeological finds at Khorsabad happened in 1844.[8]

5. This name has to be repeated a few times in order to understand the meaning of its mention in this passage.

6. See lastly Sharp 2006, 63–76. These essays have to be equated, for their fairness and accuracy, to the three pamphlets against the detective literature of Edmund Wilson edited in *The New Yorker* (1944–1945): (1) "Why Do People Read Detective Stories?" (2) "Who Cares Who Killed Roger Ackroyd: A Second Report on Detective Fiction," and (3) "Mr. Holmes, They Were the Footprints of a Gigantic Hound."

7. So, Matthiae in his foreword to Nadali and Polcaro 2015, 15, chooses 1842 as the year in which "si aprì la grande stagione di una vera epopea di rinascita archeologica del mondo mesopotamico."

8. For the exceptional contribution supplied by the Italian Paolo Emilio Botta to the birth of Assyriology, see Bergamini 1984–1987, 5–16.

So, it is not a strain to maintain that these two extraordinary intellectuals' adventures started at the same time. But, in my opinion, the influence of the Assyriology on mystery literature is to be assigned chiefly to the opening of the first sections of Assyrian antiquities at the Louvre and the British Museum (in May 1847 and October 1848, respectively). Now, let me consider how writers of mystery stories have dealt with Assyriology, Assyriologists, and Assyriologica.

Figure 3. Paolo Emilio Botta (16 December 1802, Torino—29 March 1870, Achères). Portrait by Charles Émil De Callande Champmartin, Musée du Louvre.

1. The Cuneiform Inscription

A collection of short stories, which was named after the first of its seven stories, *The Bradmoor Murder* (1929),[9] of Melville Davisson Post includes a tale titled "The Cuneiform Inscription." The author had published eleven years before *Uncle Abner*, in all probability the best collection of American detective short stories after the above-mentioned Poe's *Tales*, but almost all the other of M. Davisson Post's tales are by far inferior to those of *Uncle Abner*,[10] including the story in question.

The cuneiform inscription is the following:

9. In the same year, in the field of Assyriology, three volumes, which had the largest diffusion and the deepest influence on the successive studies, were published: Barton 1929; Budge and Gadd 1929; Cuq 1929.

10. In my opinion, only the thirteen tales of Col. Baxton (*The Silent Witness*, 1930) and the three tales of Judge Pendleton's diary (*The Sleuth of St. James Square*, 1920), set, like the stories of Uncle Abner, in the state of Virginia, are high-grade.

It has been drawn up by sir Hector Barthlett, the most eminent Assyriologist of Europe. He has deciphered the inscription of Darius I at Behistun and has swept away Halévy's thesis that the cuneiform writing was a mere graphic artifice of the Sumerian priests. Sir Hector, while deciphering the Persian inscription, has found a treasure and, in the absence of any antiquities law, has seized it. Then he has concealed it, but has indicated its position by the above-mentioned cuneiform inscription. It is considered by the other Assyriologists an absurdity because of the drawing of two heads of a king and the impossible inclination of two wedges. However, Sir Hector has retorted that the Assyriological knowledge of his colleagues is limited to the Holy Writ and therefore he has left a message equal to their limited intelligence.

The household of Sir Barthlett, too engaged in deciphering ancient inscriptions, is ruined, but luckily for the niece, heir of the dissipated estate, the girl's godfather enters. He takes a look at the inscription and immediately realizes that the two heads of the king refers to the book of 2 Kings, while the following cuneiform signs are the rough rendering of three Roman numerals, XVI, XVII, and V. He consults a Bible and reads at 2 Kings 16:17: "and set it on a stone base." Now, is there a stone base in the old Assyriologist's country house? Yes, in the terrace, and on top of it a square of tiles. And, having raised a few of them, he finds the treasure, succeeding where all the savants of Europe have failed. While the girl opens the only just found copper basket, where layers and layers of enormous emeralds are arranged, he leaves forever. The tale is of scant value and interest, apart from the cuneiform inscription and the precise mention of Halévy's thesis.

2. *The Seal of Nebuchadnezzar*

In the same year of the edition of M. Davisson Post's tales, *The Seal of Nebuchadnezzar* of R. A. Freeman was published. Here Dr Thorndyke's investigation regards an Oriental find of great value, namely, a seal of King Nebuchadnezzar. It is not told exactly to whom of the four homonymous rulers this object belonged, but the hint to a "great king in those remote, almost mythical times" rules out Nidintu-Bēl and Araha and, given the enthusiasm with which rich American collectors pursue the seal, it is unlikely that his ancient owner was Nebuchadnezzar I, who defeated the Elamites. Thus, remains the most famous of the Nebuchadnezzars, the conqueror of Jerusalem.

Major Cohen has picked up in the neighborhood of Baghdad a small gold cylinder seal, engraved with minute cuneiform signs and a hole bored through its axis from end to end. Unaware both of Assyriology and of sphragistics, Cohen has sold it for twenty pounds to a dealer of antiquities, Maurice Lyon, expert in restoring and faking antiques, but almost as ignorant in Babylonian artifacts as the good major. Now, the seal is shown by Lyon to a collector of Babylonian antiquities, Martin Rowlands, who, seeing that it is genuine and valuable, hastens to buy it for forty pounds. Then, rolling the seal on a molding wax, he learns that the name of his ancient owner is Nebuchadnezzar, as it is soon confirmed to him by the keeper of Babylonian antiquities at the British Museum. Meanwhile, Cohen has made a number of impressions of the seal on clay and sold them also to Lyon. An American Assyriologist buys the rollings and, acquainted with Cohen's name and address, learns of the existence of the seal. So, Cohen, Lyon, and some wealthy American collectors, friends of the American Assyriologist, vie for the seal, which is worth anything up to ten thousands pounds. Finally, Lyon murders the lucky (?) owner of the seal and replaces it with a fake. But Dr Thorndyke, inspecting the little object shown by the dead man's brother, and measuring it with his pocket caliper-gauge, notes that there was a difference of nearly two millimeters as regards the measurements taken on the true seal by the keeper of the British Museum, and besides, the perforation is too bright in the middle for an artifact almost two millennia and half years old. Therefore, it is a fake and, of course, made by an expert, who has both a seal rolling, from which an electrotype can be made, and the skill necessary to turn a flat electrotype into a cylinder. When, the day after, Lyon is caught carrying a case with a rather damp plaster copy of Donatello's *St. Cecilia,* Dr Thorndyke must only drop the statuette, pick up among the hundred snowy fragments a little yellow cylinder, and entrust the murderer and faker to a superintendent of Scotland Yard.

R. A. Freeman was indeed fond of Assyriology. Under the pseudonym Clifford Ashdown (and in collaboration with John Pitcairn), he published twenty-seven years prior in *Cassell's Magazine* a dozen tales with the protagonist Romney Pringle, a jobless literary agent and amateur cracksman. Among them is "The Assyrian Rejuvenator," in which our hero strips a Mr Jacobs, who sells off a miraculous specific, of his illicit gains. However, apart from the name of the elixir, the only Assyriological element of the tale are "the curly locks and the beard which suggested the winged bulls of Nineveh" of the "Assyrian looking" charlatan.[11] In *The Red Thumb Mark* (1907), the first novel with Dr Thorndyke as protagonist, the main course of the supper prepared by him for his assistant, Dr Jarvis, is a steak—"food meet for the mighty Šamaš"—and this pun is indeed a mystery. What could have inspired the author? The Cruciform Monument (fig. 4) with its Pantagruelian diet for Šamaš and his spouse Aya[12] will be translated nearly forty years after the publication of the novel (see Gelb 1949, 346), and in no other inscription, to the best of our knowledge, does the god of the sun and justice stand out for being a gourmet or a glutton.

Finally, in the second novel with Dr Thorndyke, *The Eye of Osiris* (1911), he investigates the disappearance of the Egyptologist John Bellingham and eventually finds out that his corpse is concealed under the bandages and in the case of the mummy of Sebek-

11. This tale and the novel of the following pages have been already quoted by Foster 2008, 66.

12. "Shamash's meal was a 3 years ox for 3 meals: I have established a 3 years ox for an only meal. I have added 10 mountain sheep to 10 mountain sheep: so, I have established 20 mountain sheep as meal of an only meal. I have added 2 talents (= about 60 kg.) of fish to 2 talents of fish: so, I have established 4 talents of fish as meal of an only day, etc." For the Cruciform Monument, see most recently Al-Rawi and George, 1994: 139–48.

Figure 4. Cruciform Monument. BM 91022. © The British Museum. King 1910, plate opposite p. 224.

Hotep, a scribe of the Twenty-Second Dynasty, while the bones of the Egyptian official have been scattered all over a watercress field by Dr Bellingham's notary, who, for evil purposes, does not wish that his client's corpse is found. Assyriology peeps out in the novel with the mention of the Tell Amarna letters, glossed to benefit the less-learned readers, as "the cuneiform tablets of Amenhotep IV." The heroine of the story, the niece of the late Egyptologist, is conducting bibliographical research about them, and these tablets have appeared at first to the narrator as "an uncouth kind of fossil biscuit suited for the digestion of a prehistoric ostrich," but the love that he begins to feel for the young Assyriologist changes them into artifacts "of supreme fascination."[13]

3. *The Assyriological Epigraphist*

Among the thirty-three novels with the protagonist Hercule Poirot, three are set in the Near East: *Murder in Mesopotamia* (1936), *Death on the Nile* (1937), and *Appointment with Death* (set in Petra; 1938), and we could add *Murder on the Orient Express* (1933), since the long travel, during which a murder will be committed by many perpetrators, starts at the station of Aleppo.

Murder in Mesopotamia, of course, has many relationships with Assyriology, since it is set at Tell Yarimjah, which had been a great Assyrian capital, with temples, palaces, and private houses, and with the addition of an early Akkadian cemetery and ceramics of the fifth millennium. The novel contains a vivid description of the life of an archaeological expedition, and a good whodunnit plot with a "locked room" mystery that is

13. In another tale of Orientalist content, *The Moabite Cipher*, a text written in Moabite characters is read by Dr Thorndyke with the simple process of putting it into a bowl of water. A second text appears on the sheet and discloses in plain English where the loot from a bank robbery has been hidden, with the bitter disappointment of Prof. Poppelbaum, Semitic epigraphist of British Museum, who had tried to decipher the Moabite text with great exertion and imagination. And I nearly forgot the fake hieroglyphics and scarab of another Dr Thorndyke's tale, *The Bleu Scarab*.

both plausible and easy to carry out. But even I, who am among the most fervent of Dame Christie's fans, have to admit that the story has an improbable starting point.[14]

The present epigraphist of the expedition should be Father Lavigny, but under the name of this wellknown scholar and his monk'r robe, a clever thief, a certain Raoul Menier, specialized in thefts from museums, conceals himself. It had happened that the official epigraphist of the mission, Dr Byrd, was suddenly taken ill, and the head of the expedition, Dr Leidner, invites Father Lavigny. He too, however, is in poor health and then forced to decline the offer, but Menier, whose attention has been attracted by the golden artifacts from the dig at Tell Yarimjah, manages to get hold of the telegram of refusal of the true Dr Lavigny and substitutes one of acceptance. Apart from the inconsistency that the renowned archaeologist of the ancient Near East does not know the renowned Assyriologist by sight, thẹ author's poor opinion of epigraphists on both their constitution (two out of two in ill health) and the intricacies of their task ("with a smattering knowledge a clever man might bluff his way through") should be noted. The false epigraphist is at last exposed by Poirot, who unveils also the mystery of the two murders: the former one is indeed a strange "crime committed to vindicate his honour" by the head of the archaeological mission.[15]

Contempt for the Assyriologist, even if tempered by irony, is shown also by another great writer of detective stories, Josephine Tey: in the novel *Miss Pym Disposes* (1946), the supremacy among the most boring lectures given in a girls' boarding school is contested by those of "an octogenarian on Assyrian inscriptions, a Czech on Central Europe, and a bone-setter on scoliosis."[16]

The Assyrian world is present in the Christie stories also with the name of the cat of the vicar's wife in the village of Miss Marple. This cat is called Tiglath-pileser in the novel *A Murder Is Announced* (1950) and in the tale "Sanctuary" of the collection *Double Sin and Other Stories* (1961). If in the latter story it is mentioned only as a fussy cat with regard to the freshness of allotted fish, in the former one it, by fusing the light, suggests to Miss Marple the way by which the murderer caused the darkness required for her criminal purposes. This for the detective side. But, for the Assyriologial one, why did Agatha Christie write more or less correctly the name of one of the greatest Assyrian kings only in the former passage? The first part of this name is Tukultī, "My

14. The victim, the wife of the head of the archaeological mission, marries for the second time her preceding husband without any suspicion that he is the same man. True, he, having become an archaeologist, has now a long beard and slooping shoulders. But nevertheless.

15. Agatha Christie certainly drew inspiration both for the setting and for single episodes of this novel (1936) from the expedition of Leonard Woolley at Ur (1922–1936), of which she was guest in Autumn of 1928 and at the beginning of 1930, and there she met her future husband Max Mallowan, a young assistant of Dr Woolley. But let us hope that neither the English archaeologist nor his wife who accompanied him had points of contact with the principal characters of *Murder in Mesopotamia*. However, it is common knowledge that Dame Christie was not very fond of Woolley's wife.

16. I owe the quotation of this passage to the courtesy of Benjamin Foster.

Trust," turned Tiglath in the Old Testament. Thus, the sh of Tiglash-pileser in the latter passage is a displeasing mistake.

In the tale with another detective, a lot less charming than Poirot and Miss Marple, Parker Pyne ("The House at Shyraz" in the collection of tales *Parker Pyne Investigates* of 1934) the hill of Behistun is mentioned as "that romantic spot where Darius describes the extent of his empire and conquests in three different languages—Babylonian, Median, and Persian." Henry Rawlinson and Edwin Norris would not be have been able to say better in so few words.

4. *The Assyriologist as Detective*

In the only detective novel written by the historian and journalist Dermot Morrah, *The Mummy Case Mystery* (1933), the protagonist is the alleged mummy of Pepi I, the most ancient royal mummy in the world purchased by the professor of Egyptology in the University of Oxford, Peter Mannington Benchley. When a fire breaks out in the Egyptologist's bedroom, in which the Egyptologist has kept the mummy, a charred and shapeless form is found in a pile of black debris. The problem for the coroner is to establish whether it is the body of the pharaoh or of the Egyptologist. The resolution of the riddle is supplied by the lecturer of Assyriology, Dr Humpfrey Considine, who owns a tablet, the official dispatch sent from the battlefield to Assyria and written the very day of the battle in Sinai where Pepi was killed. The Assyriologist picks up this tablet among a number of small objects of baked clay filled with small wedged-shaped characters and translates it by sight, for the benefit of Prof. Sargent, a friend of his and amateur detective of the story:

> In the wilderness of Sinai[17] I laid low Pharaoh and all his host, I the High Priest. King Pepi, king of the Egyptians, with my right hand I slew him. With my axe I smote him, I clave him from the crown even unto the chin, so that his brains gushed forth, so that the right ear of Pharaoh fell a cubit's span from the left, so that men took up the head of Pharaoh in two pieces. I the High Priest destroyed him with my own hand. So perish all the enemies of the great god! (p. 121)

"Indeed a vigorous work for a clergyman!" exclaims Sargent (or in Italian "All'anima della botta!," as it is written in a tale of Achille Campanile, Papirio, in reference to the stroke inflicted by a Roman senator over the head of a disrespectful Gaul). Since the skull found in Prof. Benchley's rooms is intact, the skeleton must belong to the poor Egyptologist. But, as Prof. Sargent's subsequent inquiries will reveal, to which the lec-

17. The site was evidently chosen as the most logical place for a fight between the Egyptian and Sumerian troops, but it may also be a nostalgic recollection of the Palestinian campaign in which the author took part during the World War I.

turer of Assyriology will make another contribution,[18] the charred remains are of the corpse of Bonoff, a Soviet Egyptologist and blackguard, killed by Prof. Benchley in a duel. Then, Prof. Benchley mummifies his wicked colleague in the full style of the Eighteenth Dynasty, also solving a number of perplexities that have always puzzled Egyptologists, since "there's nothing like the empiric method in archaeology." Lastly, Prof. Benchley, disguised as Bonoff, is traced by Sargent and Considine to a ship, but he is spared by his two Oxford colleagues, who are convinced of his *bona fides*.

It remains to be established who this strongest High Priest of Uruk was. I incline to exclude Enmerkar, able in the solution of riddles; Lugalbanda, whose preeminence was the running speed; and Dumuzi, "the fisherman," who "was taken captive single handed by Enmebaragesi," a king of Kish (see Klein 2008, 78). The most likely candidate is definitely Gilgamesh: as a matter of fact, an en of Uruk capable of seizing an ax of the weight of two hundred kilograms in order to kill the Bull of the Heaven, should not have found it difficult to smash the thin skull of a decrepit Pharaoh. I present it as a mere working hypothesis, but, if confirmed by successive research, it would supply a synchronism between the fifth ruler of the First Dynasty of Uruk and Pepi I. In any case, it seems unlikely that Dermot Morrah, in ascribing such an accomplishment to a priest of Uruk, did *not* have in mind Gilgamesh. Therefore, it is odd that he had resisted the temptation to quote the name of Gilgamesh in the translation of the passage.

5. *The Amateur Assyriologist*

No detective boasts such multiform knowledge as Philo Vance. He made his debut in *The Benson Murder Case* (1926), beat every record of sale with the second novel (*The Canary Murder Case*, 1927) and went on to be the central character of eleven more novels, but the last (*The Winter Murder Case*, 1939) was left at the stage of a long outline by the death of the author, S. S. Van Dine. He had declared that no writer had in his pen more than six good novels, and, at least with regards to his own work, was absolutely right.[19]

For a brief overview of his expertise, Philo Vance knows a lot about Chinese and Japanese engravings (*The Benson Murder Case*), monochrome porcelain Sung and Ming (*The Kennel Murder Case*), Egyptian papyri of Menander (*The Scarab Murder Case*), chronology of ancient and middle Egyptian kingdoms (*The Scarab Murder Case*), electrodynamic (*The Bishop Murder Case*), breeding of Scottish terriers (*The Kidnap Murder Case*), *Aeneid* (*The Garden Murder Case*), and the fall of the Roman

---

18. He detects the anachronism of canopic jars of the Eighteenth Dynasty sealed by the cartouche of a pharaoh of the Sixth Dynasty, a feat in which not many Assyriologists today would succeed.

19. For an interesting coincidence, the far better (in my opinion) Vance novel is the sixth, *The Kennel Murder Case* (1933), with two perfect "murders of the locked room," and not *The Greene Murder Case* (1928) with the too long series of murders. However, the latter story is many critics and fans' favorite: see, e.g., Dickson Carr 1963, 98; Symons 1959, 7.

Empire (*The Greene Murder Case*).[20] Was Babylonia left out from his interest? Of course not: at the beginning of the story of *The Casino Murder Case*, Philo Vance appears at the breakfast table wearing a sumptuous Chinese dressing gown and reveals to his friend Van Dine:

> Just awake, I felt depressed. I could not resolve some doubts of mine about the recent Ur excavations so that last night I have not slept well. Thus, I have adorned myself with these Chinese ornaments in an attempt to improve my state of mind.

What were the doubts about? Since the novel was published in 1934 and in the same year appeared L. Woolley's two splendid volumes, *Ur Excavations* II, *The Royal Cemetery: A Report on the Predynastic and Sargonid Graves Excavated between 1926 and 1931*, dedicated to the Ur royal tombs, the findings in them must have been the cause of Vance's sleepless night. And I think I can be more circumstantial, supposing that the detective's interest pinned on the "multiple deaths." Although L. Woolley used over and over again the term, "human sacrifice," he admits that the word is misleading. Woolley's reconstruction (1934, 41–42) is that the female courtiers, musicians, high officials, soldiers, and grooms, who were found in the "royal tombs," were not killed in honor of the king or the queen but drank quietly of the poison provided in order to accompany their masters in their last journey and to be translated to a higher sphere of service. So, their death was a privilege, rather than a doom, reserved to the best ones in the king's court. The little cups found at their side and the big copper pot in the Great Death-Pit of PG/1237, which may have contained the poison or soporific drug, suggest confirmation of this hypothesis. But, while Woolley pointed out that there seems to have been no violence done on the courtiers, recently the skull of a female wearing an elaborate headdress and that of a soldier with the remains of a crushed copper helmet, coming respectively from the above-mentioned PG/1237 and the king's grave PG/789 and now belonging to the University of Pennsylvania, were radiographed and subjected to Computed Tomography (CT)-scans at the hospital of the University of Pennsylvania. Among the types of fragmentation patterns, which are visible on the CT scans of both the skulls, there are three cases (two on the male skull and one on the female skull) of what appear to be blunt-force trauma, producing circular holes in the flat neurocranial bones. The size and morphology of all three marks of trauma indicate that the instrument used to inflict the injury had a small pointed striking end with sufficient weight to have penetrated the skull at close range (see Baadsgaard, Monre, and Zettler 2012,

---

20. This exceptional extent of Vance's learning may be attributed to the fact that at the university "he had courses in the history of religions, the Greek classics, biology, civics, and political economy, philosophy, anthropology, literature, theoretical and experimental psychology, and ancient and modern languages" (*The Benson Murder Case*). From it comes the general admiration for his unusual culture, well synthesized by Ogden Nash's dystich "Philo Vance needs a kick in the pance."

140–44): therefore, a death extremely violent, and not very quick and painless, given that the soldier's skull was hit twice. Is it possible that Philo Vance had sensed or inferred something like that?

6. *The Detective as Assyriologist*

Unlike the omniscient Philo Vance, Mr Holmes was proud of his ignorance no less than of his knowledge. As he expressed himself excitedly to Dr Watson, straight after their first encounter (*A Study in Scarlet*), "a man's brain originally is as a little empty attic, and you have to stock it with such furniture as you choose ... Now the skillful workman is very careful indeed as to what he takes into his brain-attic. He will not have nothing but the tools which may help him in doing his work." Mr Holmes's work was that of consulting detective. This happened in January of 1881. But in spring of 1897, Mr Holmes and his friend were settled in a cottage at the extremity of the Cornish peninsula (*The Adventure of the Devil's Foot*). Here they had been driven by the positive injunctions of a doctor of Harley Street to a change of air and scenery. Mr Holmes spent his time in solitary walks upon the moor, but also in a research on the relationships between the ancient Cornish language and the Chaldean[21] from the Phoenician traders in tin. This complex study, for which Mr Holmes got some books of philology, was abruptly suspended by the investigation on the "Cornish Horror," a dreadful tragedy in which two brothers lost their lives. But Mr Holmes must have returned to his research, since in the list of his publications (see Baring Gould 1962, 326–27), in addition to specialist studies on detective work (essays on the tobacco ashes, characteristics of handwriting and typewriting, footprints, simulation of the diseases, recourse to the dogs for investigations, tattoos) and others dedicated to his hobbies (music and beekeeping), we find the monograph *A Study of the Chaldean Roots in the Ancient Cornish Language*, published in London in 1898. To the best of my knowledge, it is the only Assyriological study written by a detective, amateur or official. But my efforts to find it have proven futile.

7. *The Historical Tale*

In the May 1954 issue of the *Ellery Queen's Mystery Magazine*, and then in the collection *The Theme Is Murder* (1967), Miriam Allen deFord published a mystery tale, "The Judgement of En-lil," set at Nippur during the reign of Ur-Ninurta (1923–1896 BCE), "based on a famous real-life case which was cited many times in later trials," as it is specified by Frederic Dannay, a valve (a half of the bivalve) of Ellery Queen, in the introduction to the tale. The murder in question is that mentioned in a fragmentary tablet published by Chiera (1922, 172–74). The cuneiform text was republished with the

---

21. The tale was published in *The Strand Magazine* in the December 1911 issue. The term "Chaldean" referred by then to the Neo-Babylonian dialect of the Akkadian language.

joins of 2N-T.54 and of other fragments, all excavated at Nippur and kept at the University Museum of Philadelphia, by Jacobsen (1959, 130–50), and reissued by Jacobsen (1970, 193–214).

DeFord's tale is anterior to Jacobsen's article, but in any case she must have based her plot not on the translation of the too-reduced fragment of Chiera (1922, 172–73), but on that of 2N-T.54.[22] It is by far more complete, in particular with regard to the position of Nin-dada, Lu-Inanna's wife: the three murderers of her husband reveal their crime to Nin-dada, for reasons not indicated and difficult to understand. For her part, she does not inform anyone of the disclosure of the secret, perhaps out of fear. But the murder is all the same disclosed (we are not told the "whys" or the "wherefores") and reported to the king, who turns the case over for judgment to the assembly of Nippur, where the murder has been committed. During the trial, the three murderers' guilt is soon ascertained, but that of Nin-dada's becomes subject for discussion. Nine members of the assembly are of the opinion that the wife is culprit in the three murderers and therefore she has to be executed together with them before the deceased's ceremonial chair. However, two other members declare themselves in favor of Nin-dada, even if with an apparently inconsistent statement: "Nin-dada, daughter of Lu-Ninurta, may have killed her husband, but what can a woman do in (such a matter) that she is to be killed?" Then, they seem to admit that the woman, though aware of the crime, did not report it, and yet they do not consider her as much of a culprit as the actual murderers and liable to the same punishment.[23]

Lastly, the assembly's judgment is that a wife may be an accessory to an enemy of her husband by providing him with pieces of information that would allow him to commit the crime with greater safety. Now, the murderer can reveal everything to his victim's wife, so that she becomes his accessory. Nin-dada, because of the strong relationship with the deceased, is judged as even more of a culprit than the three murderers, who might have had grounds for their crime, which no wife must have. Therefore, she is put to death together with the men.

This is the real life case. Miriam deFord in her tale keeps the principal characters—Lu-Inanna, Enlil's chief accountant; his wife, Nin-dada; and the first of the murderers, Nannasig—but eliminates the other two. Since the cuneiform text does not reveal

22. In the introduction to the tale it is added that the author had received information on the tablet from a newspaper, and then wrote to a professor at the University of Pennsylvania, "who had once been in charge of archeological researches at Nippur" and who sent to her a translation of the tablet, alas "mutilated and incomplete." The author owes in all probability the reading of the victim's name as Lu-Inanna, and not as Lu-^{d}Ninni (thus in Chiera's translation), to this Assyriologist. He may be identified with Francis Steele who both worked at the University of Pennsylvania and was epigrapher during the first season of the Joint Expedition at Nippur of the University of Pennsylvania and the Oriental Institute of Chicago.

23. A different translation of the objection of Šaliqulum and Ubar-Sîn, still more at Nin-dada's defense, is presented by Kramer 1956, 54 ("The First Legal Precedent").

the motive for the crime, the author supplies Nannasig with two reasons: first, he is Lu-Inanna's assistant, who wants his superior's place, and then he had a slave-girl, Gim-Nunsina, whom Lu-Inanna has compelled Nannasig to sell to him. This woman does not exist in the story of the cuneiform tablets. Lu-Inanna's purpose in the tale is to take the pretty girl as concubine who will bear him a child in place of the sterile Nindada. Lu-Inanna has not told the young woman yet of her luck, but he is going to do that on his return from Drehem.

Nin-dada, a governor's daughter, who has married Lu-Inanna, a commoner, has always despised her husband, but, at the news that a slave-girl is going to be his new concubine, her spite becomes hate. She sends Gim-nunsina to bring Nannasig to her and informs him that Lu-Inanna has gone to Drehem with a single servant, neither of whom is armed. Thus, Nin-dada suggests to her husband's enemy the means of eliminating him, exactly as it had been supposed by the assembly of Nippur in 2N-T.54. Nin-dada also provides Nannasig with a knife, and he, after a moment of doubt, goes straight to his deed, overtakes Lu-Inanna by a swift horse, and trails him to an unfrequented place, where he eliminates both him and his servant. But the latter is still alive when a physician, who is passing through to visit a patient, stoops over him, and he is able to say the murderer's name to the physician. Therefore, Nannasig is brought to trial and confesses his crime but reveals also his instigator's name. However, Nin-dada declares to have sent for Nannasig only in order to entrust him with the official seal, which Lu-Inanna had left behind him, and to demand to follow after him and give it to his superior. Nin-dada's justification, supported both by her father's prestige and by the well-known Nannasig's hate for his victim, assures her acquittal, while Nannasig is executed.

No member of the assembly evidently has thought of looking for the victim's seal in his luggage, in confirmation or not of Nin-dada's declaration. Nevertheless, the story does not end with the woman's triumph. Gim-Nunsina has understood that because of Nin-dada she has become the agent by which her former master Nannasig, whom she has loved tenderly since her childhood, died. She goes to her master and, having learned from her also that with Lu-Inanna's death she has lost her emancipation, stabs the widow with the same knife that had caused three men's death, crying: "This [*and not that of the assembly*] is the judgement of the god Enlil."

The tale has a few Assyriologist mistakes. Drehem (the modern name of Puzriš-Dagan, a few kilometers southeast of Nippur-Nuffar) is indeed "the receiving station for the immensity of offerings in cattle, sheep, pigs, and goats." But Drehem, at the time in which deFord's tale is set, did not exist for about a century, more precisely since the third year of Ibbi-Sîn. Besides, neither Lu-Inanna nor Nannasig could use horses but only asses, and it is highly unlikely that a judge of Nippur had the same name as the infamous king of the Gutians Tirigan. On the contrary, it seems to be appreciable the idea of giving to a physician the Sumerian name of Ziusudra, "Life of long days," but perhaps it is only an example of serendipity.

8. *The Historical Novel*

Il segreto dello scriba by Paolo Lanzotti (Casale Monferrato 2004) is set in the capital of a small northern province of the Neo-Sumerian state, Nim, with Enki as its city god, and is dated at the middle of Shulgi's reign.[24] In this period the king was forcing his great administrative reform, mentioned in the name of his twenty-first year of reign, to all the temple households of his state. This reform is an important part of the story, since the scribe Mebarasi, the investigator in the novel, is sent by the king to Nim to control the carrying out of his directives. But Mebarasi and his assistant, as they have only just arrived, get involved with the murder of another royal scribe, Niši, who, sent from the capital Ur, had the task of recording the land of the temple households before their change of ownership to the crown. This murder is twice over a mystery. The corpse presents thirty-two (!) slashes over all the body, a rope round the neck, the skull crushed, and a bronze nail driven into the mouth, while the carcass of a cat lies in the room. Besides, from the time when Niši has been escorted to his lodgings by Akurgal, the captain of the guards, and two soldiers to the time when his corpse had been found by the sentinels, who had continuously looked after scribe's house, nobody had entered or exited his lodgings. Indeed, a mystery of the locked room.

The only possible explanation of the murder is of the supernatural kind: Shulgi's agent, entrusted with a sacrilegious task, had been punished by gods' will. The governor Ebgal, worried by possible riots, asks Mebarasi to investigate the mystery of Niši's death, to which the other three murders follow in quick succession. However, just when the scribe is reaching the solution, Akurgal confesses his guilt: he has learned of Niši's corruption and has intended to punish the culprit by his own hand. Then, after proclaiming his faithfulness both to the king and to the governor, the captain stabs himself.

But the governor is not convinced of this confession, and Mebarasi reveals only to him the truth, which is as intricate as it is bitter: the culprit of Niši's murder is the governor's wife, who, first seduced and then spurned by Niši, had poisoned him, causing also the death of the cat, which had eaten the leftovers. Terror-stricken for her crime's consequences, the woman turned to Akurgal, whose loyalty she knew well. He went quickly to Niši's lodgings, getting past the sentinels without any difficulty, since they reckoned that the scribe was alive and awake because of the oil lamp's light. Akurgal treated Niši's body with a stab, big tablet, rope, and nail, and at last left a corpse that no one could consider a victim of poison. But Akurgal realized too late that he had become the only suspect of the murder, when the day after the sentinels found Niši's corpse. So, with a brilliant idea, probably inspired by Enki, he went to the scribe Kaku, who had a certain resemblance with Niši, and with the promise of a big reward persuaded him to take the part of the departed. Then, he had ordered three gendarmes to relieve the three

24. Another mystery novel by the same author, *Due misteri per Kengi il pensieroso* (2014), too, is set in the Neo-Sumerian period. The leading character, an apprentice scribe, has a name that seems to be rather a toponym, since Kengi (> ki-en-ĝir$_{15/x}$) designates Sumer.

sentinels at Niši's lodgings. During the changing of the guard, Kaku sneaked into Niši's room, and soon after he went out in order to go together with Akurgal and two guards to a field. The third guard had been left before Niši's lodgings with the order of blocking the entry to everyone. In the evening, when the small group had returned, Akurgal rebuked a sentinel for his muddled outfit with such a violence that no guard realized that Kaku, after entering Niši's lodgings, had immediately gone out, leaving behind a nearly insoluble mystery. However, Mebarasi unravels it: among the other elements, he detected that the notes Kaku had written on a tablet in regard to the field that he, instead of Niši, would have measured, were meaningless. Of course, Kaku, as well as two other characters who knew too much, had been subsequently removed by Akurgal.

From the Assyriological side, the novel does not have serious mistakes. Of course, I would have preferred that the tablet stained with blood in the dusk jacket was a *Runde Tafel*, for example, AnOr 45, thirty-five of the twenty-seventh of Shulgi, and not an extract of the bilingual vocabularies of Ebla (the reverse of MEE 4, 75, to be precise), and that, among the hundreds and hundreds of good Neo-Sumerian anthroponyms, the author had chosen names more reliable than Chere, Equi, or Obarage.[25] However bigger faults can be found in the plot. Five dead bodies seem too many for one novel; although, I must admit, S. S. Van Dine did worse. And the two detectives, the old man with exceptional gifts of observation and deduction but disillusioned with life and an alcoholic, and the young man who is enthusiastic and naive and finds love, is almost annoying for lack of originality. But, most of all, what would John Dickson Carr, Clayton Rawson, Hank Talbot, or Edward D. Hoch have thought of a murder in a locked room, in which three sentinels do not realize that a man is going in and out of the room they are supposed to look after?

9. *The Detective of Baghdad*

The mentions of Assyriology are not numerous in the thirty-four tales written by Ch. B. Child between 1947 and 1969. This is surprising, as these tales have as leading character the Inspector (and then Chief Inspector) Chafik J. Chafik and are set in Baghdad. The mentions of Assyriology regard above all the Inspector's appearance: he has "the eyes of a people who had seen the rise and fall of the Chaldeans, the Hittites, the Assyrians and the Babylonians," "the dignity of a Babylonian god-king," "the indulgence of a Babylonian king," "the profile of a plate from the 'grave-shafts' of Ur," "the resemblance with an ancestor who had lived before Noah." But in "There Is a Man in Hiding" (*Collier's*, 29 September 1951)[26] the motive for the crime is the funeral cup of lapis and gold

25. Besides, considering the city gods of Nim, I should have appreciated some personal names with the theophoric elements Enki-Ea and Damkina-Damgalnuna: alas the author has missed an opportunity to give a touch of Assyriological likelihood to his story.

26. It has been reissued with the title of "The Army of Little Ears" in *Ellery Queen Mystery Magazine*,

belonging to a Sumerian prince, "worked so fine it shames eggshell."[27] The Sumerian nobles were in the habit of being buried with one of these cups, filled with wine, in their hands.[28] The object of enormous value has been stolen by an assistant archaeologist during the excavations of the Ur royal tombs in the 1920s and now he tries to sell it to an Armenian antique dealer. But Dr Ghaffari from London University takes possession of the cup, killing the archaeologist and thief with a bronze club shaped like a lion's paw and kidnapping the Armenian dealer. Improper behavior, one may say, but is should be considered that Dr Ghaffari was not rich enough to purchase the cup and, on the other hand, he could not let it go far from his land. Lastly, he is tracked down at his home by Inspector Chafik, whom he attempts to strike with an ancient battle-ax. But the policeman is faster and fires twice with a modern gun. The dying man takes the chalice and, holding it with both hands, sits in a chair. The closing eyes look for an escort to the netherworld.

Another tale by Child, "The Invisible Killer" (*Collier's*, 21 January 1955) is set at Akkar,[29] an ancient city not far from Baghdad, recently uncovered by Dr Julius Anton. An assistant of his, Mr Jamil Goury, has been strangled in the strangest occurrences. A row of archaeologists was crawling through the narrow part of the shaft; Goury was first in line and Dr Anton followed him. The lights went out and all a sudden the place was completely dark. Goury cried: "Let go!" and threw himself forward, apparently to grasp his enemy. Then, his legs thrashed, like he was being choked and Dr Anton tried to haul him out by the legs, but he could not move him. Lastly, Goury's body became limp and Dr Anton reached over him to grapple with whatever was holding the unfortunate assistant. But, when the body was removed, everyone could ascertain that nothing and no one was in the grave, except for a corpse dead four thousand years, the resident of the tomb. An hour later, this ancient corpse presents a modern knife between the shoulder blades. As every fan of the "mystery of the locked room" may easily conceive, the culprit is the person nearest to the victim. For his part, Insp. Chafik notes some oddities: a forked twig and a small bead left upon the floor of the shaft and no traces of thumbs in the contusions on Goury's throat. Dr Anton had prepared a noose of wire weighed with lead beads, spaced like the fingers of an hand, and the twig of peach so that Goury would blunder against it and drop the noose around his neck. The remainder had been accomplished by his hauling of the trapped man's legs. But why? Simply enough, Goury had to die since he knew that Dr Anton had found the gold hidden in a tomb by Nazi

---

November 1954, and then in the anthology *The Sleuth of Baghdad: The Inspector Chafik Stories* (2002), 86–100.

27. A likely reference to the many ostrich shells used as a cup and colored or encrusted with gold, lapis lazuli or mother of pearl found in the Ur tombs by Woolley 1934, 280–83, et passim.

28. As for the wine, I do not know of any ancient parallels, but a gold cup was found in the hands of Mesundu, the prince of PG/755 (Woolley 1934, 157), and probably in those of the princess of PG/1054 (Woolley 1934, 99).

29. This name is probably inspired from Akkad, the capital of the first empire of the world.

parachutists during the war and intended to use it for continuing the excavations of his beloved Akkar. And the stabbing of the old corpse? Goury's servant had intended to avenge his master, knifing his supposed murderer.

10. Perfect Crimes and Not

In all, Assyriology with its characters, artifacts, and stories does not seem have been worthily treated in the works of mystery literature, even by its greatest writers, such as Melville Davisson Post and Agatha Christie. The best detective story of Assyriology is, in my opinion, the article of Parpola (1980, 171–82). Our Finnish colleague has not only disclosed the name of the murderer of Sennacherib, that is his son Arad-Mullišši, but has also demonstrated that this discovery agrees with the evidence both in the Bible (2 Kings 19:36; Isaiah 37:38) and by Berosus in the *excerpta* of Alexander Polyster and Abydenus. Besides, Simo Parpola has held accountable Sennacherib's two high officials, Nabû-šuma-iškin and Ṣillâ: they intercepted and removed the prospective disclosers of the plot and so ensured its success. Of course, Parpola has not been able to bring about the punishment of the culprits, but, before the court of history, he has both exposed the conspirator and his accessories[30] and rid the innocent Asarhaddon of unfounded suspicions. The latter one is the proper detective's task, since it is even more important than the guilty party's capture.[31]

Arad-Mullišši's murder was not a perfect crime since his conspiracy was soon revealed to his contemporaries and, even though with a good deal of delay, to posterity. Besides, he made very little of his crime: he did not ascend the throne, from exile learned about his hated half-brother's triumph, and, seven years later, was captured at the far Šubria, where he had retired, put to death together with his accomplices, and then taken back to Assyria—at least what was left of him, considering that his nose, ears, and hands had been cut off and his eyes gouged (see Leichty 1995, 955). On the contrary, the deaths of Amar-Suena and Erra-imittī may be considered perfect murders, from both viewpoints (concealment of the truth and attainment of the goal).[32] The plots of Šū-Sîn and of Enlil-bani respectively, in order to eliminate those who blocked their way to the throne, reach perfection, considering also the low costs of the means (the nail of a shoe and a hot soup), not to mention an agreeable touch of black humor.

But perhaps another murder lies hidden among the folds of the most ancient Mesopotamian history. Enkidu's death has without doubt obscure aspects. Gilgamesh,

30. Greater attention would have perhaps to be shown to the action of Arad-Mullišši's brother, Šarra-uṣur.

31. This matter has been treated over and over by Agatha Christie; see, e.g., the tale "The Four Suspects" in the short story collection *The Thirteen Problems* (1932).

32. On the death of these two kings, see Pomponio 1988, 52–57 and 2010a, 3–12, respectively. Amar-Suena died from the "bite" of a shoe, that is likely for an infection of a foot, and Erra-imittī for having gobbling a too hot soup, both departures not honorable, especially for two god-kings.

while generous with advice and lessons, does not seem to have had the common sense to take a physician to his friend's sickbed or to turn to Gula, the medicine goddess. In addition, his hurrying off after his friend's death to the pursuit of the immortality resembles to an escape in order to avoid questions and inquiries and calls to mind the terror of the culprit, who gets away even if he is not pursued. Gilgamesh's empty-handed return to Uruk, too, after a long time, raises grave doubts on the sincerity of his travel's aim, which he flaunted to whomever he met with exaggerated promptness and the literal repetition of a memorized story. We do not know the motive for this murder, but jealousy and secret conflicts are plausible reasons, as well as Gilgamesh's wish of displaying at long last his bravery, though without Enkidu's backing. Now, it is not likely that this latent, and unilateral, hostility wholly escaped Uruk courtiers' notice. At this regard, the poem *Gilgamesh, Enkidu, and the Netherworld* should be considered. We don't know whether the author of its was Lugal-gabagal or another bard, but definitely no one other than a court poet, for both the closeness to the main characters of the event and the sensibility of feeling, could realize what had happened. And the poem's message, apart from the mythological proem and the tale of the Euphrates poplar, is plain enough: Gilgamesh sent Enkidu to the Netherworld! As a matter of fact, Gilgamesh's moans and his desperate search for a someone to recover his *pukku* and *mekkû* were directed exclusively to Enkidu: the en of Uruk had enough knowledge of his friend's unselfish and innocent soul to reckon that Enkidu would have been the only volunteer for that mad enterprise.[33]

A perfect murder, sure, and yet what a lot of resemblance between the deaths of Enkidu and Gilgamesh, in their way, including the accompanying of dreams, and the obscurity of its causes. Divine retribution? Yes, it is possible, but I wonder whether Šamhat, who must never have forgotten her simple, wild lover, just as he never forgot her, even on his deathbed, having left her profession due to age, did not work in the royal kitchens of Uruk.[34]

Bibliography

Al-Rawi, F. N. H, and A. R. George. 1994. "Tablets from the Sippar Library. III. Two Royal Counterfeits." *Iraq* 56:139–48 .

Baadsgaard, A., J. Monre, and R. L. Zettler. 2012. "Bludgeoned, Burned, and Beautified: Reevaluating Mortuary Practices in the Royal Cemetery of Ur." In A. M. Porter and G. M. Schwartz (eds.), *Sacred Killing: The Archaeology of Sacrifice in the Ancient Near East*, 125–58. Winona Lake: Eisenbrauns.

33. The theory put forward in the latest edition of the poem (Gadotti 2014), that Enkidu was not dead and he, alive and well, perhaps not very well, was blown by the wind out the hole excavated by Utu, is suitable to the prudence of the bard, eager not to overdo in the openness of his statement.

34. Other motives may be inferred by the analysis of the relationship between the two heroes in Walls 2001, 50–68.

Baring-Gould, W. S. 1962. *Sherlock Holmes of Baker Street. A Life of The World's First Consulting Detective*. New York: Bramhall House.

Barton, G. A. 1929. *The Royal Inscriptions of Sumer and Akkad*. New Haven: Yale University Press.

Budge, E. A. W., and C. J. Gadd. 1929. *The Babylonian Story of the Deluge and the Epic of Gilgamish, with an Account of the Royal Libraries of Nineveh*. London: British Museum.

Bergamini, G. 1984–1987. "Paolo Emilio Botta e la scoperta della civiltà assira." *Bollettino della Società Piemontese di Archeologia e Belle Arti*, n.s. 38–41:5–16.

Chiera, E. 1922. *Old Babylonian Contracts*. Publications of the Babylonian Section 8/2. Philadelphia: University Museum.

Cuq, É. 1929. *Études sur le droit babylonien, les lois assyriennes et les lois hittites*. Paris: Geuthner.

Dickson Carr, J. 1963. "The Grandest Game in the World." In E. Queen (ed.), *Mystery Mix*, 96–101. London: Four Square.

Foster, B. R. 2008. "Assyriology and English Literature." In M. Ross (ed.), *From the Banks of the Euphrates: Studies in Honor of Marie Louise Slotski*, 51–82. Winona Lake, IN: Eisenbrauns.

Gadotti, A. 2014. *"Gilgameš, Enkidu, and the Netherworld" and the Sumerian Gilgamešh Cycle*. Berlin: de Gruyter.

Gelb, I. J. 1949. "The Date of the Cruciform Monument of Maništušu." *Journal of Near Eastern Studies* 8:346–48.

Greene D. G. 1987. *Death Locked In*. New York: International Polygonics.

Jacobsen, Th. 1959. "An Ancient Mesopotamian Trial for Homicide." In *Studia Biblica et Orientalia 3: Oriens Antiquus*, 130–50. Analecta Biblica et Orientalia 12. Rome: Institut Biblique Pontifical.

———. 1970. *Toward the Image of Tammuz and Other Essays on Mesopotamian History and Culture*. Cambridge, MA: Harvard University Press.

King, L. W. 1910. *A History of Sumer and Akkad*. London: Chatto & Windus.

Klein J. 2008. "The Brockmon Collection Duplicate of the Sumerian King List (BT 14)". In P. Michalowski (ed.), *On the Third Dynasty of Ur. Studies in Honor of Marcel Sigrist*, 71–91. JCS Supplement Series 1. Boston: American School of Oriental Research.

Kramer, S. N. 1956. *From the Tablets of Sumer*. Indian Hills, CO: Falcon's Wing.

Leichty, E. 1995. *Esarhaddon, King of Assyria*. In J. M. Sasson (ed.), *Civilizations of the Ancient Near East*, 949–58. New York: Scribner's Sons.

Nadali, D., and A. Polcaro. 2015. *Archeologia della Mesopotamia antica*. Roma: Carocci.

Parpola, S. 1980. "The Murderer of Sennacherib." In B. Alster (ed.), *Death in Mesopotamia*, 171–80. Mesopotamia 8. Copenhagen: Akademisk Forlag.

Pomponio, F. 1988. "Presagi ingannevoli." *Die Welt des Orients* 29:52–57.

———. 2010a. "Antichi re e liquidi bollenti." In M. Caltabiano, C. Raccuia, and E. Santagati (eds.), *Tyrannis Basileia Imperium: Forme, prassi e simboli del potere politico nel mondo greco e romano*, 5–14. Messina: Dip. Scienze dell'Antichità, Università di Messina.

———. 2010b. "Assiriologia e letteratura poliziesca: rapporti tra due nobili avventure intellettuali." In M. G. Biga and M. Liverani (eds.), *Studi dedicati al Padre Werner R. Mayer, S.J. da amici e allievi*, 293–306. Rome: Università *di Roma La* Sapienza.

Queen E. 1969. "A Ghost Haunting America". In E. Queen (ed.), *In the Queen's Parlor and Other Leaves from the Editor's Notebook*, 78–79. New York: Biblo & Tannen.

Sayers, D. L. 1928. *Great Short Stories of Detection, Mystery, and Horror*. London: Victor Gollancs.

Sharp, R. 2006. "Poe's Duplicitous Dupin". In B. F. Fisher (ed.), *Masques, Mysteries, and Mastodons*, 63–76. Baltimore: Edgar Allan Poe Society.

Symons J. 1959. The Hundred Best Crime Stories. In The Sunday Times. Manchester: Withy Grove Press.

Thomson, H. D. 1978. *Masters of Mystery: A Study of the Detective Story.* Mineola: Dover.
Walls, N., ed. 2001. *Desire, Discord and Death: Approaches to Ancient Near Eastern Myths.* Boston: American Schools of Oriental Research.
Woolley, L. 1934. *Ur Excavations* II, *The Royal Cemetery: A Report on the Predynastic and Sargonid Graves Excavated between 1926 and 1931.* London: Publications of the Joint Expedition of the British Museum and the Museum of the University of Pennsylvania to Mesopotamia.

Ancient Aliens, Modern Cosmologies

Zecharia Sitchin and the Transformation of Mesopotamian Myth

Ryan Winters

It is not uncommon for scholars and teachers of the ancient world to encounter people who bring up the topic of "aliens" and the influences such beings may have had on ancient civilizations. This is actually a quite widespread cultural phenomenon as far as the modern reception of the ancient past goes, and scholars should, to some degree, reckon with this.[1] Whatever the reason might be, many today entertain the notion that humans in ancient times were influenced by aliens from outer space. Some would even credit the rise of humanity and ancient civilization itself to contact with these interplanetary travellers. Most paradigmatic of this phenomenon is the popular American television series *Ancient Aliens*, which premiered on the "History Channel" in 2010, and is now in its twelfth season, with new episodes continuing to air as of late 2017.

As silly as it may seem to some, I think that the popularity of modern "ancient alien" beliefs may have something to teach us about certain human and civilizational universals concerning mythology and cosmology and the role these play in shaping the perception of the past. Modern cosmological notions, which society at large accepts as factual—"The Big Bang" and "The Heliocentric Model"—have in a sense made it inevitable that ancient mythologies, themselves stemming from an entirely different cosmological basis, would be reinterpreted to fit the modern system. Because of the important role that the concept of "Outer Space" plays in modern consciousness, for some, the ancient gods have been transformed into modern space aliens.

By studying the myths, pantheons, and religious practices of an ancient culture, scholars can reconstruct that culture's "cosmology." A cosmology is a set of fundamen-

1. For an extensive analysis by a scholar in religious studies of the modern belief that ancient peoples had contacts with space aliens, see Richter 2012 and 2017, with further references. The present communication is by a student of ancient Mesopotamian language, history, and religion, and is intended to be more limited in scope. The focus is specifically on the differing cosmological perceptions of ancient Mesopotamians and modern humans.

tal assumptions that address such notions as how the universe and all the forces within it came to be, the outer shape and form of the world, and the origin and destiny of mankind. One of the most famous ancient cosmologies is the one expounded by the composition *Enuma Elish*,[2] which promoted the Babylonian city-god Marduk to the chief of the pantheon, and made his city Babylon into the center of the universe. *Enuma Elish* represented essentially a literary restructuring, in response to the political exigencies of the time, of the inherited Babylonian cosmos, as represented by earlier myths such as, in particular, *Inuma Ilu* (aka *Atra-Hasis*). Marduk, formerly a deity of only local importance, took over and combined the titles and functions of older chief deities like Enlil and Enki.

Scholars do not know for certain exactly what effects *Enuma Elish* had on the beliefs and practices of society at large, or to what degree the composition came about as a result of trends already in progress. But it is quite clear that the cosmology promoted by *Enuma Elish* served the interests of the Babylonian political and religious elite (Michalowski 1990, 389–93).

In modern times as in ancient, we too feel and experience our place in the cosmos, the world, and the course of history, based on the prevailing culture. Today this can be influenced by everything from education to politics, religion, media, and pop culture. Needless to say, none of these forces exists in a vacuum, and various interests will seek to promote views they find agreeable, be this in pursuit of profit and power, or in order to promote this or that ideology. Although it is unlikely that any two individuals in modern times will share the same "cosmology"—with so many religions, ideologies, and educational backgrounds coexisting—prevailing cultural trends still play a major role. One of these trends is the importance attached to outer space and space exploration. For some, the idea of outer space is so prominent that it has conditioned their reception and experience of the ancient past. "Ancient aliens" authors have thus taken advantage of our cosmological preconditioning by reinterpreting ancient mythology in a way that fits with modern assumptions about the nature of the universe.

If the name of the ancient "Sumerians" has in pop culture become particularly strongly associated with "ancient aliens," this is almost entirely due to the writings of a Russian-American named Zecharia Sitchin (1920–2010). A prolific writer, Sitchin authored over eleven books between 1976 and 2010 (fig. 1). Sitchin's books have sold millions of copies worldwide, and have been published in more than twenty-five languages.[3] Sitchin's ideas have also been receiving a further popularity boost from the *Ancient Aliens* television program, where at least three entire episodes have been devoted to his theories about an alien race called "Anunnaki," said to be responsible for the creation of humanity. The 2012 movie *Prometheus* revolves around a humanity-

2. See Kämmerer and Metzler 2012 and Lambert 2013 for the most recent scholarly editions, and Gabriel 2014 for an analysis of Enuma Elish and the *Weltordnung* ("Pax Mardukiana") it promoted.

3. See "Zecharia Sitchin," Wikipedia, https://en.wikipedia.org/wiki/Zecharia_Sitchin.

creating alien race of "Engineers," who seem in part to have been inspired by Sitchin's Anunnaki. Significantly, at the beginning of this film, fictional ancient artwork in a style clearly imitative of ancient Mesopotamian artwork, said to depict contact with aliens, was shown. In October 2017, the Google search results for "Anunnaki" still seemed almost entirely dominated by content related to Sitchin's idea of the Anunnaki as an alien race. A YouTube search for "Anunnaki" returns alien content with hundreds of thousands, some even with millions of views. In 2016, the Iraqi Minister of Transport, at a press conference for the opening of a new airport, claimed, citing Sitchin, that ancient Sumerians had built and used the world's first airport in what is now Iraq, some five thousand years ago (Speigel 2016).

It is perhaps easy to understand why "aliens" have been invoked as a convenient way to explain how ancient civilizations were, without modern technology, able to achieve impressive technical and architectural feats, like the Egyptian pyramids or Stonehenge.[4] But it is a bit more surprising that Mesopotamian civilization has become, in popular culture, so strongly associated with "aliens," considering that this land has bequeathed far less immediately impressive architectural and visual remains.

In the case of Zecharia Sitchin, it has been not the visual remains, but the Mesopotamian mythological heritage,[5] that has inspired a modern "ancient aliens" belief. In general, Sitchin's books, although they are presented as the result of scholarly research, are written with a tone and style that more closely resembles that of a mystery novel, which in part explains their appeal. But at the same time there seems to be little doubt that Sitchin was familiar with several Mesopotamian myths through their modern scholarly editions. Although he never seems to have received any formal education in

4. Richter 2017, 142–43 and Richter 2012 discuss the use by prominent Swiss theorist of ancient aliens (for Richter and others, "ancient astronauts") Erich von Däniken, of what Richter calls an *interpretatio technologica*. This constitutes a form of modern mythmaking whereby the supernatural phenomena occurring in ancient myths are made understandable by explaining them in a modern technological language. For Richter, it is the technological explanation that lies at the root of Däniken's ideas and which best explains their cultural currency: "Däniken is only part of a larger tradition of speculation that, in turn, has roots not only in our intellectual history and literature, but also relates to the success and influence of science and technology which pervades our lives today" (Richter 2012, 224).

5. Ceccarelli (2016) discussed the use of biblical texts by Marco Biglino, an Italian ancient aliens author who has been quite active in the past decade. According to Ceccarelli, the "method" employed by Biglino and similar authors can be compared to "cargo cult science" as described in a story told by renowned physicist Richard Feynmen. This story describes a group of Pacific island natives who, apparently having witnessed the landing of cargo planes during World War II, attempt to recreate a primitive landing strip in the hope that now, with similar conditions having been created, planes will begin to land again. Ancient aliens theorists demonstrate a similar type of "logic" that, though it may seem sound to them, is based on fundamentally false assumptions about the nature of what they are dealing with. In the case of Biglino, this manifests itself in the discrepancy between his pretense of a proper philological analysis, and his attempts to use the "results" to argue in favor of an "ancient aliens" interpretation (Ceccarelli 2016, 957).

Figure 1. Cover images of Sitchin's "Earth Chronicles" series, 1976–1996. https://www.amazon.com/Complete-Zecharia-Sitchin-Chronicles-Nine-Book/dp/B00MRH7E1W.

ancient Near Eastern studies,[6] Sitchin displays a somewhat surprisingly high level of familiarity with the extant myths, their themes, and even their thematic connection with other traditions such as the biblical and classical ones. Among others, he drew

6. According to https://en.wikipedia.org/wiki/Zecharia_Sitchin, Sitchin was born in Soviet Azerbaijan, and raised in what was at the time Mandatory Palestine, later to become the state of Israel. He received a degree in economics from the University of London, and worked as journalist in Palestine/Israel before moving to New York in 1952. It remains unknown, whether or not Sitchin was actually a

upon the myth *Inuma Ilu* (aka *Atra-ḫasis*)[7] and used this text as a cornerstone for the creation of his own mythos.

The foundation of Sitchin's mythos is that the "Anunnaki" (which in the Mesopotamian tradition referred to a group of gods), was actually a real race of alien spacefarers—according to Sitchin, the same one referred to by the biblical Nephilim. The home planet of this race (which is called "Nibiru"[8] and is alleged to have a 3,600-year orbit around our sun) was depleted of resources, and so the Anunnaki launched an expedition to earth, above all to mine gold, which was necessary for their space-travel technology. The aliens who had been assigned this arduous mining task, however, were not too pleased with their lot, and a rebellion ensued. The solution was to create a new race of slaves to do the work, which would be a hybrid of the Anunnaki-aliens themselves and preexisting simian animals that had already existed on Earth (Sitchin 1976, 2010).

Here it is easy to see how Sitchin reimagined the ancient Mesopotamian *Inuma Ilu* myth for his purposes. He has essentially retold the same ancient myth, in an updated, modernized, and dramatized fashion but with the former gods now understood as space aliens (see in particular Sitchin 2010, 145–51). Extra details have been added to make the myth appeal to modern senses, such as the idea that humanity was created using genetic engineering on apes. The idea of space aliens—of which nearly everyone today will already have some clue from pop culture, movies, etc.[9]—turns out to be a convenient, even plausible way to allow moderns to imagine ancient myths as literally happening, in a way that fits with modern assumptions about the shape and nature of the universe.

Perhaps the same themes that made *Inuma Ilu* alluring for its ancient audience—the concept of a rebellion by a divine race against imposed labor, and the creation of mankind as a result—are those that we find so intriguing today, even if we read the myth only as moderns should—"academically."[10] But by recasting the gods as aliens,

---

believer in his own theories, and what motivated his prolific output—whether it was his own passionate belief, a simple desire for profit, or other reasons. On the internet, it is possible to find claims about a potentially nefarious background for Sitchin and his activities; among the allegations are that he was a high-ranking Freemason, or a CIA operative, tasked with spreading occult disinformation.

7. The edition of Lambert and Millard 1969 was published only a few years before the appearance of Sitchin 1976.

8. The existence or nonexistence of "Planet Nibiru" continues to be a hotly debated topic. As recently as November 2017, Forbes magazine devoted an entire article towards debunking the existence of Nibiru (Mack 2017). The Sitchtian "Nibiru" is likely derived from Akkadian *nēberu*, from the root *ebērum* "to cross over," which was one of the names of the planet Jupiter (*CAD* N/2: 147).

9. For a thorough review of the history of belief in space aliens and how this relates to ancient astronaut mythologies, see Richter 2012, 224–27.

10. That is to say, understanding the myth as reflecting the history, culture, and worldview of the past society that produced it. This same method of analysis is also applied to texts that still hold cultural currency, such as the Bible.

Sitchin has given modernity a chance to understand the ancient myth literally and so experience it "directly," in a way perhaps analogous to how the ancients themselves might have.[11] This is precisely so because, for many today, the idea of an alien is more believable than the idea of a god.

Although not everyone today would agree that they firmly believe in the existence of extraterrestrial life, few would disagree with the idea that the earth rotates, revolving around the sun within outer space as part of the milky way galaxy, an almost incomprehensibly vast system containing many other suns with many other planets. The ancients, in contrast, did not think of planets and stars as worlds or as *Terra Firma*, but as part of a system that was Earth- and human-centered. The modern concept of a very vast outer space leaves plenty of room for beings, more-or-less humanlike but much more advanced, originating from other planets and traveling around in spacecraft. Along these lines, alien-believers invoke the so-called *Drake equation*[12] to estimate the probability of the existence of extraterrestrial civilization, which, by all modern cosmological parameters, should be very high. On the other hand, the so-called *Fermi paradox*[13] describes the contradiction between these high probability estimates and the apparent lack of hard evidence for alien life.

The perception of the vastness of space, it should be noted, is not the recent result of modern technology or of new observation techniques, but was already a mathematical consequence of the most fundamental modern cosmological notion—that of heliocentrism. Because there is not any observable parallax or shift between stars of the winter and summer night skies, for the heliocentric model to be geometrically feasible the stars must all be located at a very great distance from the earth. In the late-sixteenth century, one of the last great geocentric astronomers, Tycho Brahe (1546–1601), considered this kind of a vast universe to be absurd, precisely because it disagreed so sharply with the biblically based cosmological notions with which he was accustomed.[14]

---

11. This notwithstanding, scholars continue to debate how literally the ancients took their myths or even if they "believed" in them at all. It could be similarly irrelevant in this context to ask whether Sitchin himself believed his own theories (I think it is actually very likely that he did not), or to ask the same question of his readers (the most passionate of which certainly do believe). On the question of "belief" among the ancient Greeks, the classic work is Veyne 1988. For ancient Mesopotamia, a "maximalist" approach to the question of belief as it relates to mythology is represented by Jacobsen 1976, 1–17, while a "minimalist" approach is often ascribed to Oppenheim 1976, 171–83. Cf. the discussion in Veldhuis 2004, 13–17.

12. "Drake equation," Wikipedia, https://en.wikipedia.org/wiki/Drake_equation.

13. "Fermi paradox," Wikipedia, https://en.wikipedia.org/wiki/Fermi_paradox.

14. Blair 1990, 364: "In the absence of any observed stellar paradox, Tycho scoffed for example at the absurdity of the distance and the sizes of the fixed stars that the Copernican [i.e. heliocentric] system required.... Tycho stressed his conviction on this point in the Progymnasmata: 'It is necessary to preserve in these matters some decent proportion, lest things reach out to infinity and the just symmetry of creatures and visible things concerning size and distance be abandoned: it is necessary to

The ancient Mesopotamians, for their own part, long before any specific myth like *Inuma Ilu* or *Enuma Elish* was composed, had their own specific ideas about how the universe looked. For them, earth was not one wandering planet among many but the center of the universe, surrounded by a cosmic ocean.[15] They believed in (or rather, they experienced knowledge of) gods, and various categories of divine beings that were, like the modern space aliens, more or less humanlike but much more advanced. They had specific ideas about where these beings fit in with the scheme of things, both in the natural and the social realms. Stars were not, as for us, distant solar systems potentially housing alien races but were seen rather as gods[16] who could even be petitioned directly through prayer and ritual,[17] and which, like other natural phenomena, could be read as signs or portents of the future to come.[18] Creation myths described the relationship between gods, the world/universe, and humans. One could say that the world according to the ancient scheme leaves plenty of room for gods to exist in multiple different forms, whether anthropomorphically, as natural or celestial phenomena, or as idols in the context of a cult. In ancient Sumer especially, it seems that almost anything could be "deified" to one degree or another.

The ancient Mesopotamian mindset could be been seen as standing in contrast to the modern "rational and scientific" conception of the universe, which includes notions like the vastness of outer space. But if the modern scientific system is itself only another set of cultural assumptions different from the ancient one, then in modern times the only real room for gods or superhuman beings is out in the vastness of space, in the form of extraterrestrial aliens. It is this fundamental distinction between conceptions of the universe, which underlies the modern retelling of ancient myths using the language of space aliens.

In the same way that the Marduk priesthood promoted a Babylon-centric cosmology to serve its own interests, the concept of outer space has often proven expedient to the modern holders of political power. Ever since the 1950s and 1960s, with the so-called "Space Race" between the Soviet Union and the United States, the importance of outer space and the pressing necessity of exploring it has been pushed from the highest levels of power, consuming vast amounts of resources, largely if not entirely for political reasons. The Soviet's launching of the Sputnik satellite in 1957 was perceived as a major defeat by Americans, even sparking widespread fear that the nation might soon

---

preserve this symmetry because God, the author of the universe, loves appropriate order, not confusion and disorder.'"

15. For an extensive study of Mesopotamian conceptions of the shape of earth and the universe, see Horowitz 1998.

16. On the relation in Mesopotamia between the cosmos and the divine, and on the stars as embodiments of deities, see Rochberg 2010, 317–38.

17. For ancient conceptions of the stars and the role they play in the determination of destiny, see Steinkeller 2005, 47, with a diagram of the Babylonian universe.

18. See Rochberg 2004 for an extensive study of the Mesopotamian sciences of celestial divination.

be vulnerable from an attack from outer space. On the other hand, the televised airing of the first moon landing in 1969 was felt as a major triumph, and sold as the "defining moment of a generation." Nor is the phenomenon of science fiction—on the one hand a profitable industry—unrelated, with the original *Star Trek* series having been broadcast from September 1966 until June 1969, just one month before the airing of the moon landing. It is of course unsurprising, then, that Sitchin's work, which is essentially well-written science fiction recasting the Mesopotamian gods as aliens, first appeared just at the tail end of the space race phenomenon. Science fiction adds to the mystique and romance of outer space. Space exploration also remains the exclusive purvey of the elite; only those with the most political and economic power are able access the so-called outer space, while the vast majority of mankind acts only as observer through a television screen.

To understand Sitchin and his success, it should be emphasized that the idea of aliens is not some fringe or marginal phenomenon in modern society, but one that is engaged with and actively promoted from the highest levels. In 2014, no less a prominent religious figure than Pope Francis entertained the notion of aliens, saying that he would be willing to baptize a "Martian" should one ever present itself before him. What some may dismiss as a whimsical comment about inclusion actually inspired an entire book with the title *Would You Baptize an Extraterrestrial?*, coauthored by the director of the Vatican Observatory, Brother Guy Consolmagno. For this prominent Jesuit astronomer, a future encounter with an alien race is not only completely inevitable, it could even take on messianic undertones, with the advanced spacefaring race teaching humanity how to dispel with all social ills.[19]

On the other hand, aliens could be seen not as saviors from above, but as a threat justifying worldwide political consolidation. In a speech before the United Nations in 1987, United States President Ronald Reagan made the following statement:

> Perhaps we need some outside universal threat to make us recognize this common bond. I occasionally think how quickly our differences worldwide would vanish if we were facing an alien threat from outside this world.[20]

Concerning this idea one cannot help but be reminded of the demonic army led by Kingu and Tiamat, the struggle against which justified Marduk's assumption of supremacy in *Enuma Elish*. More recently, in 2014, former President Bill Clinton echoed the

19. Sadowski 2014: "Jesuit Brother Guy Consolmagno, the new president of the Vatican Observatory Foundation, has no doubt that life exists elsewhere in the universe and that when humanity discovers it, the news will come as no big surprise.... Brother Consolmagno suggested the idea of discovering extraterrestrial life may be so appealing to humanity, with all its pain, injustice and disease, that there is hope that 'any race advanced enough to cross the stars to visit us must also be advanced enough to show us how to overcome all those human ills. They look to the aliens to be saviors of mankind.'"

20. Ronald Reagan, United Nations Address 1987; see Koenig 2013.

same sentiment almost verbatim in a more informal setting, on an evening television program, and provided some more extensive commentary of cosmological relevance:

> We know now that we live in an ever-expanding universe, we know that there are billions of stars and planets—literally—out there, and the universe is getting bigger. We know from our fancy telescopes that just in the last two years more than twenty planets have been identified outside our solar system, that seem to be far enough away from their suns and dense enough, that they might be able to support some form of life. So, it makes it increasingly less likely that we are alone ... but if we were visited someday I wouldn't be surprised. I just hope it's not like [the movie] *Independence Day*, a conflict. It may be the only way to unite this increasingly divided world of ours ... think of how all the differences among people on earth would seem small if we felt threatened by a space invader.[21]

Thus, whether they be seen as demonic threat or as Christ-like savior, or even somehow as both in one, there can be no doubt of the salience of the alien phenomenon at the highest echelons of society.

In this light, the recasting of the Mesopotamian gods as aliens emerges not as an unexpected pseudoscientific aberration, but instead as the natural consequence of our widely agreed-upon image of the universe. So long as prominent voices like former US presidents and top Vatican astronomers see alien encounters in our near future, then at the very least there will be mystery-novel salesmen ready to project alien encounters onto the ancient past, if not also a public ready to eagerly buy into such notions. Notions of ancient aliens will continue to "leak," from time to time, into the world of scholarship, or at least into scholars' everyday lives, whether in the classroom, in the museum, or at the pub.

I think the best we can do as scholars is to try to ensure that everyone has access to accurate information. If people wish to believe in aliens then they will, but it should be made clear that space aliens are a product of the modern perception of the cosmos and cannot have been conceived of by the ancients in the same way. Although ancient peoples experienced the world as replete with spiritual and divine forces (and often used their perception of such forces to guide their lives, such as through omens), mythology *sensu stricto* and mundane life are nevertheless always kept completely separate in our ancient sources. Supernatural events as such were not a daily occurrence. One might interpret some event as an omen or sign from the gods, but one did not see "gods" encased in flames flying around the streets of Sumer. The basis of society was cereal agriculture, and chariots were definitely animal-drawn wagons, and not space ships. An Assyrian king might claim to have received divine encouragement before leading his

21. Bill Clinton on *Jimmy Kimmel Live!* (2014) [TV program], 2 April 2014, 21:30.

armies on a campaign, but he did not claim to fly, or to wield supernatural powers of fire or lightning against his enemies.

If heliocentrism robbed humanity of its unique position in the cosmos, then ancient aliens cheapen the value of humanity in ancient history, which otherwise provides a chance to glimpse mankind in its rawest form. Explaining ancient technical and cultural achievements through ancient alien contact completely removes the human nature of these achievements, which were often in the face of significant environmental hardship, and formidable external and internal threats, political and socioeconomic. On the other hand, by reading ancient myth as a record of an ancient encounter with real extraterrestrials, one completely fails to even begin to understand the complex yet fundamental role of mythology in human thought and society.

Sadly, I think alien beliefs are more popular than many scholars might think, and they may even be growing more popular, especially among the undereducated. Aliens are not fringe, but rather mainstream. They are actually a product of rather fundamental modern assumptions about the universe, and ideas about aliens are promoted from a high level.

Those who study ancient belief systems are in a better position than most to demonstrate that conceptions about the universe are not merely sets of facts, purely objective and sovereign, but exist within the cultural and individual mind. As such, cosmology can be influenced by various factors, including perhaps even political and ideological agendas.

Bibliography

Blair, A. 1990. "Tycho Brahe's Critique of Copernicus and the Copernican System." *Journal of the History of Ideas* 51:355–77.

Ceccarelli, M. 2016. "Tra paleoastronautica, secolarizzazione, individualizzazione religiosa e quasi-religione: Il 'fenomeno Biglino.'" *Studi e Materiali di Storia delle Religioni* 82:952–75.

"Drake equation." n.d. *Wikipedia*. Accessed February 2018. https://en.wikipedia.org/wiki/Drake_equation.

"Fermi paradox." n.d. *Wikipedia*. Accessed February 2018. https://en.wikipedia.org/wiki/Fermi_paradox.

Gabriel, G. 2014. *Enūma Eliš: Weg zu einer globalen Weltordnung*. Orientalische Religionen in der Antike 12. Mohr Siebek: Tübingen.

Horowitz, W. 1998. *Mesopotamian Cosmic Geography*. Mesopotamian Civilizations 8. Winona Lake, IN: Eisenbrauns.

Jacobsen, T. 1976. *The Treasures of Darkness. A History of Mesopotamian Religion*. New Haven and London: Yale University Press.

Jimmy Kimmel Live! 2014. TV program. 2 April 2014, 21:30.

Kämmerer, T., and K. Metzler. 2012. *Das Babylonische Weltschöpfungsepos Enūma elîš*. Alter Orient und Altes Testament 375. Münster: Ugarit Verlag.

Koenig, K. 2013. "Flashback: Reagan's Vision for a Unifying Alien Invasion." *MSNBC*, 24 September. Accessed February 2018. http://www.msnbc.com/msnbc/flashback-reagans-vision-unifying.

Lambert, W. 2013. *Babylonian Creation Myths*. Mesopotamian Civilizations 16. Winona Lake, IN: Eisenbrauns.

Lambert, W., and A. Millard. 1969. *Atra-Hasīs: The Babylonian Story of the Flood*. Oxford: Clarendon.

Mack, E. 2017. "November 19 Came And Went With No Sign of Nibiru (Once Again)." *Forbes*, 19 November. Accessed February 2018. http://www.forbes.com/sites/ericmack/2017/11/19/nibiru-planet-x-november-19-nasa-space/.

Michalowski, P. 1990. "Presence at the Creation." In T. Abusch, J. Huehnergard, and P. Steinkeller (eds.), *Lingering over Words: Studies in Ancient Near Eastern Literature in Honor of William L. Moran*, 381–96. Atlanta: Scholars Press.

Oppenheim, A. L. 1976. *Ancient Mesopotamia: Portrait of a Dead Civilization*. Chicago: University of Chicago Press.

Richter, J. 2012. "Traces of the Gods: Ancient Astronauts as a Vision of Our Future." *Numen* 59:222–48.

———. 2017. *Götter-Astronauten. Erich von Däniken und die Paläo-SETI-Mythologie* Perspektiven der Anomalistik 5. Freiburg: Gesellschaft für Anomalistik.

Rochberg, F. 2004. *The Heavenly Writing: Divination, Horoscopy, and Astronomy in Mesopotamian Culture*. Cambridge: University Press.

———. 2010. *In the Path of the Moon: Babylonian Celestial Divination and Its Legacy*. Studies in Ancient Magic and Divination 6. Leiden and Boston: Brill.

Sadowski, D. 2014. "Vatican Astronomer: Just a Matter of Time until Life Found in the Universe." *Catholic News Service*, 19 September. Accessed February 2018. http://www.catholicnews.com/services/englishnews/2014/vatican-astronomer-just-a-matter-of-time-until-life-found-in-universe.cfm.

Sitchin, Z. 1976. *The 12th Planet*. New York: Stein and Day.

———. 2010. *There Were Giants Upon the Earth: Gods, Demigods, and Human Ancestry; the Evidence of Alien DNA*, Rochester, VT: Bear and Company.

Speigel, L. 2016. "ET's Built Earth's First Airport, Iraqi Transport Minister Says." *HuffPost*, 13 October. Accessed February 2018. https://www.huffpost.com/entry/first-airport-on-earth-iraq_n_57fbb625e4b068ecb5e05fed.

Steinkeller, P. 2005. "Of Stars and Men: The Conceptual and Mythological Setup of Babylonian Extispicy." In A. Gianto (ed.), *Biblical and Oriental Essays in Memory of William L. Moran*, 11–47. Biblica et Orientalia 48. Rome: Biblical Institute Press.

Veldhuis, N. 2004. *Religion, Literature, and Scholarship: The Sumerian Composition Nanše and the Birds*. Cuneiform Monographs 22. Leiden: Brill.

Veyne, P. 1988. *Did the Greeks Really Believe in their Myths? An Essay on the Constitutive Imagination*. Chicago: University of Chicago Press.

"Zecharia Sitchin." n.d. *Wikipedia*. https://en.wikipedia.org/wiki/Zecharia_Sitchin.

The (In)visibility of Archaeology

Davide Nadali

The question of visibility is at the center of archaeological debate and methodology: as ancient ruins are covered by the dust and layers of time and later occupations, archaeology itself is the practice that reveals that past and discovers ancient traces; in other words it makes the past visible. The contrast between invisibility of the past (before the discovery) and visibility of the past (once it has been unearthed) seems to define the basic principles of archaeological thought and theory. If the process of discovering ancient traces (making them visible) seems to be the main result of an archaeological excavation, the action of making what has been brought to light invisible seems to be more illogical and, to a certain extent, contradictory. However, since archaeology as practice in the field and the subsequent archaeological interpretation by archaeologists lie exactly inbetween the will of making things either visible or invisible, the dialectic opposition intrinsically concerns archaeology and archaeologists, even if the latter are not always aware of it. Nevertheless, as we will see, they are responsible for the (in)visibility of what they have discovered.[1]

The need for visibility of the results of archaeological excavations generates different solutions: actions in the field (restorations, integrations, reconstructions)[2] and publication of data. In both cases, the ideas of archaeologists stem from the necessity and will of making their stories and discoveries available to the general public and the scien-

1. The need for making archaeological discoveries invisible depends on several factors, being the result of, for example, explicit choices by the archaeologists, the need for preservation and protection (the archaeological evidence is discovered, studied, photographed, drawn, and published, but then covered again) or even external impositions due to political, cultural, and religious reasons.

2. The three terms are not synonyms but rather they imply a different degree of intervention on the archaeological records to make them visible to the general public (tourists) and scholars or even to make them invisible—that is, the nature and result of the intervention are so imposing that the traces of the past are concealed, reinvented, and misinterpreted. Integrations (the filling-in of missing elements) and reconstructions, if they are not based upon scientific principles and approaches, can result in aberrant new realities that have little or nothing to do with the original: in this respect, if the intention was to make the original look better and more engaging for the viewers, the final result is exactly the contrary, that is the creation of a package that hides the original and presents a false reality or, even worse, a deliberate fake.

tific community, with different aims. On one hand, the presentation and visualization of data for a general public can be heavily imbued with preconceived interpretations and images in the head of both the creator and the beholders: it means that the final presentation reflects more what we wish the past was or what people expect it was, rather than its actual character. At the same time, even in the case of the publication of data for scholars and colleagues, presentation of what has been excavated reflects the analysts' understanding of a specific context or building, with selection of data.

As a consequence, each choice in visualizing the discovery has a specific target and audience: it is quite natural that each archaeologist wants to broadcast the results of her/his work;[3] it is quite another matter when she/he imposes her/his view of the past through the crystallization of an image that eventually enters our system of reference and interpretation, which happens when we intentionally or unintentionally refer to it whenever we are dealing with that particular archaeological context or we are facing and studying a similar one.

In this respect, old images of ancient Near Eastern cities that were conceived in the nineteenth century soon after the first discoveries are still used today because they entered our mnemonic process of identification to which we refer almost automatically. This happens even when we use those images to point out that they give a false and misleading view of the ancient Near Eastern ruins. In any case, we are still using them as part of the archaeological archive, one could even say as a heavy legacy, as a way of representing the ancient Near East.

Near Eastern archaeology has always faced the problem of visibility since the very beginning: the first explorers of ancient Mesopotamian ruins had to deal with the difficulty of making their discoveries clear, readable, and understandable for a general public of nonspecialists. This is particularly true if we take into consideration the shape and morphology of ancient sites in the Near East: the artificial mounds (*tulūl* in Arabic) are hills of earthen strata that have been created by the continuous anthropic action of construction and leveling mud-brick architecture. The use of mud bricks therefore increases the instability of ancient Near Eastern architecture. In fact, if mud bricks are not conveniently protected (by the presence of roofing or plaster), the action of wind and rain actually dissolves the bricks producing heaps of shapeless soil. Mud bricks are also a thorny issue in field archaeology because archaeologists must be very careful during the excavation, distinguishing bricks that kept their original shape and place from bricks that collapsed and bricks that no longer exist and have been reconverted into soil. Due to the fragile condition of adobe architecture, archaeologists often discover few preserved bricks. As a consequence, they have to resort to hypothesis for imaging and representing the original shape and height of the walls. If classical ruins, made of baked bricks and stones, were well-visible to travelers and explorers, the ruins of

3. This also happens in the choice of wording and definition as in the case of the definition and creation of the seductive model of the "empire." See Matthews 2003, 127–32; Liverani 2005, 228–30.

ancient Near Eastern civilizations were on the contrary mostly invisible or they were visible in the shape of hills; even after the excavations, they could still be invisible and therefore mostly incomprehensible.

The present analysis retraces the ways of archaeologists in representing the past and making it visible with the identification of six phases:

- phase 1: the discovery of the ancient Near Eastern past;
- phase 2: the invention of the past;
- phase 3: the scientific approach to the invention;
- phase 4: the manipulation of the past;[4]
- phase 5: the preservation of the original data;
- phase 6: the new frontiers of the visualization of the past.

In the end, it will be clear how archaeologists are still dealing with and are still bothered by the necessity of making their discoveries visible. The problem is still the same, but the aims and methods have changed.

1. Phase 1: The Discovery of the Ancient Near Eastern Past

In 1842, Paul-Émile Botta, French consul at Mosul in northern Iraq, started the exploration of the ancient hills of Quyunjiq that he abandoned immediately afterwards because of the mediocre results; he then moved farther north to the hills of Khorsabad, thus discovering Dur Sharrukin, the ancient Assyrian capital that was founded by Sargon II in the eighth century BCE. Soon after the achievements of Botta, British explorer Austen Henry Layard started his work at Nimrud, another Assyrian city, actually the first Assyrian capital in the era of the so-called Neo-Assyrian period that was refounded by the king Assurnasirpal II in the ninth century BCE.[5]

In the mid-nineteenth century, the West finally met, concretely and physically, the civilizations of the ancient Near East that were, up to that time, mostly known via indirect references in the Bible and in classical sources. Indeed, the discovery of Nineveh and Assyria in general by the French and British explorers opened a renewed season of interest in the ancient Near East, emphasized by the opening of the Assyrian galleries in the Louvre Museum in Paris and the British Museum in London, where people could directly look in the eyes of the Assyrian kings and they could also be astonished

4. Manipulation can, to a certain extent, be seen as a pejorative derivation of the invention. Invention, one can say, is an innocent process, at least in its primary intention, while manipulation implies the use of the invention but deviated and charged with heavy political and ideological symbolism.

5. For a history of the discoveries in Assyria in the nineteenth century, see Larsen 1996 and Liverani 2013, 3–66 (especially 25–42).

and scared by the huge colossi of human-headed bulls and lions. At that time a real Assyromania affected architecture, costumes, and the way of life.[6]

Just because archaeology in the Near East started in Assyria, whose culture was largely well-known from the Bible, the concrete and vivid representation of the ruins of the ancient Assyrian cities, from the sculptures that were visible in Paris and London were taken, became immediately necessary and urgent: What did an ancient Assyrian city look like? Which references did the first explorers have at their disposal? A few years later, towards the end of the nineteenth century when the explorations in southern Iraq started, leading to the discovery of the Sumerians, there was a completely different emphasis: the fact that the Sumerians were not referenced in the Bible caused different interpretations by the explorers who were engaged with the translation of Sumerian texts and the question of the origin of this population.[7] Moreover, the absence of long sculpted walls like those found in the Assyrian palaces made the exploration of the Sumerian sites more difficult because of the extreme complexity of identifying the walls, which were made exclusively of mud bricks. In the end, one might roughly sum up that the absence of walls and buildings as well as the remote antiquity of the Sumerians, whose memory was not preserved in the Bible, did not impel the represention and comprehension of those spaces within the urban place.

2. *Phase 2: The Invention of the Past*

The results of the French and British excavations of the Assyrian cities raised the question of the visibility of those discoveries: if the Assyrian bas-reliefs were clearly visible and, one might say, understood even outside their context, the visibility of the general outline of the cities and their architecture was the real problem. Moreover, this challenge was worsened by the rudimentary techniques of excavations employed by both French and British explorers. Once the perimeter of walls and, consequently the bas-reliefs that lined the walls, were detected, the excavation proceeded through the use of pits and tunnels that followed the limits of the rooms, discarding what was in the rooms and what covered (later strata) the archaeological deposits. The words of Layard (1853, 69) clearly describe the method:

> The accumulation of soil above the ruins was so great, that I determined to continue the tunnelling, removing only as much earth as was necessary to show the sculptured walls.

---

6. On the impact of Assyrian discoveries in Europe, see Bohrer 2003, 2008; Micale 2008; Pedde 2015.

7. The question about the origin of the Sumerians led to research on the physiognomy of Sumerian men. Scholars attempted to use the Sumerian sculptures discovered at that point, in comparison with images of other populations, in order to determine what they looked like. See for example Evans 2012, 15–45; Verderame, in this volume.

Figure 1. Eugène Delacroix, *Death of Sardanapalus*. Louvre Museum.

The need for visibility of the discoveries was harmed by the natural invisibility of the ruins (hidden below the mounds) and the invisibility caused by the inadequate excavation techniques. In other words, contents were discovered, but the space where the contents were found was roughly excavated and analyzed. In the end, one could say that Assyrian cities were still unknown after the French and British efforts, but surely the knowledge of the urban organization, the shape of the city, and the relationship of the different buildings and their components were still missing and, I would say, impossible to grasp at that time with the approach in the field, which was merely devoted to the removal and cleanliness of the deposits of soil covering the sculptures.

Due to the lack of direct archaeological information (plans of buildings were heavily schematic with hypothetical reconstructions based on symmetry and misleading analogies), the representation and visibility of Assyrian cities were only possible thanks to the imaginary reconstructions of James Fergusson and Thomas Man Baynes that were used to illustrate Layard's books. Looking at the paintings of Fergusson and Baynes, it is immediately clear that archaeological reality has been bent in favor of and adapted to the stereotypical idea of an Oriental city, as formulated in paintings before the archaeological discoveries, such as *Belshazzar's Feast* (1826; see fig. 2 in McGeough this volume) and *The Fall of Nineveh* (1830) by John Martin and the *Death of Sardanapalus* (1827) by Eugène Delacroix (fig. 1; see also Bohrer 2003, 50–55; Bahrani 2001; Micale 2005, 144–46). Compared to the totally imaginary paintings of Martin and Delacroix,

Figure 2. *The Palaces of Nimroud Restored*, James Fergusson. Chromolithograph. Published in Austin Henry Layard, *The Monuments of Nineveh* (London, 1853).

the reconstructions of Fergusson (fig. 2) and Baynes were somewhat more Assyrianized, that is, elements of the Assyrian culture (namely, the sculptures and other decorative elements) were added to and inserted into a fictitious background that mixed up Egyptian and Persian elements of architecture and invented second and third stories.

Elements of other cultures were thus used to fill in the missing parts of the Assyrian buildings and cities: the reconstructions of Fergusson and Baynes were the result of a fusion of styles, cultures, and historical periods, but they finally complied with what people were expecting. In some ways, archaeological discoveries did not change the stereotype. On the contrary they helped to crystallize and reinforce it because sources got the better of archaeology, that is, the Assyrian city finally looked as one expected, wanted, and thought.[8] This process is particularly evident when one looks at the realization of the Assyrian Court for the Crystal Palace in London: Assyrian elements were freely used and adapted not to represent an Assyrian real space, but rather to reproduce what people pretended was an Assyrian space, finally creating an Assyrian nonplace (Micale 2010, 95).

8. The same happened for the Egyptian antiquities when Auguste Mariette had to rethink the reconstruction of the Egyptian monument for the *Exposition universelle* in Paris in 1867 to comply with the general idea of Egypt in people's minds (Mariette 1867, 11). See also the use of antiquities in staging operas and how the discoveries in Assyria after 1842 entered theatres to stage the "correct" scene (Nadali 2013a), with Egypt and the use of Persian elements still predominant. Finally, the new entries from Assyria were adopted even to represent non-Assyrian contexts, such as Babylon in the opera *Nabucco* (Nadali 2013b).

3. Phase 3: The "Scientific Approach" to the Invention

Strongly imbued with stereotyped images of the past, Mesopotamian archaeology had, and still has, to deal with that imaginary background, where desires of the artists and, in the end, of the archaeologists prevailed upon the archaeological reality of the excavations with its imperfections, incompleteness, and void of information. The real problem is the attempt to fill that void. There was a moment, in the history of the exploration of the past of ancient Mesopotamia, when attention to the details and the methods of construction of ancient buildings entered the vocabulary of field archaeology and led to what has been labeled "the discovery of mud-bricks" (Liverani 2000). The work by Robert Koldewey and Walter Andrae at Babylon and Assur respectively, deeply changed the approach to the excavation, the study of the context, the analysis of architecture, and, finally, the reconstruction of the ancient buildings. The education of both Koldewey and Andrae as architects deeply affected their methods of excavation and observation of the archaeological context (Micale 2007; Micale and Nadali 2008). Indeed, it would be much more suitable to speak of an architectural context. In fact, the section drawings made by the German scholars at Babylon and Assur clearly reproduce the superimposition of different architectural elements (foundation, elevation, type of materials, etc.) rather than what we now precisely define and intend as an archaeological stratification. At Babylon, Koldewey also operated excavations through pits and tunnels, exactly as Layard did at Nimrud. Nevertheless, his architectural attention to the elevation of structures was in some way transformed and adapted to observe the elevation of the archaeological deposits, thus giving the first examples of section drawings of the sequence and superimposition of the deposits. Architecture, however, always prevailed: this is clear in the observation of the same drawings, where the details for the microanalysis of strata strongly rely upon the presence and preservation of architectural features (Micale and Nadali 2008, 412–13, fig. 4).

The scientific approach of Koldewey and Andrae to archaeology was therefore mainly architectural. In this respect, although innovative in the review of previous and contemporary excavations in Mesopotamia at that time (Matthews 2003, 14), the final result was a combination of archaeological data (reality) and a preconceived idea of the architecture (integration and imagination). In the end, although based on a careful observation of the architectural elements in the field (plans), the reconstructions integrated what was missing with elements and details that were mostly in the mind of the archaeologists (or architects) rather than what actually existed. Observing the documentation of the German scholars, it seems to denote a discrepancy between plans and section drawings and the reconstructions of architecture: the former gives the reality of findings while the latter represents what the monuments originally looked like. Actually, the first attempt to distinguish between what archaeological excavations produced (i.e., the state of preservation of the ruins at the moment of discovery) and how later

Figure 3. The temple and palace at Assur. From Andrae 1938, 44, Abb. 24.

representations integrated to show the original aspects of ancient buildings was made by the French archaeologist Victor Place (Micale 2005, 142–43; 2007, 120).

Beyond the single building, Koldewey and Andrae also presented the general outline of the cites of Babylon and Assur, with a representation, or at least an attempt to represent, the dimension of the two oriental cities. If anachronism and loans from the contemporary oriental cities were finally avoided (Liverani 2013, 79), the representations of Babylon and Assur, however, were too rationalist with a tendency to emphasize the monumental architecture. The general views of Assur by Andrae (fig. 3), for example, represent a city where monumental buildings (palaces and temples) stand out above a flat urban area just filled in with patterns of indistinct buildings without any specific or remarkable features (towers, niches and buttresses, decorations, protruding elements). Even people are absent, except for a few gathering of people next to the main and important buildings. The shapes of the oriental cities by Koldewey and Andrae are, one would say, less Orientalist (in the terminology of Edward Said), nevertheless they are the result of the application of a mental idea.[9]

9. Interestingly enough, the power of mental idea or ideal mental images of the ancient Oriental cities also affected photography, with photos of ancient ruins that were purposely taken as to give and represent a reality that was however filtered and that needed to be in compliance with the idea in mind. See the contribution of Di Paolo in this volume.

4. Phase 4: The Manipulation of the Past

In a certain way, one could assert that each representation of the ancient Orient is a kind of manipulation, that is the past is distorted and adapted to the present for the needs and wills of the people that are looking at and benefitting from it; however, manipulation becomes more invasive and dangerous when political implications are clearly and deliberately addressed.

The nature of archaeology in the Near East is indeed political if one takes into account that the so-called pioneers of the explorations of the ancient Mesopotamian past were first and foremost diplomats and politicians of the European states in the Ottoman Empire who then decided to serve as archaeologists.

In analyzing the attitude of scholars studying the Mesopotamian past, Zainab Bahrani (1998, 161) observed that "the relationship between politics and archaeology has meant two things only": the first tendency was related to the study of ancient Babylonians and Assyrians as a manifestation of propaganda and oriental despotism, with clear political and moral judgments compared to the rational world of Greece and partially of Rome; the second tendency was even more political as it touched on the question of how the Iraqi Baathist regime reused and employed the pre-Islamic past for propagandistic purposes. In both cases, the Mesopotamian past was overloaded with targeted objectives that aimed to represent the past as both a mirror of the ancient society and a reflection of the modern one.

The discovery of the Mesopotamian past has been perceived as different from the classical tradition of Greece and Rome but at the same time as the prelude to Western civilization. In this respect, ancient Near Eastern civilizations have gained an importance because they have been viewed as the ancestors of the West, which then improved on the earliest achievements through invention and originality. Thus, from the moment of discovery, representations and manipulations of the past were useful for judging and interpreting dissimilarities with the West and its cultural points of reference and acknowledged values.

On the other hand, the use of the Mesopotamian past by the Baathist regime was, of course, politically instrumental and it became a key to interpreting the present. Surely it was a manipulation, with a representation of Saddam Hussein acting as an Assyrian king (shooting the enemy from a chariot while surrounded by modern war machines—helicopters, planes, ships, and missiles) or next to Hammurabi and the stele of his Law Code as a symbol of justice for his nation and people (Heinz 2002, 79–80). Beyond these iconographic re-/mis-interpretations of ancient Mesopotamian images, modern architecture also tried to replicate the shape of past buildings. Even the choice of the place was strategic, for example Saddam's palace on the ruins of Babylon. The intensive program of restoration and reconstruction of the ancient archaeological heritage aimed to revitalize the past and make it clearly visible again. The decayed mud-brick structures were heavily rebuilt and, interestingly, the reconstructions actually followed the drawings of the Babylonian monuments made by Koldewey, as also happened for the temple *Emakh* of Babylon (Micale 2005, 152). So, what is wrong if the model for the reconstruction exactly followed the drawing by the European archaeologist who excavated the temple?

If reconstructions and imaginary representations of the nineteenth century were imbued with stereotypes of the ancient Orient, modern Iraqi reconstructions and representations were based on the archaeology as if they wanted to go back to the originality and reliability of the data. The interest in the Mesopotamian past was used for representing and exalting the national identity via the reappropriation of their archaeological heritage. I wonder whether this return to traditional (Mesopotamian) architecture might be interpreted as the reaction to the realization of projects by modern European and American architects who were active in Baghdad in the 1940s, 1950s, and 1960s, and who imported, with adaptations to the local environment, an international style of architecture that was then perceived as alien.[10]

5. Phase 5: The Preservation of the Original Data

Far from the exciting moment of the discovery and the political implications of the representation of the past, archaeology as a discipline finally developed an additional phase to its mission, that of restoration, as a way not only of preserving the original data but to make them visible without altering their nature, shape, and function. The basic rule is to respect the reality and state of preservation of the archaeological findings, aiming to present and preserve them as they were found without any additional superimposition or desire to make them more alluring and fantastic for the general public. Today, archaeology no longer considers the desires and expectation of people, at least as a matter of principle: of course, much depends on the general political and cultural situations archaeologists are facing, with the need, at times, of a free concession or the forced compliance of a compromise. Rather archaeology aims to teach people to understand the complexity of archaeological findings even in their precarious state of preservation. Integration and restoration aim to show how the datum was found by the archaeologists and how it can potentially be interpreted, reconstructed, and made visible and comprehensible while avoiding any distortion. The process of making archaeology visible must respect the originality of the datum, giving visitors the opportunity and means to discern and distinguish the original from the integrated elements, replicas, and reconstructions (G. Buccellati 2017, 150).

To exemplify the approach to restoration, which aims both to make archaeological discoveries visible and to protect them (with a consequent and unavoidable process of invisibility of the datum), I will consider two cases: Tell Mardikh, ancient Ebla, and

10. On the transformation and modernization of the urban architectural landscape of Baghdad between the First and Second World Wars, see Pieri 2015.

Tell Mozan, ancient Urkesh, both in Syria. It is not coincidental that this new approach to restoration in archaeology began in Syria, in a context in which the heavy legacy of Mesopotamia (both discoveries and tradition of study) was not influential: solutions had to rethink the standards and traditions dictated by the fanciful reconstructions and representations that beleaguered Mesopotamian archaeology, which, as we have seen, was sometimes translated into reality (of which Babylon, the walls of Nineveh, and the ziggurats of Ur and Dur Kurigalzu are the best known and notable examples).

Ebla and Mozan used two different approaches that led to the same endpoint: the archaeological record has been protected, partially integrated and consolidated, respecting the discovery as it was found. That is, the buildings have been restored to the state they were in upon excavation and not as they would have been in antiquity. At both sites the idea of total integration and reconstruction has been avoided, preferring a system of preservation that reflects the condition of the remains as they were at the time of the discovery.

At the end the 1990s, the Italian Archaeological Expedition of Sapienza University of Rome to Syria initiated a program of restoration and rehabilitation of the archaeological areas so far excavated for the creation of an archaeological park. The main, and most difficult, task concerned the preservation of the mud-brick structures, which, if not suitably protected and consolidated, easily collapse. The plan, however, did not encompass the reconstruction of the original mud-brick walls—that is, the process of restoration was not used to recreate the shape of decayed or lost walls. Rather, the restoration aimed to preserve the existing remains, showing the state of walls exactly as they were found by the archaeologists. Thus, attention focused on choosing the most suitable methods and techniques for preserving the original structures and evaluating the effectiveness of these interventions.

Most importantly, the goal of the restoration was to make the site and its mud-brick structures visible and comprehensible without affecting the urban landscape of the site. As a consequence, it was necessary to hide the original mud-brick structures (they were thus made invisible to visitors) in order to preserve them so that they would be still visible in the future. Beyond the consolidation of the original mud-bricks (fig. 4),[11] operations were principally devoted to covering the ancient walls with a layer of newly fashioned mud-bricks made of the same soil from the site but with a different color so that the original sections would always be distinguishable from the restored sections (figs. 5, 6, and 7). Another solution that also considered the invisibility of the original walls was the use of traditional local system of a mud plaster, directly applied to the bricks.[12]

---

11. On the techniques used at Ebla, see Mari et al. 2000.

12. This technique was employed, for example, in the restoration of Royal Palace G and the massive mud-brick walls of the Temple of the Rock (Area HH). See Ramazzotti 2010.

Figure 4. The consolidation of a mud-brick wall using ethyl-silicate and primal solutions at Tell Mardikh/Ebla (© Missione Archeologica Italiana in Siria).

Figure 5. The making of new mud bricks at Ebla using soil from the site (© Missione Archeologica Italiana in Siria).

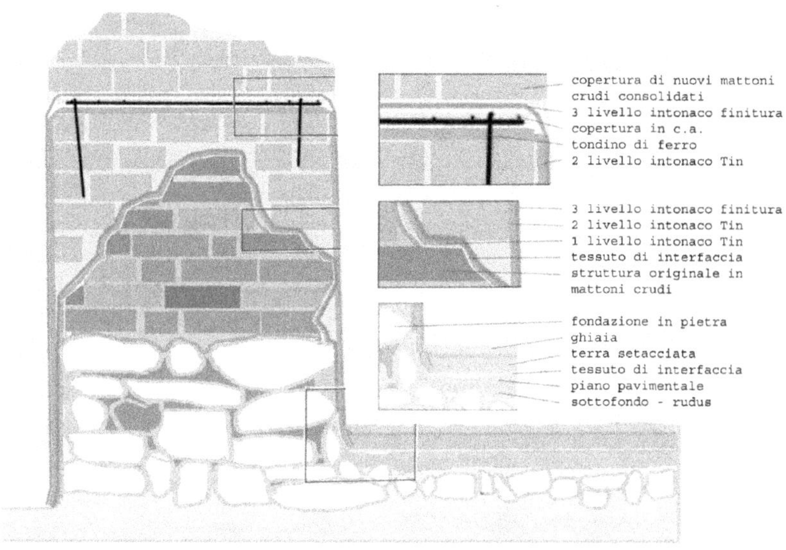

Figure 6. Section drawing of a mud-brick wall with the detail of the protective materials used to preserve the original inner core. Elaboration by Ugo Capriani (© Missione Archeologica Italiana in Siria).

Figure 7. Red and yellowish original mud bricks, covered with new mud bricks, in the area of Western Palace Q, Tell Mardikh/Ebla (© Missione Archeologica Italiana in Siria).

Since 2004, a restoration program has been carried out at the site of Tell Mozan. Different solutions from those at Ebla have been applied for the conservation of the original mud-brick structures, but the same philosophy can be recognized: restoration aimed at the preservation of the original walls without any alteration of their shapes and state of preservation. Again, restoration aimed to preserve and show to visitors exactly what the archaeologists found and identified in the field. The necessity of presenting and "staging" the discovery must not exceed the limits of interpretation and force the data. This is particularly true if one takes into consideration that "restoration affects very concretely the perception one has of the data" (G. Buccellati 2017, 142). For that reason, Buccellati (150) rightly argues:

> Excavators should therefore be clear as to what their particular staging is intended to be and articulate it in such a manner that the visitors may benefit from the mediation offered, while allowing at the same time the benefit of an immediate confrontation with the original, such as it is after it had been properly selected and preserved.

The special attention to the distinction between the original and restored part is indeed the distinctive style of the restoration program at Tell Mozan. In fact, the boundary between visible and invisible is tiny since the American expedition introduced a new experimental system of curtains (fixed on metal structures that circumscribe the walls as a cage) that can be pulled sideways to reveal the original mud-brick walls underneath (figs. 8 and 9).[13] The cover was also colored. In that way, archaeologists not only protected the original walls but they could also use this device for scientific and didactic purposes (fig. 10): curtains were differently colored according to the function of the sectors of the palace (e.g., service vs. formal wing; G. Buccellati 2006, 79).

The restoration projects of both Ebla and Mozan have been based on true respect for the original structures, on the one hand, and the general outlook of the sites, on the other. When found collapsed or destroyed, original walls have not been rebuilt but have simply been covered with a special balance between the question for visibility of the ruin and the unavoidable effect of invisibility for the purpose of protection. At Ebla, mud-brick walls have been physically covered and touched with new mud-bricks, while at Mozan a superstructure has been created above the walls for the positioning of the curtains: in any case, archaeological records have become visible and comprehensible only through a partial process of invisibility that has allowed the protection and conservation of the original fragile data.

Finally, both systems are characterized by a process of reversibility, because the restored elements can easily be removed to make the original elements visible once again. In fact, both systems are so uninvasive that continued maintenance and renewal

---

13. On the restoration choices and methods for mud-brick structures at Tell Mozan, see G. Buccellati 2000; Buccellati and Kelly-Buccellati 2005, 44–46; G. Buccellati 2006.

Figure 8. The installation of the metal structures on the mud-brick walls of the palace of Tell Mozan/Urkesh (© IIMAS – International Institute for Mesopotamian Area Studies).

Figure 9. The curtains covering the metal structures in the area of the palace of Tell Mozan/Urkesh (© IIMAS – International Institute for Mesopotamian Area Studies).

Figure 10. The curtains identify the functional sectors of the palace of Tell Mozan/Urkesh (© IIMAS – International Institute for Mesopotamian Area Studies).

of the restored parts are required (remaking of mud plaster, integration of the new mudbricks, replacement of curtains, etc.).

6. *Phase 6: The New Frontiers of the Visualization of the Past*

Staging the past has recently moved into the realm of 3D and virtual representation. New technologies have effectively opened up and fostered intriguing possibilities and perspectives in the (re-)presentation of the archaeological records for the general public (tourism) but even for scientific and didactic purposes (Bonde and Houston 2013; G. Buccellati 2017, 165).

The main task is the visualization of the archaeological record by translating that record into pictures, with the passage from what is visible or even invisible in the field into virtual reality where archaeology is made accessible though movement. Is there a difference between the new methods and the old graphic systems conceived, for example, by the first explorers of ancient Assyrian cities and the representations of Babylon and Assur by the German archaeologists? It is always a matter of visual representation, more precisely of making the archaeological discoveries visible and therefore tangible through the (integrated) use of different media (Shanks and Webmoor 2013, 144–45). One could even say that, although the methods are different, the problems are still the same: objectivity of the representation, respect for the archaeological context, and the fidelity of the reconstruction. One might run the risk that new 3D and virtual reality solutions are considered more reliable because of the technological elements they employ, and it is important to distinguish the medium from the final product. It may be that new and alluring computer images are useless and distort reality with the creation of an idea that has little or nothing to do with the archaeological contexts it pretends to visualize and present. In the process of filling the gaps to make everything clearly visible, we must be mindful of what we integrate and how we fill in the missing information without taking for granted that our reconstruction is necessarily true and the only valid one. Because of the free circulation of these new reconstructions on laptops, smartphones, and other interactive tools (Shanks and Webmoor 2013, 148), these images might in the end be much more dangerous in disseminating and replicating errors than even the old drawings of the nineteenth and early-twentieth centuries.

If virtual reality and the use of motion pictures of archaeological records can have a cognitive validity as a research tool, it is important to base the model upon rigorous and well-established data so that the final result will not be a fanciful, unreliable product where the aesthetic appeal prevails over the archaeological evidence (F. Buccellati 2015, 162–63; Nadali 2015, 100–101; G. Buccellati 2017, 163).

New instruments for preparing, and new devices to disseminate, pictures of the past open innovative and fresh paths for the comprehension of archaeological evidence and contexts on the one hand and the dissemination of the archaeological results (making them largely visible and attractive) to a wider public on the other. In particular, the question of the correctness and truthfulness of what is made visible is essential, even outside an academic context. One might be tempted to accept that images of the past for nonspecialists should be more alluring and attractive, with a certain degree of completion, and involving some invention. This, however, brings us back to the same set of problems that has affected the representation of the archaeology of the ancient Near Eastern since the very beginning of the discoveries of the mid-nineteenth century: the need to make ruins visible for the general public affected representations and reconstructions of the past and impacted archaeological evidence even in academic circles.

7. Conclusion

Archaeology and visibility are closely connected. Each archaeological discovery must be made visible for scholars and the general public alike; this is even a financial necessity, as the publicizing of archaeological work through the use of flashy images and reconstructions is essential for raising funding to pursue research in the field. In the end, the methods and tools have changed, but archaeologists are still in the business of making the archaeological data visible. Indeed, they are ever more engaged in the chase for the most current technologies and devices.

Speaking from a strictly archaeological point of view, I think it is essential to keep in mind the importance of the archaeological context and the type of message one wants to convey. Each reconstruction, physically in the field or by the creation of images, has to comply with a balanced critique that takes into account (1) what we have (the archaeological reality); (2) how we want the past to be (being aware of how our personal and subjective desires can clash with data in the field); (3) the purposes of the reconstruction we want to promote (being explicit if the intention is overtly for promotion); (4) the evaluation of the choices and the resulting limits of the interpretation and representation (images cannot in the end prevail over the facts).

Each effort to make archaeology visible must be cognizant of the limits of the invisibility of some archaeological data: as for the case of the restoration in the field, invisibility indeed has become an obligation in the effort to preserve the future visibility of delicate contexts. Conservation is a commitment that should lead to a conversation on possible and more appropriate methods of preservation, and not to a conversion of the archaeological reality into a fixed and unshakable (mis)representation of the past.

Bibliography

Andrae, W. 1938. *Das wiedererstandene Assur*. Leipzig: Hinrichs.

Bahrani, Z. 1998. "Conjuring Mesopotamia: Imaginative Geography and A World Past." In L. Meskell (ed.), *Archaeology Under Fire: Nationalism, Politic and Heritage in the Eastern Mediterranean and Middle East*, 159–74. London: Routledge.

———. 2001. "History in Reverse: Archaeological Illustration and the Invention of Assyria." In T. Abusch et al. (eds.), *Historiography in the Cuneiform World: Proceedings of the XLV[e] Rencontre Assyriologique Internationale*, 15–28. Bethesda: CDL.

Bohrer, F. N. 2003. *Orientalism and Visual Culture: Imaging Mesopotamia in Nineteenth-Century Europe*. Cambridge: Cambridge University Press.

———. 2008. "Inventing Assyria: Exoticism and Reception in Nineteenth-Century England and France." In S. W. Holloway (ed.), *Orientalism, Assyriology and the Bible*, 222–66. Sheffield: Sheffield Phoenix.

Bonde, S., and S. Houston. 2013. "Re-Presenting Archaeology." In S. Bonde and S. Houston (eds.), *Re-Presenting the Past. Archaeology Through Text and Image*, 19–29. Oxford: Oxbow.

Buccellati, F. 2015. "What Might a Field Archaeologist Want from an Architectural 3D Model?" In M. G. Micale and D. Nadali (eds.), *How Do We Want the Past to Be? On Methods and Instruments of Visualizing Ancient Reality*, 157–69. Regenerating Practices in Archaeology and Heritage 1. Piscataway, NJ: Gorgias.

Buccellati, G. 2000. "Urkesh: archeologia, conservazione e restauro." *Kermes* 40:41–48.

———. 2006. "Conservation qua Archaeology at Tell Mozan/Urkesh." In N. Agnew and J. Bridgland (eds.), *Of the Past, for the Future: Integrating Archaeology and Conservation; Proceedings of the Conservation Theme at the 5th World Archaeological Congress, Washington, D.C., 22–26 June 2003*, 73–81. Los Angeles: Getty Conversation Institute.

———. 2017. *A Critique of Archaeological Reason: Structural, Digital and Philosophical Aspects of the Excavated Records*. Cambridge: Cambridge University Press.

Buccellati, G., and M. Kelly-Buccellati. 2005. "Urkesh as a Hurrian Religious Center." *Studi Micenei ed Egeo-Anatolici* 47:27–59.

Evans, J. M. 2012. *The Lives of Sumerian Sculpture: An Archaeology of the Early Dynastic Temple*. Cambridge: Cambridge University Press.

Heinz, M. 2002. "Bild und Macht in drei Kulturen." In M. Heinz and D. Bonatz (eds.), *Bild—Macht—Geschichte: Visuelle Kommunikation im Alten Orient*, 71–94. Berlin: Dietrich Reimer.

Larsen, M. T. 1996. *The Conquest of Assyria: Excavations in an Antique Land*. London: Routledge.

Layard, A. H. 1853. *Discoveries in the Ruins of Nineveh and Babylon: With Travels in Armenia, Kurdistan and the Desert; Being the Result of a Second Expedition Undertaken for the Trustees of the British Museum*. New York: Putnam.

Liverani, M. 2000. "La scoperta del mattone: Muri e archivi nell'archeologia mesopotamica." *Vicino Oriente* 12:1–17.

———. 2005. "Imperialism." in S. Pollock and R. Bernbeck (eds.), *Archaeologies of the Middle East: Critical Perspectives*, 223–43. Malden, MA: Blackwells.

———. 2013. *Immaginare Babele: Due secoli di studi sulla città orientale antica*. Rome: Laterza.

Mari, C., U. Capriani, F. Finotelli, and S. Marabini. 2000. "Restauro e valorizzazione turistica del sito di Ebla (Siria): Prime fasi sperimentali di restauro, consolidamento e protezione." in P. Matthiae et al. (eds.), *Proceedings of the 1st International Congress on the Archaeology of the Ancient Near East, May 18th–23rd, 1998, Università di Roma "La Sapienza,"* 929–44. Rome: Università di Roma "La Sapienza."

Mariette, A. 1867. *Description du Parc* égyptien *de l'Exposition universelle de 1867*. Paris: Dentu.

Matthews, R. 2003. *The Archaeology of Mesopotamia: Theories and Approaches*. London: Routledge.

Micale, M. G. 2005. "Immagini di architettura: struttura e forma dell'architettura mesopotamica attraverso le ricostruzioni moderne." In A. Di Ludovico and D. Nadali (eds.), *Studi in onore di Paolo Matthiae presentati in occasione del suo sessantacinquesimo compleanno*, 121–66, Contributi e materiali di archeologia orientale 10. Roma: Sapienza Università di Roma.

———. 2007. "Riflessi d'architettura mesopotamica nei disegni e nelle ricostruzioni architettoniche di Assur e Babilonia: tra realtà archeologica e mito dell'architettura monumentale." *Isimu* 10:117–40.

———. 2008. "European Images of the Ancient Near East at the Beginnings of the 20th Century." In N. Schlanger and J. Nordbladh (eds.), *Archives, Ancestors, Practices. Archaeology in the Light of Its History*, 191–203. Göteborg: Berghahn.

———. 2010. "Designing Architecture, Building Identities: The Discovery and Use of Mesopotamian Features in Modern Architecture Between Orientalism and the Definition of Contemporary Identities." In P. Matthiae, L. Romano, et al. (eds.), *Proceedings of the 6th International Congress on the Archaeology of the Ancient Near East 5–10 May 2008, 'Sapienza'—Università di Roma, Volume 1*, 93–112. Wiesbaden: Harrassowitz.

Micale, M. G., and D. Nadali. 2008. "'Layer by Layer...' Of Digging and Drawing: The Genealogy of an Idea." In R. D. Biggs, J. Myers and M. T. Roth (eds.), *Proceedings of the 51st Rencontre Assyriologique Internationale Held at the Oriental Institute of the University of Chicago July 18–22, 2005*, 405–14. Chicago: University of Chicago Press.

Nadali, D. 2013a. "Invented Space: Discovering Near Eastern Architecture Through Imaginary Representations and Constructions." In L. Feliu et al. (eds.), *Time and History in the Ancient Near East. Proceedings of the 56th Rencontre Assyriologique Internationale at Barcelona 26–30 July 2010*, 391–404. Winona Lake, IN: Eisenbrauns.

———. 2013b. "Nebuchadnezzar, King of Assyria: Rewriting Ancient Mesopotamian History in Fiction." *Res antiquitatis* 4:11–28.

———. 2015. "The (Dis)Embodiment of Architecture: Reflections on the Mirroring Effects of Virtual Reality." In M. G. Micale and D. Nadali (eds.), *How Do We Want the Past to Be? On*

Methods and Instruments of Visualizing Ancient Reality, 89–105. Regenerating Practices in Archaeology and Heritage 1. Piscataway, NJ: Gorgias.

Pedde, B. 2015. "Mesopotamia: A Source of Inspiration for the Architecture in the 20th Century." In M. G. Micale and D. Nadali (eds.), *How Do We Want the Past to Be? On Methods and Instruments of Visualizing Ancient Reality*, 27–47. Regenerating Practices in Archaeology and Heritage 1. Piscataway, NJ: Gorgias.

Pieri, C. 2015. *Bagdad: la construction d'une capitale moderne (1914–1960)*. Beyrouth: Presses de l'Ifpo.

Ramazzotti, M. 2010. "The Ebla Archaeological Park: Natural, Archaeological and Artificial Italian Portrait of the Ancient Syrian Capital." In P. Matthiae, L. Romano, et al. (eds.), *Proceedings of the 6th International Congress on the Archaeology of the Ancient Near East 5–10 May 2008, "Sapienza"—Università di Roma, Volume 2*, 581–97. Wiesbaden: Harrassowitz.

Shanks, M., and T. Webmoor. 2013. "A Political Economy of Visual Media in Archaeology." In S. Bonde and S. Houston (eds.), *Re-Presenting the Past: Archaeology Through Text and Image*, 142–81. Oxford: Oxbow.

Imagining the Tower of Babel in the Twenty-First Century

Is a New Interpretation of the Ziggurat of Babylon Possible?

Juan-Luis Montero Fenollós

Who has not heard of the Tower of Babel?[1] In Western imagination, the construction of this universal building is linked to the myth of confusion and human pride. In the Bible, the Tower of Babel appears at the center of a dramatic episode that affects the future of humanity. Yahweh punishes human beings for having committed a sin whose nature is unknown.

Since Late Roman times, always with considerable imagination, humankind has attempted to reproduce the image of this universal monument (Magness et al. 2018). Its appearance evolved at the same pace as artistic and architectonic styles. In the sixteenth century, the simple quadrangular Romanesque towers led to enormous buildings being made with superimposed colonnades of a circular structure (De Coster 2016, 242). All the images recreated by artists are colossal and infinite towers whose excess honors the biblical myth: "Come, let us build ourselves a city with a tower that reaches to the heavens," says Gen 11:4.

There is no doubt whatsoever that the Tower of Babel is the most represented building in the history of architecture. Humankind continues to this day to reflect on the myth of Babel and its tower, a monumental structure that seems to defy the laws of nature. Modern examples of structures that also seem to defy these laws are the skyscrapers built in the United States in the second half of the nineteenth century and the

1. I am grateful to Martin Schøyen, owner of the collection, and professor Jens Braarvig, of the Cultural Studies Department of the University of Oslo and chief editor of the Schøyen collection, for the facilitated photographs. We are also very grateful to Professor Andrew George, of the University of London (SOAS), who sent us an unedited sketch of the stele. Ana García reworked the drawing published by George 2011, pl. LIX and photographs of the stele to create the drawing we present here. The plans and 3D reconstructions have been carried out by José Antonio Hidalgo and María Miñarro.

Figure 1. The ziggurat of Babylon. Photograph by P. Modlinski (2004). From Montero Fenollós 2010, 92.

start of the twentieth (Pedde 2001), or the Burj Khalifa in Dubai, called by its sponsors the Emir of Abu Dhabi, which, when built in 2010, broke all records with a height of 828 meters.

The tragic fiction of Babel continues to be a recurring theme in the reflections of artists and architects of our time, as cities have lost their human dimension. Two recent exhibitions (2012–2013) were held about Babel and its tower as the central axis of its reflections: "Towers and Skyscraper: From Babel to Dubai" in Barcelona, Madrid and Brussels (Albaric, Dulau, and Mory 2012) and "Babel" in Lille (Tapié and Cotentin 2012). Today, the myth of Babel continues to fascinate humanity in a world marked by chaos, excess, intolerance, and conflict. Its universal iconography is alive and renewed in a world scenario in constant change. The discourses on Babel in artistic western representations in the twentieth and twenty-first centuries have undergone an evolution that is the consequence of a new reading of the biblical myth. One of the most striking features of contemporary Babel is the total absence of God. The Tower has been laicized (Aujoulat 2015).

Nevertheless, behind the myth there is a historical reality, currently transformed into an archaeological reality. What we now know universally as the Tower of Babel was known by the Babylonians as the Etemenanki, the "House which is the Platform of Heaven and Earth." It was the ziggurat of Babylon. Today, this ziggurat is a monument in ruins, destroyed and sacked (fig. 1). All that remains is its negative imprint on the ground of the Babylonian site. Since its discovery by German archaeologists in 1913, such a precarious state of conservation has caused a debate among specialists of Mesopotamia as to what its original appearance must have been.

1. The Textual, Iconographical, and Archaeological Sources on the Etemenanki

The most detailed description of the general structure and the dimensions of the Etemenanki come from the so-called Esagil tablet, of which two manuscripts have been preserved, the most complete of these being located in the Louvre (George 1992, 109–12). This is a cuneiform text dating from 229 BCE and copied in Uruk from a more ancient original of the city of Borsippa. The text gives us a description of the main monuments of the sanctuary of Marduk in Babylon, including the ziggurat. Until recently, it was the only reliable testimony of what the Babylonian tiered tower must have been like above its first story. All modern hypotheses of reconstruction of the monument have been based on the figures contained in this document (Schmid 1995, 29–40).

Lines 36 to 42 of the Esagil tablet give us the dimensions of the different stories of the ziggurat of Babylon, according to the Babylonian metric system (George 1992, 117):

> l.36: The dimensions, length, breadth and height, (of the ziggurat): its name being Ziqqurrat-Temple of Babylon;
>
> l.37: 15 *nindanum* the length, 15 *nindanum* the breadth, 5.5 *nindanum* the height: the bottom platform;
>
> l.38: 13 *nindanum* the length, 13 *nindanum* the breadth, 3 *nindanum* the height: the second story;
>
> l.39: 10 *nindanum* the length, 10 *nindanum* the breadth, 1 *nindanum* the height: the third story;
>
> l.40: 8,5 *nindanum* the length, 8.5 *nindanum* the breadth, 1 *nindanum* the height: the fourth story;
>
> l.41: 7 *nindanum* the length, 7 *nindanum* the breadth, 1 *nindanum* the height: the fifth story;
>
> <5.5 *nindanum* the length, 5.5 *nindanum* the breadth, 1 *nindanum* the height: the sixth story>;
>
> l.42: 4 *nindanum* the length, 3.75 *nindanum* the breadth, 2.5 *nindanum* the height: the upper sanctum, the seventh story (and) the *šaḫûrum*.

To date, this description has been the key to be able to reconstruct the Etemenanki three-dimensionally. According to the traditional reading of the document, the tower was made up of six terraces and a temple at the summit. Taking into account that a *nindanum* is equivalent to six meters, these are the dimensions of the ziggurat of Babylonia:

Story	Length	Breadth	Height
1st	90 m	90 m	33 m
2nd	78 m	78 m	18 m

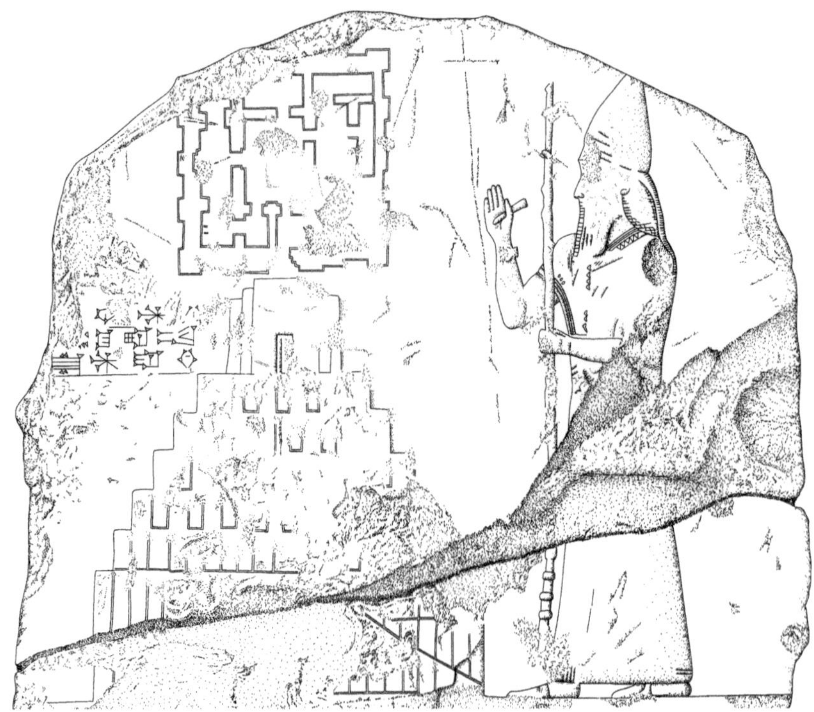

Figure 2. Drawing of the Stele of Tower of Babel. Schøyen collection (Oslo). Drawing by A. George, adapted by A. García.

Story	Length	Breadth	Height
3rd	60 m	60 m	6 m
4th	51 m	51 m	6 m
5th	42 m	42 m	6 m
6th[2]	33 m[?]	33 m[?]	6 m[?]
Upper temple	24 m	22.5 m	15 m
Total height	–	–	90 m (15 *nindanum*)

The collection of documents of Martin Schøyen in Oslo includes a stone stele that is very interesting for the study of the ziggurat of Babylon (George 2011, 153–65): in fact, it is known as the "Stele of the Tower of Babel" (fig. 2). It is made up of two fragments of black stone, possibly basalt, which fit perfectly together. The conserved part of the stele measures 47 cm high, 25 cm wide, and 11 cm thick, and it is partially damaged. It contains two types of information: on one hand, iconographical (there is a bas-relief

2. It appears that the scribe has forgotten a line with the figures for this story (George 1992, 430–31).

on the upper part of the stele) and, on the other, epigraphical (on the lower part there is a damaged cuneiform inscription that is typical of the Neo-Babylonian period).

The bas-relief is made up of a ziggurat, the plan of two temples, and a man represented in different scales. On the left side of the stele, the ziggurat is engraved with a completely frontal perspective. A cuneiform inscription located near the top of the sixth terrace allows us to identify this monument as "Etemenanki, the ziggurat of Babylon" (George 2011, 154). This artistic representation, which is only a simplified outline, contains various relevant data.

The ziggurat of the stele was formed of a temple and only six stories, not eight as Herodotus (1.181) and other, modern authors have asserted (Parrot 1949, 191). The tower of the stele appears to be represented with a height that is similar to the width of its base. Unfortunately, the stele makes no contribution to solving the ancient debate on the height of the ziggurat of Babylon. Nevertheless, one must consider that this was not a scaled architect's plan. The artist's objective was to represent the general structure of the monument that best defines it, that is, a tiered tower of six stories with an upper temple. The comparison of this representation with the dimensions provided by the Esagil tablet for the Etemenanki does not fit at all as, in the tablet, the first two stages were notably taller (33 and 18 m) than the rest. In contrast, on the stele, the first story is the tallest and the upper levels are identical in height (George 2011, 156).

The walls of the six terraces were embellished and reinforced with a "niche-and projection" articulation (called *ḫipšum* and *dublum* in Akkadian), which was typical of Babylonian religious buildings. The high temple was located at the top of the sixth story with a tiered façade with a central doorway flanked by stepped projections, called *dublum āsûm* ("projecting pilaster") in Akkadian (George 2011, 157). The façade is high enough to correspond to a building with two floors, as was common in many Mesopotamian temples.

Importantly, in the lower right-hand corner of the ziggurat is an oblique line that reaches the center of the top of the first stage. This is the representation of one of the stairways of the monument, known from archaeology, which indicates that the relief of the stele shows us the southern façade of the tower.

In the upper part of the stele, above the ziggurat's high temple, the floor plan of a building appears to be engraved on the other scale, which, due to its characteristics and the context in which it is inserted, can only be the plan of "the ziggurat temple," the Etemenanki proper. Although the plan is not totally preserved, we know this is a building with a square base whose four façades present its walls with recesses and projecting articulations (as is characteristic of Babylonian temples). The drawing presents a door flanked by stepped projections on the lower side. A second floor-plan, also partially conserved, is engraved on the shoulder of the stele. This plan may well correspond to another building that is not the high temple of the Etemenanki. The best candidate seems to be the upper temple of the ziggurat of Borsippa, the Eurmeiminanki, whose construction is referred to in the text of the stele (George 2011, 159). These two temples, constructed at the same time by King Nebuchadnezzar II (604–562 BCE), may well have had an identical floor plan.

The overlay of both plans allows us rather reliably to reconstruct what the floor plan of this religious building was like, with two doors, one in the southern façade and the other on the northern façade. The Esagil tablet states that this temple had four doors, named according to the cardinal points. Other texts indicate that the temple of the ziggurat had only two outer doors called Ka-unir or "Door of the ziggurat," in the southern façade, and Ka-Etemenanki or "Door of Etemenanki," in the western façade (George 1992, 90; 2011, 158).

According to the reconstruction, which we have deduced from the stele, the plan of the temple was made up of twelve rooms, whereas the Esagil tablet described nine (George 1992, 117; Schmid 1995, plans 17–18). We should also mention that in the western wall, there is a niche, which must represent the very holy place where the throne of Marduk was found. To the south of this holy space, there is a small square room where two small outlines can be seen. These are engraved on the plan located on the main face of the stele. This could be a schematic representation of the divinity's bed-chamber.

The discrepancies between the textual information of the Esagil tablet and the relief of the stele of the Tower of Babel are clear. Both the tablet and the bas-relief may well show us an idealized ziggurat of Babylon (George 2011, 156). However, as we have seen, the nature and the function of both documents are distinct. The tablet is a compilation of mathematical exercises with possibly ideal figures. On the contrary, the stele is a first-hand document created to commemorate the finalization of the works of Etemenanki by King Nebuchadnezzar II around 590 BCE. The construction of the ziggurat and its upper temple is the central motif of the stele. For this reason, the artist must have been obliged to give all types of details of the structure and the floor plan of the sacred house of the god Marduk in Babylon. To summarize, as well as being the only known contemporary representation of the ziggurat of Babylon, it is our most reliable iconographical source.

On the right side of the ziggurat and of a greater size, there is a figure. It is a bearded man wearing a long robe with a conical Babylonian royal crown (called *agûm* in Akkadian). He is holding a long staff in his left hand (*ḫaṭṭum* in Akkadian), and a small conical object, which is difficult to identify, in his right, and wearing a bracelet on his wrist. The man has some parallels with other representations of Babylonian monarchs dated between the ninth and seventh centuries BCE (George 2011, 154). The royal symbols (crown or staff) and the context leave no doubt as to the identity of the person of the bas-relief, namely, King Nebuchadnezzar II.

Finally, on the lower part of the stele there is a long cuneiform inscription in three columns and incompletely conserved. The text, which recounts the culmination of the works of the ziggurats of Babylon and Borsippa, is very similar to the inscriptions made by Nebuchadnezzar II to commemorate the construction of Etemenanki (George 2011, 159–62).

As the Schøyen collection's Stele of the Tower of Babel was obtained from the antiquities market, a debate was initially raised between specialists on its authenticity. Once this question was rapidly dealt with, the main discussion focused on discovering whence the document could have come. The most likely original location of the stele must have been some cavity within the structure of the ziggurat of Babylon, where it was placed as a foundation deposit by its royal builder. We are unaware, however, of any reference to the existence of a deposit of this type in Etemenanki, although we are confident that by the time the German archaeologists arrived in Babylon, a large part of the ziggurat had already been dismantled.

Andrew George (2010, 477–80) suggests that the stele was not discovered in Babylon in modern times but could have been recovered from the ruins of the ziggurat in antiquity. In his opinion, the stele could form part of a war booty, obtained in the time of the Achaemenid king Xerxes (486–465 BCE), who had to deal with two revolts in Babylon in 484 BCE. According to this theory, the stele would have been kept as a treasure in Susa, in Iran (George 2011, 165).

Until the start of the German excavations in Babylon, European travelers had suggested three possible locations for the Tower of Babel: Birs Nimrud, 'Aqarquf, and Tell Babil. This confusion was explained by the poor state of conservation in which the ziggurat of Babylon must have been found. From the twelfth to nineteenth centuries, there must have been hardly any visible remains of the Babylon tower, so it was difficult to finalize its identification. After centuries of abandonment, pillage, destruction, and reuse of materials, far from being the impressive monument described in Genesis, the tower was no more than a modest mound of mud bricks. Its ruins did not correspond to what human imagination had built. Furthermore, European travelers reached the city of Bagdad via one route that came from the north and passed near the ruins of 'Aqarquf and via another route from the south that ran close to Birs Nimrud (Montero Fenollós 2011). Naturally therefore, both ziggurats were identified (due to their monumental appearance) with the Tower of Babel, that is, the ziggurat of Babylon.

The foundation in 1898 of the Deutsche Orient-Gesellschaft, under the auspices of Emperor Wilhelm II, marked the start of German archaeological research in Babylon under the direction of Robert Koldewey (1914). It was a huge program, as excavations began on 26 March 1899 and continued until 7 March 1917, right in the middle of World War I.

The remains of the Etemenanki were soon identified in the topography of the huge field of ruins of Babylon. They were found in an area that, due to its general appearance, the Arabs called *as-Saḫn*, "the grill": a large square (the core of the ziggurat) with a "handle" on its southern side (the large central stairway). The excavation of the ziggurat of Babylon was carried out between 11 February and 7 June 1913 under the supervision of Friedrich Wetzel, taking advantage of a reduced water level (Wetzel and Weissbach 1967). Later, in 1962 and 1968, other German researchers carried out verification works in the infrastructure of the ziggurat (Schmid 1981a, 1981b, Schmidt 2005).

In 1938, Wetzel published the first detailed plan of the ziggurat of Babylon (Wetzel and Weissbach 1967), which was later corrected thanks to the works of Hansjörg Schmid (1995). The final plan, published in 1995, is of extraordinary quality and offers us a true approximation of the construction of this famous monument. The height, dimensions, materials used, shadows cast, and other annotations present in the plan provide spatial dimension and evoke the construction technique and processes. This graphic documentation has led to the archaeological basis from which the hypothesis of reconstruction of the Etemenanki has been made.

In this floor-plan, the first stage is embellished with a pattern that represents the "niche-and projection" style typical of Babylonian sacred architecture. The terrace had practically square dimensions: 91.66 m on the northern side, 91.48 m on the western side, 92.20 m on the southern side, and 91.52 m on the eastern side. The central core of the monument, which was made with mud brick with hardly any added straw, could belong to a more ancient ziggurat. It had the following measurements on each one of its façades: 61.10 m, 61.15 m, 61.20 m, and 61.15 (Schmid 1995).

The ziggurat of Babylon is made up of a core of mud brick, encircled by a perimeter layer, 15 to 18 meters thick, of baked mud brick and mixed with asphalt mortar with small bits of reed whereby essentially the negative imprint was preserved, having been left on the ground (Marzahn 1993, 38). The bricks of the outer walls of the ziggurat had been extracted since the medieval period and, primarily, were removed during the nineteenth century. Apparently, both baked and unbaked bricks were square and had the same dimensions 31.5–32 cm on the side and 9–9.5 cm thick. The existence of larger mud bricks was also noted (55 cm by 9 cm), used above all in the side stairways but also in the projections. Another important feature of the monument is the verification that the conserved external walls of the first story have no incline or slope, but are perfectly vertical, an observation that appears to contradict initial expectations (Wetzel and Weissbach 1967, 33).

The 1962 excavations documented various remains of the ziggurat's organic structure. In the core, traces of wooden framework of palm trunk (25 to 30 cm in diameter) were found. These were placed in a horizontal position and probably also vertically, with a 3 meter distance between them (Schmid 1981b, 45). These wooden elements indicate knowledge of the structural pressure of the mass of these dimensions and consequently the concern to resist its lateral impact. On the other hand, inside the core, every seven courses, a fine, black horizontal line could be seen: the layers of the reeds had been completely corroded by humidity (Schmid 1981b, 44).

On the southern façade of the ziggurat, Wetzel excavated the beginnings of the two lateral stairways that ascended from each corner of the first story. There were seven in the southeastern corner (Wetzel and Weissbach 1967, 33; Schmid 1995, tables

17–19). These stairways were 8.20 to 8.27 meters wide and had an outer wall that was one meter thick and 95 centemeters high. The steps were made up of two baked mud bricks (55 by 9 cm), mounted, 32 centemeters in width and an approximate height of 18 centemeters. On the same façade, a large frontal stairway, 51.61 m long and 9.35 m wide, was oriented perpendicular to the tower. On both sides, was a protection wall, similar to that described above.

2. A New Hypothesis

The first actual investigation into the structure of the ziggurat of Babylon was that of William Lethaby. In 1892, he put forward the silhouette of a tower with seven stories, where the height and base measured the same (90 m). The British architect's reconstructed relief on the figures in the Esagil tablet, but despite the data of the cuneiform text, Lethaby thought that the result obtained was that of an enigmatic monument with respect to its volume and stability (Vicari 2000, 30).

All attempts to reconstruct the total height and that of the different terraces of the ziggurat of Babylon were subject to the figures provided in the Esagil text. The hypotheses made to date were slaves to this cuneiform text, according to which the total height of the tower was 15 *nindanum* or 90 meters. Clearly a building with such dimensions is a spectacular monument, which honored the grandeur of Babylon. However, a 90-meter tower built of earth is an anomaly in the annals of Mesopotamian architecture, leading me to ask, Does this traditional hypothesis correspond to an ancient reality?

A reflection on the nature of the Esagil tablet is needed. According to Andrew George (2005–2006, 77; 2011, 155–56; 2013, 39), most researchers have misunderstood the function of this document. In his opinion, this is neither a descriptive text nor an objective one, as it does not provide the necessary information derived from direct knowledge of an actual monument. The text is inscribed in the long tradition of Babylonian science: that is, it is a compilation of mathematical exercises and so it is highly likely that the tablet's figures are hypothetical and not real. The tablet thus refers more to an abstract and academic ideal than to an architect's blueprint for an eventual construction. The text's real interest does not come from the practical description of a building but from the metrological systems that Babylonian scholars must have learned. This is actually a key document for Babylonian metrology as it describes two monuments (the Esagil and the Etemenanki) following two measurement systems: the Kassite system and the Neo-Babylonian and Standard Neo-Babylonian system, which differ from one another by the length of the cubit (Powell 1982).

Some Neo-Babylonian inscriptions refer to the reconstruction work on the ziggurat of Babylon that was begun by King Nabopolassar (626–605 BCE) and completed by his son Nebuchadnezzar II. According to this documentation, Nabopolassar "fixed on the breast of the underworld, whose four walls he raised in bitumen and baked brick to a height of thirty cubits on the outside, but which he did not finish to the top" (George 2011, 167). The same text mentions that Nebuchadnezzar II continued his father's work: "I conscripted for labour in the building of Etemenanki and imposed corvée-duty on them. Its base filled out to make a high terrace of thirty cubits. I coated sturdy cedars and great beams of *musukkannum*-wood with bronze and set them copiously in rows ... On top of it I built for my lord Marduk a holy sanctum, a chamber of repose as in bygone times" (George 2011, 167). So, if Nabopolassar raised the structure of the ziggurat to a height of 30 cubits (15 m) and his son added a further 30 cubits before building the upper temple (of unknown dimensions but which could have measured 15 m in height), the sum gives us a height of 45 meters. Where are the missing 45 meters to achieve the 90 meter height stated in the Esagil tablet?

The Neo-Babylonian construction was not entirely new, as it was made on the remains of an older ziggurat, which was in the process of reconstruction after the reign of Sennacherib (r. 704–681 BCE; George 2005–2006, 86–88 and 92). In other words, the works of Nabopolassar did not begin at ground level but were built on the preexisting mud-brick mass, the height of which is unknown. According to the figures of the Esagil tablet, we can deduce that this archaic ziggurat also measured 45 meters in height, which, added to the 45 meters constructed by the two Neo-Babylonian kings, would give us a total height of 90 meters. The problem would thus appear to be resolved.

However, it is very unlikely that the ziggurat of Babylon would have reached 90 meters high, despite what the Esagil tablet says. No one can confirm that this monument was built following the figures inscribed in this cuneiform text. In fact, a ziggurat of these dimensions would defy the laws of statics and of resistance of materials (Vicari 2000, 30–32). A structure with these proportions could not have been made with the materials and techniques of the period, in my view. There is no doubt that archaeology has confirmed that the dimensions of the base of the ziggurat described in the Esagil tablet (15 *nindanum* or 90 m) practically coincide with the actual ones. Excavations have confirmed a square tower base of over 91–92 meters. But this does not mean we should definitely accept the other figures of the terraces of the Etemenanki recorded on the tablet. In our opinion, this would lead to impossible architecture.

If we look for comparanda among the the ziggurats of Mesopotamia, we are hindered by their very poor state of preservation, which leaves us with incomplete documentation. The following table shows the dimensions of a selection of the main ziggurats:

City	Base (m)	Height of the first story (m)	Height preserved (m)
Eridu	61 x 46	–	–
Ur	62 x 43	11	20
Larsa	43 x 40	–	18
Uruk	56 x 48	11	14
Nippur	57 x 38	–	–
Borsippa	90 x 90	15	48

Kish (Uhaimir C)	53 x 43	–	16
Sippar	34 x 33	–	15
Dur Kurigalzu	80 x 80	19	46
Assur	60 x 60	–	20
Kar Tukulti Ninurta	31 x 31	–	8
Kalhu	51 x 51	–	–
Dur Sharrukin	43 x 43	6	–

The data in the table show that, as far as the base is concerned, Dur Kurigalzu, the current ʿAqarquf, and Borsippa, today Birs Nimrud, were two of the largest Mesopotamian ziggurats. Both monuments had a base (80–90 m) comparable to that of the ziggurat of Babylon (90–92 m). Furthermore, these two had the highest core, at almost 50 meters high (46–48 m).

The Kassite ziggurat of Dur Kurigalzu (fig. 3) was subject to a photogrammetric study of its four façades by an Italian team to formulate a hypothesis on its original appearance. The study suggests that its tower comprised three stories, successively 19.80 m, 14.85 m, and 11.80 m in height (Gullini 1981; Gullini, Parapetti, and Chiari 1987, 250–51). It does not provide, however, any data on what the upper temple would have

Figure 3. The southeast face of the ziggurat of Dur Kurigalzu. Photograph by J. Margueron.

look like, the height of which could probably not have exceeded 12 meters. This would give a total height of approximately 58 meters for a three-story monument and an 80 meter base.

The ziggurat of Borsippa has been excavated and analyzed in detail by an Austrian team since the 1980s, despite the one hundred thousand cubic meters of rubble that covered the ruins of this enormous structure, which has frequently been confused with the Tower of Babel (Allinger-Csollich 1991 and 1998; Allinger-Csollich, Heinsch, and Kuntner 2010). The researchers used mechanical excavators to reach the base of the monument, which measured 90 meters on each side. Further, we know that the superstructure is preserved a height of around 48 meters. The work on the eastern corner of the tower allowed the excavation team to document that the first terrace of the ziggurat at the time of Nebuchadnezzar II was 15 meters in height (Allinger-Csollich, Heinsch, and Kuntner 2010, 31).

The Austrian team concluded that the Tower of Borsippa would have been composed of seven terraces with a total height of 70 meters. The name of the ziggurat, Eurmeiminanki ("House that Controls the Seven *me*'s of Heaven and the Underworld") appears to allude to these seven levels. Borsippa's ziggurat is a monument with a long and complex construction history that extends from the Third Dynasty of Ur to the Neo-Babylonian period (ca. 2112–539 BCE). A cuneiform inscription found on the ziggurat describes the restoration works carried out by Nebuchadnezzar II on the monument (Beaulieu 2000, 309–10).

Outside of the core Mesopotamian territory is another relatively well-preserved ziggurat: the Elamite ziggurat of Choga Zanbil, ancient Dur Untaš, in southern Iran, part of whose first three terraces still survives (25 m high in total). According to R. Ghirshman, the director of the French archaeological mission in Iran, the monument was composed of four stories, each 12 m in height, and constructed on a square base of 105.20 m. At the top of this 48 m tower, was a chapel consecrated to the Elamite deities Napiriša and Inšušinak (Ghirshman et al. 1966).

The analysis of these three ziggurats gives us some useful data. According to the three reconstructions suggested based on archaeological documentation, these are monuments whose base is always greater than the height. The reason for this difference between the base and the height is clear: since a large base could better support the tension of the construction, they ensured the stability of these solid constructions. These comparanda suggest that a ziggurat of Babylon whose height could have matched the dimensions of its base would be unlikely.

From a structural point of view, these monuments made of earth were under the pressure of the weight of the materials that gave them their form. The Mesopotamian ziggurat is the result of the vertical accumulation of earthen materials (mud brick and baked mud brick) and the first terrace had to support the weight of the materials of all the upper terraces. This tension had to be lower than the degree of strength of the material used in the construction of the monument. If this were not the case, the monument would collapse. These tensions and forces of the structure of the ziggurat were counteracted partly with the use of wooden armature, layers of reeds, and an external layer of baked mud bricks (Sauvage 1998, 379; Schmid 1981b, 44–45). According to the studies carried out by the Centre international de la construction en terre (*CRAterre*) of Grenoble, the compressive strength of the mud brick with organic fibers is from 5 to 20 kg/cm^2. In humid conditions, this is reduced by a half (Doat et al. 1979, 185).

As can be seen in the table above, none of the assessed monuments supported on their lower terrace a tension comparable to what a 90 m high ziggurat of Babylon would impose, which would be 6.38 kg/cm^2. In the ziggurats studied, this compressive strength was always below 4 kg/cm^2. Furthermore, one must consider that this tension was transmitted finally to the soil on which the monument was built. The terrain made up of alluvial deposits, as occurs in the plain of Babylon (Sanlaville 2000, 102–3), cannot support a tension above 4–5 kg/cm^2 without threatening the stability of the construction (Vegas, Mileto, and Busto 2010, 115).

In conclusion, technical and construction-related arguments show that a 90 m-high ziggurat of Babylon was not possible for the time, despite the figures in the Esagil tablet. The height of the ziggurat must have corresponded to 50 to 70 percent of the length of its base, that is, it would measure between 45 and 63 m approximately. Another question to clarify is the distribution of this height between the different terraces that made up the monument.

Having discarded the validity of the Esagil tablet as offering only an ideal and unrealistic model, we move on to examining the Stele of the Tower of Babel preserved in Oslo. Unlike the text of the Esagil tablet, the stele was carved to commemorate (around the year 590 BCE) the finalization of the construction of the Etemenanki and its upper temple by King Nebuchadnezzar II. This is, therefore, an exceptional document, which to date no one has used to propose a new hypothetical reconstruction of the ziggurat of Babylon. Although simplified, this image seems to be the closest to reality. In fact, it is the only one we have. The problem resides in transitioning from this iconographic representation to an actual metric reality.

In principle, due to the previously presented technical arguments, we can propose a ziggurat with a maximum height of 60 m (66.66% of its base), raised on a square base of 90 m per side. To reconstruct the measurements of the six terraces and the high temple, we put forward a theoretical exercise using three elements: the silhouette of the Etemenanki carved on the stele of Oslo, a height of 60 m and the Babylonian metrological system (1 *nindanum* = 6 m). The terraces, from the second to the sixth, are represented with an identical height on the stele (1 *nindanum* for each appears coherent); the first terrace measures approximately three times that of the upper terraces, that is, 3 *nindanum*. For the temple at the top, we propose 2 *nindanum,* which gives a total height for the monument of 10 *nindanum* (60 m). According to our hypothesis, from the base of the ziggurat, which measures 15 *nindanum* (90 m), the length and the width of each story is regularly reduced by 2 *nindanum*. Following this logic, the upper temple would measure 3 *nindanum*. The following table summarizes the hypothetical restitution of the dimensions of the ziggurat of Babylon from the schematic carved on the stele of Oslo.

Story	Long / wide		Height	
	nindanum	meters	*nindanum*	meters
1st	15	90	3	18
2nd	13	78	1	6
3rd	11	66	1	6
4th	9	54	1	6
5th	7	42	1	6
6th	5	30	1	6
Ziggurat temple	3	18	2	12
Total height			10	60

The proposed hypothesis produces a ziggurat whose metric parameters must have been very similar to those of the ziggurats of Dur Kurigalzu and Borsippa. In our opinion, the amorphous core of mud brick that remains of both monuments, approximately preserves the original height of these Mesopotamian towers. On these massifs (of 46 to 48 m of preserved height) the upper temple was located, which would translate into buildings that rarely surpass 60 m. In fact, the compressive strength calculated for a 60-meter ziggurat of Babylon (3.58 kg/cm^2) is very similar to that of the Italian hypothesis of reconstruction of the ziggurat of Dur Kurigalzu (3.81 kg/cm^2). The reconstruction work on the Eurmeiminanki, the ziggurat of Borsippa, was done in parallel with that on Etemenanki, according to Neo-Babylonian texts (George 2011, 160). Both monuments, the first consecrated to Nabu and the second to his father, Marduk, probably had a very similar architectonic structure. They were constructed on a base of identical dimensions (i.e., 90 m).

Another one of the problems to resolve with respect to the ziggurat of Babylon, is its access system, that is, how one moved around on the monument. Given the almost total disappearance of the tower, accesses are only incompletely known. Thanks to the archaeological work of the German mission (Schmid 1995, table 17), we know that the southern façade had two lateral stairways whose steps were 18 cm high and 32 cm wide. If we do a step-by-step reconstruction in order to decipher the maximum height they could reach, we observe that the stairways could not have exceeded 25 meters. If the first terrace was 33 meters high, as indicated in the Esagil tablet, the visitor could not reach the top of this terrace, as the stairway would stop in front of an impassable wall of approximately 8 meters in height. This is further evidence of the idealized nature of the figures of the tablet. The access system was completed with a frontal stairway, which began 60 meters distant from the southern façade.

On the right-hand side of the first terrace, the stele of the Tower of Babel shows the presence of a ramp or lateral stairway that leads to its top. Unfortunately, the central and left-hand area of the first terrace are very deteriorated so it is impossible to identify other accesses in this bas-relief. On the other hand, the upper terraces (second to sixth) carved on the stele are not totally horizontal, but reveal a slight incline. This may be a graphic and schematic representation of the spiral ramp of which Herodotus (1.181) wrote.

Finally, the upper temple of Babylon was built on the summit of the sixth terrace of the ziggurat of Babylon. Given its location, crowning the construction, archaeological remains of the plan of this building have not been preserved. The overlay of two floor-plans engraved on the stele helps us see that the temple at the top had two doors, one on the south (towards the Esagil) and another on the north (towards the southern palace). The ziggurat-temple has a square layout with walls decorated outside with niches and projections that were typical of Neo-Babylonian sacred buildings (fig. 4).

The temple floor plan is probably made up of twelve rooms. In the wall, there is a niche that must represent the "very holy place," with the statue of the god Marduk. The central space of the temple was covered with a type of skylight that illuminated the interior of the building, which must have had an upper floor. According to the Esagil tablet, the temple at the top of the Etemenanki was called *kiṣṣum elûm*, a term that could have been a synonym of *gigunûm*, that is, a chapel elevated on a terrace or a tower (George 1992, 43 and 431–32). The ziggurat temple was also named *nuḫar* or *bīt ziqrati* in Akkadian (George 1992, 89 and 424). According to the same tablet, this temple would have a *saḫurum*, a concept that is interpreted as an upper story that was accessed via an

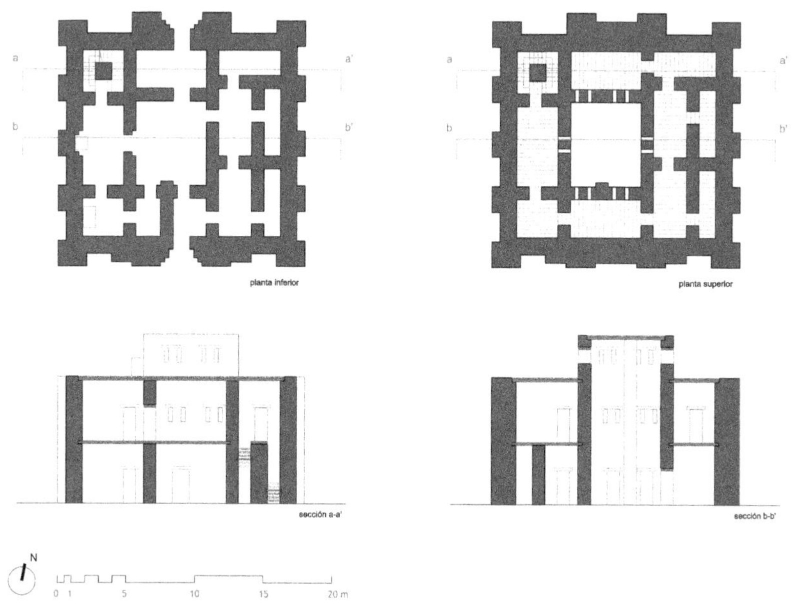

Figure 4. The upper temple of the ziggurat of Babylon. New hypothesis.

inner staircase (George 1992, 433). Finally, the façades of the temple were decorated with blue lapis lazuli (George 2011, 168–69), with glazed bricks similar to those used on the Ištar Gate.

3. Conclusion

To summarize, we propose a 60 meter-tall ziggurat of Babylon, distributed over six terraces, which come to a total of 48 meters and an upper temple of 12 meters. According to the Stele of the Tower of Babel, all the terraces had walls decorated with niches and projections. Due to its small dimension, these architectural elements did not respond to a structural need; rather they must have had a more decorative function as these long walls, articulated in this way, produced a play of shadows and lights, depending on the time of day.

Access to the first terrace of the Etemenanki was guaranteed by a central stairway and two lateral stairways located in the southern façade. From here, the way to the upper temple was guaranteed by ramps, well organized in a zigzag format on the main façade (fig. 5) or well distributed in a spiral through the four façades of the monument (fig. 6). In both cases, the ramps were 3 m wide and had an inclination that would vary between 5 and 13 degrees. This new proposal, which reopens the debate about the nature of the ziggurat of Babylon/Tower of Babel, has been endorsed by other researchers (Matthiae 2018, 414–20). According to this new hypothesis, the ziggurat of Babylon was an impressive monument, built with almost 400,000 tons of earth and approximately 25 million pieces of mud brick. These figures do justice to the greatness of Babylon and its builders, who, with such humble materials as earth were able to construct a monument that is still alive through myth over two thousand years after its construction. This is the greatness of Babylon and its famous tower.

Bibliography

Albaric, M., R. Dulau, and P. Mory. 2012. *Torres y rascacielos: De Babel a Dubái*. Barcelona: La Caixa.

Allinger-Csollich, W. 1991. "Birs Nimrud I." *Baghdader Mitteilungen* 22:384–499.

———. 1998. "Birs Nimrud II." *Baghdader Mitteilungen* 29:97–330.

Allinger-Csollich, W., S. Heinsch, and W. Kuntner. 2010. "Babylon: Past, Present and Future; The Project Comparative Studies Babylon-Borsippa: A Synopsis." In P. Matthiae and L. Romano (eds.), *Proceedings of the 6th International Congress of the Archaeology of the Ancient Near East*, Vol. 1, 29–38. Wiesbaden: Harrassowitz.

Aujoulat, A. 2015. "De l'Antiquité à la science-fiction: la réinvention de Babylone dans les représentations artistiques occidentales des XXe et XXIe siècles." *Cahiers de l'École du Louvre* 6:71–80.

Beaulieu, P. A. 2000. "Nebuchadnezzar II's Restoration of E-urimin-anika, the Ziggurat of Borsippa (2.122B)." In W. Hallo (ed.), *Context of Scripture*, Vol. 2, 309–10. Leiden: Brill.

De Coster, X. 2016. "De la réalité au mythe: la tour de Babel, de la Bible à nos jours." In Ph.

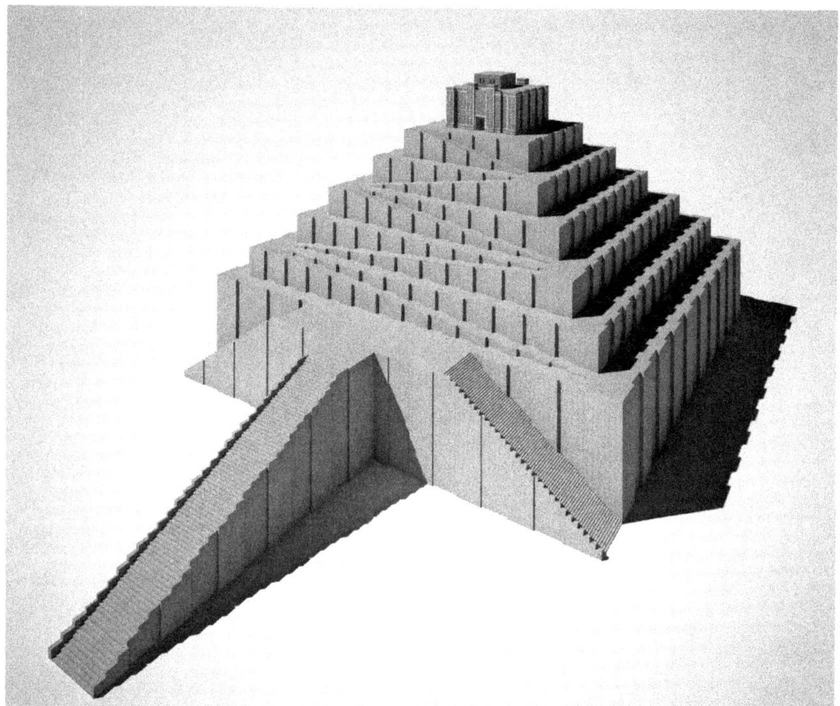

Figure 5. The Etemenanki, the ziggurat of Babylon (Hypothesis a).

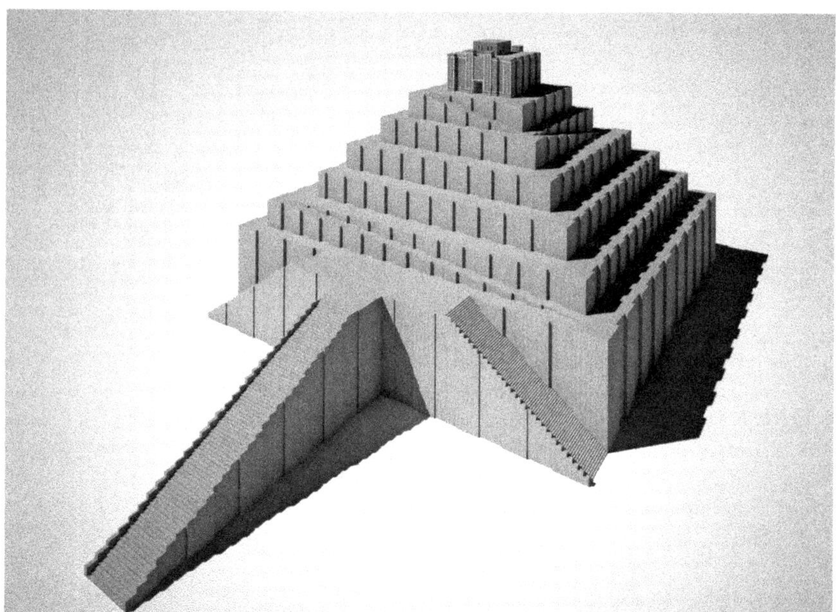

Figure 6. The Etemenanki, the ziggurat of Babylon (Hypothesis b).

Quenet (ed.), *Ana ziqquratim: Sur la piste de Babel*, 241–47. Strasbourg: Presses Universitaires.

Doat, P., A. Hays, H. Houben, S. Matuk, and F. Vitoux. 1979. *Construire en terre*. Paris: Alternatives.

George, A. R. 1992. *Babylonian Topographical Texts*. Leuven: Peeters.

———. 2005–2006. "The Tower of Babel, Archaeology, History and Cuneiform Texts." *Archiv für Orientforschung* 51:75–95.

———. 2010. "Xerxes and the Tower of Babel." In J. Curtis and J. Simpson (eds.), *The World of Achaemenid Persia*, 472–80. London: Tauris.

———. 2011. *Cuneiform Royal Inscriptions and Related Texts in the Schøyen Collection*. Bethesda: CDL.

———. 2013. "La porte des dieux: la topographie cultuelle de Babylone d'après les textes cunéiformes." In B. André-Salvini (ed.), *La tour de Babylone*, 20–42. Rome: CNR and Louvre.

Ghirshman, R. et al. 1966. *Tchoga Zanbil (Dur-Untash)*. Volume I. *La ziggurat*. Paris: Geuthner.

Gullini, G. 1981. "New Suggestions on Ziggurat of Aqarquf." *Sumer* 41:133–37.

Gullini, G., R. Parapetti, and G. Chiari. 1987. "Attività di consulenza, progettazione e collaborazione scientifica." In *La terra tra i due fiumi: Venti anni di archeologia italiana in Medio Oriente*, 241–52. Rome: Quadrante.

Koldewey, R. 1914. *The Excavations at Babylon*. London: MacMillan.

Magness, J. et al. 2018. "The Huqoq Excavation Project: 2014–2017 Interim Report." *Bulletin of the American Schools of Oriental Research* 380:61–131.

Marzahn, J. 1993. *La Porte d'Ishtar de Babylone*. Mainz: von Zabern.

Matthiae, P. 2018. *Dalla terra alla storia : Scoperte leggendarie di archeologia orientale*. Torino: Giulio Einuadi.

Montero Fenollós, J. L. ed. 2010. *Torre de Babel, historia y mito*. Murcia: Tres Fronteras.

———. 2011. "The Tower of Babel before Archaeology: The Ziggurat of Babylon according to European Travelers (XII–XVII Centuries)." *Res Antiquitatis* 2:31–49.

Parrot, A. 1949. *Ziggurats et Tour de Babel*. Paris: Albin Michel.

Pedde, B. 2001. "Das Neue Babylon." *Alter Orient Aktuell* 2:8–12.

Powell, M. A. 1982. "Metrological Notes on the Esagila Tablet and Related Matters." *Zeitschrift für Assyriologie* 72:106–23.

Sanlaville, P. 2000. *Le Moyen-Orient arabe: Le milieu et l'homme*. Paris: Armand Colin.

Sauvage, M. 1998. *La brique et sa mise en oeuvre en Mésopotamie*. Paris: Éditions Recherche sur les Civilisations.

Schmid, H. 1981a. "Ergebnisse einer grabung am kernmassiv der zikurrat in Babylon." *Baghdader Mitteilungen* 12:67–137.

———. 1981b. "The History of the Construction of the Ziggurat in Babylon according to the Results of the Excavations in 1962." *Sumer* 41:44–47.

———. 1995. *Der Tempelturm Etemenanki in Babylon*. Mainz am Rhein: von Zabern.

Schmidt, J. 2005. "Babylon." In *German Archaeological Institute Orient Department-Baghdad, 50 Years of Research in Iraq 1955–2005*, 63–67. Berlin: Deutsches Archäologisches Institut.

Tapié, A., and R. Cotentin. 2012. *Babel*. Lille: Invenit.

Vegas, F., C. Mileto, and J. Busto. 2010. "Arquitectura de tierra: Materiales y técnicas de construcción de la torre de Babel." In J. L. Montero Fenollós (ed.), *Torre de Babel: Historia y mito*, 107–18. Murcia: Tres Fronteras.

Vicari, J. 2000. *La Tour de Babel*, Paris: Presses universitaires de France.

Wetzel, F., and F. H. Weissbach. 1967. *Hauptheiligtum des Marduk in Babylon, Esagil und Etemenanki*. Osnabrück: Zeller.

Athletic Disciplines in the Ancient Near East

Representation and Reconstruction

Silvia Festuccia

The deliberate pursuit of sports for their own sake is a global phenomenon that has its beginnings earlier in human prehistory than was believed until recently (Pope and Nauright 2011).[1] The question is: To what point in human history can we assign the shift from physical activity as a mechanism of defense and self-preservation to the more intentional practice of athletic disciplines? Studies on the history of sports conducted in the second half of the nineteenth century have offered several responses to this question, displaying in the process strong influences from their respective historical, political, and cultural backgrounds.

Physical activity in prehistoric societies was originally interpreted more as a natural impulse to hunt and to protect oneself from animals and from other humans rather than as a leisure activity. Running, jumping, and climbing were the first acts of athleticism that humans practiced, driven by the instinct for self-preservation and defense, just as was the case for any other animal. Physical activity was the expression of the human instincts to fight and play, which ultimately gave rise to athletic competitions. The rules for these activities channeled physical energy by means of preestablished codes that were strictly and temporally adhered to. Peace must be secured outside the competition, such that breaking the rules and violating the limitations set during the competition necessitated sanctions and even expulsion from the system.

The relationship between sport and religion has been much discussed, both by scholars of ancient sports and by anthropologists and students of sports in general. Specialists have debated extensively about the origin, meaning, and importance of the link between sport and religion and have reached various conclusions. While some scholars, like Gardiner, argue that the practice of sport was originally a profane act, the result of human pleasure in exhibiting physical qualities, and that only later was it incorpo-

1. Abbreviations used in this essay: UET = Loding 1976; MVN = Owen 1975.

rated into religious contexts, other authors want to see a primary relationship between sport and religion. Thus, David Sansone, in his book *Greek Athletics and the Genesis of Sports* (1992), generally interprets sporting practices as a "sacrifice of human energy," which aimed at celebrating the vigor that Paleolithic populations needed to ensure successful hunts. Other authors, specifically studying the origins of Greek sports festivals, relate them, for example, to funerary games in honor of local heroes, or to initiatory rituals that lead to adulthood.[2]

Some scholars (Neuendorf 1973; Eppensteiner 1973) have suggested that sports culture was influenced by social, political, and historical factors from the very beginning. The Marxist influence in the study of sports is evident in the interpretation of movement as the primary function of physical exercise intended to improve work performance and military prowess (Eichel 1973; Lukas 1973).

Popplow (1973) assumed that physical activity existed in the Middle Paleolithic as a consequence of three factors: body movements, unconscious rhythmic movements, and games, and considered athletic activity to be the result of recreational and cultural considerations. Physical activity is therefore not only associated with the fight for survival but also with a spiritual component. This gave it an idealistic connotation that influenced subsequent studies for a long time.

Diem's (1966) monumental history on sports begins with the statement, "all physical exercises were originally cultic." This forms the basis of his interpretation and plays a crucial role in the development of a religious, worship-oriented conception of the Olympic Games. Pierre de Coubertain, inspired by the discovery of the site of Olympia by Richard Chandler in 1766 and the archaeological excavations by Ernst Curtius between 1875 and 1881, revived the modern Olympic Games. He believed that sport was a "religion" with its related church, dogma, and cult, but, above all, he thought it was driven by religious feelings. De Coubertain saw the Olympic Games as an instrument of devotion, ethics, and nobility. They were sacred and gave sports a sacred dignity even after three thousand years.

Other scholars (Van Dalem, Michell, and Bennett 1973) believed that in its early stages, physical exercise was aimed at increasing confidence and adapting to the physical and social environment. The components of the original sporting instinct were rather focused on obtaining optimal physical abilities to secure the survival of the family group or to strengthen the relationship and the participation of the group members through recreational competitions.

The research into athletic disciplines has expanded significantly both geographically and chronologically, and has recently and necessarily assumed a strong interdisci-

2. For a discussion of religion and Greek sports in particular, see Murray 2014.

plinary character, promoted by European scholars,[3] as well as by US scholars.[4] In some cases, the approach is clearly revisionist and demythological, as in the book published by H. W. Pleket and M. I. Finley in 1976, *The Olympic Games: The First Thousand Years*, which describes the ancient Olympic Games without any educational filters. These ancient Games were extremely violent, and mercenary interests and political abuse were exercised by both the athletes and the financers of the games.

Among the numerous studies by F. García Romero, one article (2013) highlights that the big sanctuaries, most notably the Olympian sanctuary, became major tourist centers owing not only to the fact that they were relevant religious sites and major centers for intellectual activity but also because they were places where one could engage in athleticism.

Many scholars have recognized the cultural and scientific value of the history of sport. From the mid-1970s and 1980s periodicals such as *Stadion: Internationale Zeitschrift für Geschichte des Sports* and *Nikephoros: Zeitschrift für Sport und Kultur im Altertum and Journal of Sports History* have provided forums for comparison and discussion, in the awareness that only multidisciplinary approaches can provide new insights into the research in this field. In the 1990s the scholars who studied ancient sports began to adopt an interdisciplinary approach and applied anthropological, sociological, and educational models to their research, thus separating the long-standing disciplines that had influenced these studies for a long time.

The practice of sports should not be considered simple entertainment. For those who practiced sports, it impacted both their individual and community identification. Games, competition, and dance celebrated the deities governing natural events. Athletic performance codified and reflected the cultural characteristics of ancient societies. The ritualized and public action of the individual was strongly communicative, and the intense physical games were vehicles of symbolic communication and culture.

In 1978, the sociologist A. Guttmann, in his book *From Ritual to Record*, a milestone in the historical study of sports, defined the features that distinguish modern sports from their ancient counterparts. Guttmann specifically pointed out that contemporary sports have lost their past relationship with ritual and religion and have taken a more secular tone.[5] Moments of gathering, public or private, such as civil or funerary celebrations, were opportunities to strengthen fundamental community identity and often provided highly symbolic activities practiced by members of the groups as well as foreigners.

---

3. In particular J. Ebert, W. Decker, M. Herb, I. Weiler, H. W. Pleket, and F. García Romero (to whom I am grateful for his generous suggestions and advice about this paper).

4. In particular M. B. Poliakoff, S. G. Miller; N. Crowther, D. G. Kyle, P. Christesen, and T. F. Scanlon, who edited a bibliographic monograph in 1984 including a list of over 1,600 monographs and articles on Greek and Roman sports, published until the early 1980s (Papakonstantinou 2010).

5. For another perspective of analysis of rituals related to sporting events, see Segalen 2002.

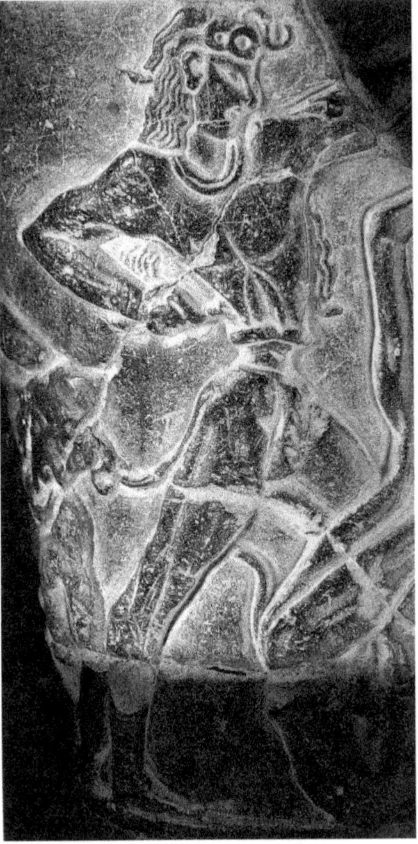

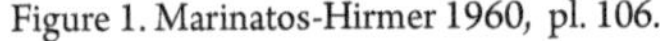

Figure 1. Marinatos-Hirmer 1960, pl. 106.

Figure 2. . The boxer fresco from Akrotiri. Marinatos 1971, pl. 119.

Several recent publications analyze the role of sports in prehistory up to the Roman period, and in some cases as far as the European Middle Ages. Only a few address the practice of sports in the ancient Near East, and they often use terms that are not geographically and chronologically precise. For example, Crowther (2010) studies the martial and recreational aspects of sports diachronically until the Byzantine period, while Kyle (2007) covers the main aspects of the history of ancient sports, mainly focusing on Greece and Rome (see also Pope and Nauright 2011).

W. Decker is the main researcher on the study of sports in ancient Egypt (see, e.g., 1992). Decker and Herb (1993) widely document testimonies of running, fighting, boxing, archery, hunting, and other sports practiced by the Egyptians. Several artifacts and painted decoration on tombs from the Old to the New Kingdom depict athletic disciplines, informing their work.

The competitive environment, which often had a central role in Minoan civilization, is depicted on several artifacts. The most frequent iconographic representations are the painted wall decorations highlighted by C. Gordon that show bull-fighting, and a rhyton from the Villa of Haghia Triada (Late Minoan IB 1500–1450 BCE), which shows boxing, bull-fighting, and additional fighting scenes in the upper register. Among the various iconographic descriptions of these findings (Militello 2003), the depicted fights occur in a competitive context and are not a part of rites of passage. The assumption is that outdoor arenas were set up to host bull fighting, gymnastic games, boxing matches, and wrestling matches.

The connection between competitive sports and military exploits in Minoan civilization was close, and the violence that could result in the death of one or more competitors was considered to be socially acceptable as it would channel destructive forces that would otherwise have been dangerous for the community. The main message conveyed in the representations is the triumph over the adversary.

Scenes depicting a standard fighting posture have been discovered on a rhyton also from Haghia Triada, but dating to the fifth century BCE (fig. 1); on a *cretula* from Knossos (Militello 2003, 4, 17, fig. 8); on three stone vases (Militello 2003, 4, 17, figs. 4–6); on three frescoes in Knossos (Militello 2003, 4, 18, figg. 10, 11, 12); on the famous fresco of the boxing boys from Akrotiri dating to the sixteenth century BCE (fig. 2); and on a miniature fresco from Tylissos (Militello 2003, 4, 18, fig. 14). Renfrew (1988) offers a summary of the sports practiced by the Minoans and Mycenaeans, and considers them to be precursors of the ancient Olympic Games and of religious festivals. He also associates them closely with Homer's epic poems, which are packed with heroic athletic activities.

In contrast, publications focusing on athletic disciplines in the ancient Near East in general are fragmented, and the epigraphic and archaeological data are rarely compared.[6]

1. *Reconstructing Sports in the Ancient Near East*

The reconstruction of sports in the ancient Near East presumes the identification of what can, practically speaking, be defined as an athletic discipline. Identifying the presence of genuine athletic activities within individual cultures, however, is not always possible, and even when it is possible, the epigraphic or iconographic evidence is often partial and inadequate, resulting in uncertain interpretations. Sporting activities in visual arts are in fact frequently mistaken for martial exercises, as in the case of wrestling, or for dancing, especially in early representations. Dancing, in particular, is often considered to be a physical activity that is practiced for the sheer pleasure of

6. The contribution of R. Rollinger, "Sport und Spiel" (2011) is an interesting synopsis accompanied by a large bibliography that was very useful for this study.

Figure 3. From Frankfort 1955, pl. 88.

rhythmic movement and through which one can release excess of energy without any competitive function.

There are still many unresolved issues in this field of study. The widely debated but still unanswered questions are, for example, How early can we date the beginning of the practice of sports as formal athletic disciplines? When can we identify the rise of sports as a profession? And a related question: Could athletes exclusively dedicate their time to working out and if so, to what extent?

The practice of sports is closely linked to its position in a particular society, in particular to its standing and importance in a religious, political, cultural, or popular context.[7] Some monuments from the seventh century BCE, for example, show wrestlers fighting to the sound of the flute, an instrument that was frequently played during sacred ceremonies (Tonini 2003). We learn from Titus Livius 1.35.8–9 (D'Amore 1937) that Lucius Tarquinius Priscus, after his accession to the throne (616 BCE), held *ludos* including horse races and wrestling matches with Etruscan contestants.

The regular practice of sports in ancient Greece is particularly linked to religious ceremonies honoring the gods. In the ancient Near East as well, beginning in the third millennium BCE there are several testaments to the widespread presence of competitions linked to particular sacred and festive events. One text on the protocol of a ritual for the goddess Ishtar, for example, establishes the close link of the cultic events with the public practice of athletic disciplines (Ziegler 2007, 261–75; Catagnoti 1997, 587). The texts mention specific physical activities that can be categorized as athletic disciplines that were consistently performed during rituals and festivals took place over the course of the year. In the following, I will discuss the evidence for three in particular, namely, running, wrestling, and swimming.

Running. Inanna/Ishtar is referred to as a runner in some hymns in her honor. In the hymn *Innin-shagura,* the goddess is repeatedly linked to the footraces. Running was an essential part of the nature of the goddess, as it demonstrated her superhuman skills. The text says: "the race to reach all belongs to you, oh Inanna/Ishtar" (Sjoberg 1975, 192; Gronenberg 1997, 45). The ritual for Ishtar cited above also included a footrace that ended at the goddess's temple (Charpin and Durand 1994, 55). The speed attributed to the runner kings Shulgi and Sargon of Akkad was elemental to worship of the divine: The king practiced sports in order to honor the goddess.

Females are almost completely missing in the evidence for the practice of athletic disciplines, with the exception of female divinities like Artemis. One of the few tes-

7. The practice of athletic disciplines in the Near East appears as the expression of different social and cultural contexts, as an integral part not only of elitist culture but also of popular culture.

timonies from the ancient Near East is a Hittite festival text that describes a woman archer taking aim at a "bear-man," that is, someone ritually playing a bear.[8]

One largely overlooked archaeological find deserves particular attention: a seal from Ishcali (fig. 3) dating to the Isin-Larsa period (2004–1763 BCE) shows a person running. Statues of runners are rare, probably because the medium used to express the plasticity of running was bronze. This material was good for conveying the sense of movement, but it was valuable and thus melted for reuse. Among the metal artworks that still survive are the Spartan female runner (520–500 BCE; fig. 4) and the statues of runners from the Villa dei Papiri of Ercolano, inspired by a Greek original from the fourth or early-third century BCE (fig. 5).

Figure 4. Running girl from Sparta. Bronze, 11.4 cm high. British Museum. http://www.bbc.co.uk/history/ancient/greeks/greek_olympics_gallery_06.shtml.

Figure 5. The runners from Villa dei Papiri di Ercolano. Bronze. 118 cm high. Napoli Museo Archeologico. © Soprintendenza Speciale per i Beni Archeologici di Napoli e Pompei. Wikimedia Commons, Roberto Fogliardi (Bobfog) [CC BY-SA 3.0 (http://creativecommons.org/licenses/by-sa/3.0/)]

Wrestling. Wrestling is one of the best-documented sporting disciplines in the ancient Near East. Wrestling competitions took place in the fifth month, the month of Abu, which corresponds to July/August in the Assyrian calendar (Rollinger 2006, 10–11). They seem to be the reenactment of divine competitions. They were in fact probably dedicated to Gilgamesh to commemorate and emulate his famous fight against Enkidu. The competitions lasted nine

8. KUB 58.14 left col. 30′–34′ (CTH 650); de Martino 2001, 74–76.

Figure 6. Seal depicting two figures wrestling while a third figure (right) watches. Amiet 1961, pl. 51, no. 712.

Figure 7. A seal depicting wrestling; on the left a figure, perhaps a referee, watches. Ascalone 2011, pl. 49, 3B.148.

days, and took place during the festival to honor the dead (Cohen 1993, 319–20, 462–63; Rollinger 1994, 38–40; George 2003, 126–27).

Wrestling scenes can be found in several media: seals from Mesopotamia and Iran always show a figure that may be a judge or referee (figs. 6 and 7) who supervised the competition to ensure that it was conducted fairly (Festuccia 2016a, 101). The consistent presence of a referee supervising the competition reinforces competitive behaviors and schemes, and it is usually defined and regulated by a cadre of rules aiming at preserving the integrity of the contestants. The contestants can and must fight for the one and only goal of the competition: supremacy. Any other expression is forbidden and regulated by written rules, laws, norms, legal procedures, and regulatory institutions. In this regard, the restraint of violence and the institution of rules for all is what is relevant.

Votive tablets provide further testimony of the representation of fights (Festuccia 2016a, 102–3), as does a stone relief (fig. 8), and a metal double vase with two semi-naked males engaged in a fight (fig. 9), both from Khafaje in the Diyala.

Swimming. At least three depictions of individuals swimming can be identified, all dating to the first half of the first millennium BCE. The orthostat reliefs of Assurnasirpal II, located in the internal courtyard XIX of the Southwest Palace in Nineveh, show soldiers swimming across the river. They are depicted using inflated animal skins as floatation devices and carrying heavy weapons. In the Throne Room of the West Palace of Nimrud more reliefs show soldiers swimming with inflated animal skins, as well as swimming freestyle,[9] a swimming technique that is still used today. Finally, in a decorative relief of a sector of the west courtyard of the North Gate of Karatepe (seventh century BCE), two people are depicted as they swim freestyle beside a boat (Rollinger 2000, 160, tab. 1; Festuccia 2016b, 166–70). No Akkadian word for swim/swimmer has been identified to date, but the word for "dive/submerge" is *šalûm* (Bottéro 1981, 1007).[10]

9. The style of swimming can be identified on the bases of other iconographic evidence, such as the Mosaic of the Baths of Neptune in Ostia (Becatti 1961).

10. For the issues related to diving activities see Festuccia 2016b, 171–72.

2. *Professional Athleticism in the Near East*

From a historical point of view, it is not clear when physical exercise intended for pleasure or physical preparation transformed into a professional activity as we lack the epigraphic and archaeological documentation that would inform us. The consistent presence of athletes in local festivals and in iconographic finds depicting sports being practiced, however, highlights the importance that the athletic disciplines had in the Near East.

Figure 8. Banquet plaque from the Sin temple at Khafaje. Frankfort 1939b, pl. 105.

Professional sports have a distinct character that separates them from athletic activities carried out on an amateur level. The practice of sports becomes a professional activity when the only objective is the desire to win, the athletes are remunerated for practicing it so that it becomes their main activity, and/or there is an economic and administrative organization supporting the athlete or the team. The professional pursuit of athleticism is easier to recognize in those sports, like running, that required the dedication of a considerable amount of time to training, as it signals time that is *not* being spent in activities connected to subsistence and directly beneficial for the community.

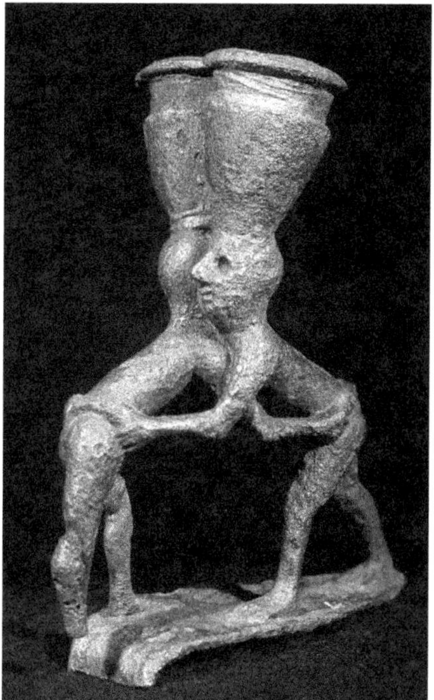
Figure 9. Metal double vase from the temple of Nintu at Khafaje. Moortgat-Correns 1989, 44.

The professional engagement in sports provided an avenue by which early communities might coalesce around the championing of a particular athlete, perhaps based on ethnicity, region, or the deity represented by that athlete. Numerous other variables that are still not understood may also have led, in the early stages of athletic competition, to the formation of confederations.

Questions about the evolution from amateur to professional sports has fed the debate over the origins and social status of the Greek athletes. The big games probably began as an informal fight where a competitor owed his victory to his natural skills. Eventually, competitive athletes became specialized and were trained intensively by their trainers, and the Pan-Hellenic winners were honored with prizes or symbolic honors. During local games, material prizes were offered for team and tribe events, but it is difficult to say how those rewards and prizes impacted the society as a whole. Those athletes who became heroes would become subjects of hero cults after their deaths. D. C. Young (1984) believes that there were already numerous nonaristocratic Greek professional athletes from the very beginning. H. W. Pleket (1976) thinks that low-status professionals started to gain a foothold only after Pindar (fifth century BCE) and that the high-class athletes continued to compete—even in sports in which fighting was involved—in imperial Roman times. The data are frustatingly inadequate, added to which, we have a rather distorted view because history usually favors the privileged and those whose social status and resources allowed them to highlight their victories and merit in the textual and material documentation.

Greece was not the first ancient civilization to organize gymnastic events, horse races, or music competitions where winners earned prizes. In Mesopotamia, the epigraphic documentation provides some useful data that testifies to the presence of professional athletes who were rewarded with objects of value. The only Mesopotamian athlete identified by name was a Sumerian wrestler known as Shulgigalzu. For his efforts, one text tells us that he received a reward: "Shulgigalzu, son of the musician Alla, received a 10-shekel-worth silver ring for fighting" (Rollinger 1994, 31). An Old Babylonian text recording payment to a list of people belonging to different categories includes ten runners or messengers who received thirteen silver shekels and ten mana of wool, and eight wrestlers who received in total seventeen shekels of silver (Feliu and Millet 2009, 97). Finally, payment of wool to wrestlers, acrobats, other unspecified professionals, and as an offering to a god are also documented. Andrews University Cuneiform Texts, no. 388 lists wrestlers who received objects as a gift for fighting one another: a silver ring and other objects mentioned in the text might have been prizes for winning. Another text mentions "clothing as a gift to wrestlers and athletes," delivered in a courtyard in the banquet room at Ur.[11]

A similar testimony documents sports competitions that took place in nearby Ga'es: "oxen for the house of wrestlers and athletes," or "wrestling matches and gen-

11. MVN 3, 331.

eral competitions," and "oil for runners, taken from Ga'es."[12] This quote is particularly significant not only because it mentions the runner (^{lú}kaš$_4$) linked to the competitions (géšba^{ba} lìrum-ma), but also because it mentions that athletes would oil themselves (ì-šeš$_4$; Lamont 1995, 209). Both beer and oil were provided by the city central administration according to a document from Ur III, which reports that five liters of plant oil were sent to runners with which to grease themselves, along with beer for the athletes (Legrain 1947, 1137). There are several interpretations as to why athletes might oil themselves up: (1) To improve the thermal regulation of the body and to warm their muscles up prior to the workout; (2) to protect the epidermis from the sun's rays and weather conditions; and (3) to prevent the loss of body fluids during strenuous activity. There is also an aesthetic benefit: Oiling would brighten up the athletes body, emphasizing their muscles and making them more pleasing to the eye.[13]

From the epigraphic data related to athletes in the Near East, the presence of different definitions have been noted, and may reflect their association with different social classes. Among those who practiced sports, were also young people who practiced athletic disciplines using weapons belonging to higher social classes (Rollinger 1994, 40–43).

3. *Conclusions*

The visual representation of sports helps us to understand the athletic displicines practiced, while the archaeological context (which in our case is usually missing) and the epigraphic data provide information on the function of the image and the reason for its creation. It is essential to understand why the images were created, how they were used to convey the religious or political ideas of a specific population with its distinct cultural and social background, and how they impacted the society that created them. The practice of athletic disciplines in the ancient Near East seems to be closely bound to religion. Indeed, though sports and religious observance are often documented together in the texts, there are scarce epigraphic data on the places where these athletic competitions took place.

The athletic disciplines that have been the focus of this essay— running, wrestling, and swimming—were practiced by gods, kings, and professional athletes mainly in the context of local festivals. As the epigraphic sources brought to bear on the evidence

12. UET 9, 1050.

13. Oil was used in some sporting disciplines practiced in Greece and some ancient sources seem to confirm these explanations. Lucian of Samosata (second century CE, *Anacharsis*, 24), for example, believed that oil is an excellent toning lotion for the skin as well as for leather as it regenerates it and makes it more resistant to rips. Pliny, instead underscored the protective characteristics of oil, specifically that it protects the body from the cold (*Natural History* 15.4.19). The use of oil might also have had a religious component whereby athletes would oil themselves as a way of devoting themselves to the god. On the reasons why Greek athletes anointed their bodies with oil, see Ulf 1979.

show, in societies where the divine forces governing subsistence and production processes made the human condition endurable, athletic competition and religious observance went hand in hand.

Bibliography

Amiet, P. 1961. *La glyptique Mesopotamienne archaïque.* Paris: Éditions du Centre National de la Recherche Scientifique.

Ascalone, E. 2011. *Glittica Elamita dalla metà del III alla metà del II millennio a.C. Sigilli a stampo, sigilli a cilindro e impronte rinvenute in Iran e provenienti da collezioni private e museali.* Rome: Erma di Bretschnaider.

Becatti, G. 1961. *Scavi di Ostia IV: Mosaici e Pavimenti Marmorei.* Rome: Libreria dello Stato.

Bottéro, J. 1981. "L'Ordalie en Mésopotamie ancienne." *Annali della Scuola Normale Superiore di Pisa* 11:1005–10.

———. 2008. *L'Epopea di Giglameš, l'uomo che non voleva morire.* Roma: Edizioni Mediterranee.

Catagnoti, A. 1997. "Les listes des ḪÚB: (KI) dans les textes administratifs d'Ébla et l'onomastique de Nagar, Mari." *Annales de recherches interdisciplinaires* 8:563–96.

Charpin, D. and J.-M. Durand. 1994. *Florilegium marianum III: Recueil d'études à la mémoire de Marie-Thérèse Barrelet.* Mémoire de NABU 4. Paris: Sepoa.

Collon, D. 1982. *The Alalakh Cylinder Seals.* B.A.R. International Series 132. Oxford: B.A. R.

Crowther, N. B. 2010. *Sport in Ancient Times.* Norman: University of Oklahoma Press.

D'Amore, L. 1937. *Tito Livio, Il Libro I delle 'Storie.'* Milan: Signorelli.

Decker, W. 1992. *Sports and Games of Ancient Egypt,* trans. by A. Guttmann. New Haven: Yale University Press.

Decker, W., and M. Herb. 1993. *Bildatlas zum Sport im Alten Ägypten: Corpus der bildlichen Quellen zu Leibesübungen, Spiel, Jagd, Tanz und verwandten Themen in pharaonischer Zeit.* New York: Brill.

Diem, C. 1966. *Historia de los deportes.* Barcelona: Diamante.

Dunand, J. M. 1998. *Les documents* épistolaires *du Palais de Mari* (2). Paris: Éditións du Cerf.

Eichel, W. F. 1973. "El desarrollo de los ejercicios corporales en la sociedad prehistórica." *Citius, Altius, Fortius* 15:95–134.

Eppensteiner, F. 1973. "El origen del deporte." *Citius, Altius, Fortius* 15:259–72.

Festuccia, S. 2016a. "Sport Representation: Transfer Images of Agonistic Context." In R. A. Stucky, O. Kaelin, and H.-P. Mathys (eds.), *9th International Congress on the Archaeology of the Ancient Near East 2014,* 99–110. Wiesbaden: Harrassowitz.

———. 2016b. "Un tuffo nell'Eufrate: le attività natatorie nella Mesopotamia Antica." In *Maria, Lacus et Flumina: studi di storia, archeologia e antropologia "in acqua" dedicati a Claudio Mocchegiani Carpano,* M. Marazzi, G. Pecoraro and S. Tusa (eds.), 163–79. Ricerche di storia, epigrafia e archeologia mediterranea 5, Rome: Bagatto Libri.

Frankfort, H. 1939a. *Cylinder Seals: A Documentary Essay on the Art and Religion of the Ancient Near East.* London: Macmillan.

———. 1939b. *Sculpture of the Third Millennium BC from Tell Asmar and Khafajah.* Chicago: University of Chicago Press.

———. 1943. *More Sculpture from the Diyala Region.* Chicago: University of Chicago Press.

———. 1955. *Stratified Cylinder Seals from the Diyala Region.* Chicago: University of Chicago Press.

Fullola, J. M. and J. Nadal. 2005. *Introducción a la prehistoria: La evolución de la cultura humana.* Barcelona: UOC.

García Romero, F. 2013. "Sport Tourism in Ancient Greece." *Journal of Tourism History* 5:1–15.
Gardiner, E. N. 1930. *Athletics of the Ancient World*. London: Oxford University Press.
Guttmann, A. 1994. *Dal Rituale al Record – La natura degli sport moderni*. Napoli: Edizioni scientifiche italiane. Translation of 1978 *From Ritual to Record: The Nature of Modern Sports*. New York: Columbia University Press.
Harris, H. A. 1972. *Sport in Greece and Rome*. Ithaca, NY: Cornell University Press.
Kyle, D. G. 2007. *Sport and Spectacle in the Ancient World*. Oxford: Blackwell.
Legrain, L. 1937, 1947. *Business Documents of the Third Dynasty of Ur*. 2 vols. London: British Museum Publications.
Loding, D. M. 1976. *Economic Texts from the Third Dynasty*. Ur Excavations Texts 9. Philadelphia and London: Published for the trustees of the two museums by the Babylonian Fund.
Lukas, G. 1973. "La educación corporal y los ejercicios corporales en la sociedad prehistórica." *Citius, Altius, Fortius* 15:273–324.
Luschen, G. and K. Weis. 1979. *Sociología del deporte*. Madrid: Miñón.
Marinatos, S. 1971. *Excavations at Thera*, Vol. 4. Athens: Archaiologike Etaireia.
Marinatos, S., and M. Hirmer. 1960. *Crete and Mycenae*. London: Thames & Hudson.
Martino, S. de. 2001. "A Fragment of a Festival of Old Hittite Tradition." In T. Richter, D. Prechel, and J. Klinger (eds.), *Kulturgeschichten: Altorientalistische Studien für Volkert Haas zum 65. Geburtstag*, 73–80. Saarbrücken: Saarbrücker Drückerei und Verlag.
Militello, P. 2003. "Il *Rhytòn* dei Lottatori e le scene di combattimento nell'Età del Bronzo Tardo I." *Creta Antica* 4:359–401.
Moortgat-Correns, U. 1989. *La Mesopotamia*. Torino: UTET.
Murray S. C. 2014. "The Role of Religion in Greek Sport." In P. Christesen and D. G. Kyle (eds.), *A Companion to Sport and Spectacle in Greek and Roman Antiquity*, 309–319. Malden, MA: Wiley-Blackwell.
Neuendorff, E. 1973. "El hombre prehistórico." *Citius, Altius, Fortius* 15:273–324.
Nitschke, J. L. N. 2007. *Perceptions of Culture: Interpreting Greco-Near Eastern Hybridity in the Phoenician Homeland*. Berkeley: University of California.
Offner, G. 1962. "Jeux Corporels en Sumer: Documents Relatifs a la Competition Athletique." *Revue d'Assyriologie et d'Archeologie Orientale* 56:31–38.
Owen D.I. 1975. *The John Frederick Lewis Collection*. Materiali per il vocabolario neosumerico 3. Rome: Multigrafica.
Papakonstantinou, Z. 2010. *Sport in the Cultures of the Ancient World*. London: Routledge.
Pleket, H. W. and M. I. Finley. 1976. *The Olympic Games: The First Thousand Years*. London: Chatto & Windus.
Pope, S. W., and J. Nauright. 2011. *Routledge Companion to Sports History*. London: Routledge.
Popplow, U. 1973. "Origen y comienzos de los ejercicios físicos." *Citius, Altius, Fortius* 15:135–54.
Renfrew, C. 1988. "Minoan-Mycenaean Origins of the Panhellenic Games." In W. Raschke (ed.), *The Archaeology of the Olympics*, 13–25). Madison: University of Wisconsin Press.
Robineau, J.-M. 1976. *Milon de Crotone ou l'invention du sport*. Paris: Presses universitaires de France.
Rollinger, R. 1994. "Aspekte des Sports im Alten Sumer: sportliche Betätigung und Herrschaftsideologie im Wechselspiel." *Nikephoros* 7:7–64.
———. 2011. "Sport und Spiel." *Reallexikon der Assyriologie und Vorderasiatischen Archäologie* 13(1–2):6–16.
Sansone, D. 1992. *Greek Athletics and the Genesis of Sports*. Berkeley: University of California Press.
Scanlon, T. F. 1984. *Greek and Roman Athletics: A Bibliography with Introduction and Commentary*. Chicago: Ares.

Segalen, M. 2002. *Riti e rituali contemporanei*. Milan: Mulino.

Überhorst, H. 1973. "Teorías sobre el origen del deporte." *Citius, Altius, Fortius* 15:9–57.

Ulf, Ch. 1979. "Die Einreibung des griechischen Athleten mit Öl." *Stadion* 5:220–38.

Van Dalen, D. B., E. D. Michell, and B. L. Bennett. 1973. "La educación física para la supervivencia del hombre primitive." *Citius, Altius, Fortius* 15:83–94.

Ziegler, N. 2007. *Les Musiciens et la musique d'après les archives de Mari*. Florilegium Marianum 9/Mémoires de Nouvelles Assyriologiques Brèves et Utilitaires 10. Paris: Societe pour l'Etude du Proche-Orient Ancien.

Afterword

Memory and Memories from the Ancient Near East to the Modern West

Frances Pinnock

Ancient Near Eastern archaeology, followed shortly after by Assyriology, started in the mid-nineteenth century,[1] with the exploration of some of the great late Assyrian royal palaces—at Nineveh, Nimrud, and Khorsabad—and with the discovery of the extraordinary carved decorations of their walls, which are the oldest evidence of the historical relief, a genre bought to a peak of accomplishment during the Roman Empire. Since its beginning, the history of the first archaeological discoveries was interwoven with the complicated diplomatic and political events[2] that characterized, in the same years and until the dissolution of the Ottoman Empire, the history of a wide area between India and Egypt.[3] On the one hand, archaeology was frequently used as a cover for activities that may—with some benevolence—be defined as diplomatic;[4] on the other hand, the decipherment of the first cuneiform documents—in particular the tablet of the legend of Gilgamesh with the Mesopotamian version of the deluge—supported the vision of those who were interested in the ancient Near Eastern past only in

1. I expressed these considerations during the seminars organized by A. Garcia Ventura and L. Verderame at the Sapienza University of Rome (2015–2016): I am very grateful to both for giving me the opportunity to take part in this volume, collecting the output of those stimulating meetings.

2. The history of the ancient Near Eastern archaeology is summarized in Matthiae 2005, 3–21, but see also, recently, Liverani 2013, 14–35, in particular on p. 28 for an interesting insight on the way Arab historians and geographers considered the antiquities of their world.

3. These events are usually called the Big Game and pivoted on the need by the great powers of the time—United Kingdom, France, Germany and, later on, Russia and the United States—to dominate the main trade routes of the most important precious and/or raw materials: For a recent presentation of these issues see Dalrymple 2013.

4. In some instances, the first explorers of the ancient Near East were really spies, at the service of their governments, like Rawlinson and, during the First World War, Lawrence; see Matthiae 2005, 25–32, about the political biases of this discipline at its beginnings.

the hope to prove the truthfulness of the biblical tales (Moorey 1991, 10–12), giving origin to the so-called biblical archaeology.[5]

After these first pioneering approaches, ancient Near Eastern archaeology followed a long path, both concerning the theoretical grounds and the practice of field archaeology, though it was not always prompt in accepting the most modern approaches of the historic and archaeological research in general. Between the end of the nineteenth and the beginning of the twentieth century we can date the birth of historical archaeology and the introduction of a kind of excavation technique, with the German explorations at Babylon in 1899 and Ashur in 1903 (Matthiae 2005, 36–42). Finally, albeit with strong discussion, the stratigraphic method was adopted for the first time by Kathleen Kenyon in her excavations at Samaria (Moorey 1991, 62), and even more importantly, at Jericho (Moorey 1991, 94–97; Matthiae 2005, 40–41). The impact of the New Archaeology of the late 1960s was only slowly and gradually felt in our field of studies, and more for the adoption of new methodologies than for the introduction of new historical perspectives.

After the Second World War, archaeologists working on the field had to face new challenges in building up relations, and eventually cooperations, with the cultural authorities of the countries that, more or less artificially created at the end of the First World War, were at that time gaining their independence and were creating structures devoted to the study of their past, frequently based on the formulations given during the mandate period (Moorey 1991, 49). Each country was different in its approach to the study of its remotest past and in its approach to the possibility, or willingness, to cooperate with foreign archaeologists.[6] Moreover, in some instances, local political authorities had their own personal agendas, which could conflict with a sound historical reconstruction, or could be superimposed over the historical reconstructions provided by archaeological and philological data.

In the last three decades, the political situation in the countries of the Near East has progressively deteriorated, leading to the present tragic situation, for which it is nearly impossible to foresee a rapid solution, in which the local populations are bearing the heaviest burden, in terms of loss of lives, loss of economic power, and loss of relevance, whereas the cultural heritage is being destroyed, looted, and dispersed. At the same time, in Europe, but not only in Europe, the study of the human past is considered less and less important, and there is a constant trend to reduce or even close courses in ancient history or whole departments.[7]

---

5. Moorey 1991, 2–4, where he also points to the different approaches to the biblical tradition, between sincere faith and some degree of cynicism.

6. These approaches varied from a real historical methodology and a great opening to cooperation, as happened in Syria, where in 2010, more than 120 foreign archaeological expeditions were active, frequently as joint expeditions, to the (temporary) rejection of the pre-Islamic past and of international cooperation, as happened in Iran after the Khomeinist Revolution.

7. For example, in Italy there has been a recent proposal to eliminate the history test in the high

The economic monoculture of modern neocapitalism isolates intellectuals, and diminishes their role, mocking their inability to produce material wealth and using the cultural heritage as a background for manifestations functional to the world of economics in the largest sense, not aiming at producing cultural curiosity and desire for knowledge. On the one hand, the cultural heritage is destroyed, or is sold on the antique market in order to produce money for guerrillas; on the other hand, funding for research is cut, but banks are supported, so, with different modes, the cultural heritage is destroyed, and a financial system is kept alive, which does not produce wealth, but only reproduces itself.

In this world, apparently so dark and hopeless, does the study of, or the interest for, the ancient Near East have sense?

It seems that, thus far, in that tormented part of the world, the temporary interruption in field activity provoked by conflicts has led to a useful period of fruitful meditation, to the refinement of methodologies and to some changes in perspectives.[8]

Another extremely positive element is the very strong interest for the ancient Near East in two different spheres: on the one hand, many young people approach the "Orientalist" disciplines, from those dealing with the oldest periods, to those dealing with the late antique and medieval times. They show passion and enthusiasm, as clearly appears from their participation in events, like the cycle of seminars organized by A. Garcia Ventura and L. Verderame, whose results are published in this volume, or from the growing interest in the series of congresses "Broadening Horizons," specifically devoted to them. Also, the participation of young and talented scholars in larger forums, like the Rencontre Assyriologique Internationale, the International Congress on the Archaeology of the Ancient Near East, or the annual meeting of the American Schools of Oriental Research. On the other hand, a peculiar, and fascinating, phenomenon is the penetration of the ancient Near East into our contemporary popular culture in different ways, sometimes with misunderstandings, sometimes with a correct knowledge: contemporary music, comics and manga, and popular literature use ancient Near Eastern characters, scenarios, and imagery, sometimes in order to create autonomous languages, and sometimes recreating old representations of the Oriental world with cultural or political bias.[9] Nonetheless, this only means that the ancient Near East, albeit

---

schools, and on 8 May 2019 an international appeal was launched against the closing of the Centre of Prehistoric Archaeology of the Near East (PANE) of the University of Brno in the Czech Republic.

8. I am thinking of the strong development in the use of satellite imagery, and particularly in their analysis and in the interest to landscape and waterscape, besides the traditional cityscapes, and I refer in particular to the works of Tony Wilkinson (2003) and Jason Ur (2010), among others.

9. There are different problems concerning the modern use of archaeology, particularly by the media, which usually prefers to talk about the "mysteries" of the ancient world, or to present everything in the light of biblical or political interpretations: Gerstenblith 2012, 22; Cline 2012; Cartledge 2012, 153–56; Pollock 2005; Bernbeck 2005.

remote in time, is still a part of a cultural background more widespread that can be imagined.

Thus, albeit facing very difficult moments, we must not despair, but rather we must still deal with the ancient Near East. We must still spread the knowledge of the ancient Near East, increase our knowledge of the ancient Near East, and, first and foremost, face the challenges of the contemporary world with an open mind and with adaptability. Certainly, the ancient Near Eastern archaeology of the twenty-first century is, and will more and more be, different from that of the nineteenth or the twentieth centuries, for several reasons.

As regards the West—or, as M. Liverani (2013, 399) recently put it, the Wests—the changes concern the differences in the scientific and methodological approaches that have always characterized Europe and the United States. One even more important change is the appearance on the scene of scholars in regions previously uninterested, or nearly completely uninterested, in our field of studies, like Central and South America, which are now starting to deal with the ancient Near East with methodologically very interesting approaches. In China there are now positions for the study of Assyriology and other subjects in local universities, which are also attracting young "Western" scholars.[10] Again, should we consider this novelty a challenge to a cultural primacy, or rather a great opportunity to confront different methodologies and theoretical approaches, which will hopefully lead to the opening of new perspectives in our field of studies? I think, of course, that the only fruitful approach is the most open and curious one.

Facing these novelties, we should be obliged to reflect on the complex nature of our behaviors, in the academy and on the field, and of our interactions. On the contrary, as I have already maintained, our universities are flustered by an economic and cultural crisis, certainly stronger in some countries than in others, and yet quite general. The economic crisis led to the decrease or annulment of funding, and most of all to the insecurity of personnel: for these reasons it is nowadays impossible, as concerns field archaeology, to plan wide-scope interventions, and it is possible to plan only small projects of short duration.

Summing up, the ancient Near Eastern archaeology in the twenty-first century, in a time of slowing down, or blocking of field operations, has the opportunity to reflect on its perspectives, to change greatly, and to find ways to face new challenges, some difficult and painful, some equally difficult but also fascinating. In a world where fear of the other, and contempt for who or what is different seem to dominate the scene and are exploited by ruthless politicians in order to gain some votes, only the development of a network of knowledge of the richness of the past from where we come and of the opportunity of the possibilities provided by the differences we face every day, may

10. Some of these "new" countries also have strong economic power, and they are also approaching the Near East and Africa with economic proposals, which can be more easily accepted because they come from nations who have themselves suffered from the colonial presence.

build up a future where everyone will be free to live one's own specificity in harmony with other specificities. The question is: will we have the intellectual and material capacities to do this?

Bibliography

Bernbeck, R. 2005. "The Past as Fact and Fiction: From Historical Novels to Novel Histories." In R. Bernbeck and S. Pollock (eds.), *Archaeologies of the Middle East: Critical Perspectives*, 97–121. Malden, MA, Oxford, and Carlton: Blackwell.

Cartledge, T. W. 2012. "Walk About Jerusalem: Protestant Pilgrims and the Holy Land." In E. M. Meyers and C. Meyers (eds.), *Archaeology, Bible, Politics, and the Media: Proceedings of the Duke University Conference, April 23–24, 2009*, 139–60. Winona Lake, IN: Eisenbrauns.

Cline, E. H. 2012. "Fabulous Finds or Fantastic Forgeries? The Distortion of Archaeology by the Media and Pseudoarchaeologists, and What We Can Do About It." In E. M. Meyers and C. Meyers (eds.), *Archaeology, Bible, Politics, and the Media: Proceedings of the Duke University Conference, April 23–24, 2009*, 39–50, Winona Lake, IN: Eisenbrauns.

Dalrymple, W. 2013. *Return of a King: The Battle for Afghanistan 1839–42*. New York: Bloomsbury.

Gerstenblith, P. 2012. "The Media and Archaeological Preservation in Iraq: A Tale of Politics, Media, and the Law." In E. M. Meyers and C. Meyers (eds.), *Archaeology, Bible, Politics, and the Media: Proceedings of the Duke University Conference, April 23–24, 2009*, 15–35. Winona Lake, IN: Eisenbrauns.

Liverani, M. 2013. *Immaginare Babele: Due secoli di studi sulla città orientale antica*. Rome and Bari: Laterza.

Matthiae, P. 2005. *Prima lezione di archeologia orientale*. Rome and Bari: Laterza.

Moorey, P. R. S. 1991. *A Century of Biblical Archaeology*. Cambridge: Lutterworth Press.

Pollock, S. 2005. "Archaeology Goes to War at the Newsstand." In R. Bernbeck and S. Pollock (eds.), *Archaeologies of the Middle East: Critical Perspectives*, 78–96. Malden, MA: Blackwell.

Ur, J. A. 2010. *Urbanism and Cultural Landscapes in Northeastern Syria: The Tell Hamoukar Survey, 1999–2001*. Oriental Institute Publications 137. Chicago: The Oriental Institute of the University of Chicago.

Wilkinson, T. J. 2003. *Archaeological Landscapes of the Near East*. Tucson, AZ: University of Arizona Press.

Contributors

Pedro Azara is an architect and professor of aesthetics at the School of Architecture (UPC-ETSAB) in Barcelona, Spain. He has published *Cornerstone: The Birth of the City in Mesopotamia* (Barcelona: Tenov, 2015 [distributed by the Chicago University Press]). He has curated *From Ancient to Modern: Archaeology and Aesthetics*, Institute for the Study of the Ancient World, New York, 2015, and *Sumer and the Modern Paradigm*, Fundació Miró, Barcelona, 2017–2018.

Paul Collins is Jaleh Hearn Curator for Ancient Near East at the Ashmolean Museum, University of Oxford. He has worked previously as a curator in the Middle East Department of the British Museum and the Ancient Near Eastern Art Department of the Metropolitan Museum of Art, New York. He is currently chair of the British Institute for the Study of Iraq. His publications include *Assyrian Palace Sculptures* (London: British Museum, 2008) and *Mountains and Lowlands: Ancient Iran and Mesopotamia* (Oxford: Ashmolean Museum, 2016).

Silvana Di Paolo is an archaeologist and art historian of the ancient Near East and a researcher at the Italian National Council of Research. Her main research interests cover the archaeology and art history of the Syro-Mesopotamian area and ancient Cyprus (third to first millennia BCE). She has participated in numerous excavations and researches in Mediterranean and Middle Eastern countries (Syria, Lebanon, Cyprus, Georgia). She coordinates the QaNaTES research program aimed to conduct archaeological investigations in the Marivan area, located in the Zagros area of north-central Iranian Kurdistan. She has written extensively on craft production in the ancient Near East (work organization, workshops, social meaning of artworks). In 2018 she edited the following volumes: *Implementing Meanings: the Power of the Copy Between Past, Present and Future* (Münster: Ugarit Verlag, 2018) and *Composite Artefacts in the Ancient Near East: Exhibiting an Imaginative Materiality, Showing a Genealogical Nature* (Oxford: Archaeopress, 2018). She is finalizing (as author) the volume *Approaching Multi-Materiality in the Ancient Near East: Divinely Inspired, Divinely Planned* (Routledge) and (as editor) *The Look of Things in the Ancient Near East: Moving from Surface toward Depth and Back Again* (Cambridge Scholars). For many years, she has worked on ancient Near Eastern collections in Italian museums in order to understand the interconnections of heritage and identity.

Kerstin Droß-Krüpe is currently a postdoctoral assistant at Kassel University. She studied classical archaeology, ancient history, and business administration at Philipps-Universität Marburg and obtained her PhD in 2010 with a thesis on textile production during the Roman Empire in the province of Egypt, which was published as *Wolle – Weber – Wirtschaft: Die Textilproduktion der römischen Kaiserzeit im Spiegel der papyrologischen Überlieferung* (Wiesbaden: Harrassowitz, 2011). In 2014 and 2016, she coedited several volumes on ancient economic history: *Textile Trade and Distribution in Antiquity* (Wiesbaden: Harrassowitz, 2014), *Textiles, Trade, and Theories* (Münster: Ugarit Verlag, 2016, with Marie-Louise Nosch), *The Cultural Shaping of the Ancient Economy* (Wiesbaden: Harrassowitz, 2016, with Sabine Föllinger and Kai Ruffing). Her current research project deals with the reception of the "Babylonian" queen Semiramis in Baroque opera.

Jean M. Evans is the chief curator and deputy director of the Oriental Institute Museum of the University of Chicago and a research associate of the Oriental Institute. Evans has been the recipient of fellowships from Ludwig Maximilian University, the Getty Foundation, the American Academic Research Institute of Iraq, the Warburg Institute, and the German Archaeological Institute. She was a curator at the Metropolitan Museum of Art from 1999 to 2008 and was ultimately a co-organizer of the exhibition *Beyond Babylon: Art, Trade, and Diplomacy in the Second Millennium BC* and coeditor of its corresponding publication. She is also the author of *The Lives of Sumerian Sculpture: An Archaeology of the Early Dynastic Temple* (Cambridge: Cambridge University Press, 2012).

Silvia Festuccia is associate professor in Cultures of the Ancient Near East, the Middle East and Africa. She teaches archaeology and the history of art of the ancient Near East at the University of Naples "Suor Orsola Benincasa" and obtained a PhD in Architecture and Heritage from the University "Alfonso X El Sabio" of Madrid, an MA and a specialization degree in Near Eastern archaeology at University of Rome "La Sapienza." She is co-director of the "Multidisciplinary Archaeological Project in Maasser el-Shouf - Qalaat el-Hoson" (MeSAP) with Myriam Ziadé (Directorate General of Antiquities, Lebanon). She has participated in different archaeological missions, directing several excavation areas and surveys at Ebla, Tell Tuqan, and Tell Denit (Syria), Monastiraki (Crete), Kharayeb and Jemjim (Lebanon), Aouam (Morocco), and Shahr-i Sokhta (Iran). She has collaborated in underwater archaeological projects, including coastal and underwater surveys in Italy and Lebanon. Author of studies on the urbanization and metallurgy for the preclassical civilizations in the ancient Near East, she has participated in international conferences and published several contributions related to archaeological excavations directed in the Near East and Italy.

Agnès Garcia-Ventura (Barcelona, 1977) was awarded her PhD in History at the University Pompeu Fabra, Barcelona, in November 2012. As a postdoctoral scholar, she worked at the Rupert Charles University in Heidelberg, Germany (2012–2013), the University Autònoma of Barcelona, Spain (2013–2014), the "Sapienza," Università degli Studi di Roma, Italy (2014–2016), and at the Institute of Ancient Near Eastern Studies of the University of Barcelona, Spain (2017–2019). Her main areas of interest are gender studies, historiography of ancient Near Eastern studies, ancient musical performance, and the organization of work in Mesopotamia. She is the editor of several volumes among which *The Study of Musical Performance in Antiquity* (coedited with Claudia Tavolieri and Lorenzo Verderame, Cambridge: Cambridge Scholars, 2018), *Las mujeres en el Oriente cuneiforme* (coedited with Josué J. Justel, Alcalá: Servicio de Publicaciones de la Universidad de Alcalá, 2018), and *Studying Gender in the Ancient Near East* (coedited with Saana Svärd, State College, PA: Eisenbrauns and Pennsylvania State University Press, 2018).

Valeska Hartmann is a doctoral candidate at the Department of Art History at the Philipps-University of Marburg. Her research project deals with the reception of antiquity and forms of Orientalism in the stage design of the *opera seria* of the eighteenth and nineteenth centuries.

Pavel Kořínek is a researcher at the Institute of Czech Literature, Czech Academy of Sciences, Prague. His work focuses on history and theory of Czech comics and popular culture studies. Recently, he served as a lead editor of the two-volume *History of Czechoslovak Comics of the 20th Century*. Currently, he is preparing a monograph about the comics magazine *Punta* (1935–1942) and its transmedial extensions.

Marc Marín is an architect and PhD candidate in Mesopotamian archaeology at the Department of Near Eastern Languages and Civilizations at the University of Pennsylvania (NELC-UPenn). He has contributed to the catalogs of the exhibitions *From Ancient to Modern: Archaeology and Aesthetics*, Institute for the Study of the Ancient World, New York, 2015, and *Sumer and the Modern Paradigm*, Fundació Joan Miró, Barcelona, 2017.

Kevin M. McGeough is professor of archaeology in the Department of Geography at the University of Lethbridge in Canada and holds a Board of Governor's Research Chair in Archaeological Theory and Reception. He has been the editor of the *Annual of the American Schools of Oriental Research*, ASOR's *Archaeological Report Series*, and is currently coeditor of the *Alberta Archaeological Review*. McGeough is the author of a three-volume series on the reception of archaeology, called *The Ancient Near East in the Nineteenth Century* (Sheffield: Sheffield Phoenix, 2015).

Eva Miller is a British Academy postdoctoral fellow in the History Department of University College London. Her project "A New Antiquity: Western Reception and Revival of Ancient Assyria in Decorative Arts and Architecture, 1850-1935" looks at the wide-ranging cultural impact of the Assyrian rediscovery. She completed her doctorate at the University of Oxford in 2017, on reliefs and texts from the reign of Neo-Assyrian king Ashurbanipal. She has previously taught at the University of Birmingham, and been Henri Frankfort Fellow at the Warburg Institute.

Juan-Luis Montero Fenollós is professor of ancient history at the University of A Coruña (Spain). He was director of the Middle Syrian Euphrates Archaeological Project between 2005 and 2011, and since 2016 has co-directed the archaeological excavations in Tell el-Far'a (Palestine).

Jana Mynářová is associate professor of Egyptology at the Czech Institute of Egyptology, Charles University, Prague. Her work focuses on relations between Egypt and the Near East in the Late Bronze Age as well as spread of cuneiform writing in the Western Peripheries in the second millennium BCE. Presently, she conducts a research project devoted to the study of Amarna cuneiform paleography.

Davide Nadali is associate professor of Near Eastern Archaeology at the Sapienza University of Rome. He received in 2006 a PhD in Near Eastern Archaeology at the Sapienza University of Rome on Neo-Assyrian bas-reliefs of the seventh century BCE, published as *Percezione dello spazio e scansione del tempo: Studio della composizione narrativa del rilievo assiro di VII secolo a.C.* (Contributi e Materiali di Archeologia Orientale 12; Rome: Università degli studi di Roma La Sapienza, 2006). Since 1998, he has been a member of the Italian Archaeological Expedition to Ebla (Syria) and in 2019 he was appointed Vice Director of the Ebla Expedition. Since 2014, he has been co-director of the Italian Archaeological Expedition to Tell Zurghul/Nigin in Southern Iraq. He has been involved in the ERC funded project on Ebla and its landscape as member for archaeological surveys in the sites of Tell Munbatah and Tell Sakka (Syria). His main interests of research concern art, architecture, and urbanism in the Assyrian period; the study of ancient warfare; the use, meaning, and reception of the production of images and pictures in ancient Mesopotamia and Syria with articles on the impact of pictures in ancient societies; the incipient urbanism in ancient Mesopotamia and the Early Dynastic period (third millennium BCE) of ancient southern Mesopotamia.

Frances Pinnock (Rome, 1950) is associate professor of archaeology and art history of the ancient Near East in the Sapienza University of Rome, and is co-director, with P. Matthiae, of the Italian archaeological expedition to Ebla, of which she has been a member since 1971. She is author of six scientific monographs and more than ninety articles in scientific journals. Her main interests are the archaeology and history of art of preclassical Syria, the transmission of iconographies and the roles of women in the ancient Near East.

Francesco Pomponio has been a full professor of Assyriology at the University of Messina since 2000. Pomponio is the author or coauthor of twenty-three monographs and about 120 articles on the administrative documentation of Early Dynastic (Šuruppak,

Ebla), Old-Akkadian (Ur, Adab), Neo-Sumerian (Umma, Girsu, Drehem, Ur), and Old Babylonian periods and on Mesopotamian and Eblaite history and religion.

Daniele Federico Rosa (Rome, 1979) is a music journalist (*Blow Up* magazine), an independent researcher in ancient Near Eastern history, and a metalhead. He wrote his PhD dissertation on Middle Assyrian geography and published a paper or two on the same topic, before deciding it was time to actually do some black metal research. He has a regular job in his free time, and he is usually dressed in black.

Luigi Turri earned his PhD in antiquities at the University of Udine and is temporary assistant professor at the University of Verona. He has been part of many archaeological missions in Italy, Syria, Iraqi Kurdistan, and Lebanon and contributed to several exhibitions. He is author of scientific and popular articles on the ancient Near East.

Lorenzo Verderame is professor of Assyriology at "Sapienza" University of Rome. He has authored several academic publications on Mesopotamian divination, rituals, and religion, Akkadian and Sumerian literature, economic texts, and technological studies. His publications include the edition of the first six chapters of the astrological series *Enūma Anu Enlil* (*Le tavole I–VI della serie astrologica Enūma Anu Enlil* [Messina: Università di Messina, 2002]), five volumes with the edition of administrative texts, and an overview of the Sumerian and Akkadian literature (*Letterature dell'antica Mesopotamia* [Florence: Le Monnier, 2016]) and civilization (*Introduzione alle culture dell'antica Mesopotamia,* [Florence: Le Monnier, 2017]). He is the epigraphist in chief of Italian Archaeological Expedition to Tell Zurghul, ancient Nigin (Iraq).

Ryan Winters received his PhD in Assyriology from Harvard University in 2019. His main interests are in the socioeconomic history of the ancient Near East and Sumero-Babylonian culture and religion. His doctoral dissertation consisted of a study on trade and international relations as attested in the palace archive found at ancient Ebla (ca. 2350 BCE, in modern-day Syria). Since 2019, he has been employed on the project *God Lists of Ancient Mesopotamia,* based out of the Friedrich-Schiller University of Jena.

Subject Index